3-

WYOMING

Time and Again

This book is dedicated to the wonderful people of Wyoming who have shared with me their time, history, and beautiful state and to the memory of my professor and friend

Robert Combs Warner
1925–1989
Cowboy, journalist, photographer, and teacher.

WYOMING
TIME AND AGAIN

MICHAEL A. AMUNDSON

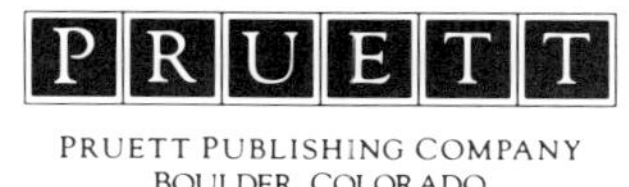

PRUETT PUBLISHING COMPANY
BOULDER, COLORADO

Printed in the United States of America
First printing May, 1991
1 2 3 4 5 6 7 8 9 10
ISBN 0-87108-803-7

Library of Congress Cataloging-in-Publication Data
Amundson, Michael A., 1965–
Wyoming time and again : rephotographing the scenes of J.E. Stimson / by Michael A. Amundson.
p. cm.
Includes bibliographical references and index.
ISBN 0-87108-803-7
1. Wyoming—Description and travel—Views. 2. Photography, Documentary—Wyoming. 3. Stimson, J. E. (Joseph Elam), 1870–1952.
I. Title.
F762.A58 1991 91-9412
978.7—dc20 CIP

Book and cover design by Jody Chapel, Cover to Cover Design, Denver, Colorado
Typography by Lyn Chaffee, Archetype, Denver, Colorado
Maps created by Linda Marston, Cartographic Services, University of Wyoming, Department of Geography and Recreation

Contents

Acknowledgements

In 1900, Joseph Stimson was hired to photograph the newly reorganized Union Pacific Railroad. With payment guaranteed for every picture he produced along the swath of the UP, Stimson was given free rein to photograph any aspect he thought would help promote the railroad. Stimson reached many of his locations not only by railcar but also by handcar, horse and buggy, and automobile.

Thanks to the grant money and confidence that I received from several groups within the State of Wyoming, I was able to enjoy many of the same freedoms that Stimson received. Without those commitments, this project could not have been completed. My first thanks go to the University of Wyoming College of Arts and Sciences' Kuehn Award Committee and the Wyoming Council for the Humanities. The first group supported me when this project was but an idea and the latter organization provided me both a Fellowship Grant to finish the project and the opportunity to present my ongoing research through their Speaker's Bureau Program. Thanks also go to U.W.'s Department of Journalism for a *Reader's Digest* grant to help defray costs. Finally, I am indebted to the American Studies Program at U.W. for their grant that helped me finally see the book become a reality.

While I owe a great deal of thanks to all of the individuals who took their time to show me sites and explain local history to me, I especially wish to express my gratitude to Mark Junge for his patience, technical advice, and guidance. Without him, this project would have been impossible. Special thank-yous also go to Paula Chavoya and LaVaughn Bresnahan of the photo section of the Wyoming Department of Commerce, Division of Parks and Cultural Resources, Museums Division, who spent many hours bringing me photographs and sharing their knowledge of Wyoming with me. Also, thanks to Jean Brainerd for her help in tracking down the history of many of the photographs in this book. Special thanks also goes to Kelly Pellisier of the Wyoming Council for the Humanities. Thank you also to the staffs of the great museums and libraries around the state and in Yellowstone National Park for their help.

I also want to thank two very special people, Stimson's daughter Josephine Love of Dayton and his grandson Richard A. Patterson of Cheyenne, for their insight on Stimson's personal life.

Regarding photographic technique, first and foremost thanks go to my late teacher and friend Robert C. Warner, who always had time for me, and to Richard Collier and Paul Jacques for their technical know-how.

I also wish to thank Eric Sandeen and John Dorst of the U.W. American Studies Program, the history department at the University of Wyoming, and the helpful people at the university's photo service. Thanks also to Rick Ewig of the *Annals of Wyoming* for his aid.

Finally, there are a few people who are very dear to me who I must acknowledge as well for their assistance and encouragement on this project. First, I wish to thank my parents Arlen and Joan Amundson and my sister Kathy Amundson for their unending support. I also would like to thank my great friend Ellie Zuber for her friendship and patience. And last, thanks to my Wyoming relatives—Al and Frances Zakotnik of Kemmerer, Gary and Joanne Zakotnik of Eden, and Doug and Rozeanne Reachard of Worland—for being there along the way.

J. E. Stimson: *Wyoming Photographer*

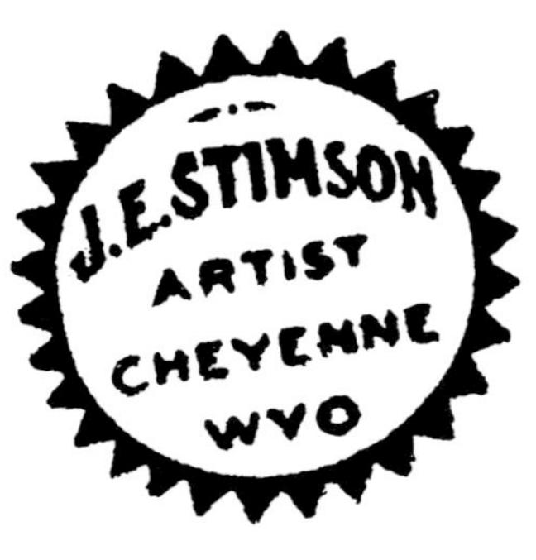

This stamp, circumscribed by the boundaries of a sun, can be found on the corner of almost eight thousand photographs that depict Wyoming during the first three decades of this century. The seal belongs to Cheyenne photographer Joseph Elam Stimson, who traveled extensively to promote the new state through photography. At first by horse and buggy, Stimson later traveled by train and automobile to capture the best that Wyoming had to offer. He photographed mining and machinery, agriculture and irrigation projects, city scenes and ranch houses, religion, medicine, politics, transportation, communication, and, of course, Wyoming's beautiful scenery. Stimson expertly photographed Wyoming for the Union Pacific, the Wyoming Department of Immigration, and various other state departments. He signed his photographs "Artist," and his use of composition and detail justify this title. His photos are not only sharp but they provide details to Wyoming life that cannot be gleaned from written history alone. Today the Stimson collection stands as a detailed glimpse into Wyoming life during the first three decades of this century.

Joseph E. Stimson was only nineteen years old when he came to Cheyenne in the spring of 1889. He had been born in 1870 in Virginia and spent most of his childhood in the southern Appalachian Mountains of South Carolina. When he was thirteen, his father moved the family to Pawnee City, Nebraska. Three years later Joseph left for Appleton, Wisconsin, to work as a photographer's apprentice for his cousin, James Stimson. While in Appleton, Joseph learned the skills of portrait photography and the details of both the collodion or wet-plate process and the new dry-plate process. He arrived in Cheyenne, probably at the suggestion of two brothers who worked for the Union Pacific, without a camera, a studio, or a clientele. He made a deal with pioneer Wyoming photographer Charles Kirkland to purchase his studio and equipment. Stimson paid $150 down and took out a small note on the remainder. In July of 1889, Stimson began making portraits in this small Cheyenne studio. The following year, Wyoming became the forty-fourth state. In January of 1894, Stimson married nineteen-year-old Anna Peterson, and the following year their first child, daughter Louise Roe Stimson, was born.

In 1894 another event occurred that would change the direction of Stimson's career. Elwood Mead, Wyoming's first state engineer, visited Stimson's studio with a package of undeveloped negatives taken in the Big Horn Mountains of northern Wyoming. Stimson developed the glass plates and was amazed by the beauty of the scenes. The following year, Mead took Stimson with him to the Big Horns, and Stimson made his first attempts at scenic photography. The results of this trip were not good; Stimson had overexposed the negatives. Four years later, Stimson was asked to accompany Wyoming's first game warden, Albert Nelson, on a trip to the Jackson Hole region. These photographs were much improved over the negatives made with Mead, although Stimson would later downgrade their value. (In fact, he kept a large print from this trip to Jackson Lake in his bedroom for many years as a reminder of what better grade of photograph he had to obtain.) Nevertheless, Stimson began selling some of his scenic prints. Over the next two years, he compiled albums of his trip to Jackson Hole as well as other, shorter trips. After one of these albums was discovered by a Union Pacific Railroad publicity agent in 1901, Stimson was hired as a publicity photographer for the railroad.

The Union Pacific was reorganizing under the direction of Edward H. Harriman and needed photographs to help change the image of the scandal-plagued railroad. Stimson was given free rein to photograph anything that might draw investors to the railway. Besides the obvious subject of the railroad itself—locomotives, train crews, rolling stock, and depots—Stimson was to photograph natural wonders, city scenes, farms and ranches, mining and irrigation projects, and anything else that might bring money to the new railroad. There were no restrictions on the number of photographs Stimson could take; he was paid for each print. His commission was set at four dollars for the first eight-by-ten-inch print received, one dollar for the next ninety-nine, and seventy-five cents for every print thereafter. Transportation along the railroad was free for Stimson, and he oftentimes used a small gasoline-powered handcar to transport his equipment to a site. The pay-per-print deal gave Stimson the freedom to shoot whatever he wanted, whenever he wanted. He was also free to sell prints made from the negatives he made for the railroad.

By 1903 Stimson's reputation as a scenic photographer had grown to the point that he was asked by the state of Wyoming to produce five hundred Wyoming scenes that would be displayed at the Louisiana Purchase Exposition to be held the following year in St. Louis. The prints were to be colored by hand, a skill that Stimson often deployed before the advent of color film. He was paid a fee of $875 and agreed to spend all of his time working on the project. During the summer of 1903, Stimson circled the state, taking scenes in the state's thirteen counties and also Yellowstone National Park. He then came back to Cheyenne and hand-painted each black and white photo. At the fair the following year, Stimson's views were displayed separately as well as with a variety of Wyoming subjects. He was awarded a silver medal for his views of mining and machinery, and two other displays that included Stimson photos won silver medals. The next year, 1905, these same views were awarded a bronze medal at the Lewis and Clark Exposition in Portland, Oregon. By 1905, after only ten years in scenic work, Stimson had gained national recognition as a photographer and artist.

In the decade that followed, Stimson continued to promote the Union Pacific through photographs. He traveled throughout UP country—Colorado, Nebraska, Kansas, Utah, Idaho, Nevada, and California—making photographs wherever he went. Agricultural scenes and shots of Union Pacific depots are common during this period. In 1905 Stimson traveled to the last American gold rush in Tonopah and Goldfield, Nevada. He also shot Yellowstone several times during this period as the park made the transition to automobile travel. Increasingly Stimson also produced negatives for Wyoming state agencies. His views were used to promote ranching and dry farming, irrigation, coal and oil production, and tourism. As with the Union Pacific, Stimson's views of Wyoming could be used by the state to bring in capital investment and settlers. In fact, Stimson worked for the state Department of Immigration for many years. His scenic views, although possibly not attracting large numbers of permanent settlers, helped establish the automobile tourist industry in Wyoming. By World War I, Stimson was producing images for both the Union Pacific and various state agencies, while selling the same prints as an independent photographer.

During the war, the federal government took control of the nation's railroads and Stimson's job was diminished. Postwar Wyoming was hit by deflation and an early entry into the Great Depression of the 1930s. For Stimson this meant fewer jobs for the railroad and the state. His portrait work increased and his hand-tinted scenes that hung in depots across the West were replaced by lithographs. In 1929 Elwood Mead, now commissioner of the Bureau of Reclamation, hired Stimson to document the bureau's western construction projects. He photographed scenes across the Rockies, including Hoover Dam. Unfortunately, these shots were retained by the federal government, and only a few have been found.

In the 1930s, while in his sixties, Stimson continued to work. He photographed Civilian Conservation Corps camps and more Wyoming ranches. In 1932, at the age of sixty-two, the photographer traveled by packhorse to the Upper Green River area of the Wind River Range. As told to Wyoming state historian Agnes Wright Spring, Stimson's story and photographs of the alpine scenery were published in *American Forests.* Six years later his wife Anna died, and Stimson went into semiretirement. Although his photographic production slowed down, he continued to hand-color prints from his files. In 1939 he traveled with his brother to their ancestral South Carolina home and then came back to Cheyenne to live out his life. In 1948, half a century after his first visit, the Wyoming Department of Commerce and Industry, predecessor to the Wyoming Travel Commission, hired Stimson to make negatives of the Tetons and Yellowstone country. Four years later, at the age of eighty-two, Stimson died of a heart attack while visiting his daughter in Connecticut. He was buried next to his wife in Lakeview Cemetery in Cheyenne.

The Stimson photo collection was purchased by the state of Wyoming in 1953 for two thousand dollars. Consisting of 7,526 photographs, many of them on eight-by-ten-inch glass-plate negatives, the collection is open to the public through the Department of Commerce, Division of Parks and Cultural Resources, Museums Division/Photographs.

Rephotography and J. E. Stimson

Rephotography is the process of trying to find exactly the spot, or vantage point, that an earlier photographer used to make an image and then duplicating that earlier image. Like the before and after X-rays that a doctor uses to examine a broken arm, rephotography captures a specific view over a period of time. It is an investigative tool that helps to illustrate the changes that have occurred. The process has many uses. For the botanist, rephotography can trace the growth or decline of plant life in a certain area. The geologist can trace the erosion process through rephotography. The historian can use the process to trace man's interaction with his environment. In this book, rephotography is used to illustrate a combination of these changes that have taken place in Wyoming during this century.

Although Wyoming is the subject of this study, the agent is Joseph Stimson. Contrary to popular belief, photography is not an indiscriminate recorder; the camera is subject to the photographer's wishes. A low camera angle might present a stronger image, while a high vantage point might suggest a less-imposing scene. The camera, like the painter's palette, is only the method used to interpret a subject. For Joseph Stimson, this subject was not just Wyoming but the best of Wyoming. Stimson was paid to promote the state, and his photographs reveal that purpose. He could have photographed the poorer sides of Wyoming, but he did not. As a Progressive Era photographer, Stimson's photos illustrate the Wyoming that his patrons wanted to show.

For this reason, I chose to concentrate my rephotographic study on how one man envisioned Wyoming during his lifetime. By retracing the vantage points that Stimson used to document Wyoming in his time, I hoped to discover what had happened to the state.

In essence, rephotography is a study of history and travel. Senior Editor Carla Davidson, of *American Heritage* magazine, said that

> history and travel have always been entwined. We instinctively knew that exploring one could only shed light on the other. This is familiar territory for me. I've always been convinced that one has only to stand on any square foot of this country—city street or farmer's field, scuff one's toe on the surface, dig a little deeper, and shortly a rich stratum of historical event will be revealed. (I've always wanted to do this with my 1904 apartment building on Manhattan's upper west side; trace its origins, find out what smaller dwelling was there first, whose farmland it was before that, and ultimately, what story was told by the rocks and sediment that came before all the rest.)

I tried to uncover the same story in Wyoming. Although every pair of photographs provides a starting and ending point to the story, each site generated questions about what had happened to Stimson's Wyoming. How is the site the same or different? Why is it this way? The landscape might hint at the reasons, but historical research closed the gaps. A thorough history completes the story. By knowing the when and why of each scene, I traveled not only geographically but also through time. I knew that there was more to each site than what I captured on film. Indeed, by uncovering the historical stratum of each site, I came away with a deeper understanding of the forces at work in Wyoming's history.

This project began in the spring of 1987, when I discovered Mark Klett's book, *Second View: The Rephotographic Survey Project.* This volume retraced the nineteenth-century geological survey photographs of William Henry Jackson, Timothy O'Sullivan, and others. Although this work described primarily the methodology of landscape rephotography, another book, Mark Junge's *J. E. Stimson: Photographer of the West,* opened my eyes to Wyoming. Stimson's turn-of-the-century images stuck in my mind, and I wanted to know what had become of each site. By synthesizing the two books, I found out.

With a background in American history and journalism, the methodology of the project was pragmatic. I began by spending three days looking through the 7,526-piece Stimson collection in Cheyenne. The vastness of the collection overwhelmed me. I knew that I had to focus the project. Because Stimson was a UP photographer, I decided to follow his route along the railroad's corridor in southern Wyoming. Stimson left no diary, letters, or maps of his photo locations. The only clues were single descriptive identification lines inscribed into each glass negative. Although a description might be exact, such as "View from Depot tower, Cheyenne," and hence easily found, many Stimson prints gave descriptions such as "Maine Rock, near Laramie." The term "near Laramie" could mean anywhere within 360 degrees of Laramie. In many instances, finding the general location of the photograph proved more difficult than finding the specific vantage point. By asking questions of the Wyoming State Archives staff, I determined which scenes might still be accessible and then photocopied the prints of these for use in the field. Although this procedure was initially used to save money, the photocopies proved to be valuable aids. They could be folded for easy carrying and gridded to help identify modern scenes. I found sixty sites that summer, but I had another two hundred views that I could not find.

To locate the general area of each vantage point, I used several books, *Wyoming Place Names,* the WPA's *Wyoming: A Guide to Its History, Highways, and People,* and state highway and topographical maps. Once in the general area, I set up my equipment. I used a 4 × 5 inch Crown Graphic view camera. The large format permitted me the "feel" of what it was like for Stimson to photograph. First, the camera required 4-by-5-inch cut sheet film that had to be loaded in a darkroom. Second, I needed a tripod to balance the camera and a black focusing cloth to see the image. When looking through the camera, the image is upside-down and backward. To compensate for this, I simply held the Stimson photocopy upside-down and looked back and forth until I had found the specific site. I used two lenses, a wide-angle 90mm and a normal 135mm lens, for all of the shots. Because the camera lacks a light meter, I made all exposures manually. I made these readings with either a hand-held light meter, the reflected light meter of a 35mm camera, or sans meter via the "sunny sixteen" rule. This last strategy simply uses the 16 f/stop at a shutter speed inverse of the film speed. Because I always used 400 ASA black and white film, this meant an exposure of f/16 at 1/500 of a second. To enlarge my depth of field, I calculated this exposure to be f/32 at 1/100. Several shots of each scene were taken to ensure a good negative, and then I would move on to the next view. On average I was able to find and photograph one scene an hour while in the field.

I brought the film back to my darkroom and developed it in tanks. This process meant total darkness; no darkroom red lights could be used. I then made the final eight-by-ten-inch prints. For this the 4 × 5 format was perfect because each print was enlarged only twofold to duplicate Stimson's eight-by-ten-inch contact print.

The following summer I repeated this process in northern Wyoming. Although again I focused mainly on townscapes, I also rephotographed many scenic views. This is easily explained by Wyoming's geography: there are more scenic places in northern Wyoming. As with the previous summer, I carried many more photocopies of scenes than I was able to find and rephotograph. As did Stimson, I traveled alone and thus enjoyed the same freedom to shoot whatever shots I might think were available.

Unfortunately there are some problems with tracing the steps of one photographer. Even in the 7,500-piece Stimson collection, there are some obvious holes. There are no photographs of Casper in this book, and the reason is simple. As the second largest city in Wyoming, Casper had its own professional photographers who documented the city's progress. To photograph Casper would have been treading onto someone else's turf. Likewise, although the Stimson collection contains many photos of the state's early oil industry, there are few, if any, shots of the Salt Creek Field north of Casper. Again, this area was someone else's territory.

After the second summer, I had located 150 sites that Stimson had photographed. Throughout that year, I presented a slide show of this work through the Wyoming Council for the Humanities. The process of choosing slides for these shows helped me to organize the photographs into the themes that appear in this book: The Natural Landscape, The Forgotten Past, The Dynamic Townscape, and A Closer Look: Interpretive Rephotography.

Each chapter begins with a brief explanation of how rephotography fits into each theme. Generally, the photographs in each chapter are not arranged in chronological, geographical, or even geological order. Subchapters such as "Dome Lake" and "Yellowstone" will be grouped accordingly.

The Natural Landscape

For the first six years of his life in Wyoming, J. E. Stimson shot portraits exclusively. A chance trip to the Big Horns took him to places in Wyoming that he probably had not even known existed. With a rural upbringing in the southern Appalachians behind him, it was natural for Stimson to gravitate to the Wyoming wilderness. His promotion work for the Union Pacific gave him the chance to work in the field, and Stimson made the most of his opportunity. The following group of photographs show not only destination stops for the railroad, such as Yellowstone, but also interesting sidelights along the way.

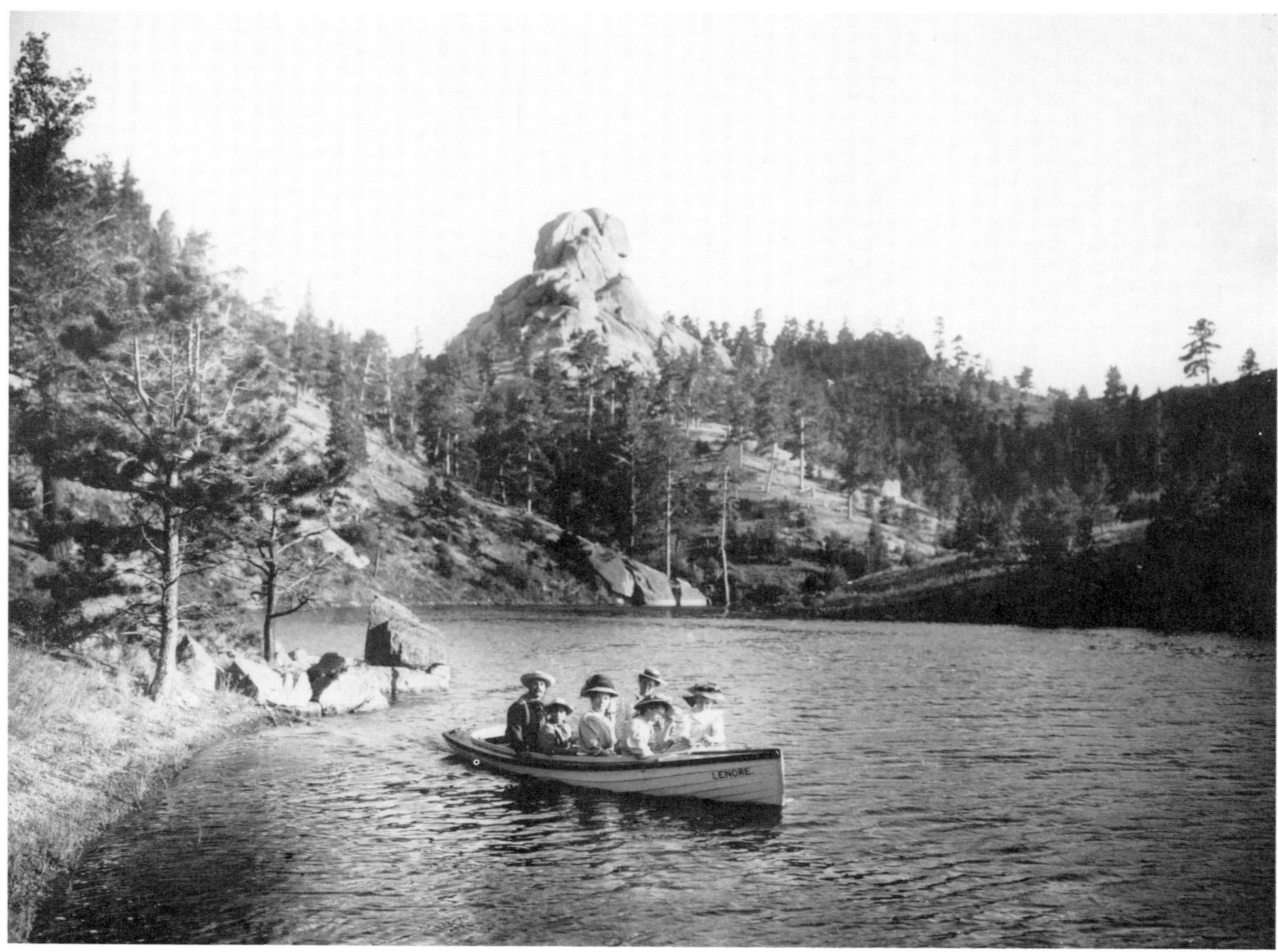

Fig. 1. Granite Springs outing, 1908.

This view looks west near the inlet to Granite Reservoir in what is now Curt Gowdy State Park. Stimson's wife, Anna, and his two daughters, Josephine and Louise, occupy the front of the *Lenore*. The large boulder at left center remains, as do the trees and rocks near the back edge of the lake at right center.

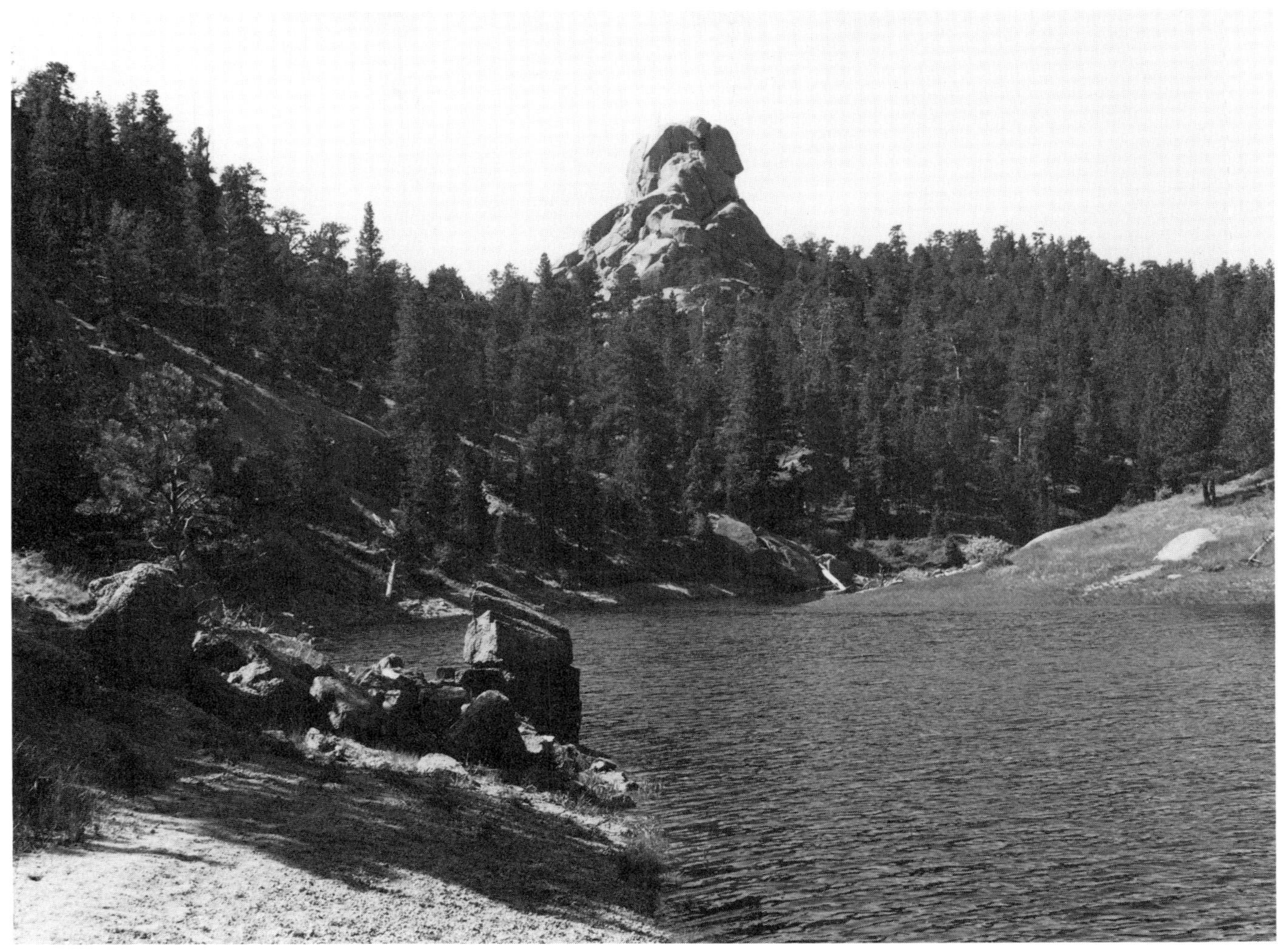

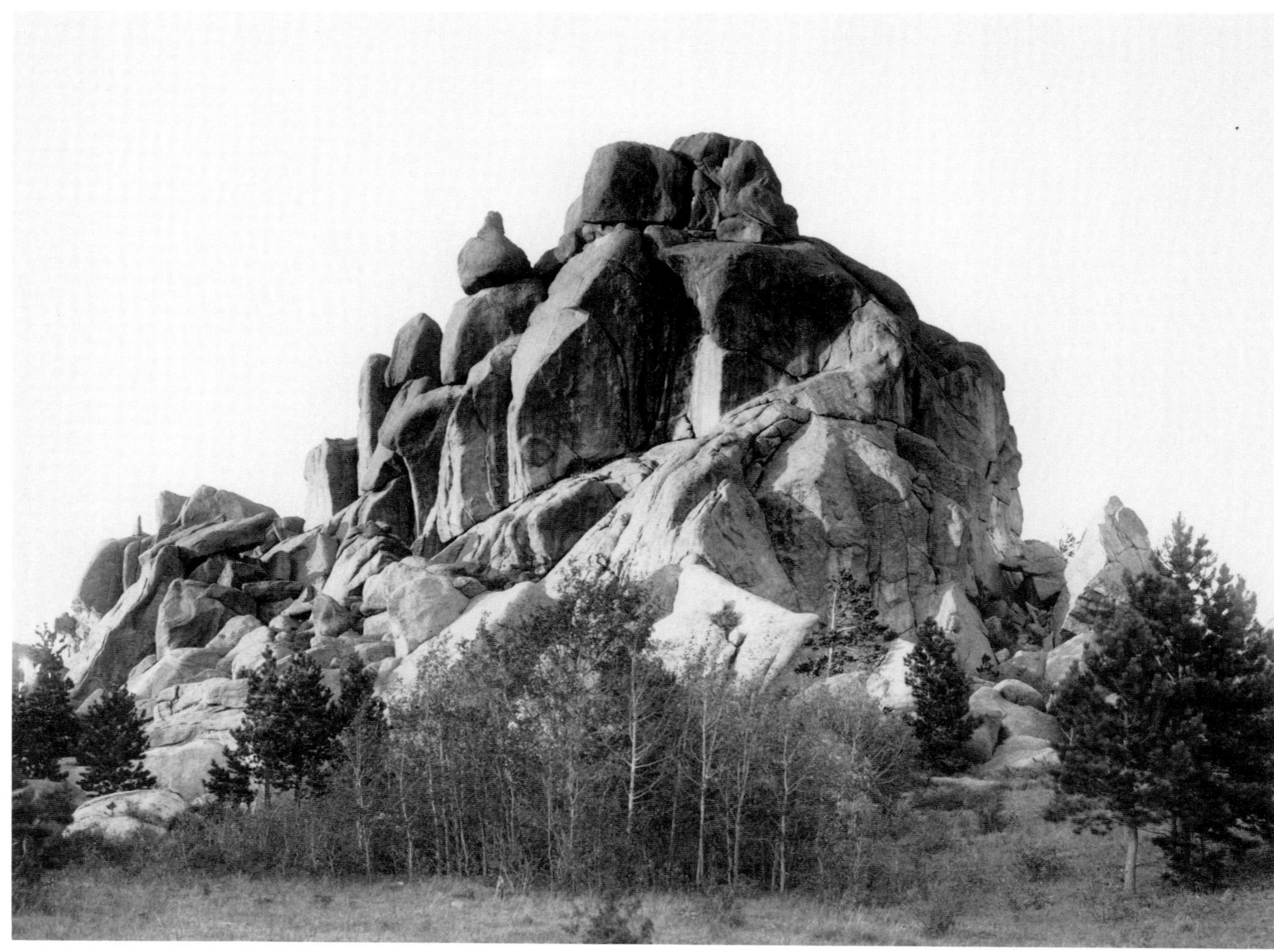

Fig. 2. Vedauwoo rock formation, no date.

Vedauwoo is a favorite picnic and rock climbing area between Laramie and Cheyenne. The name Vedauwoo comes from the Arapaho word meaning "earth born." Stimson's photograph, however, is not in the main section of Vedauwoo but on the Happy Jack Road to Cheyenne near the Hynds' Lodge. I took my rephotograph approximately fifty yards behind the original so that the aspen grove would not interfere. The small needle of rock is still in place at left center.

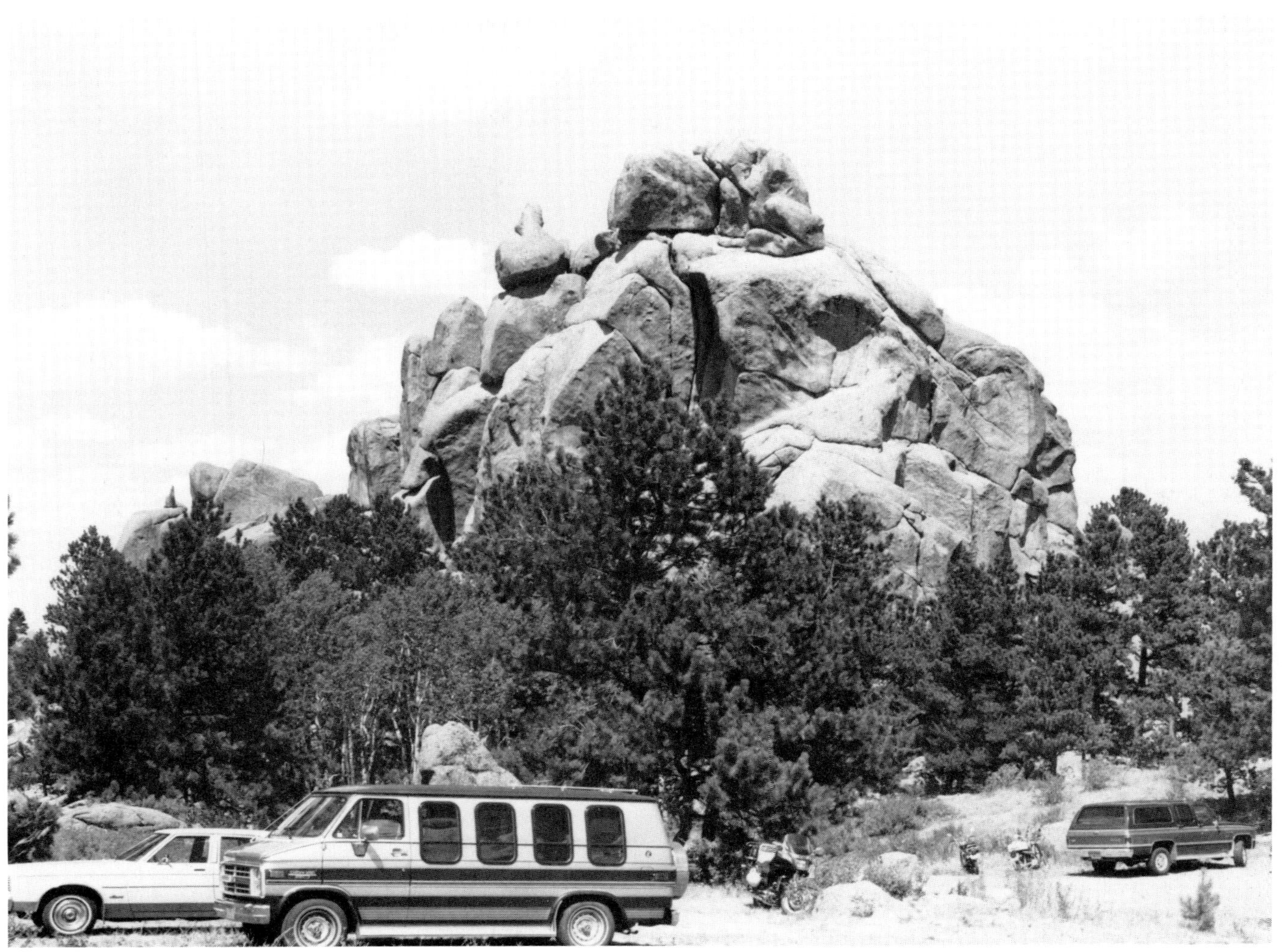

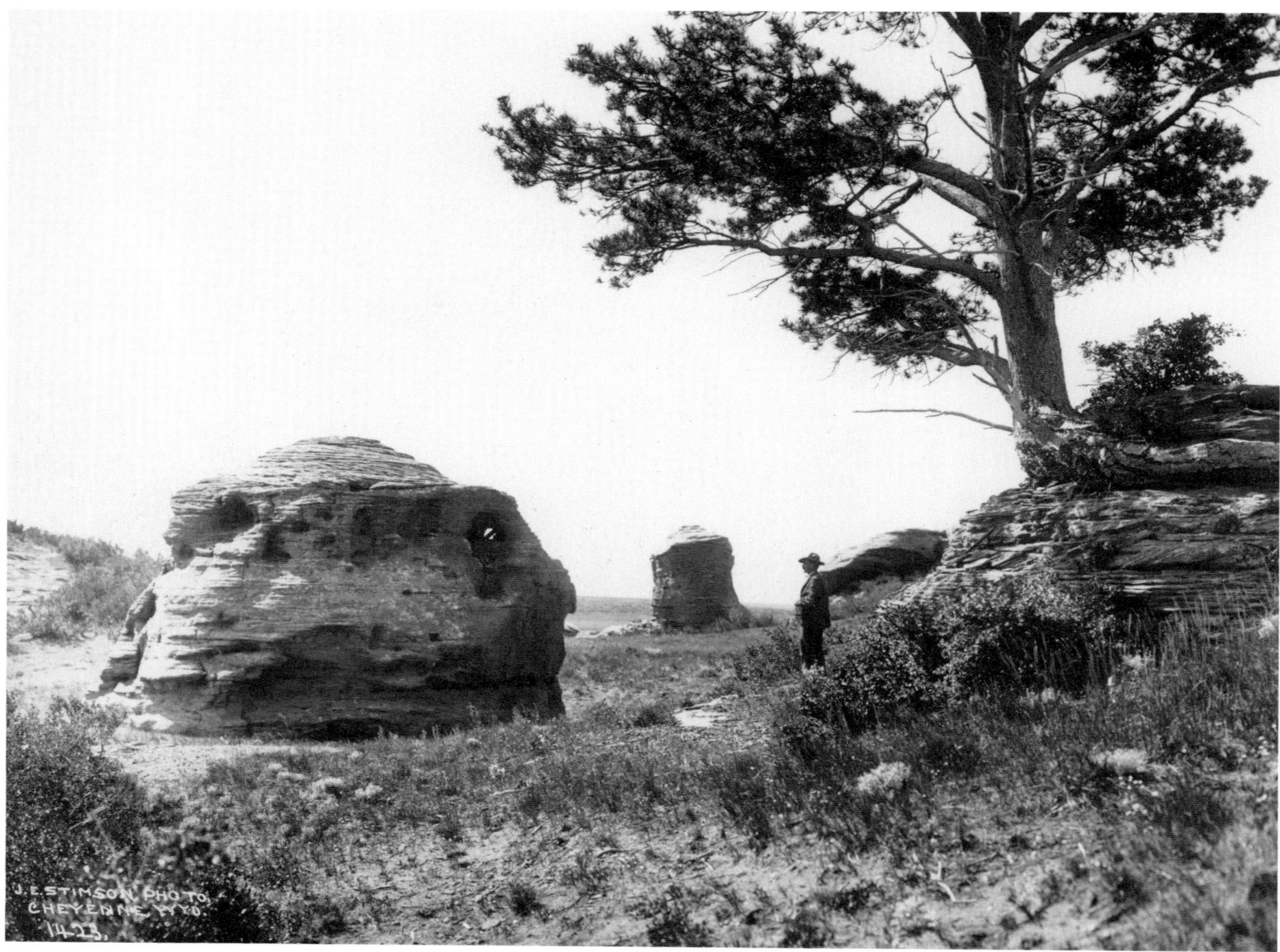

Fig. 3. Scene in the Red Buttes country, near Laramie, 1906.

The Red Buttes country that Stimson refers to is located approximately thirteen miles south of Laramie between Highway 287 and the Union Pacific tracks. Earlier the poet Walt Whitman had passed by the area and described the scenery in his poem, "Passage to India":

> I hear the locomotives rushing and roaring, and the
>   shrill steam whistle,
> I hear the echoes reverberate through the grandest scenery
>   in the world,
> I cross the Laramie plains, I note the rocks in grotesque
>   shapes, the buttes, . . .

The beehive-shaped rocks were eroded by winds. Although very little has changed in either the rocks or the trees over the last eighty years, the uniformity of the rocks made it difficult to identify Stimson's views. To solve this problem, I did what Stimson had done. I started near the railroad track and moved out from there. Sure enough, all of the photos were taken near the tracks.

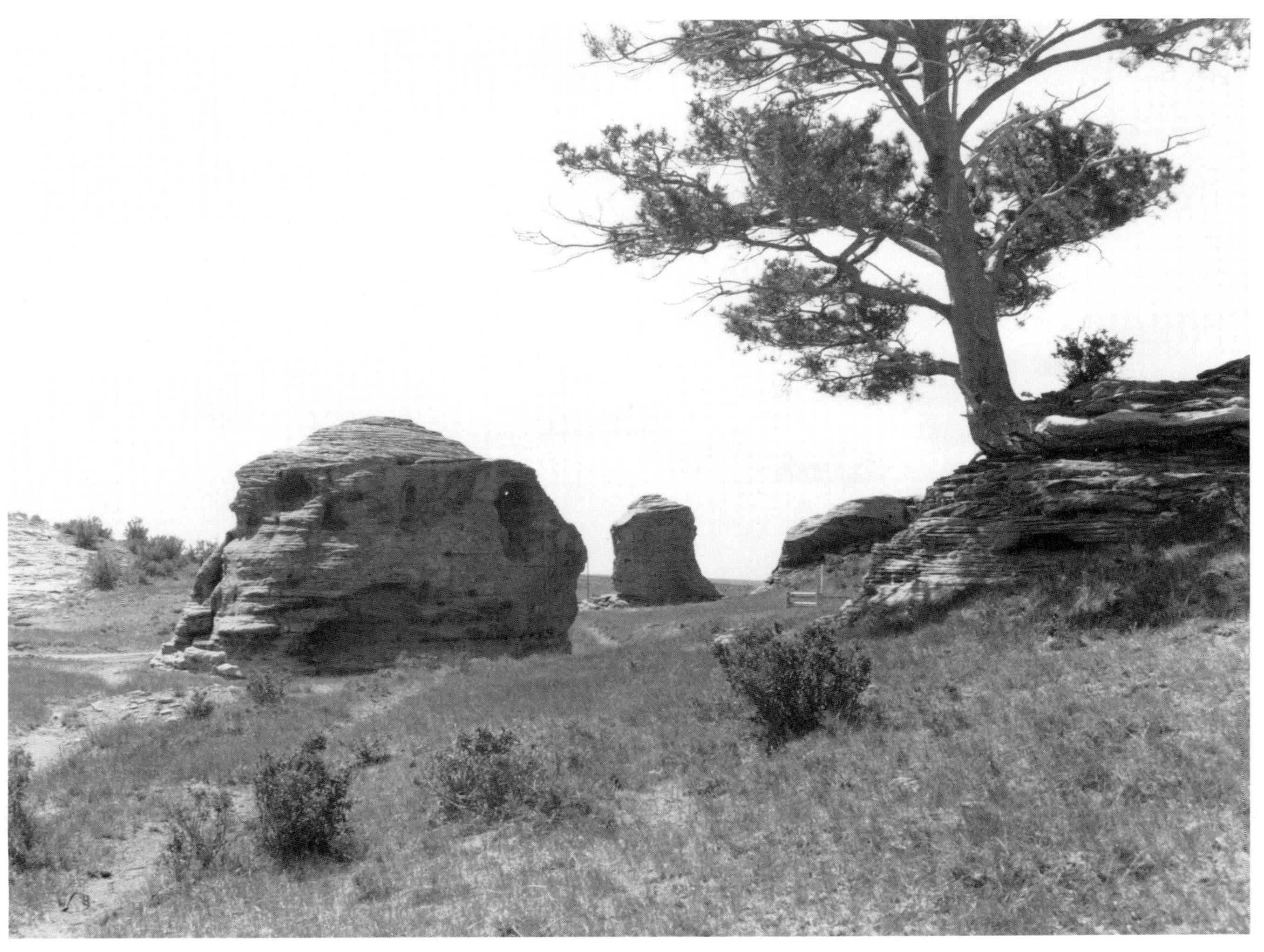

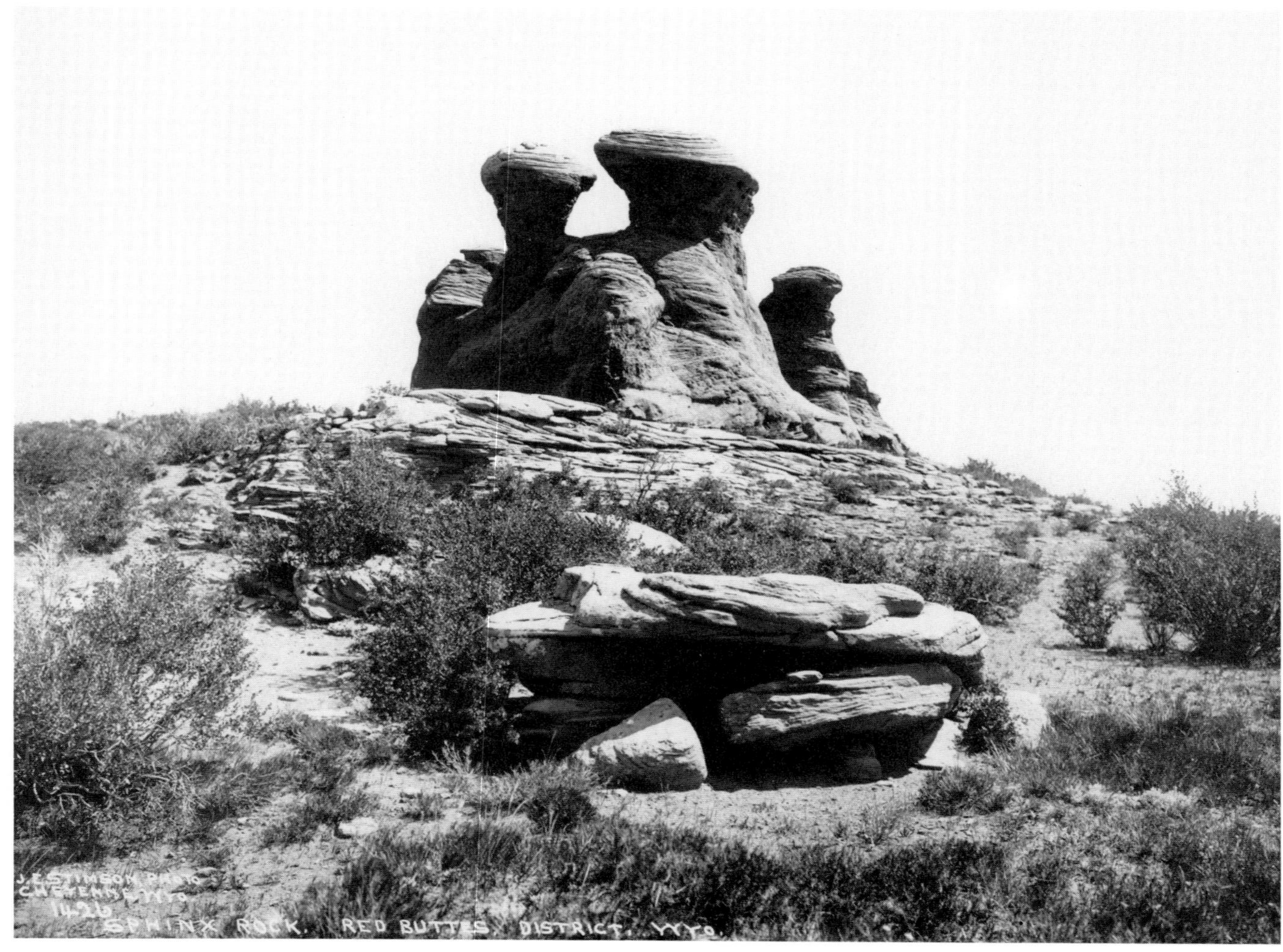

Fig. 4. Sphinx Rock, Red Buttes, 1906.

The Sphinx Rock, as Stimson called it, is also known locally as the Camel Rock. Inside this toadstool-shaped formation are various inscriptions from earlier visitors. This prominent formation can be seen east of Highway 287, thirteen miles south of Laramie.

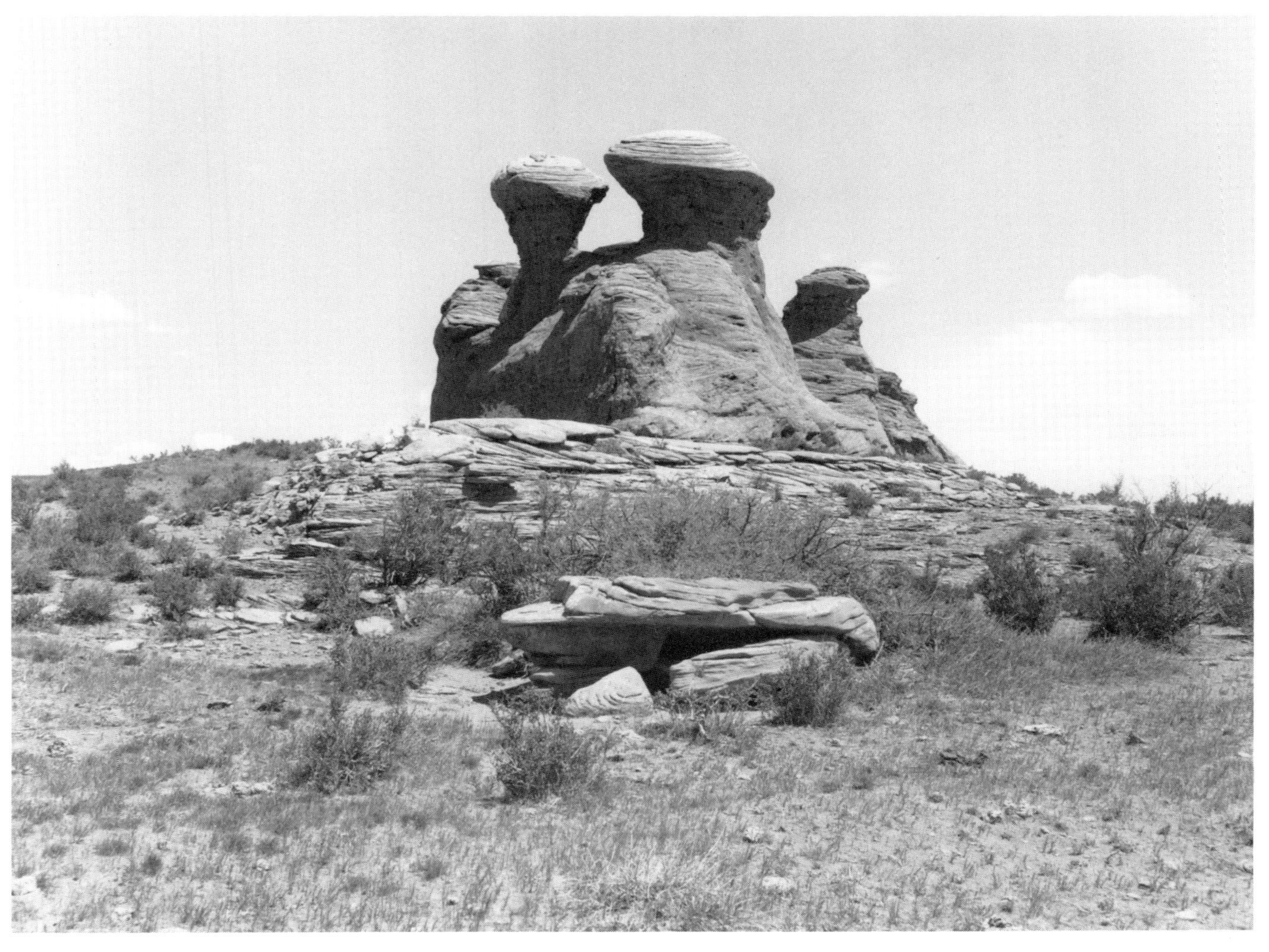

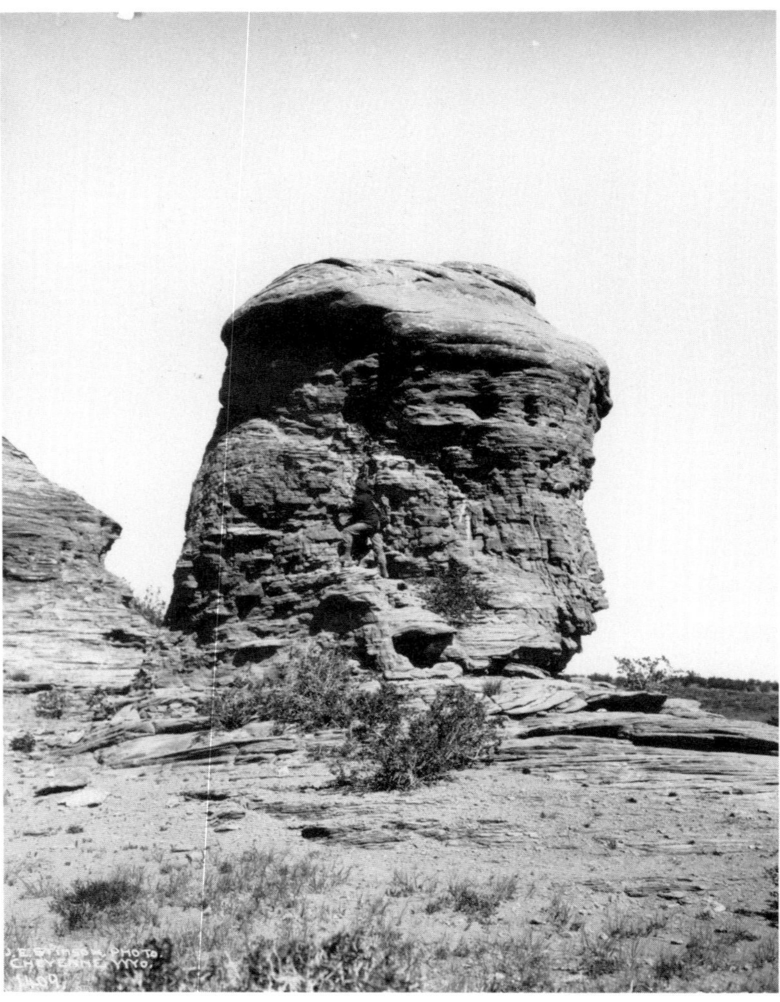

Fig. 5. Castle Dome, Red Buttes, 1906.

As with the other photographs taken in the Red Buttes area, rephotography illustrates that wind erosion is a very slow process. Except for the climber, little has changed in eighty-two years.

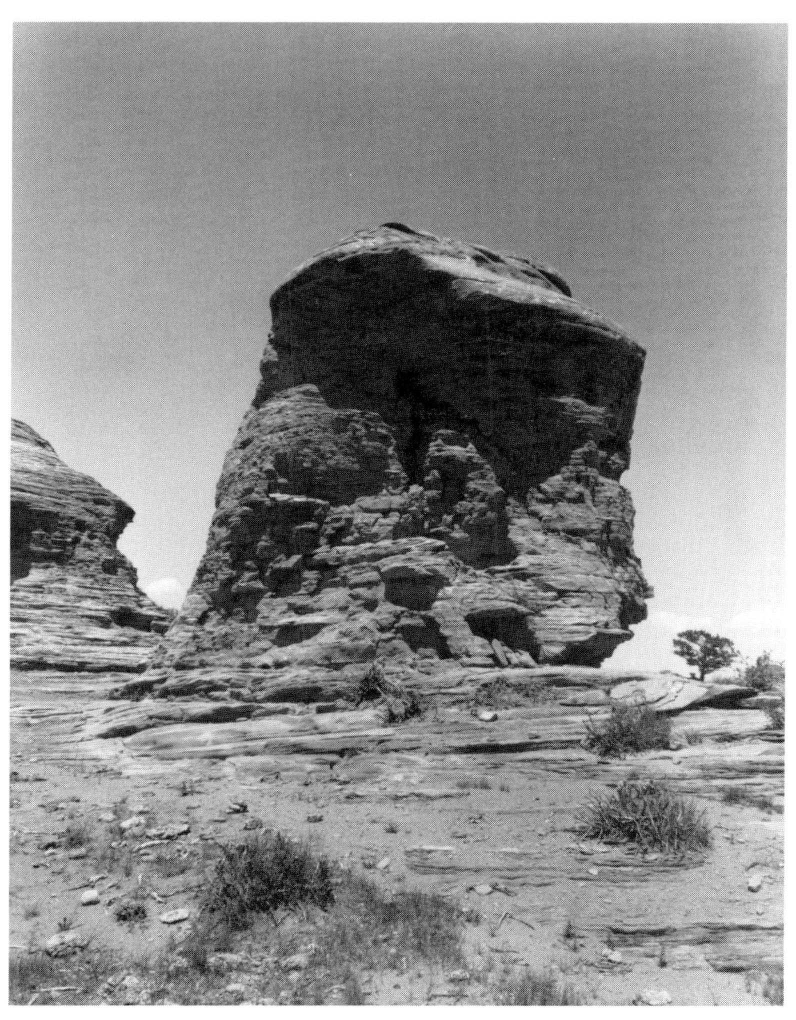

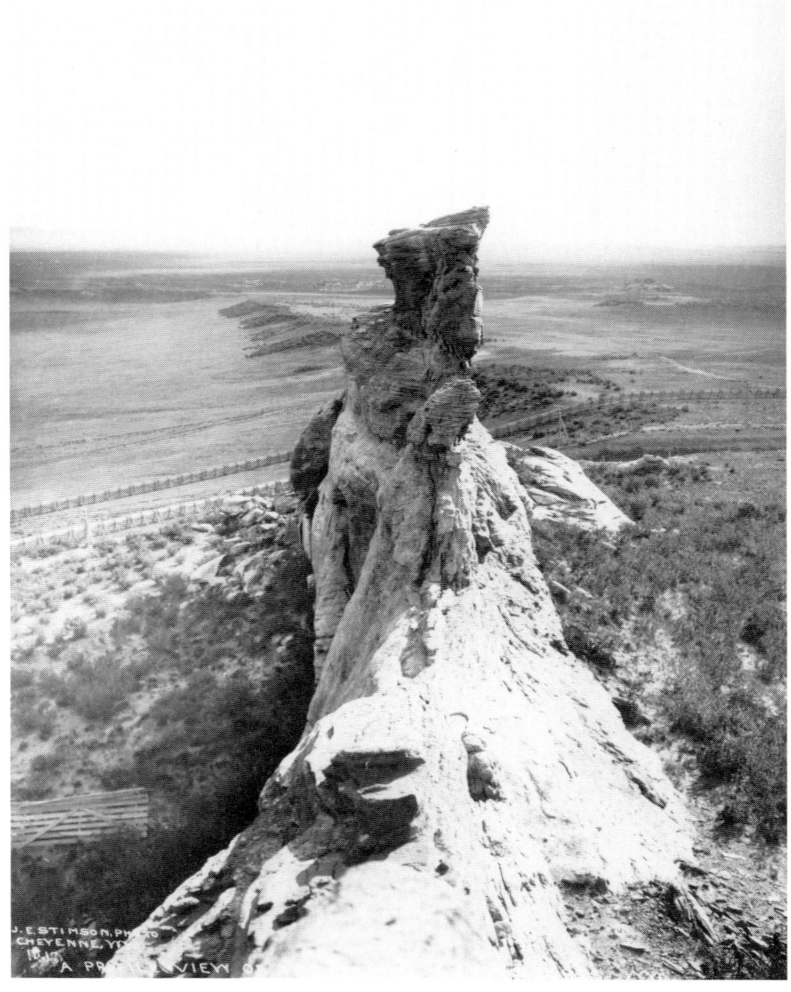

Fig. 6. A profile of the Maine Rock, Red Buttes, 1906

The "Maine" probably refers to the likeness of this formation to the sunken U.S. ship of the Spanish-American War, but this "Maine" proved difficult to find. Located near Colores, an old point on the Union Pacific near Red Buttes, the formation is rather dull-looking from Highway 287. Although the snow fence in the old photo guards the hidden tracks of the Union Pacific, the modern view shows the tracks but no snow fence.

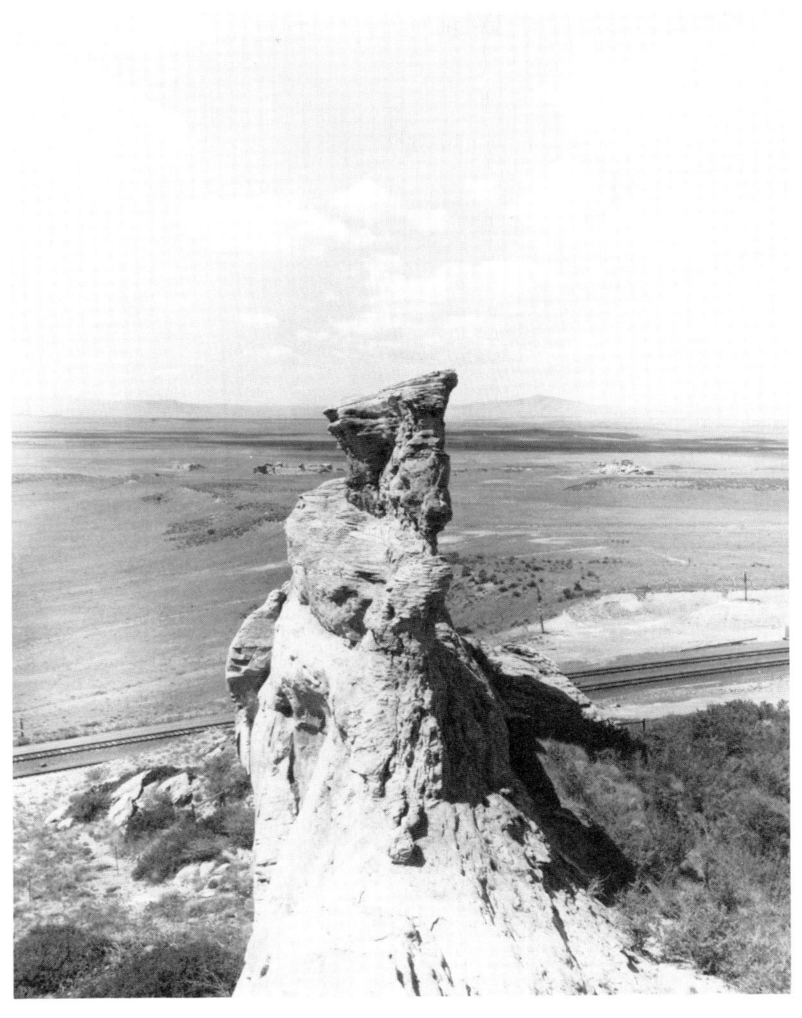

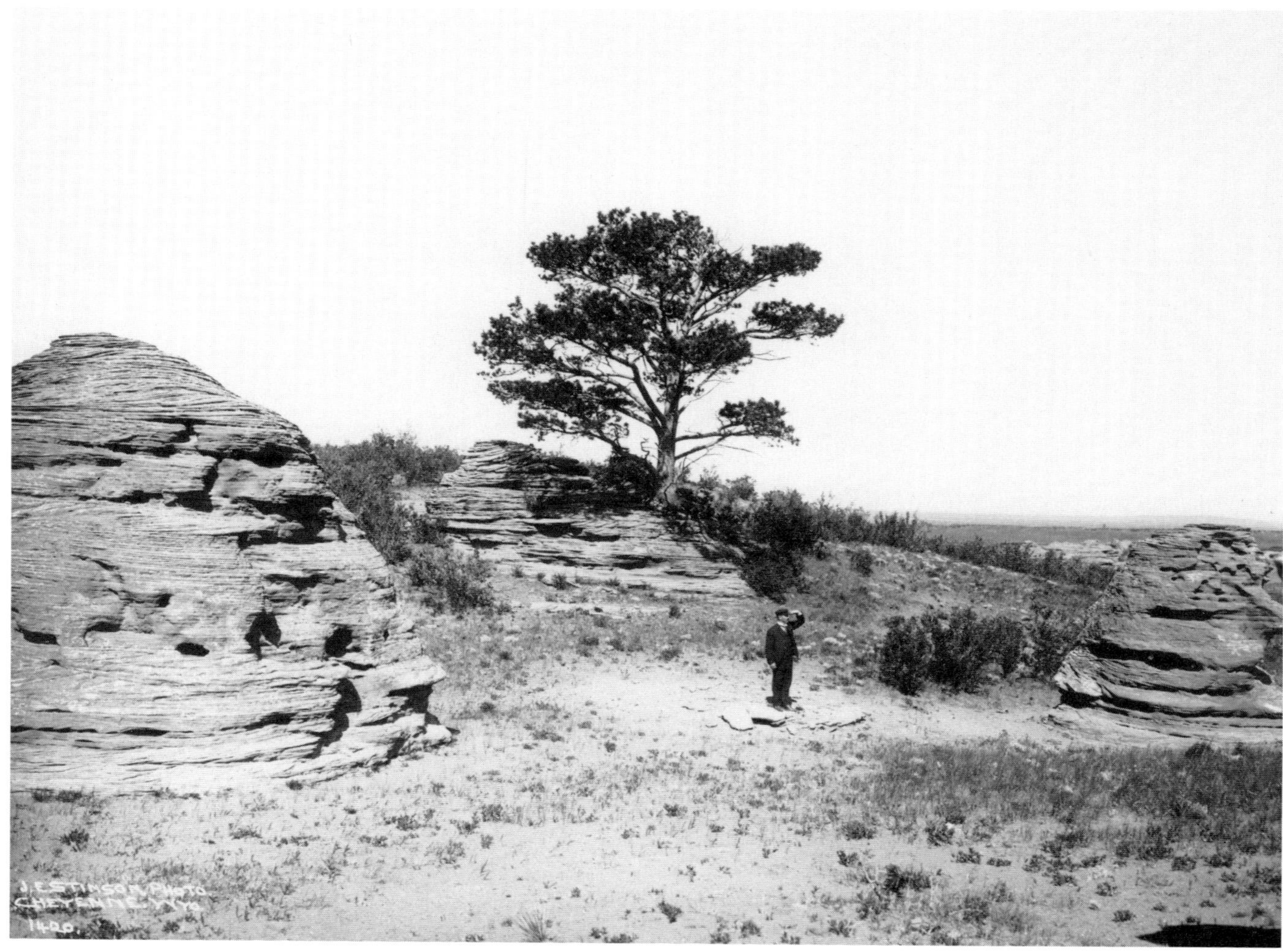

Fig. 7. The Beehive Rocks, Red Buttes, 1906.

In this view a new guide wire at center right and the road, foreground, are the only changes in the scene. The man in the center is probably a railroad conductor. The greater sensitivity of modern film captures the far-off Snowy Range in the right background.

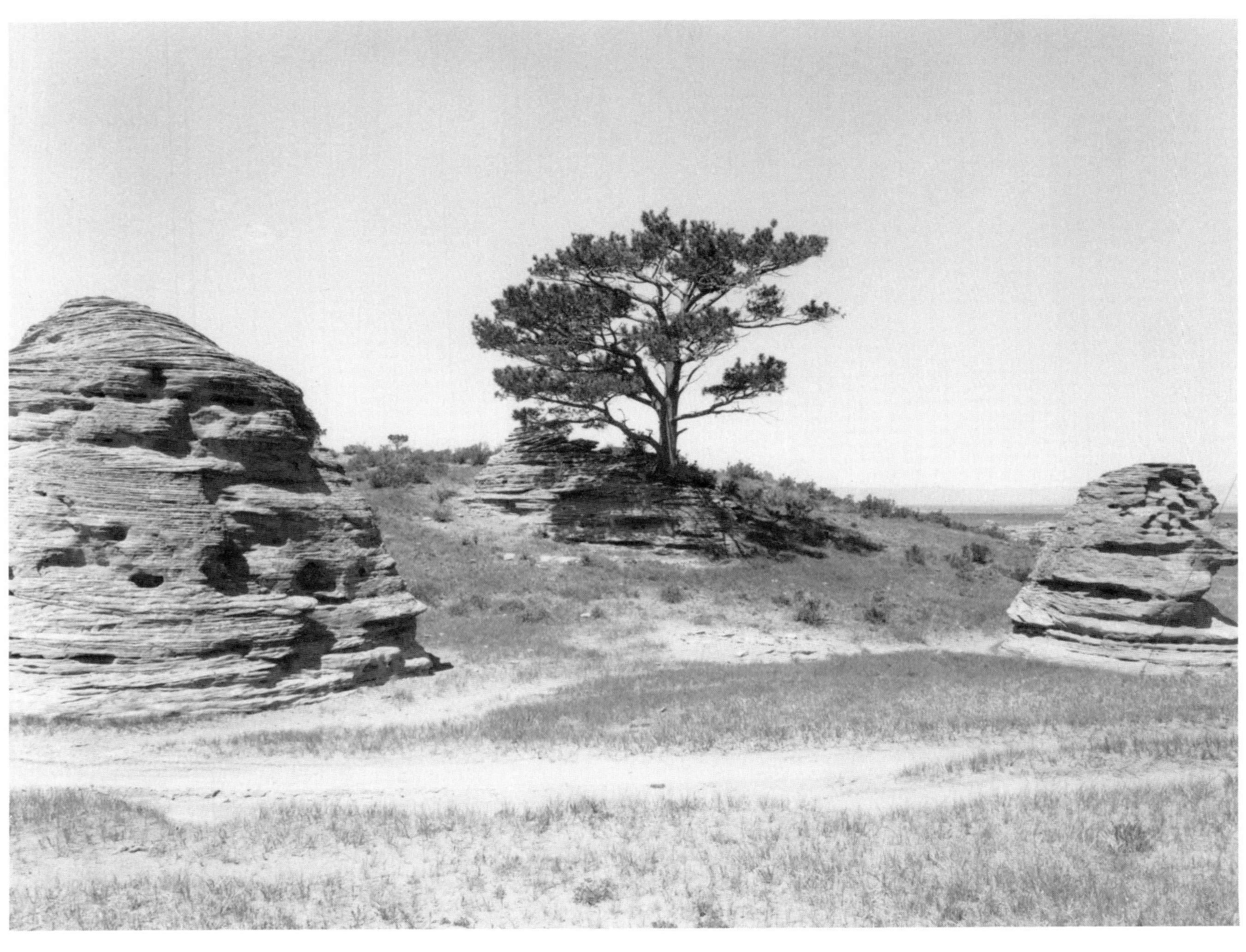

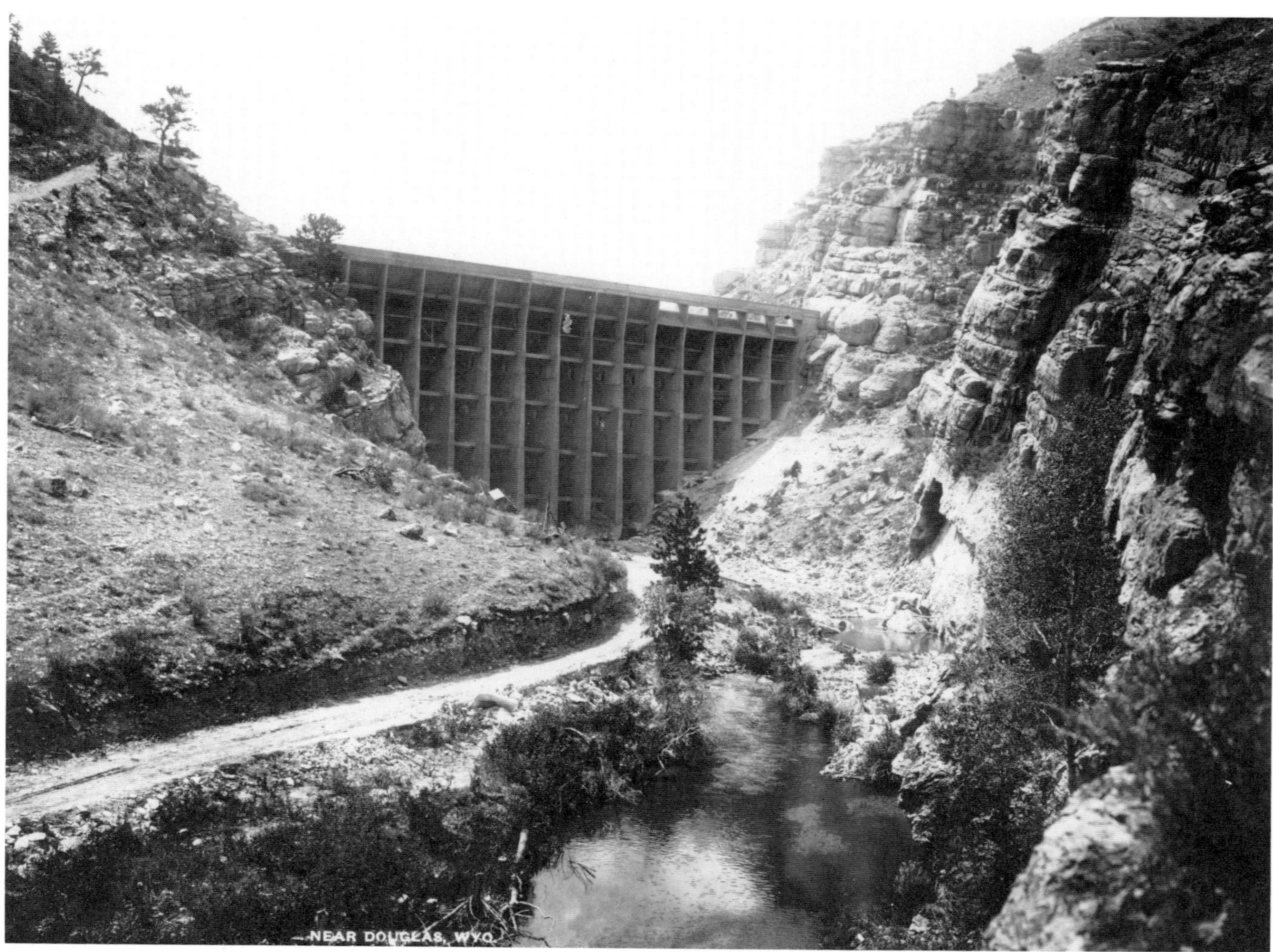

Fig. 8. La Prele Dam, near Douglas, 1910.

Located on La Prele Creek between Douglas and Glenrock, the dam was constructed in 1907–08 as part of a local irrigation project. The dam is about one mile upstream from Ayre's Natural Bridge. In *Wyoming Place Names* Mae Urbanek says that La Prele Creek was named by early trappers for the scouring rush or horsetail grass, called *la prele* in French, that grows on its banks.

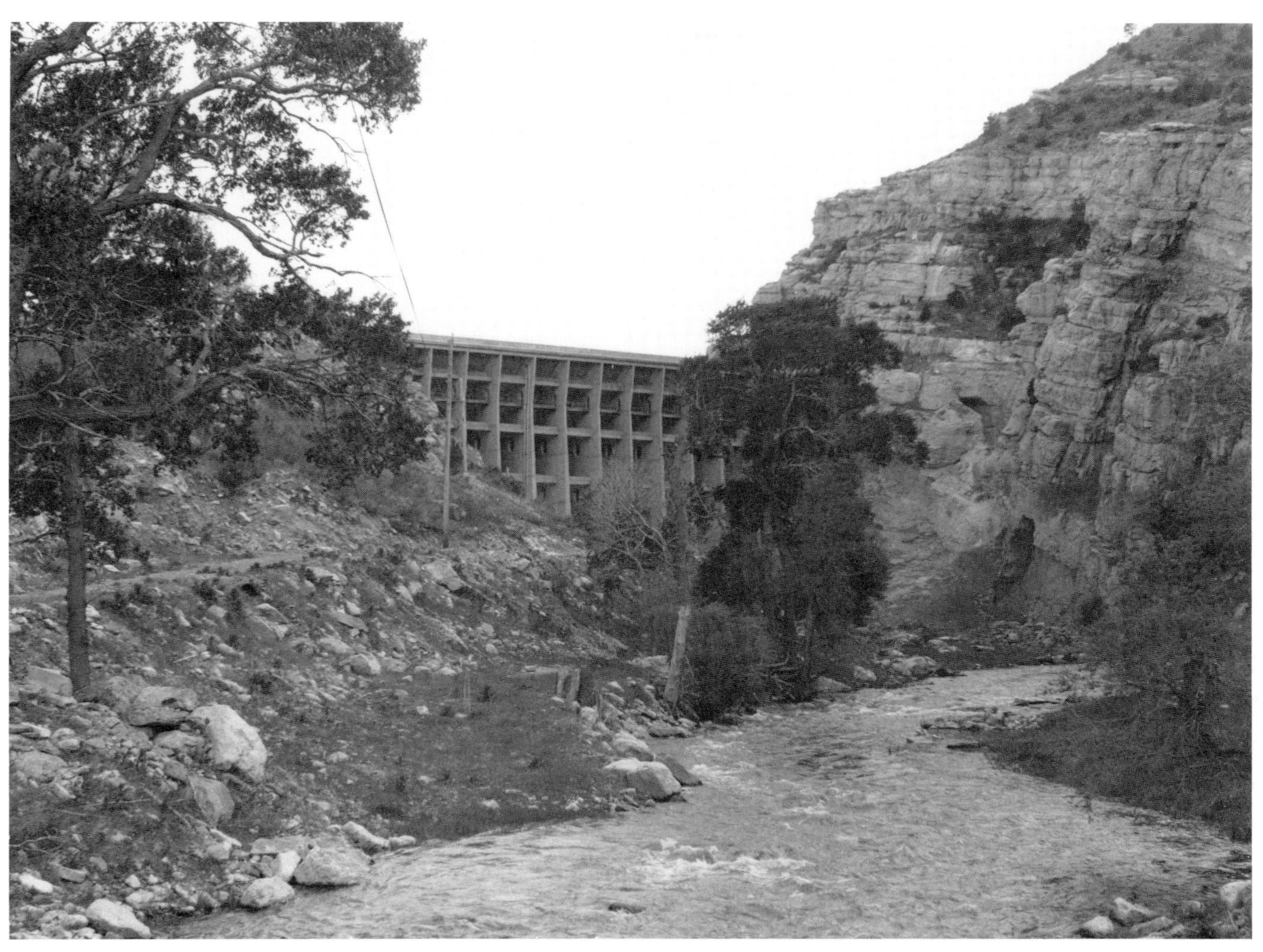

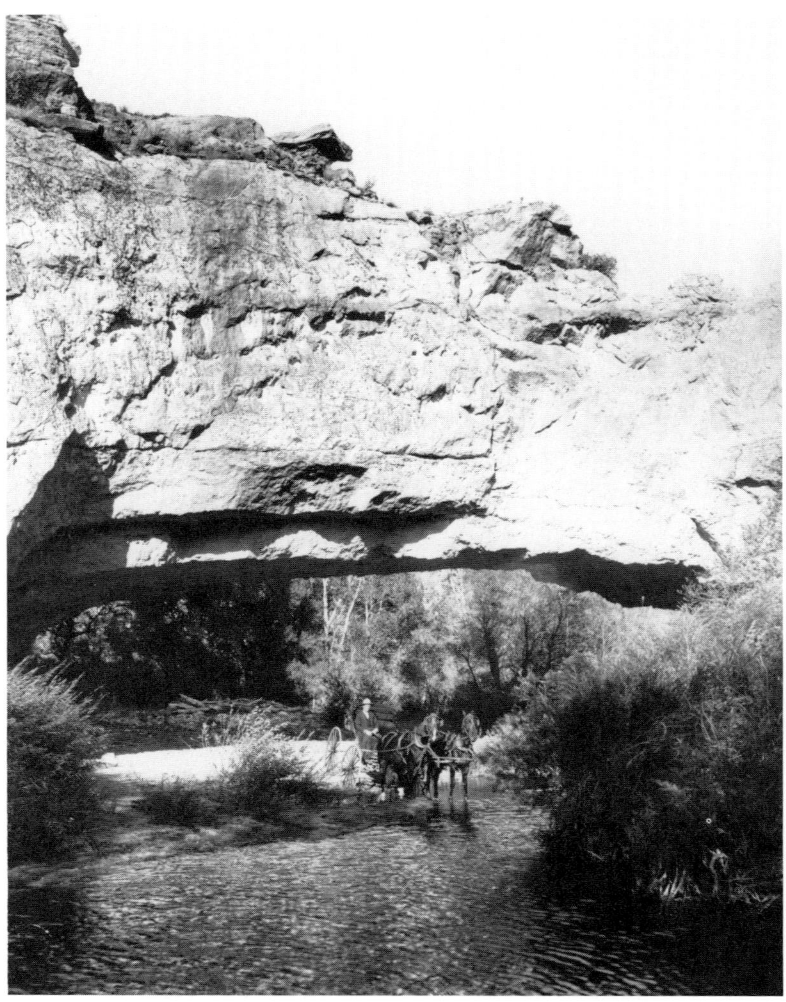

Fig. 9. View of Natural Bridge, near Douglas, 1903.

The natural bridge spans La Prele Creek about a mile below La Prele Dam. Composed of red sandstone, the bridge is thirty feet high and ninety feet across. William Henry Jackson first photographed the spot in 1870. It is now known as Ayre's Natural Bridge for early resident Alva Ayres, who owned the land. It was donated by the family to Converse County in 1921 for a public park. The horse and buggy in Stimson's view probably belonged to his guide.

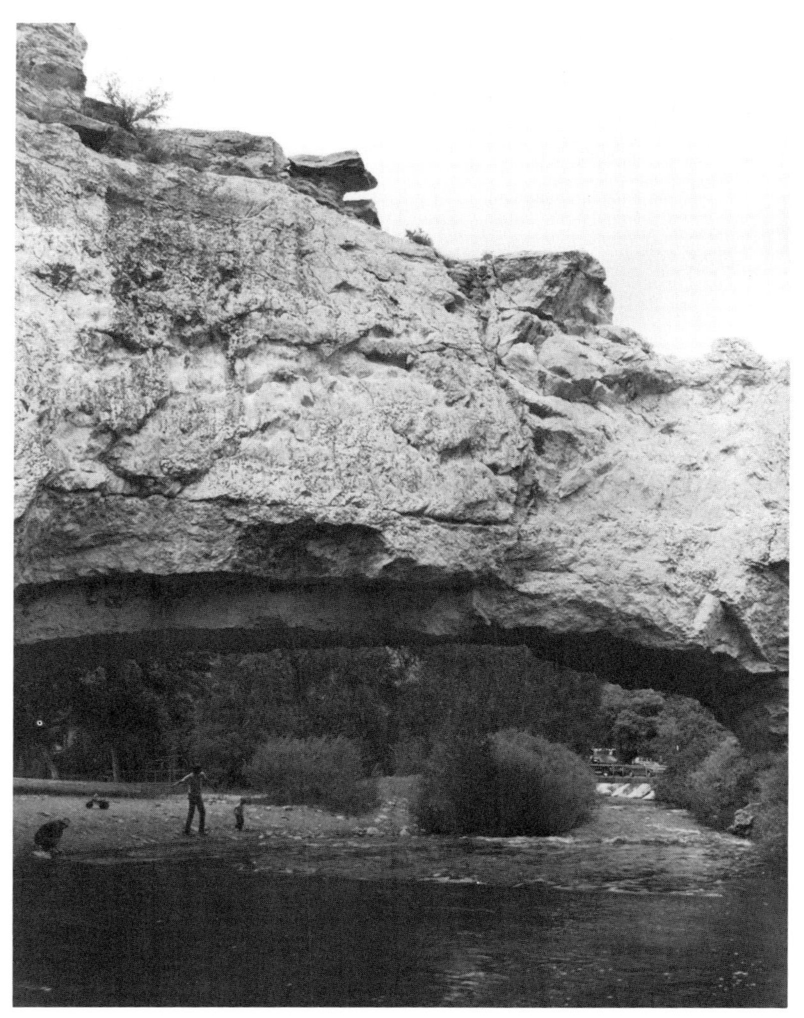

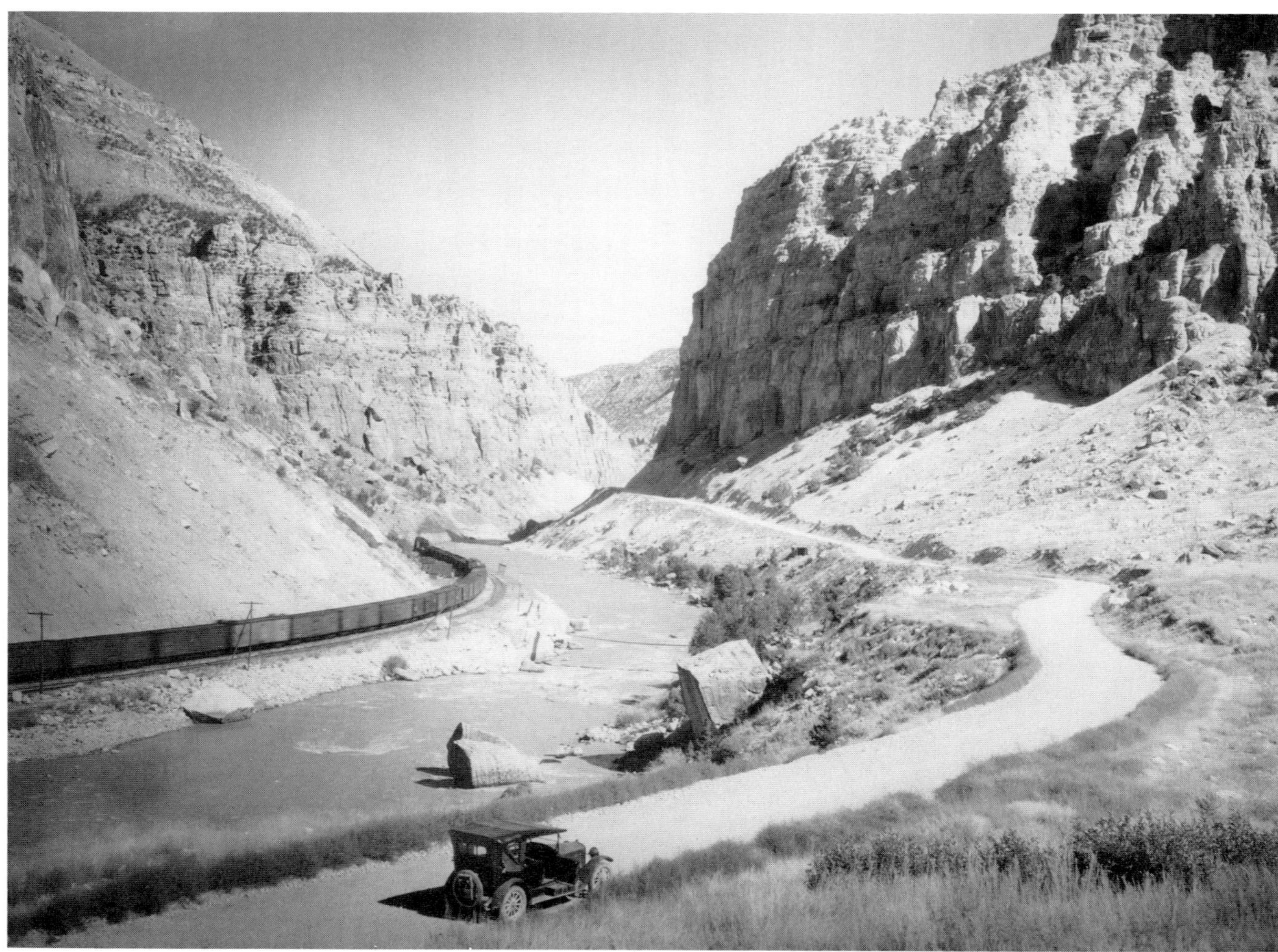

Fig. 10. Wind River Canyon, no date.

This view, looking north, is about four miles south of Thermopolis. The large river boulders in Stimson's photograph are still there, partially covered by the new highway. The Burlington Northern blasted a right-of-way through the canyon in 1913, and the highway was opened to travel in 1924.

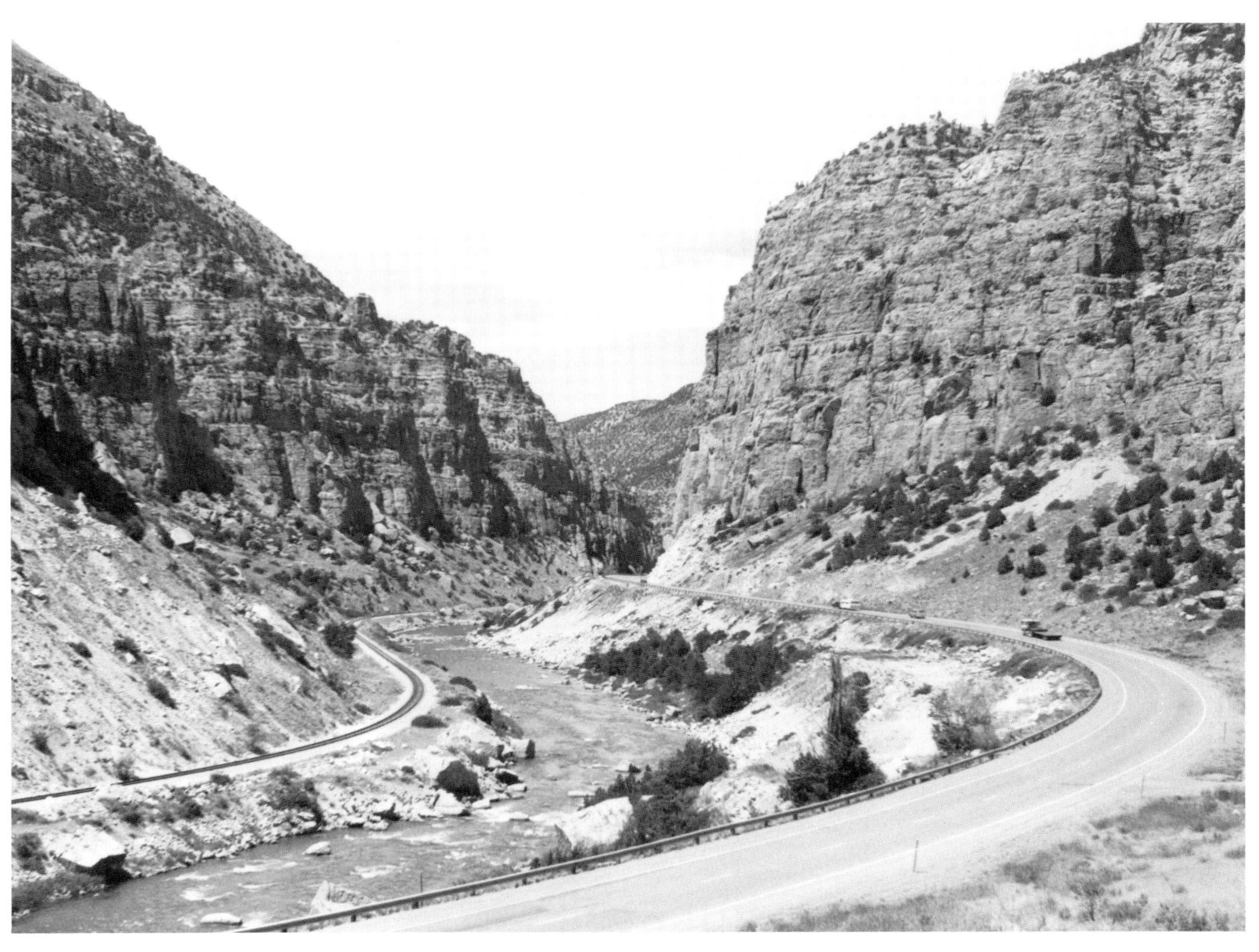

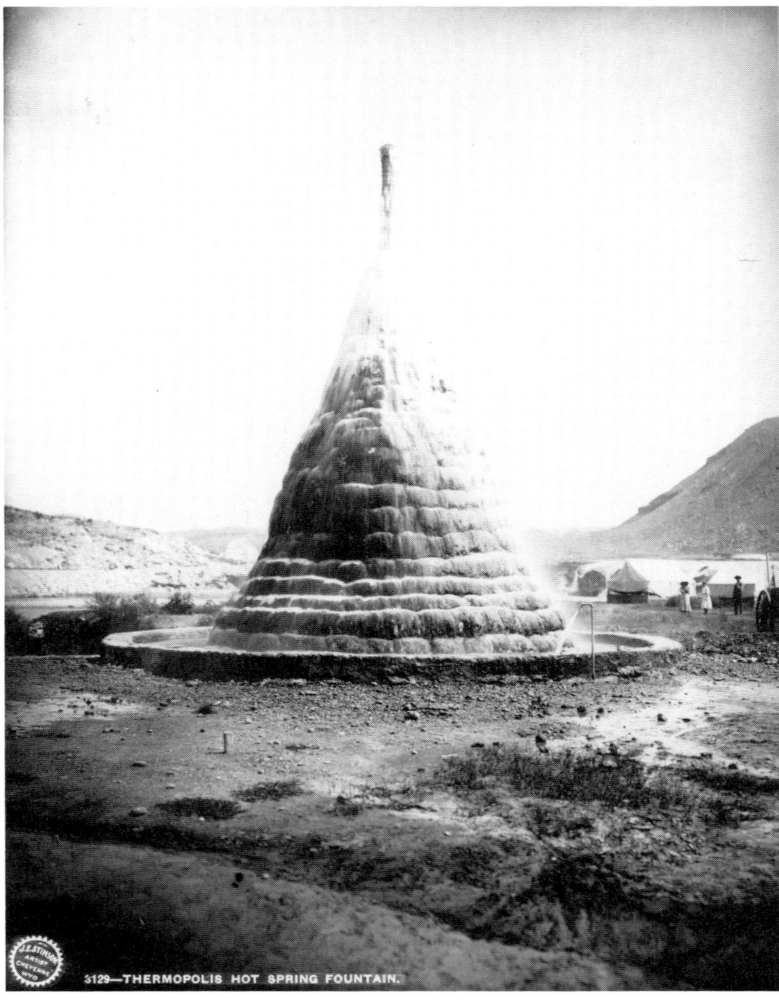

Fig. 11. Thermopolis Hot Springs Fountain, 1911.

This view illustrates the buildup of mineral water over seventy-seven years. The original fountain, a man-made cone with an inserted pipe to draw water to the top, has been drastically altered by the mineral waters. Almost eight decades later, water still trickles down the side of the fountain.

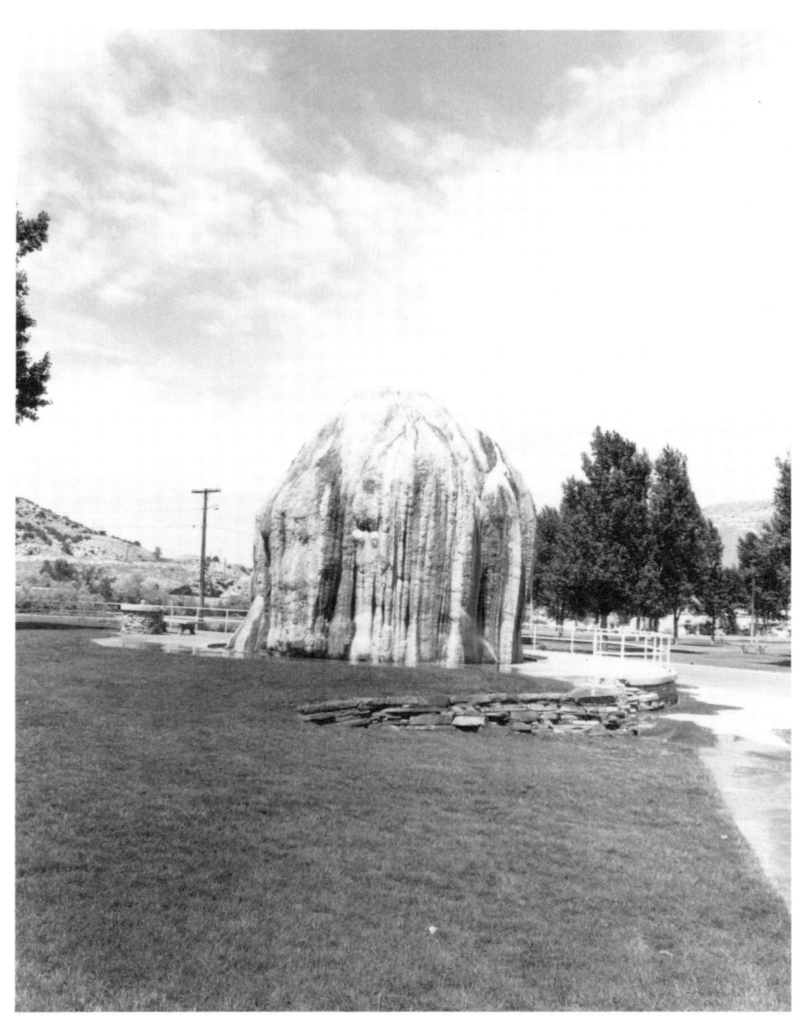

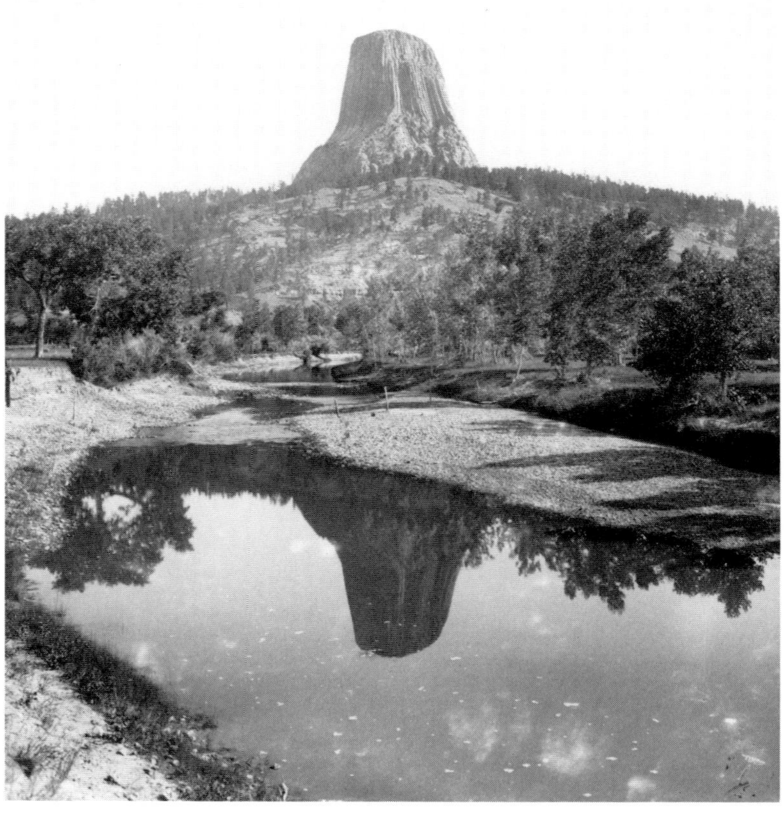

Fig. 12. Devil's Tower, 1903.

This view of Devil's Tower was taken looking north along the banks of the Belle Fourche River. Stimson made his view three years before President Teddy Roosevelt declared Devil's Tower the country's first national monument. Although Stimson's view is in the morning, the modern view was taken near dusk. The modern photo also shows that the river has shifted within its flood plain. The large rocks on the exposed hillside, center, are also visible.

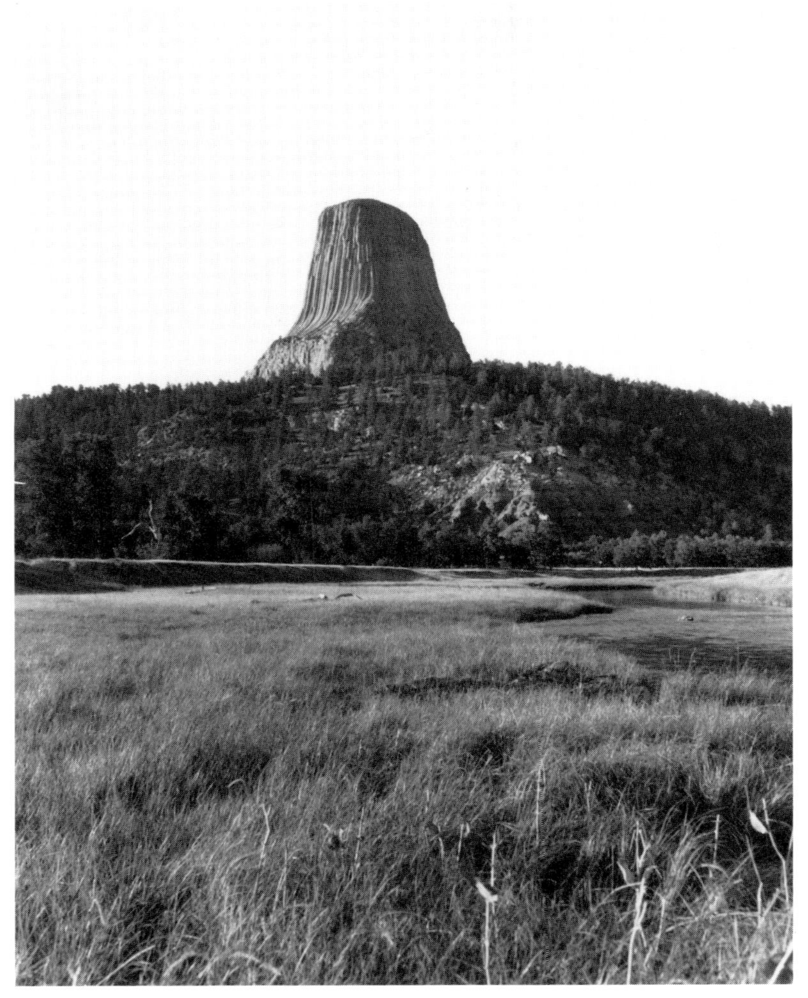

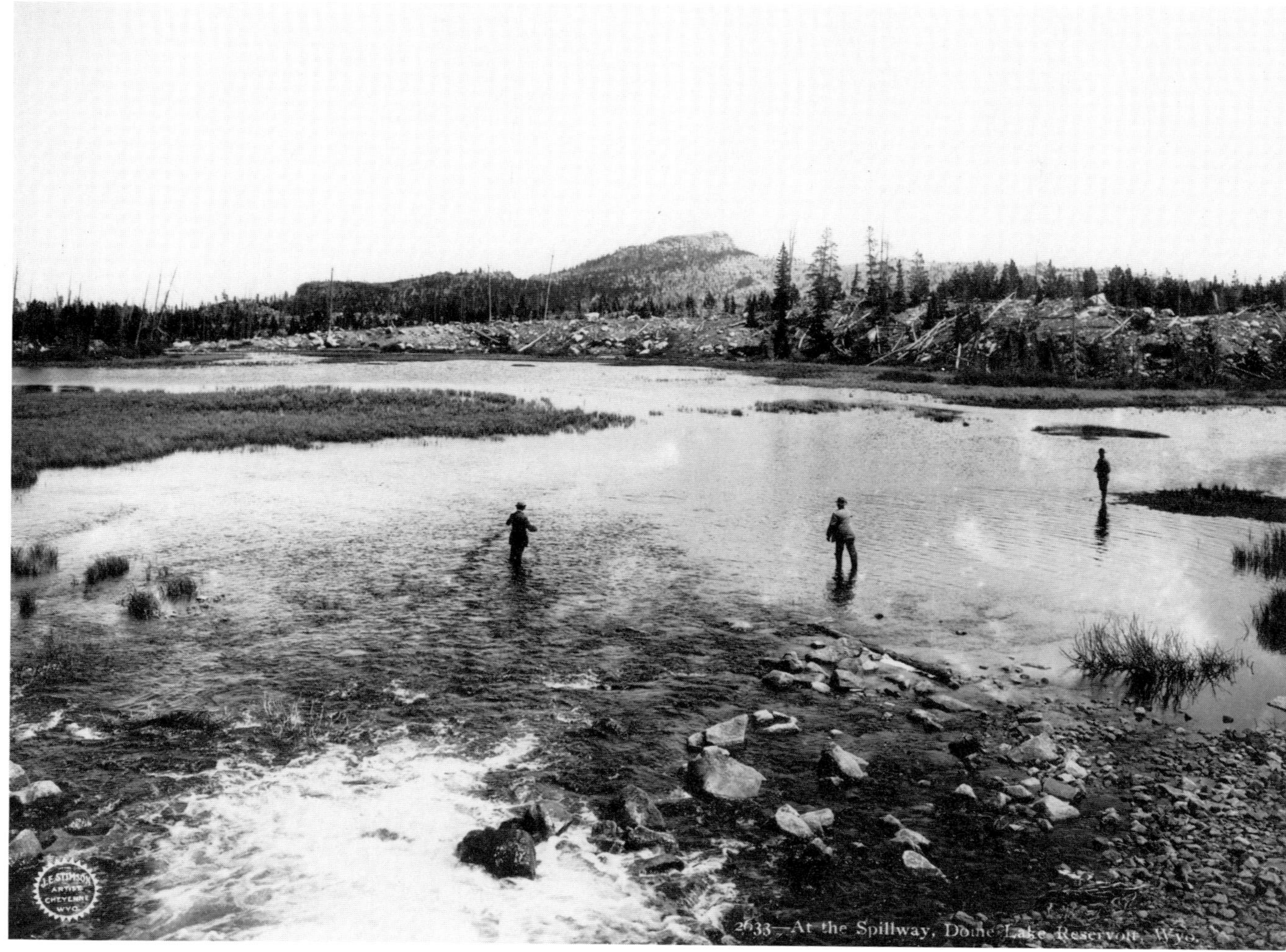

Fig. 13. At the spillway, 1909.

Dome Lake is connected to Dome Lake Reservoir by a dam. On the opposite end of Dome Lake Reservoir is this spillway. Dome Rock can be seen in the distance. Legend has it that the great Sioux chief Red Cloud burned down much of the Bighorn forest during his war with the whites over the Bozeman Trail in the 1860s. Today the forest that Chittenden described as "burned off" has fully recovered.

Dome Lake

Dome Lake is situated in the Bighorn National Forest, thirty-seven miles southwest of Sheridan. It has been a private summer resort since 1895. The land, 1040 acres, was purchased two years before the national forest was created. The Dome Lake Club controls three lakes including Crescent, Dome, and Dome Lake Reservoir. In 1894–95 a huge log lodge was built to house visitors, and the lake was stocked with trout. On August 19, 1897, one of these visitors, western historian Hiram Martin Chittenden, recorded his thoughts in a journal entry:

> Arrived at Dome Lake 9:30 am and remained 'til 2 pm. Took several pictures. This place has been turned into a summer resort under the patronage of the B&M RR [Baltimore & Missouri] but it can never be a success as it lacks the essential elements of attractive mountain scenery. The lake itself is surpassed by thousands of mountain lakes. The timber is all burned off its mountains around about, and the means of access are simply abominable.

Other private cabins were soon built. In 1908 a club member recorded a catch of twelve rainbow trout weighing between two and four pounds each. By 1915 the resort had grown into a small summer community, complete with black servants, a private telephone system, electricity, and ice houses. Members of the club included such business-

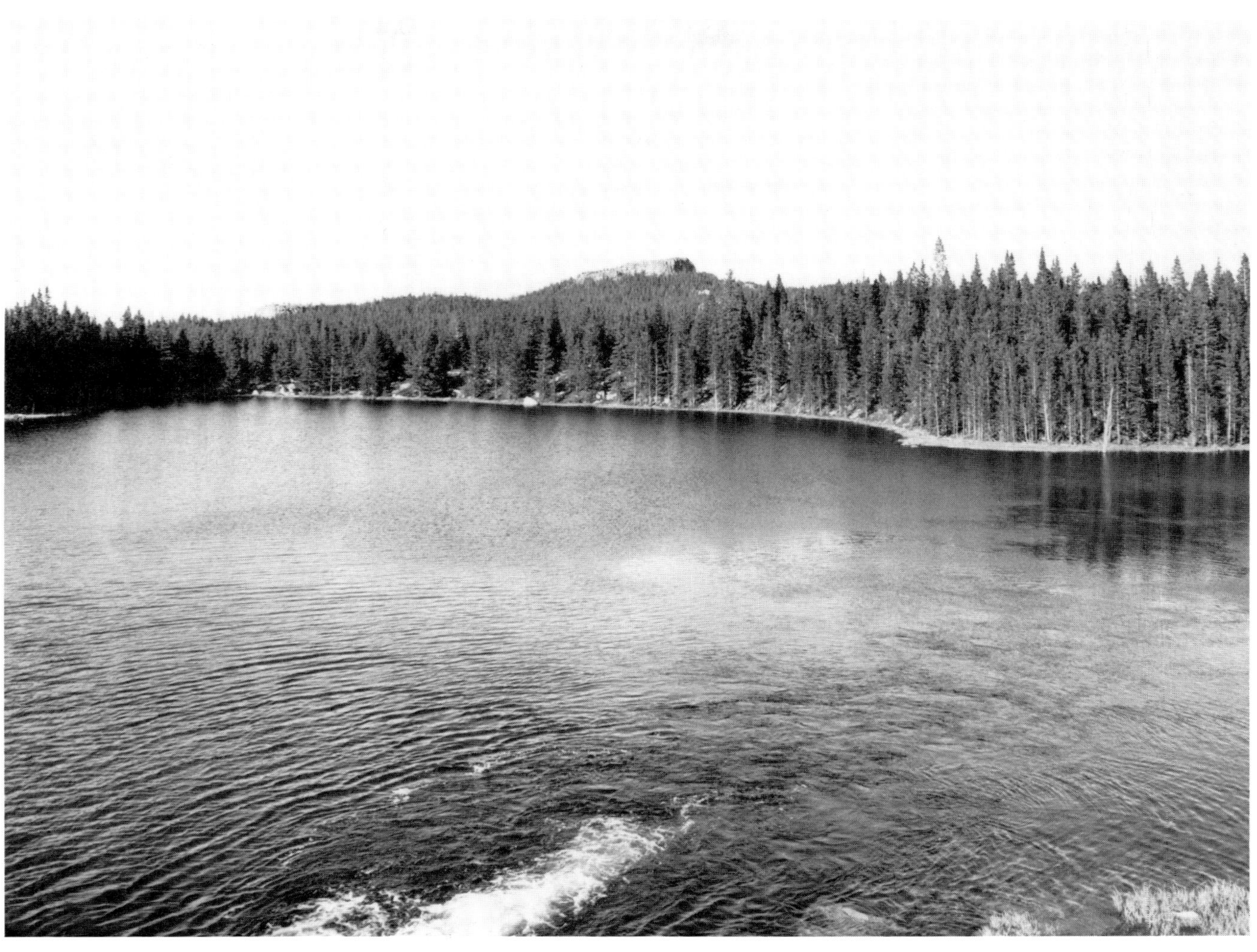

men as: C. N. Dietz and Edward Gillette of Omaha, Nebraska; W. Cameron Forbes of Boston; and John B. Kendrick of Sheridan.

In the summer of 1988, I visited Dome Lake to try to rephotograph some of Stimson's views. After making arrangements with the club caretaker, via shortwave radio, I found a friend with a four-wheel drive to make the climb through Big Horn, Wyoming up the Red Grade road to Bighorn National Forest. The mountain scenery was spectacular. Cloud Peak and Black Tooth rise from the south. After passing local dude ranches, we found the Dome Lake road. At this point, Chittenden's remarks still proved to be true. The four-mile road into the lake was certainly abominable. Twenty minutes later, we were at the locked gate of the Dome Lake Club. The view was again breathtaking. Dome Rock rose above the tree line to the northeast, and the Big Horn Mountains rose to the south and west. We saw elk, deer, and ten moose that day. The trees that Chittenden had reported burned (probably by the Sioux in the 1860s) had fully recovered. I learned that the lake is still in private hands and that most of the members stay at the lake for the entire summer. The road is kept in poor condition to help maintain privacy, but some members bypass this by flying in by helicopter. At the end of the day, we were treated to a guest gourmet chef's leg of lamb.

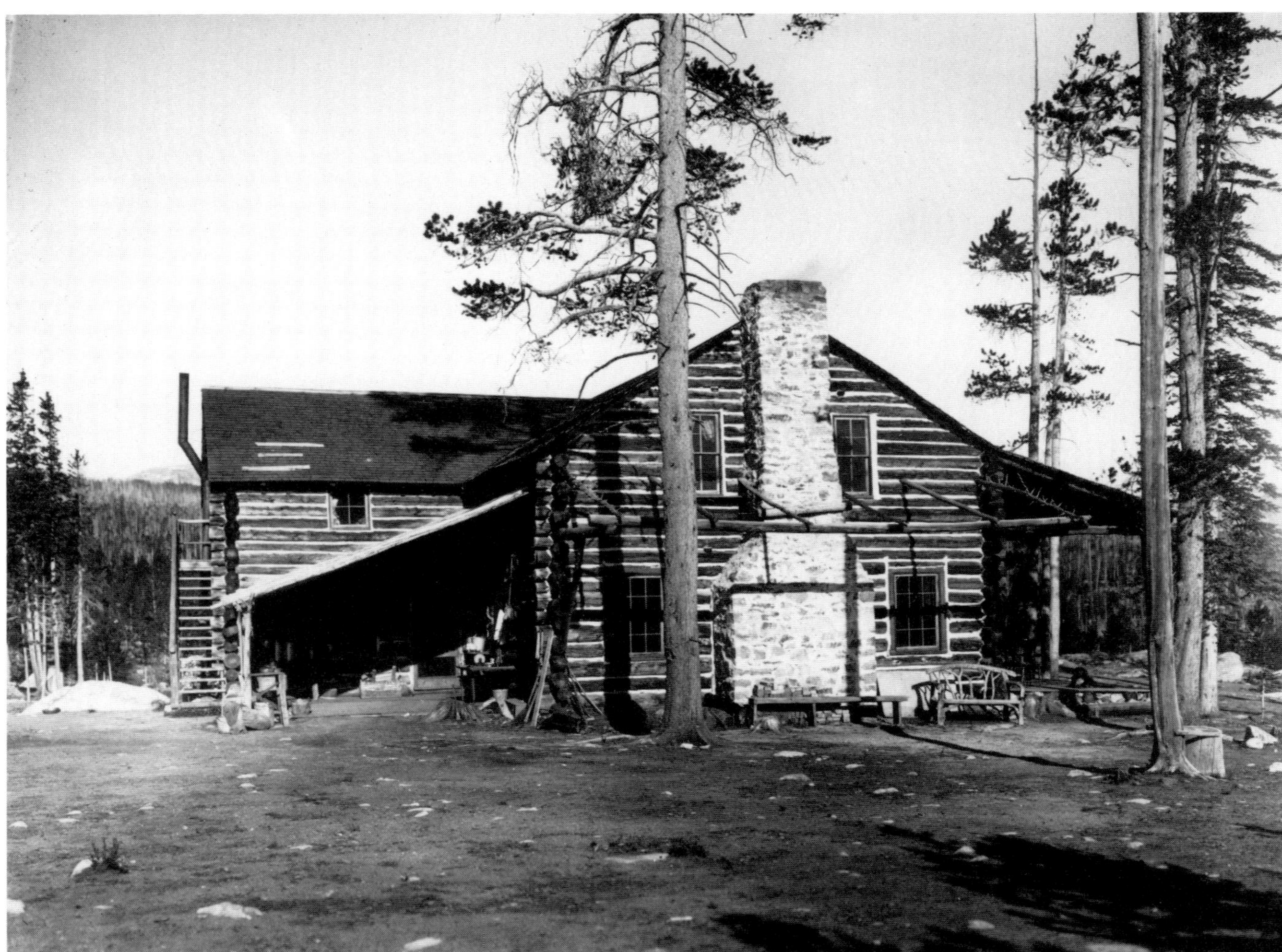

Fig. 14. Club house, 1899.

This early view of the club house is looking to the west. For many years this building was the main lodge for summer guests. It also housed a community kitchen. Separate rooms were included for black servants who were brought to work for the summer by the railroad. The original windows and chimney remain as well as an additional back wing.

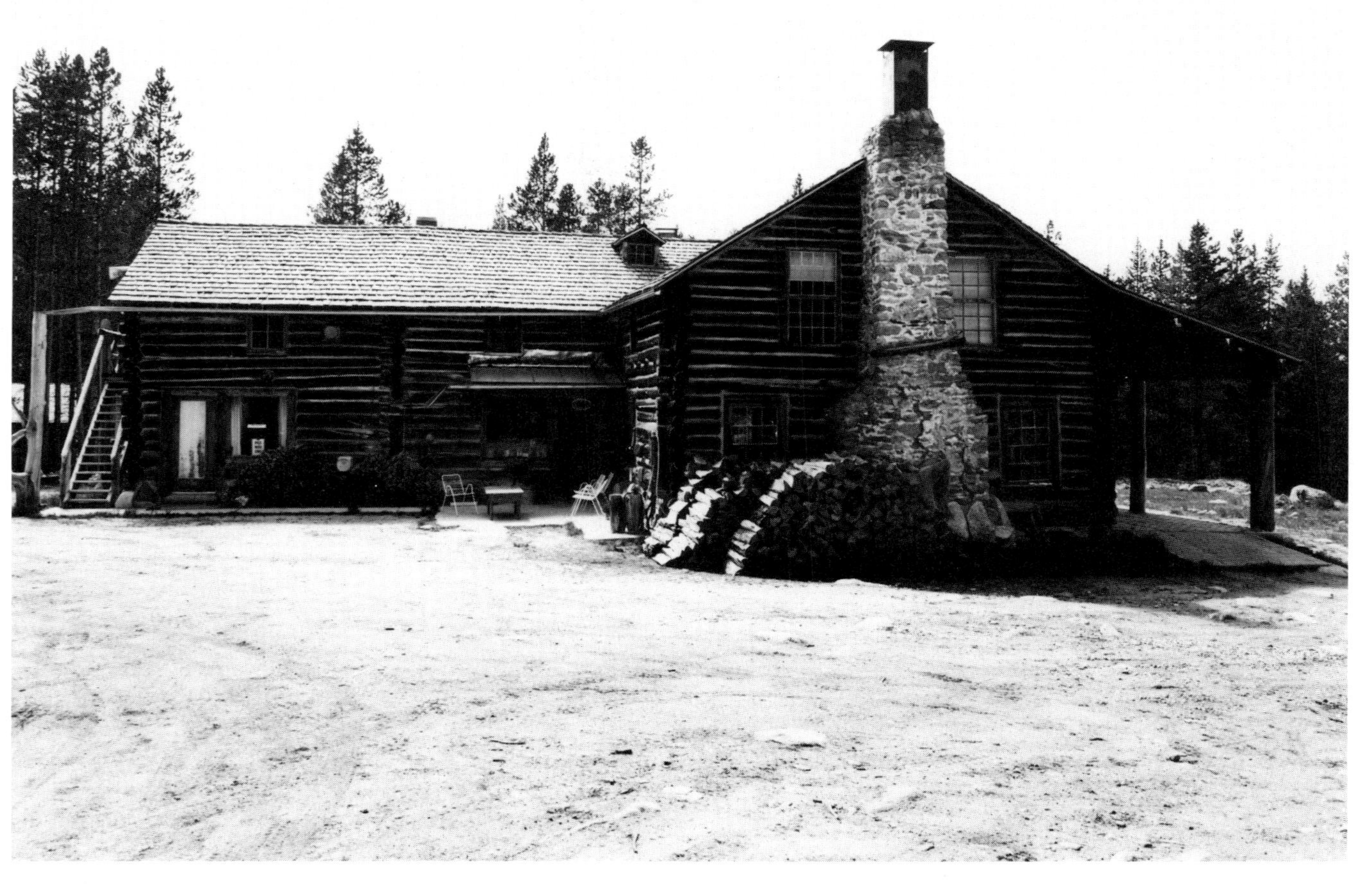

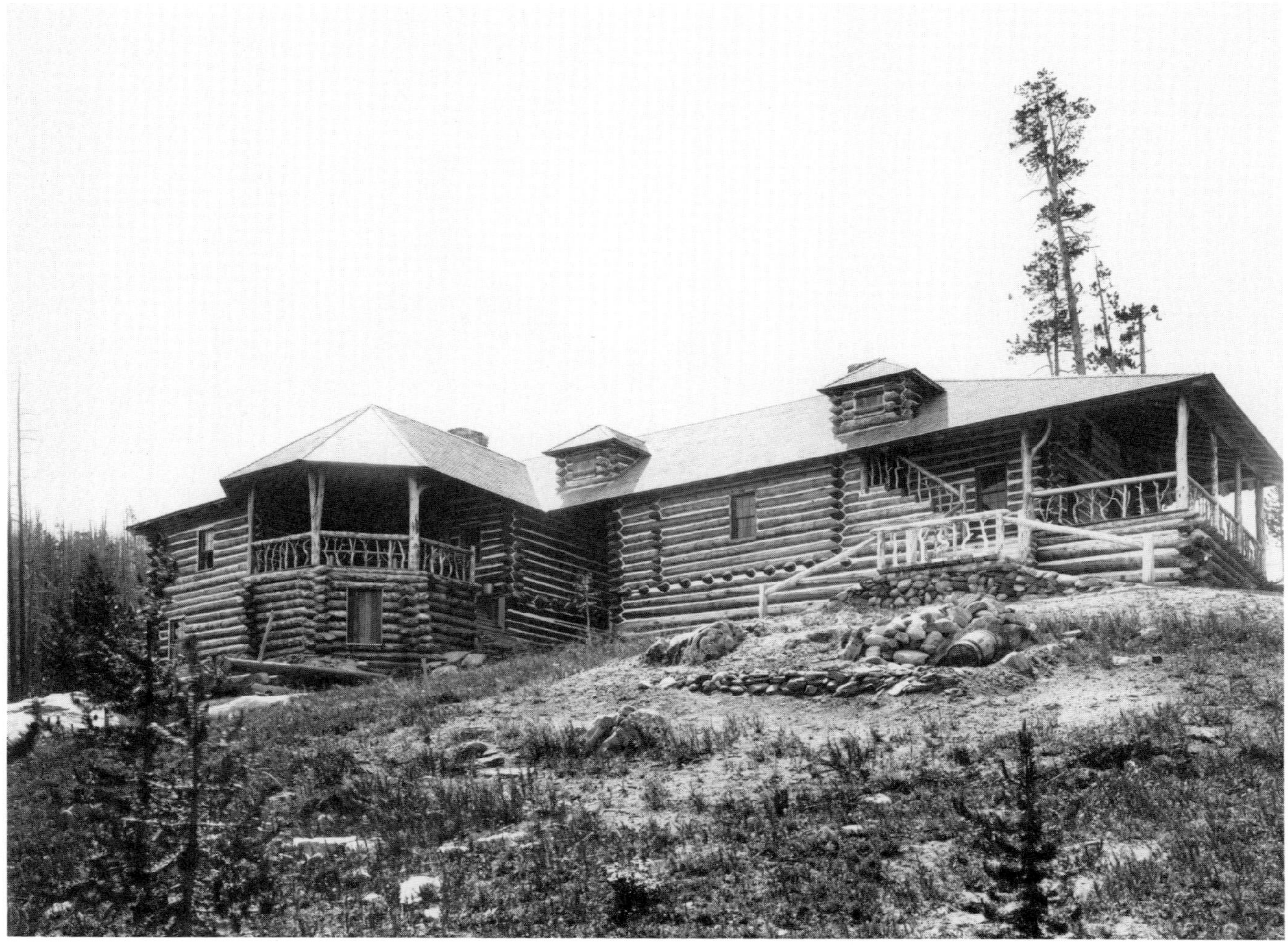

Fig. 15. Holdridge's cottage, 1899.

This cabin is actually two separate dwellings connected by a breezeway just to the right of the enclosed porch at center left. The original log lattice support has survived the renovations.

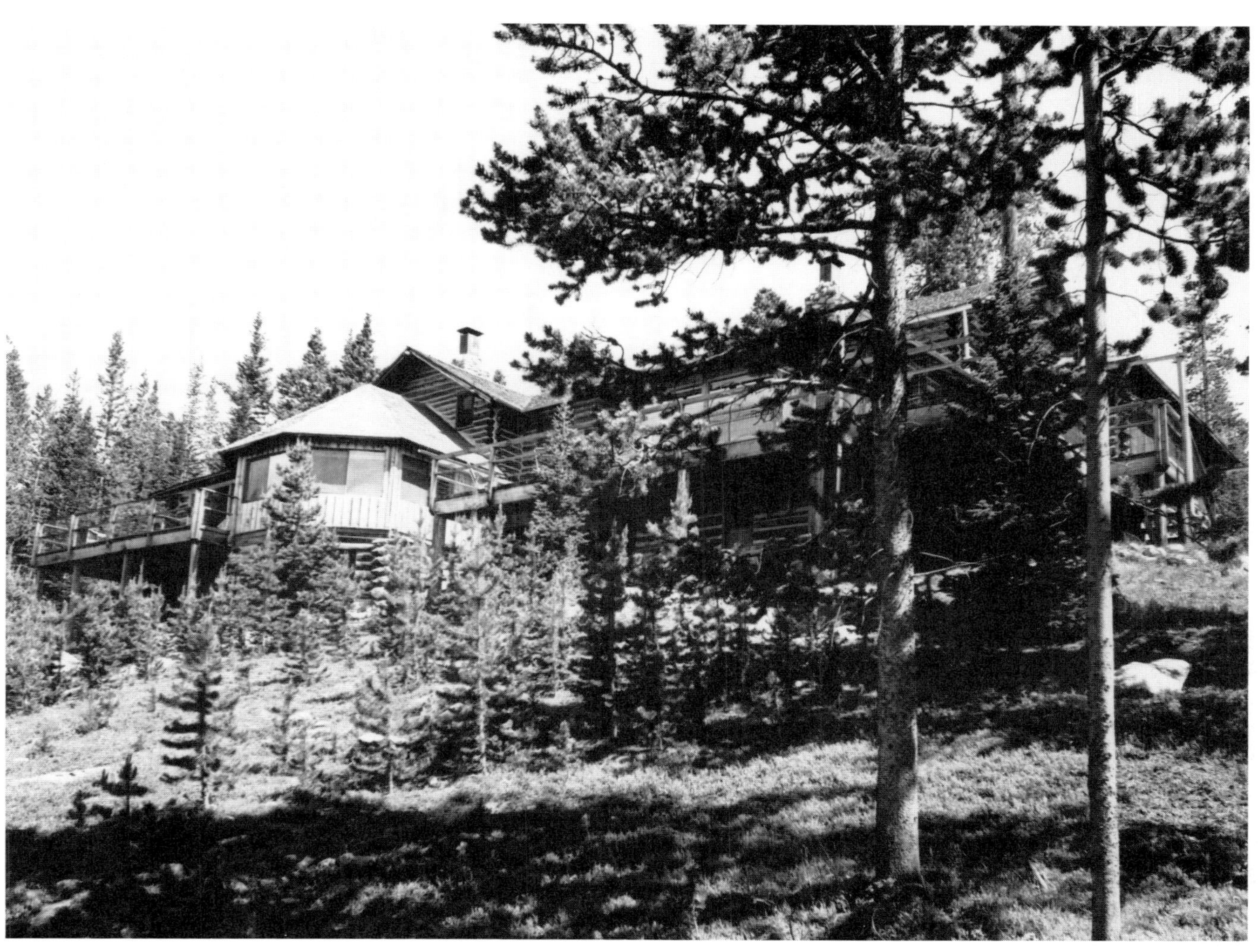

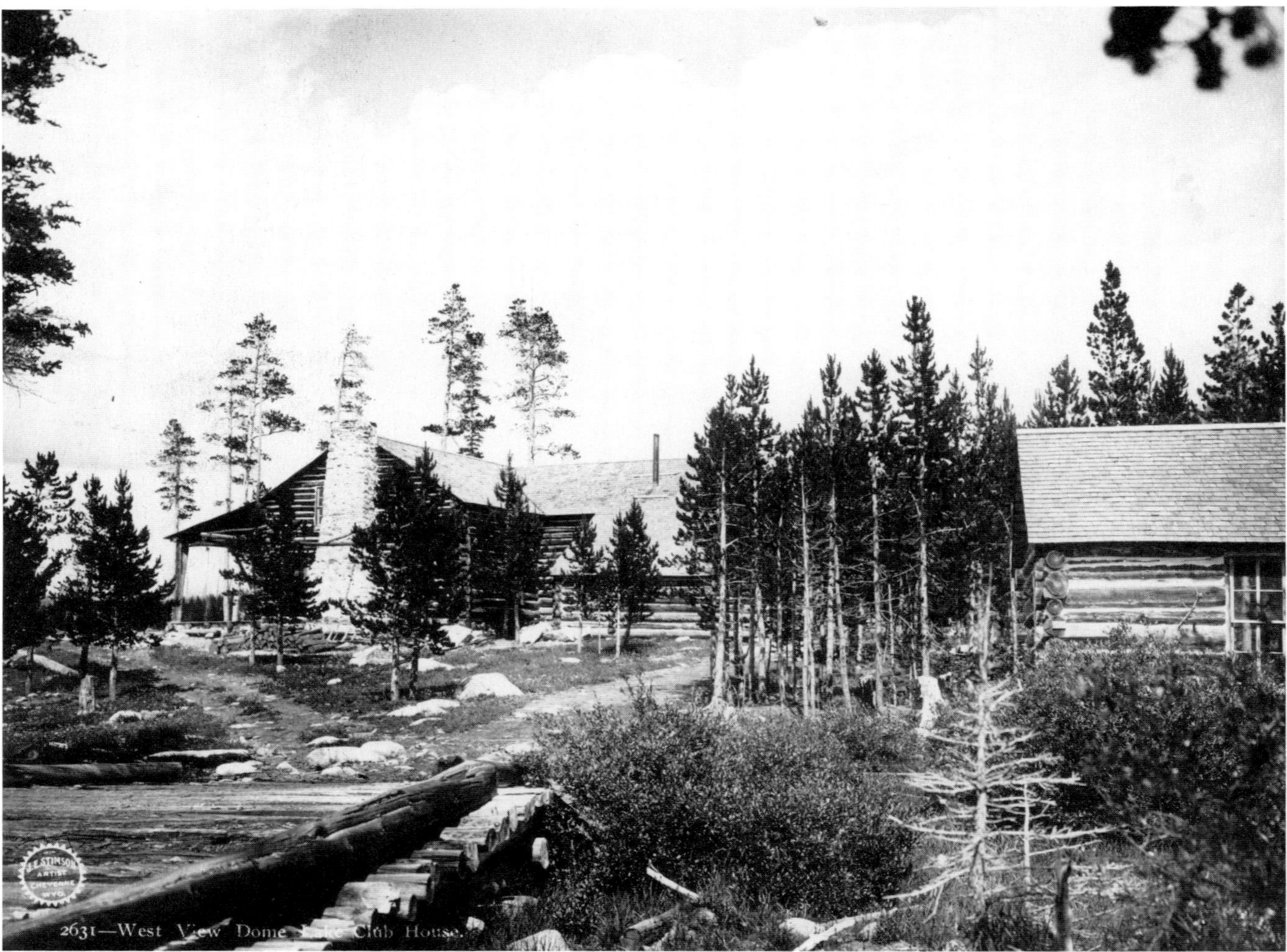

Fig. 16. West view Dome Lake Club House, 1909.

The Dome Lake Lodge is almost hidden by the growth of trees in this view from the west. The cabin at center right was one of the first structures built at the lake to house the lumbermen as they built the lodge in 1894–95. Today this building is used for storage.

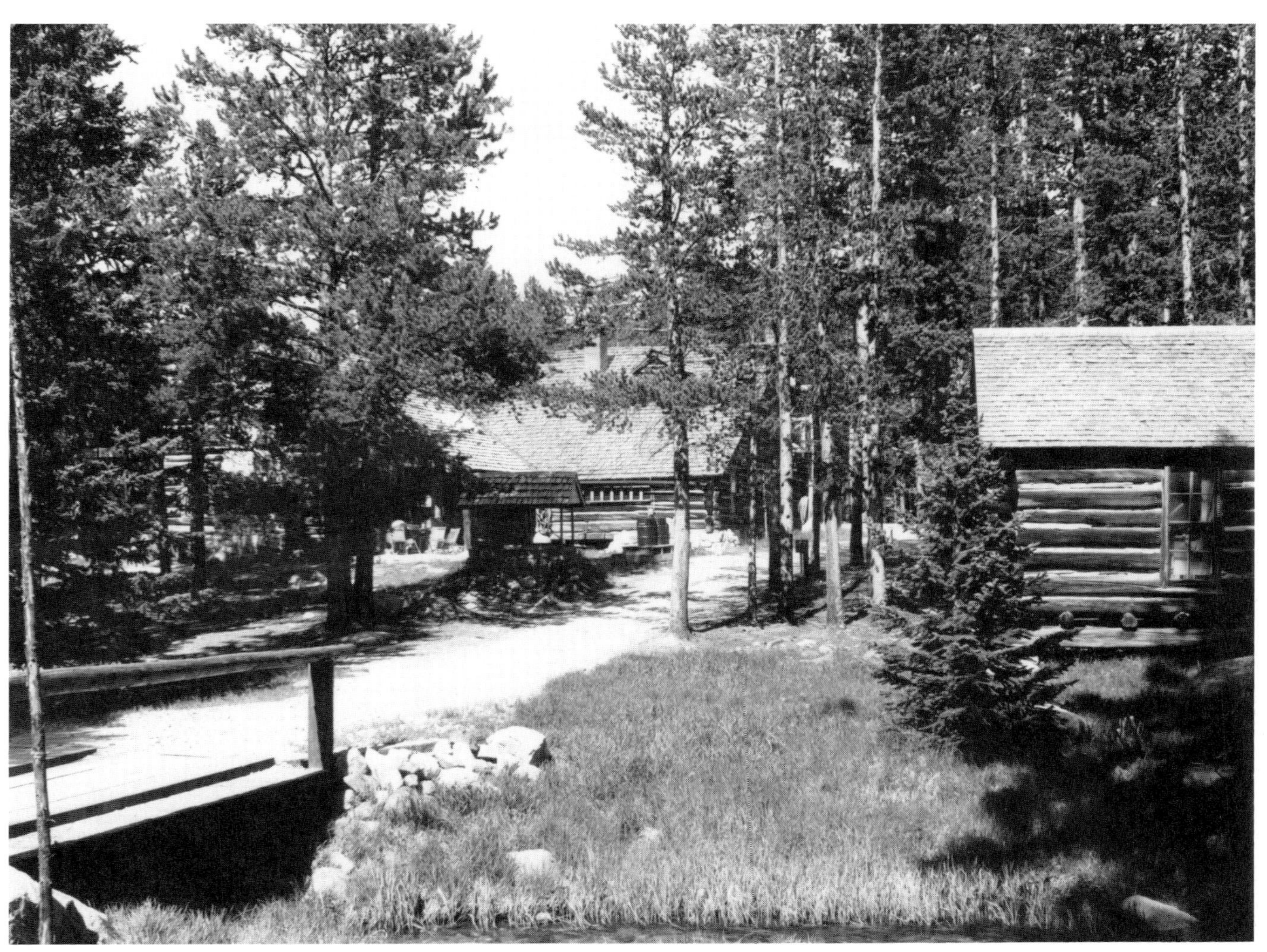

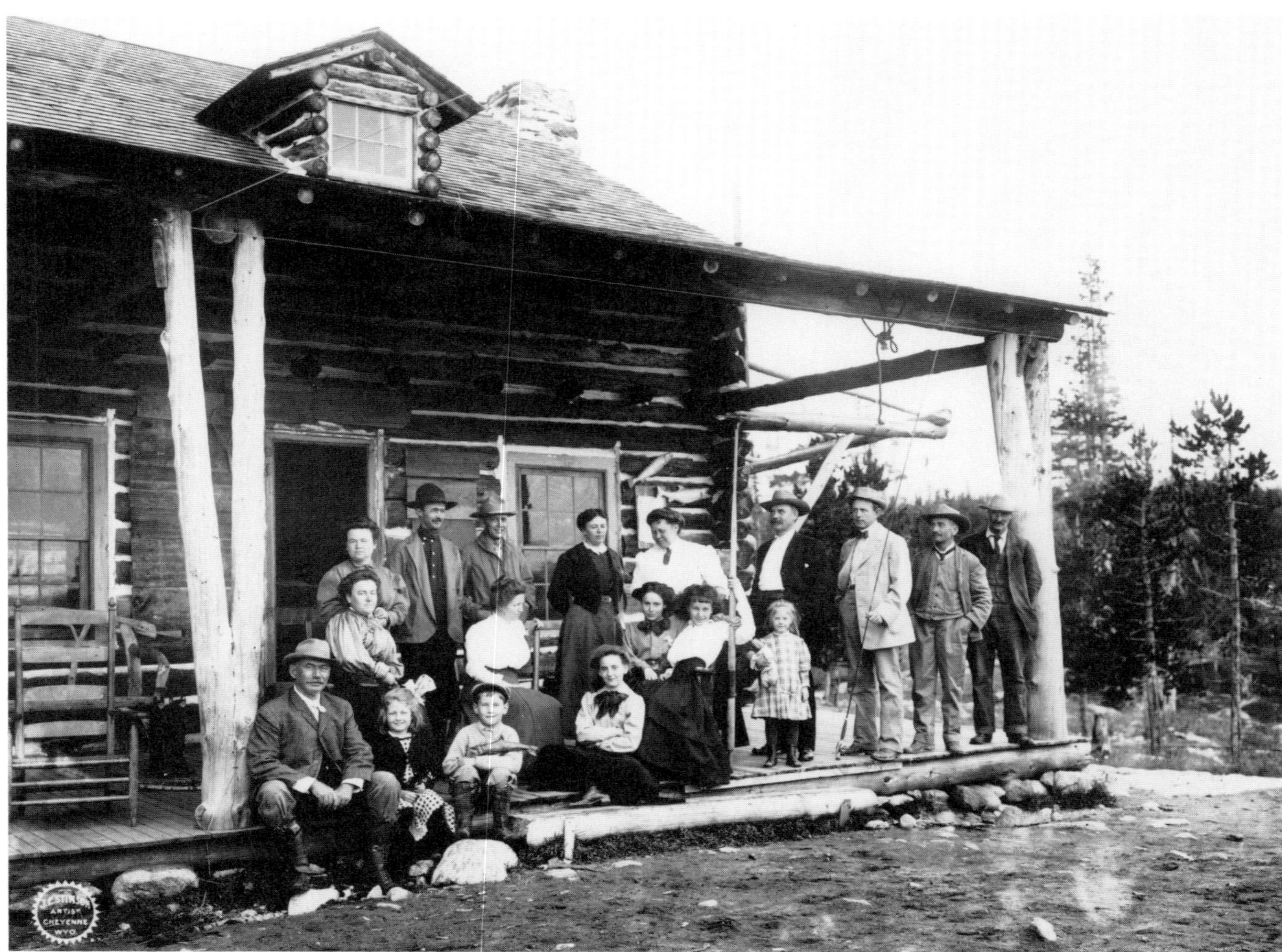

Fig. 17. Guests at Dome Lake, 1909.

Stimson's 1909 view shows some of the guests on the porch of the main lodge. Unusual log support posts, a stone patio foundation, a long fishing pole, and a boy with fish in hand can all be found in Stimson's scene. The modern view shows some of the renovations to the building, including a new foundation and support columns. A new roof and dormer have also been added. The modern guests, all eleven of them, were on a weekend fishing getaway.

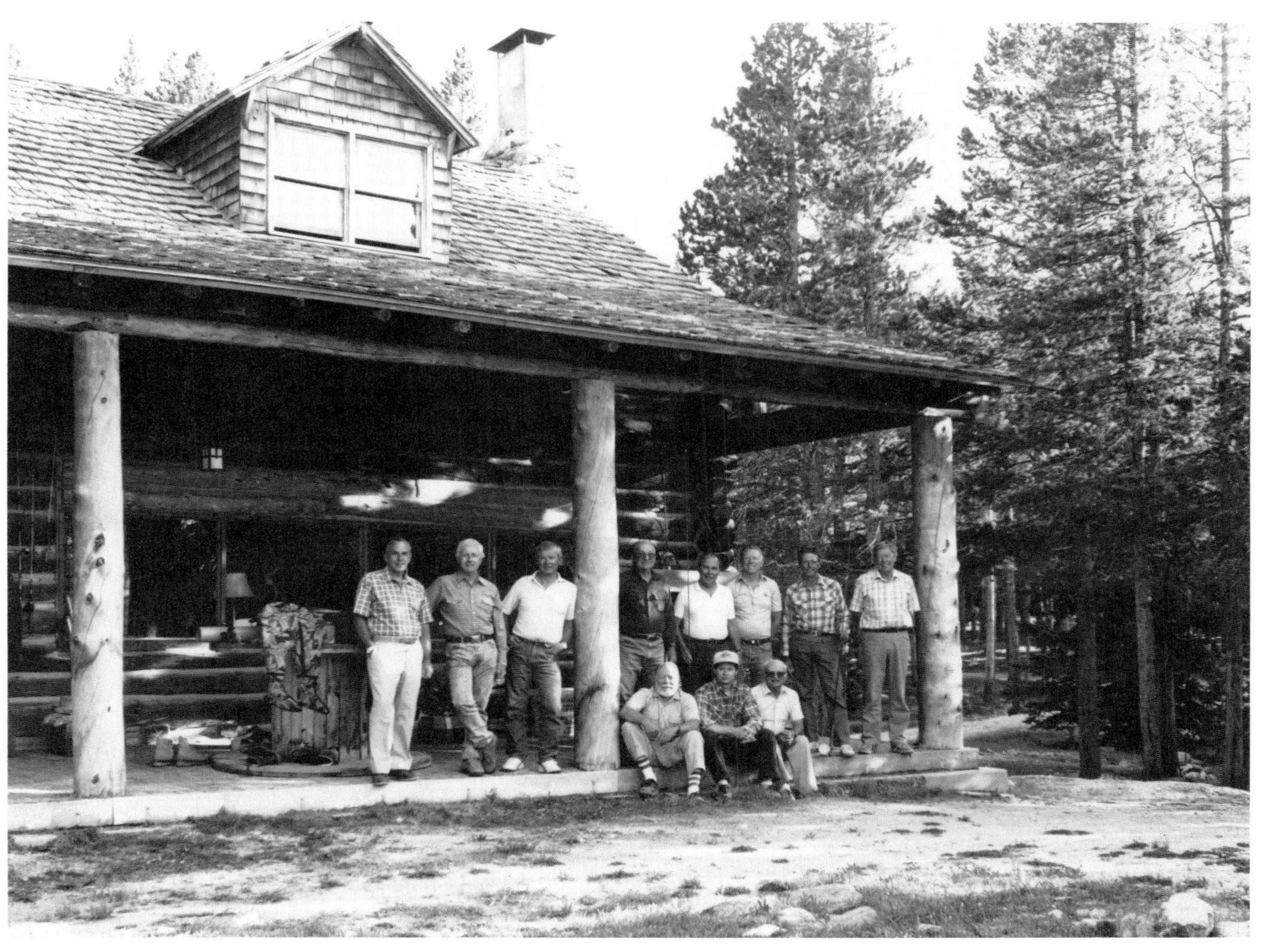

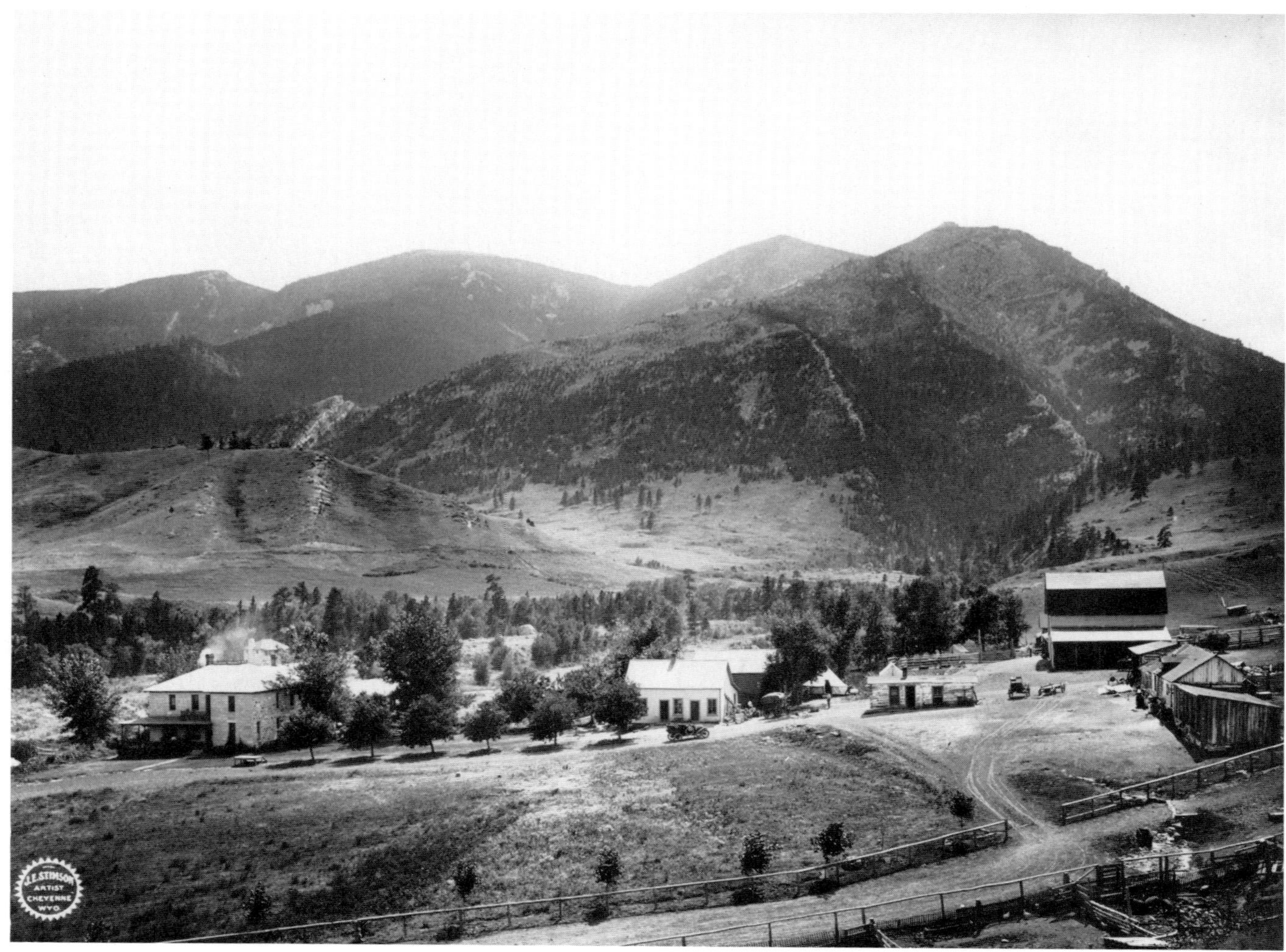

Fig. 18. Eaton Bros. Ranch, near Dayton, 1909.

Located at the mouth of Wolf Creek Canyon west of Sheridan, the Eaton Ranch was one of the earliest dude ranches in Wyoming. Howard Eaton and his brothers began their dude business at their Custer Trail Ranch near Medora, North Dakota, in 1879. They moved to Wolf in 1904 and built the large main ranch house at left center in Stimson's view. In 1927 a fire destroyed this building. The modern view shows the rebuilt house. The guests, or dudes, often come to the ranch as children and continue to spend their summers at Wolf. Some even build their own private cabins. Because of its popularity in the summer, the ranch has its own post office. Life at the ranch has been described in many magazines as well as in the writings of Mary Roberts Rinehart.

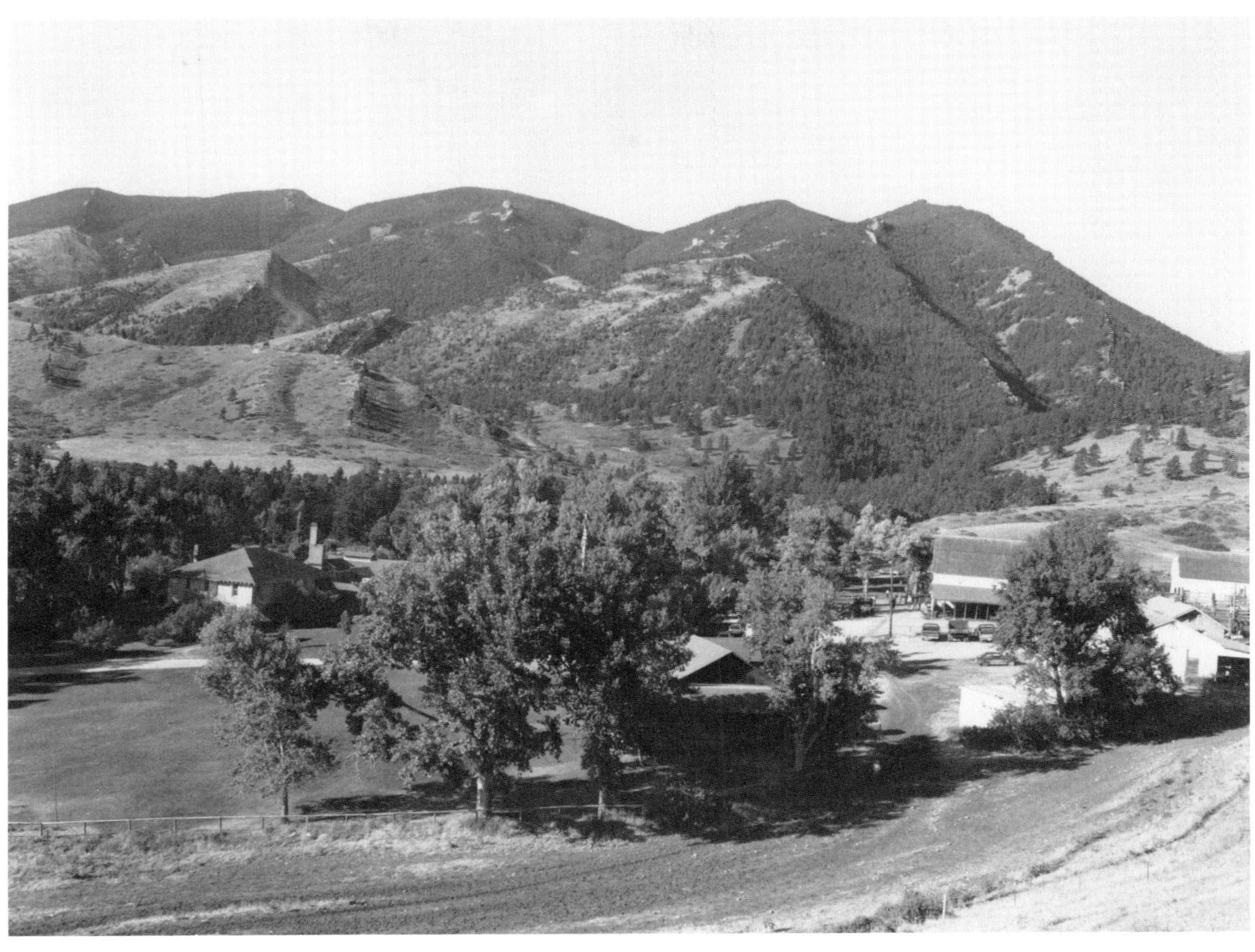

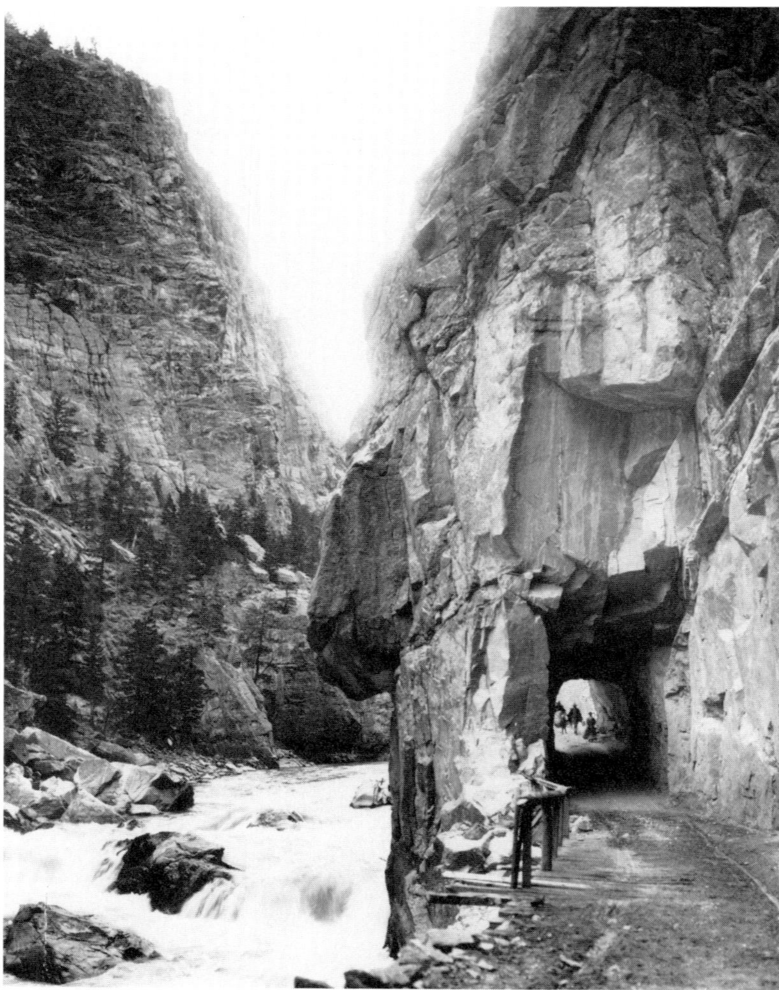

Fig. 19. Shoshone Canyon and Tunnel, 1910.

This tunnel, west of Cody, is on the old roadway leading to the Buffalo Bill Dam. The dam is one-quarter of a mile upstream. The current highway runs several hundred feet above this location. Close examination of Stimson's view reveals several people just emerging from the western edge of the tunnel. The wooden bridge in Stimson's shot, right foreground, is now gone.

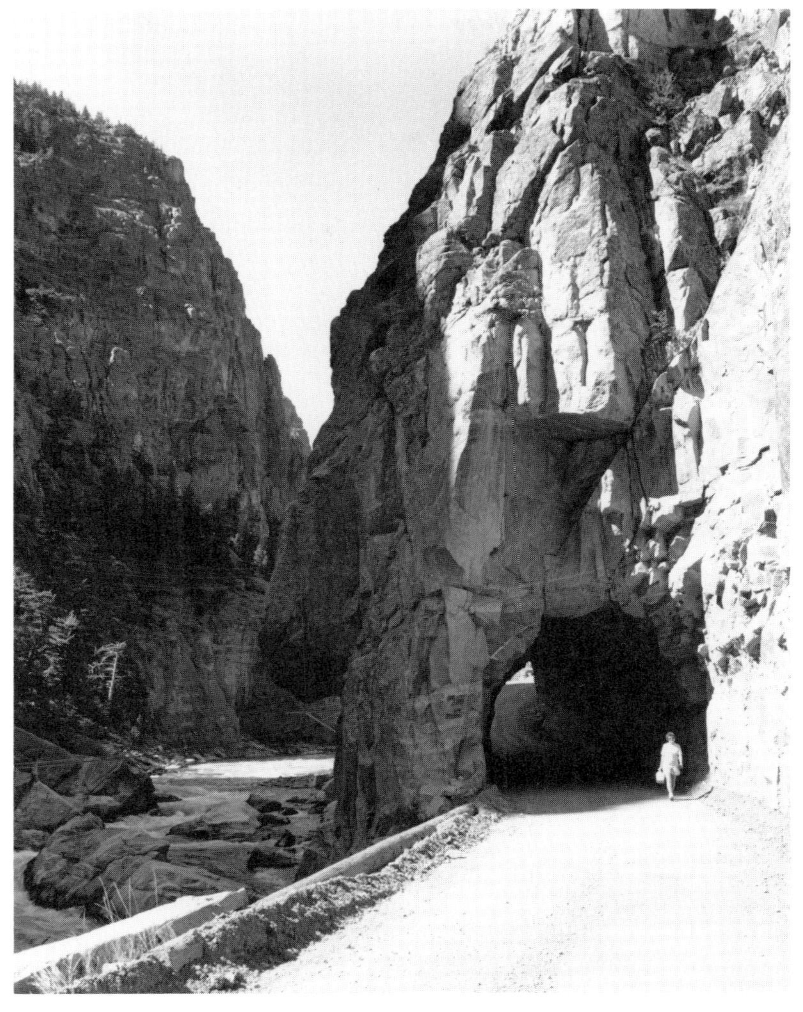

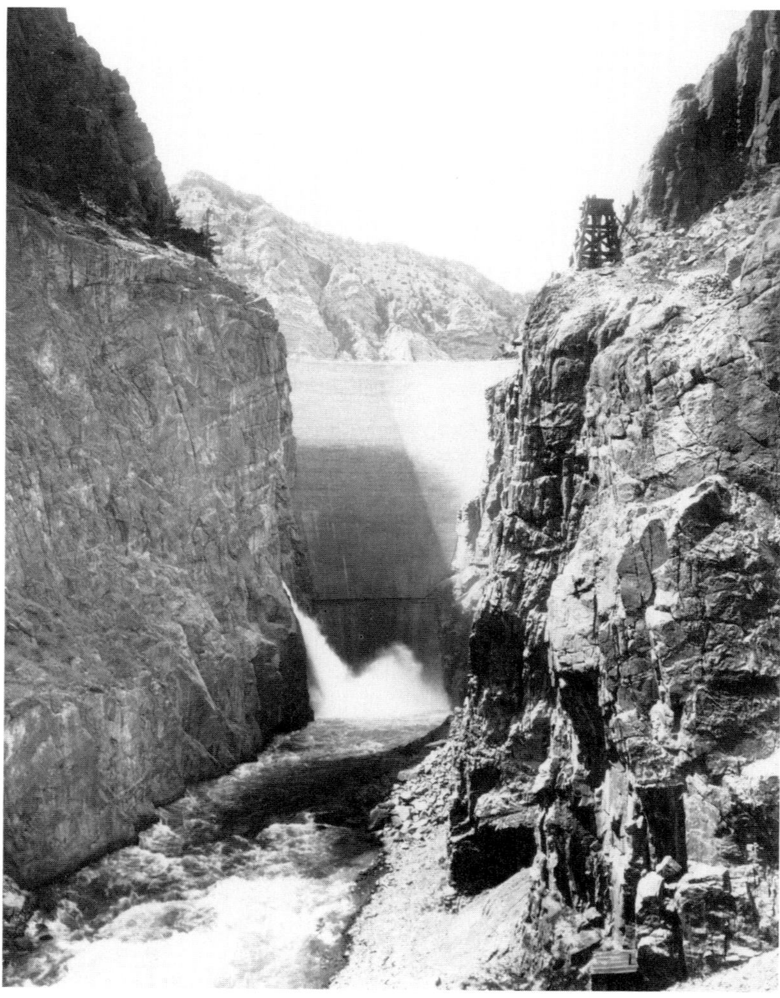

Fig. 20. Shoshone Dam, near Cody, 1911.

Now known as the Buffalo Bill Dam, the Shoshone Dam was completed in 1910 for water power, irrigation, and recreation. The dam was 328 feet high but has recently (since the modern photo was taken) been raised.

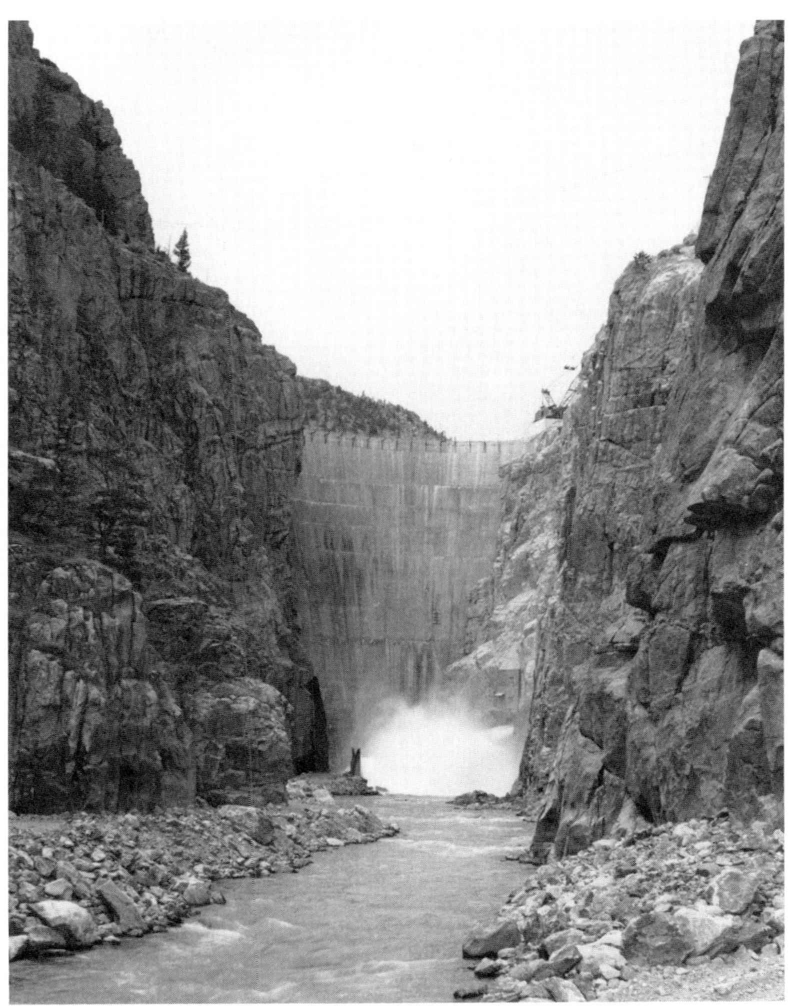

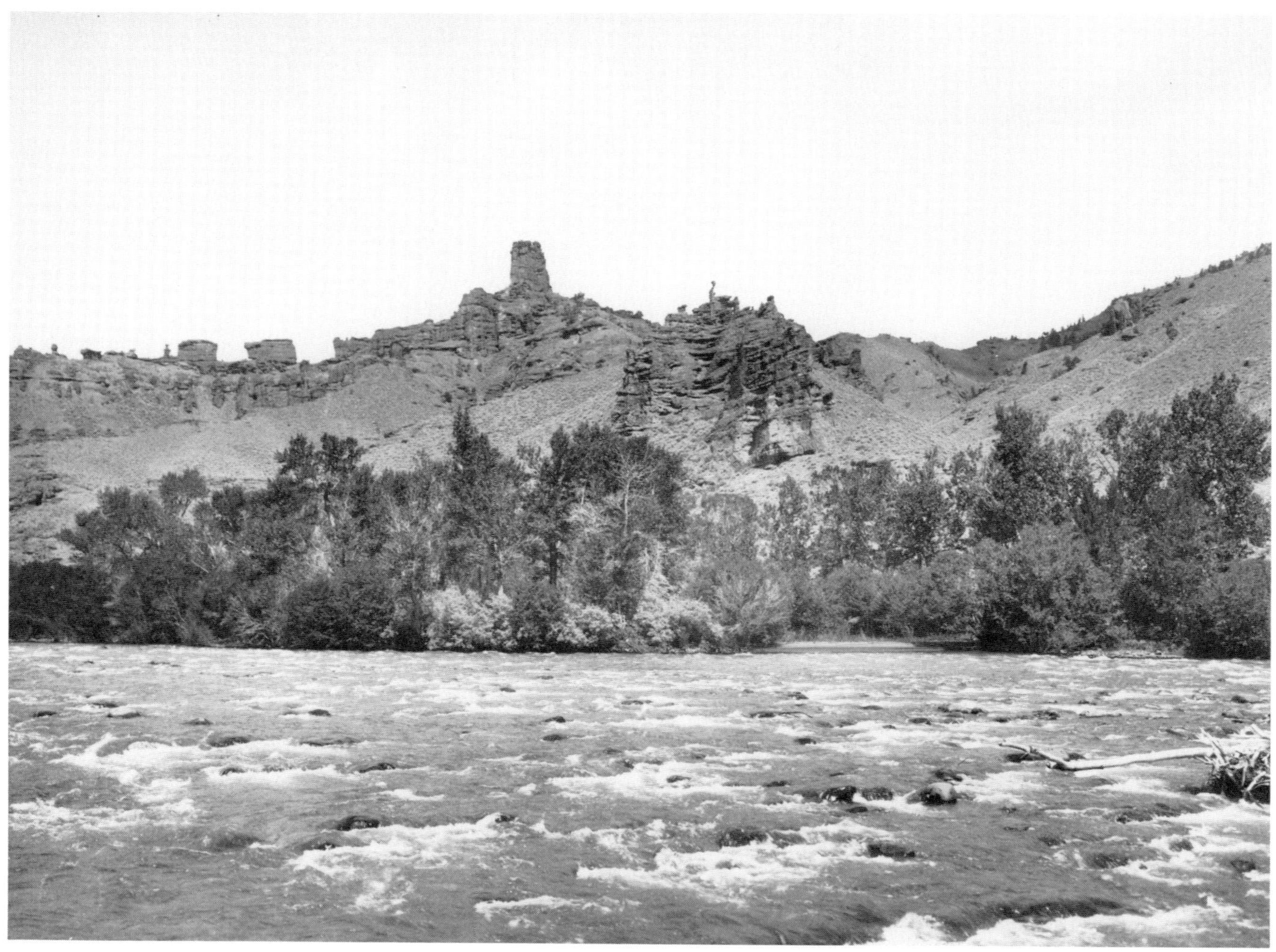

Fig. 21. Diablo Castle and North Fork of the Shoshone River, 1903.

This view is along the Cody Gateway to Yellowstone National Park. A nearby rock formation is known as the Holy City. While the higher water level in the Stimson photo is probably due to spring runoff, the lack of trees in the modern view suggests a drier environment. The delicately balanced rock formations are still intact eighty-five years later.

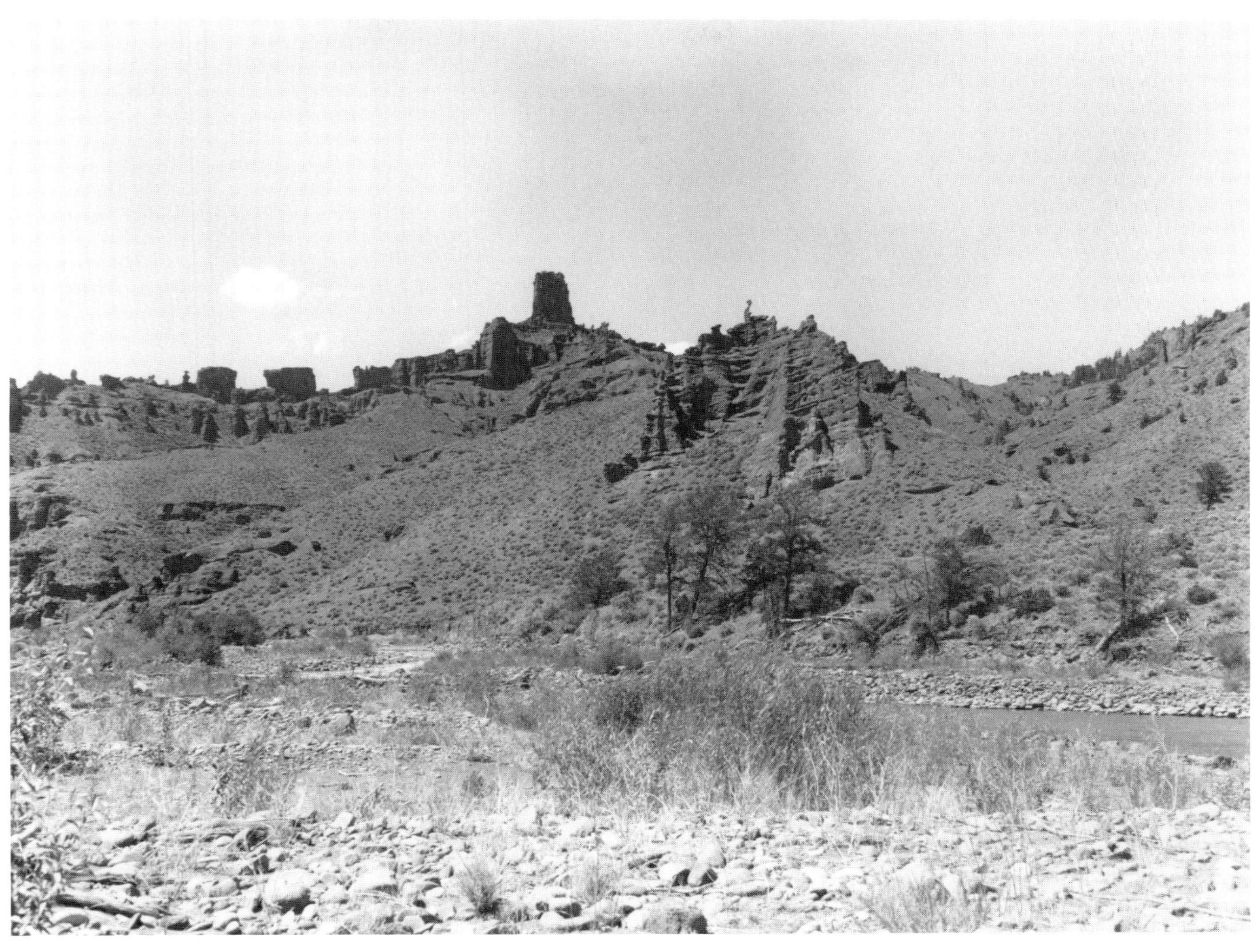

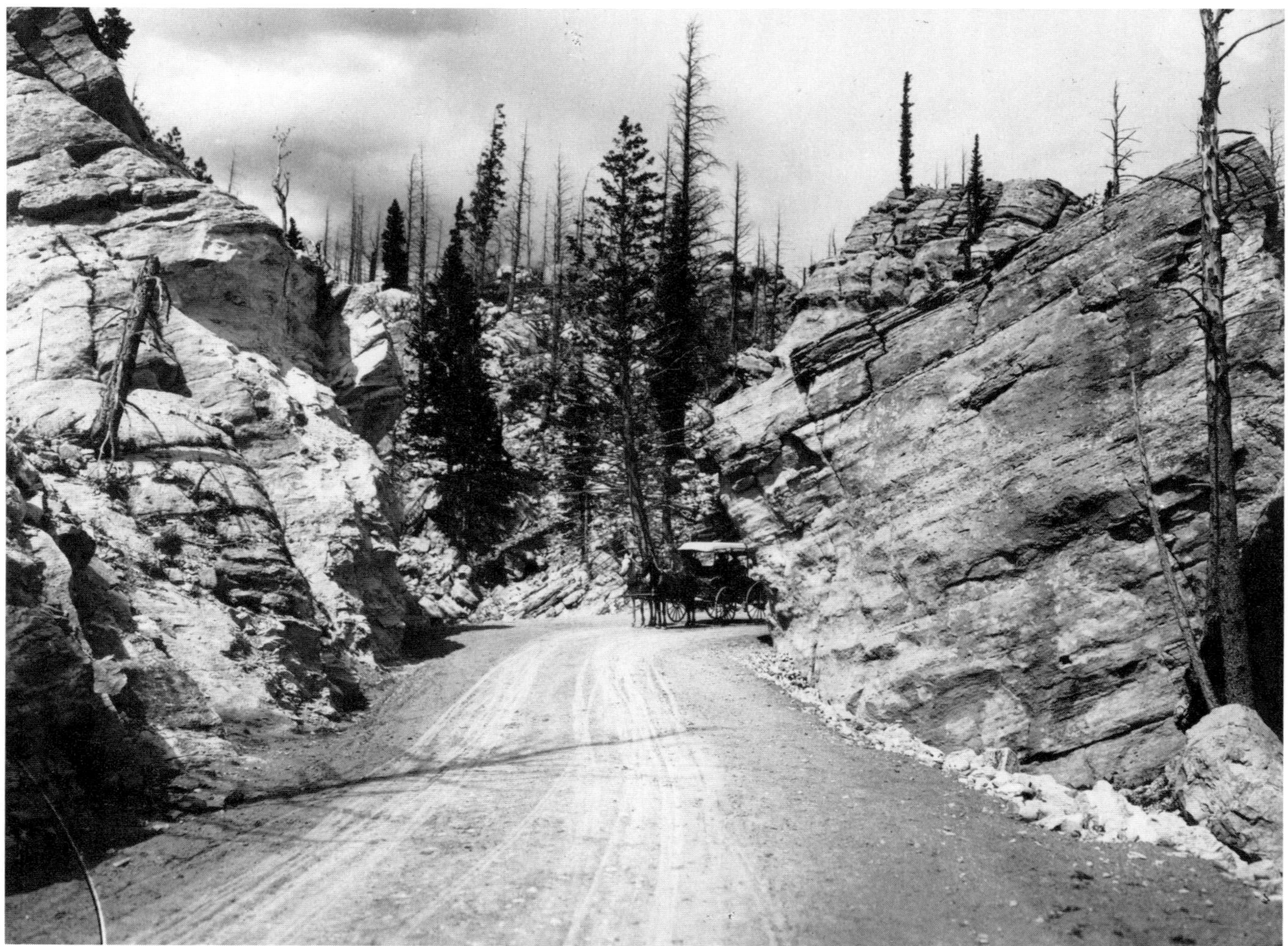

Fig. 22. Silver Gate, 1902.

This road lies three miles south of Mammoth Hot Springs near Yellowstone's famed Golden Gate. The road passes through Hoodoo Basin, an area named for its weird-shaped rocks that resemble human forms. The grove of trees in the background, burned out in Stimson's view, has thickened considerably.

Yellowstone

Joseph Stimson made his first visit to Yellowstone Park in 1903. In those days, access to the park was much different than it is today. Although the park was more than thirty years old, visitors were brought via horse-drawn carriages from the boundary railheads at Cody, Gardiner, and West Yellowstone. Once in the park, a system of coach houses and hotels provided stopovers as the tourists bounced along the roads from place to place. A site such as the Yellowstone Falls or Old Faithful could be reached by stage or private pack trip. The *Zillah,* a former Great Lakes steamship, hauled passengers around Yellowstone Lake. Thus many of Stimson's views, although easily accessible by car today, were reached by a much different method eight decades ago.

Still, although travel around the park was much more difficult than it is today, interaction with the park was greater. Once a site was reached, there were few fences and restraining devices to keep people off of the attraction. Many early photos show tourists sitting on the geysers, a practice the National Park Service would never allow today. But in those days, there were no park rangers; the U.S. Army patrolled the park until 1916.

Stimson's views of Yellowstone, then, are historically important because they depict an early stage of the evolution of the park from natural wilderness to its present stage as a controlled experience. They were also an important selling point for both the Union Pacific and the Wyoming

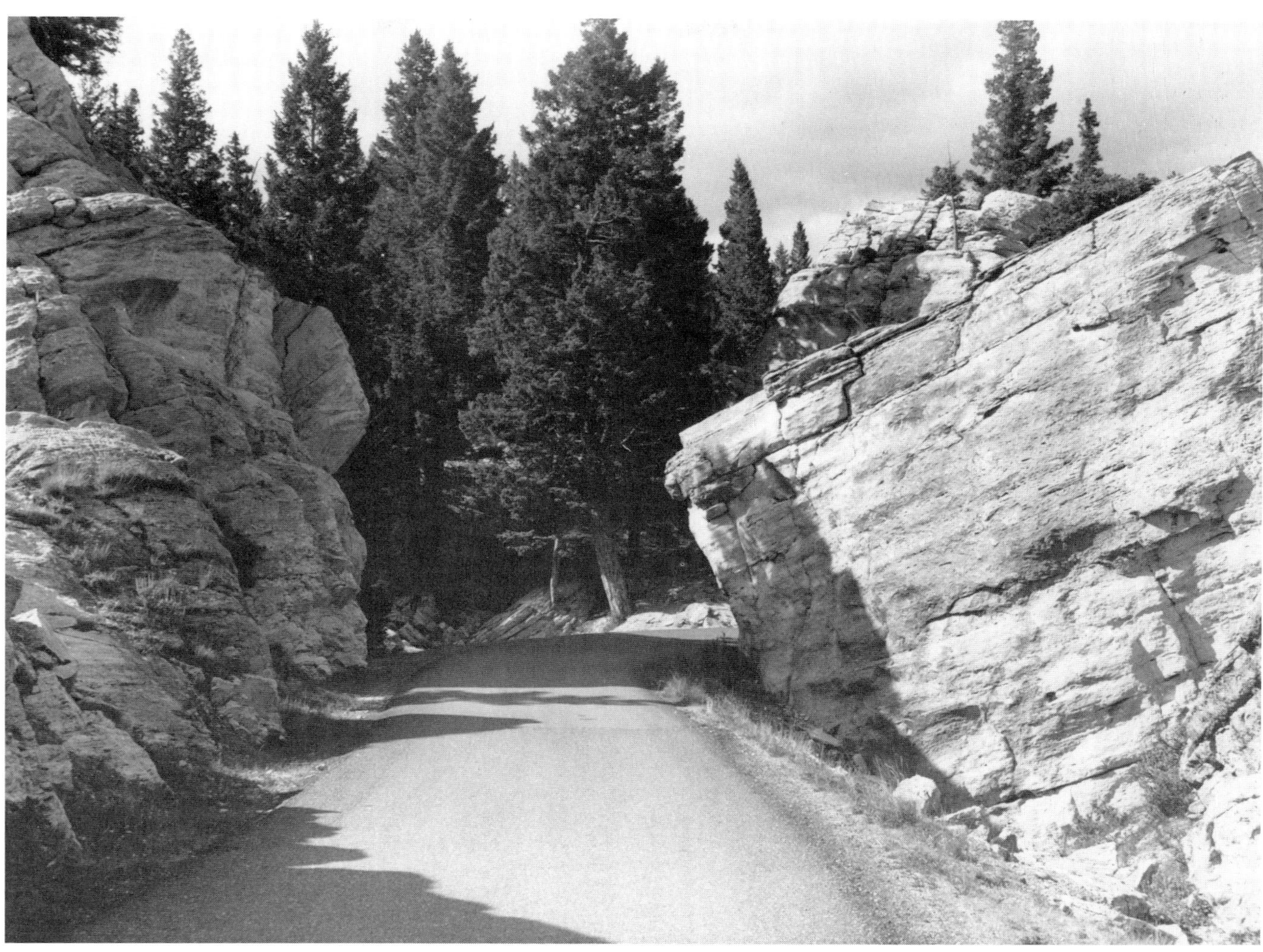

towns along the route into the park.

All of the photographs in this section were taken early in July 1988, before the devastating fires burned large sections of the park. Some of the modern views may be different today than they were just three years ago. In the future, I might go back and rephotograph these same sites to study the effect of fire on the park.

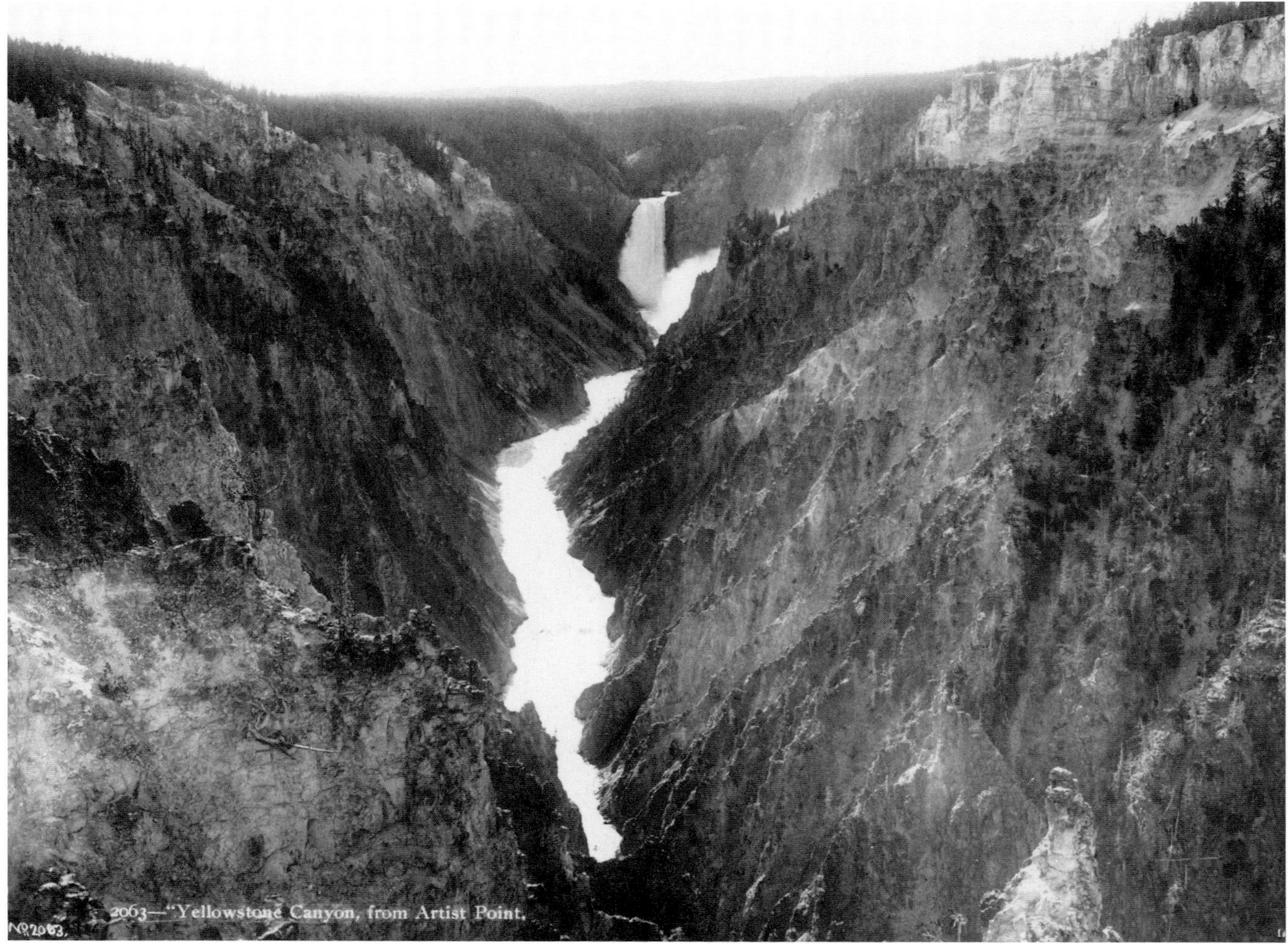

Fig. 23. Artist Point, 1907.

This is one of the most spectacular views of the Lower Falls of the Yellowstone. It is thought that this point is where Thomas Moran first painted the falls in 1872. The wagon road to Artist Point was completed along the south edge of the canyon in 1904.

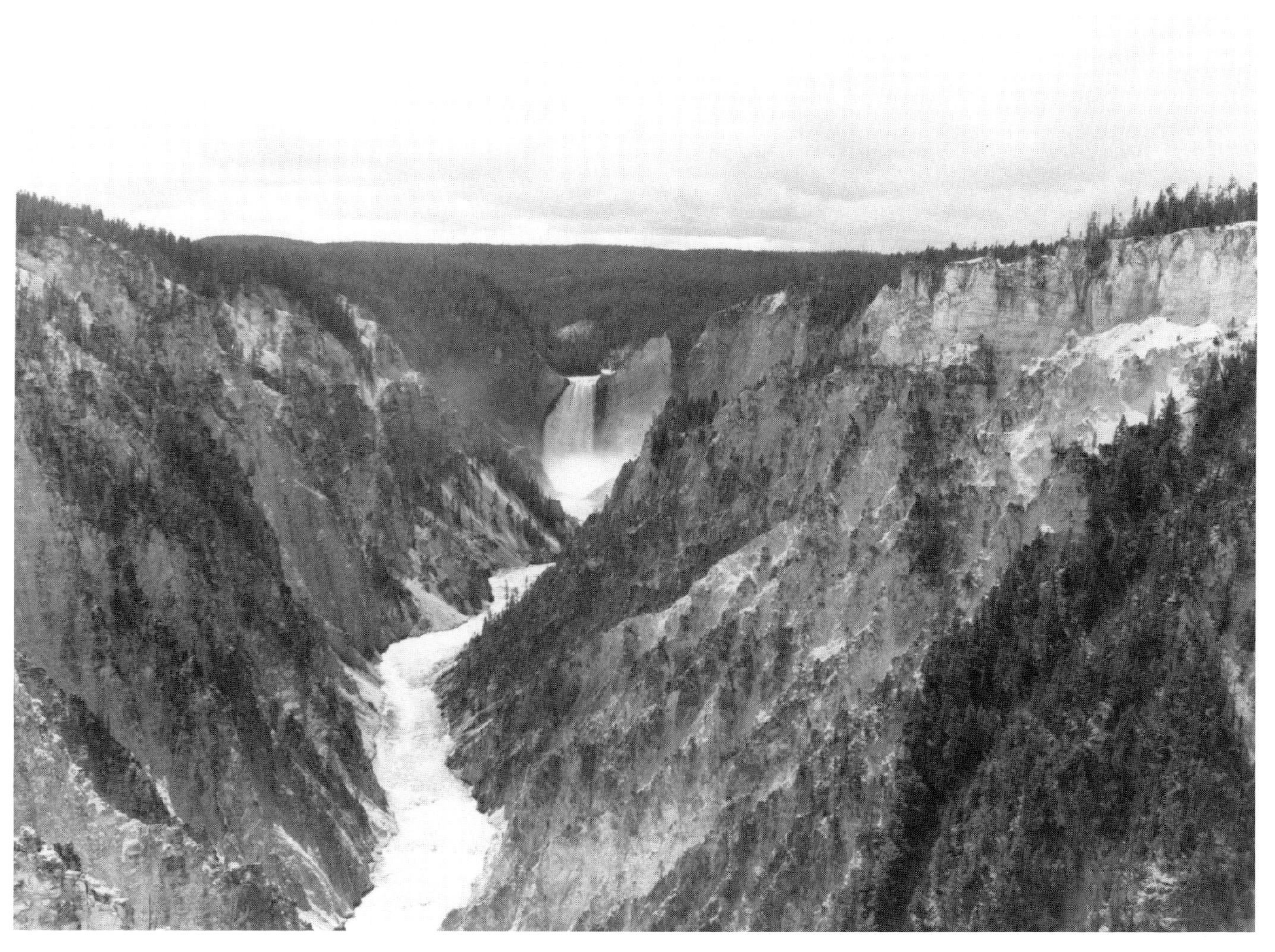

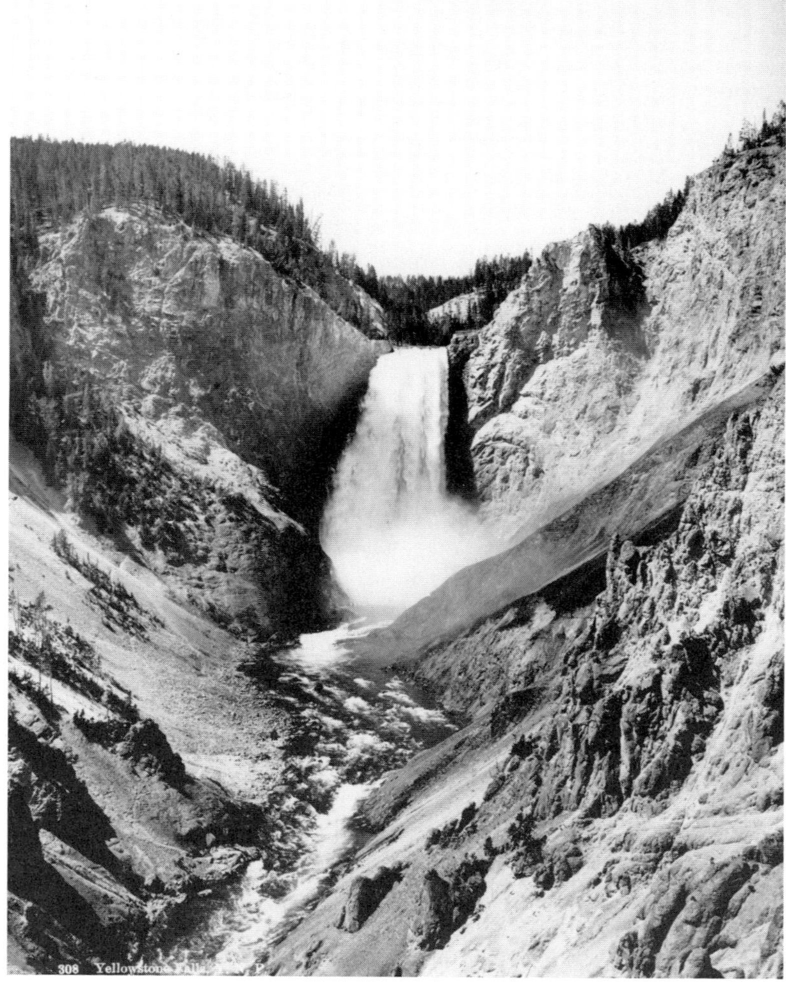

Fig. 24. Yellowstone Falls from Grand View, 1902.

This view is along the north rim of the Grand Canyon of the Yellowstone. A large growth of pine trees can be found along the right side of the canyon wall. Also, the Brink of Falls observation point is visible at the top right of the falls.

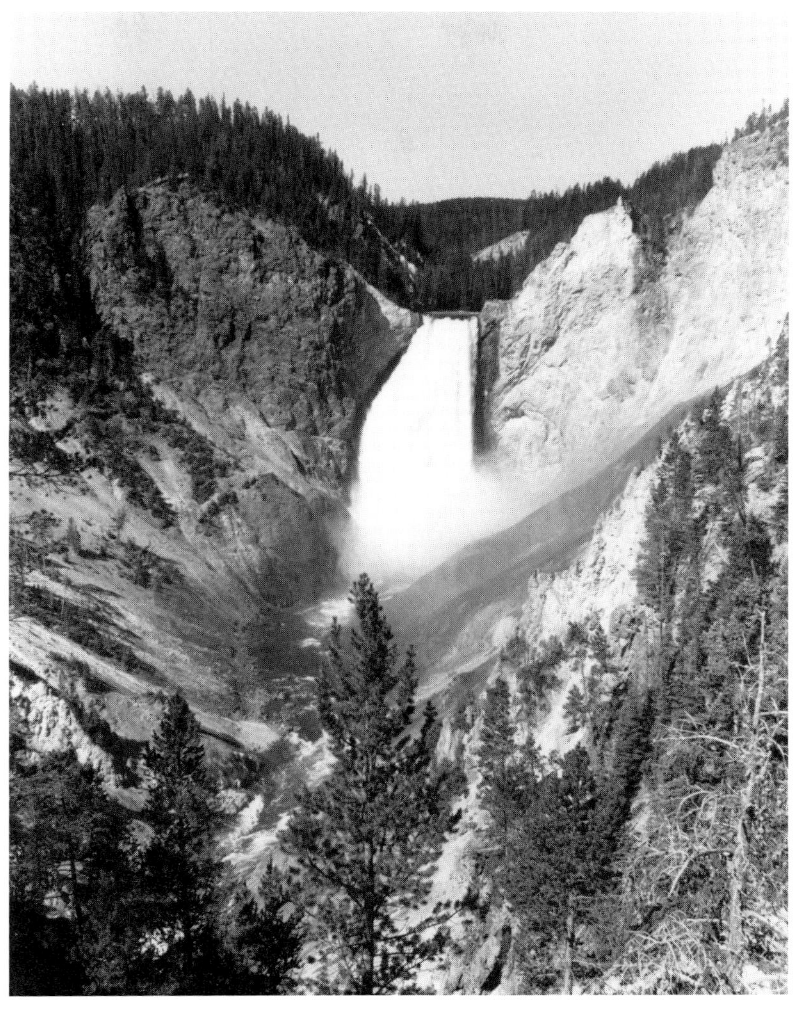

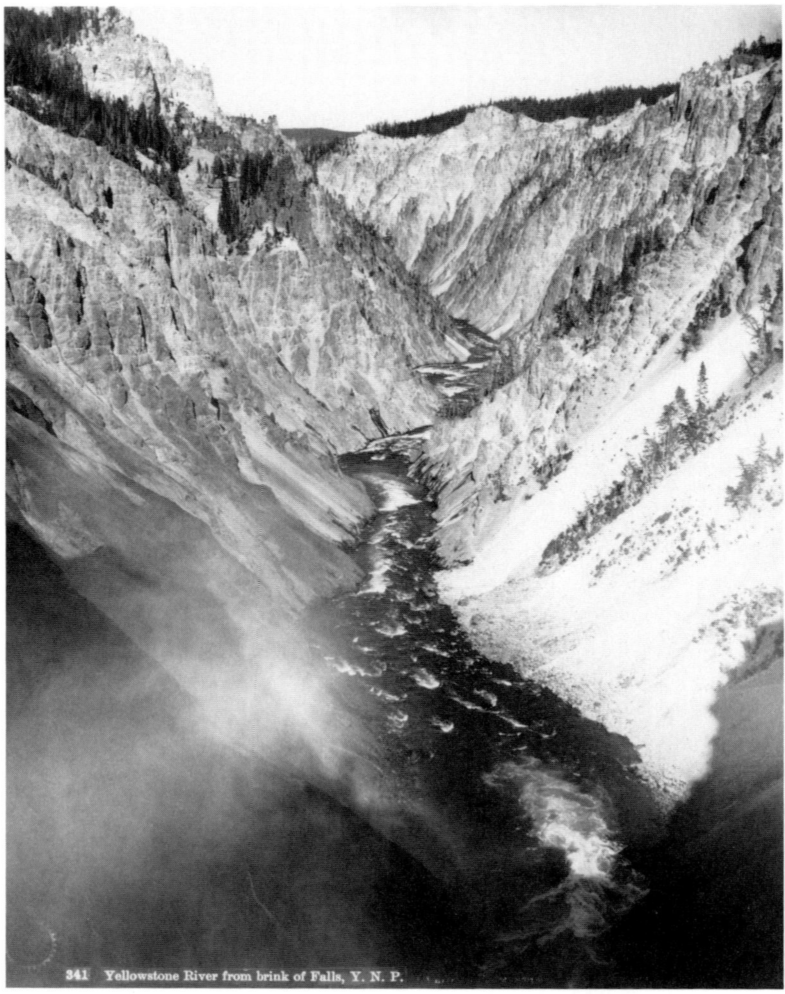

Fig. 25. Brink of Falls, 1902.

This view of the canyon was taken from the viewing platform on the north side of the lower falls. A close look shows the trail to Grand View Point, upper left, descending the left wall of the canyon.

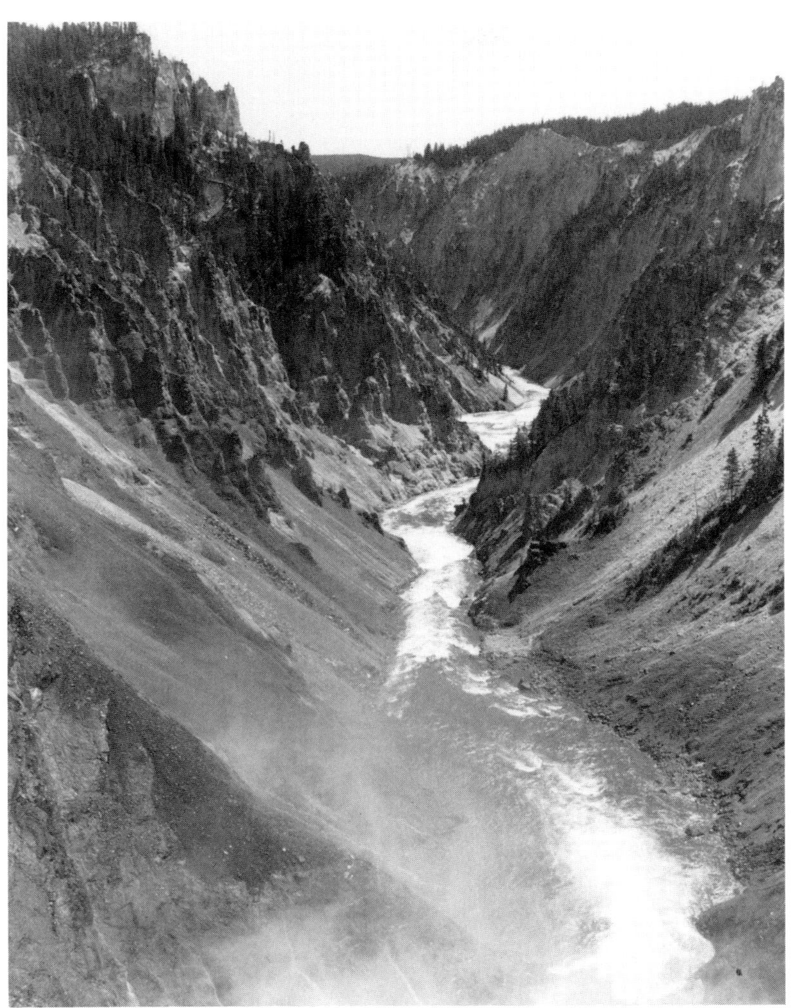

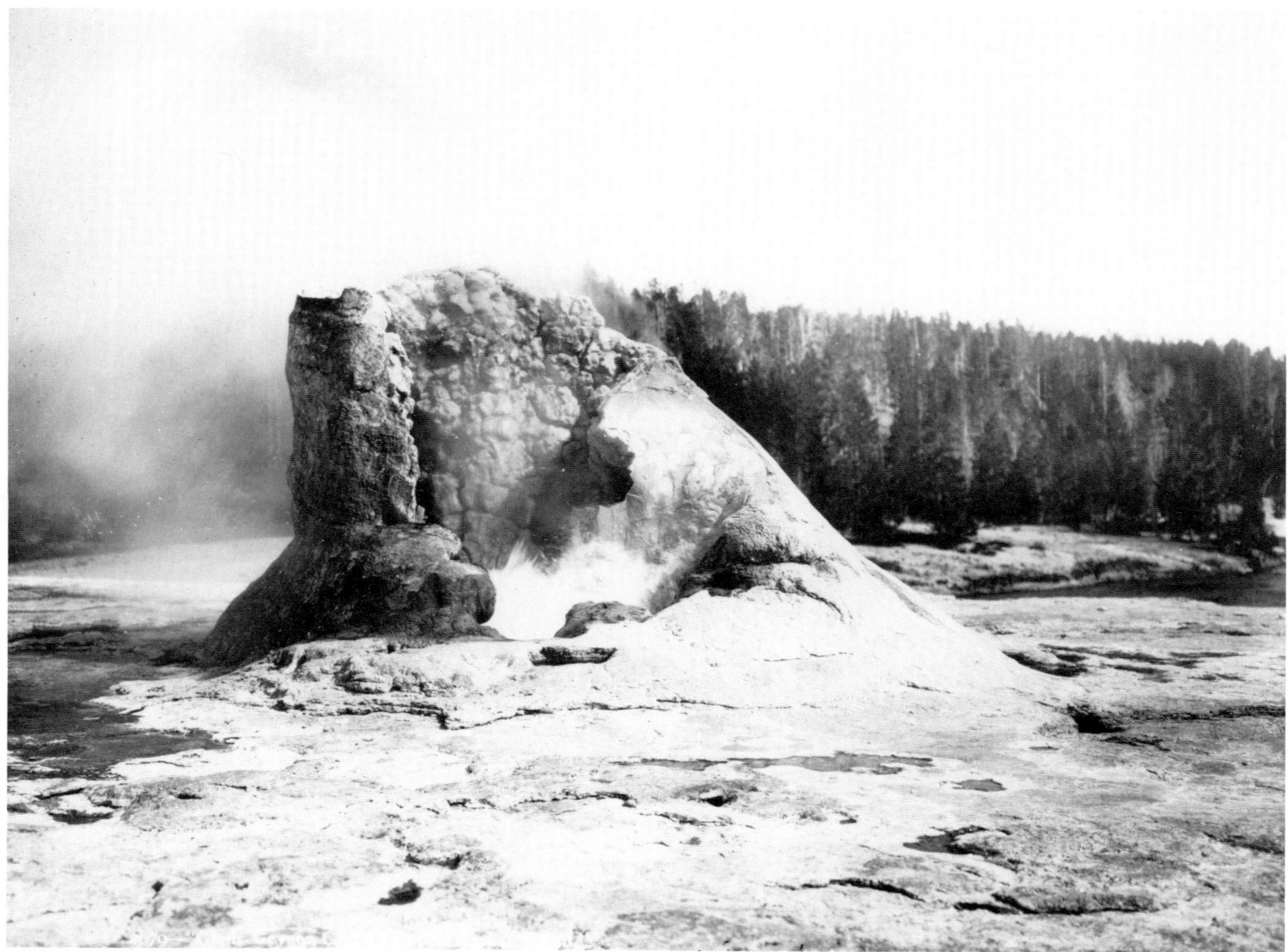

Fig. 26. Giant Geyser, Upper Geyser Basin, 1907.

Named by the Washburn–Doane expedition of 1870, the Giant Geyser is located in the Upper Geyser Basin near Old Faithful.

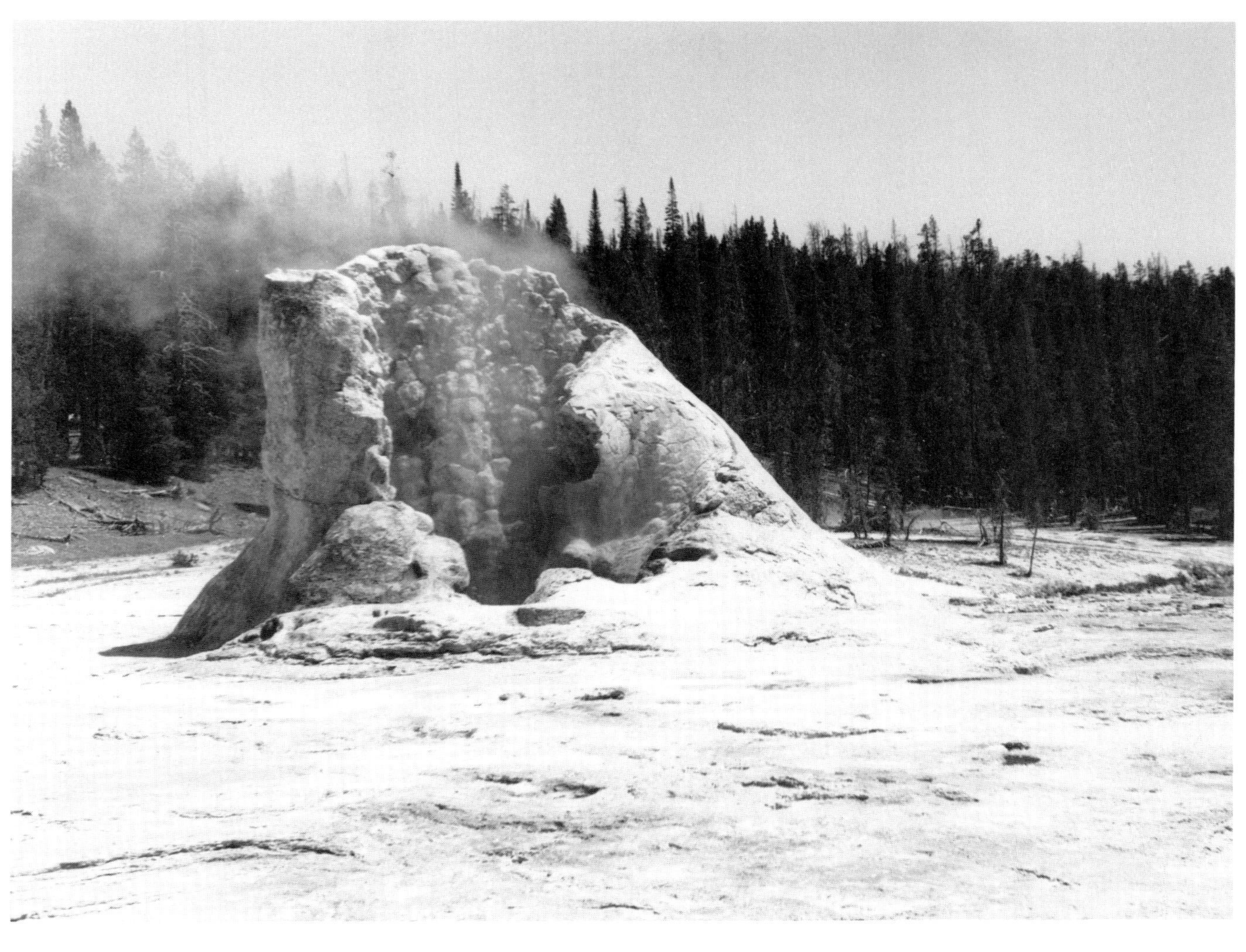

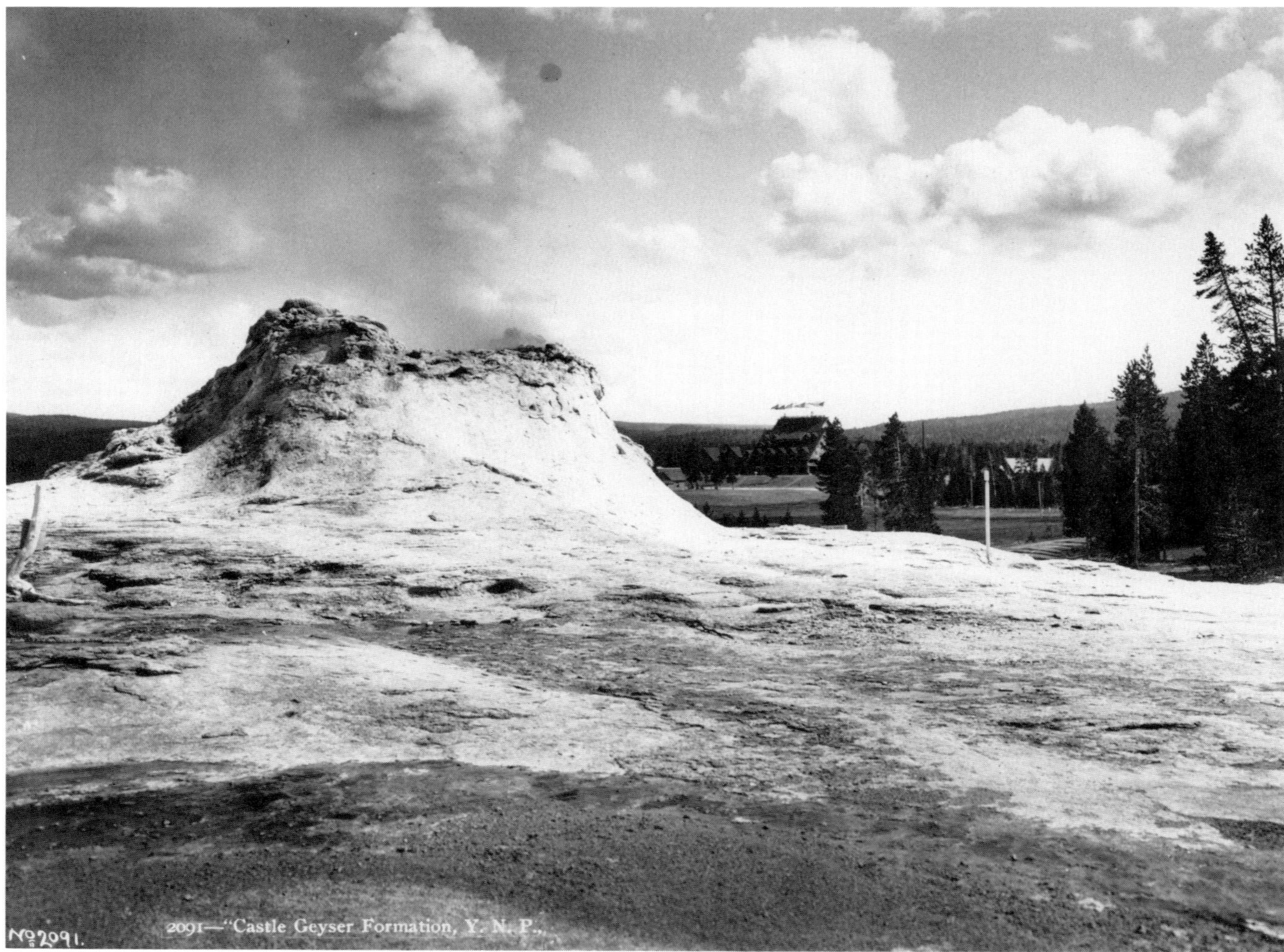

Fig. 27. Castle Geyser, Upper Geyser Basin, 1907.

Also located in the Upper Geyser Basin, Castle Geyser was named in 1870 for its resemblance to a medieval castle. In the distance, right background, are the flags atop the Old Faithful Inn.

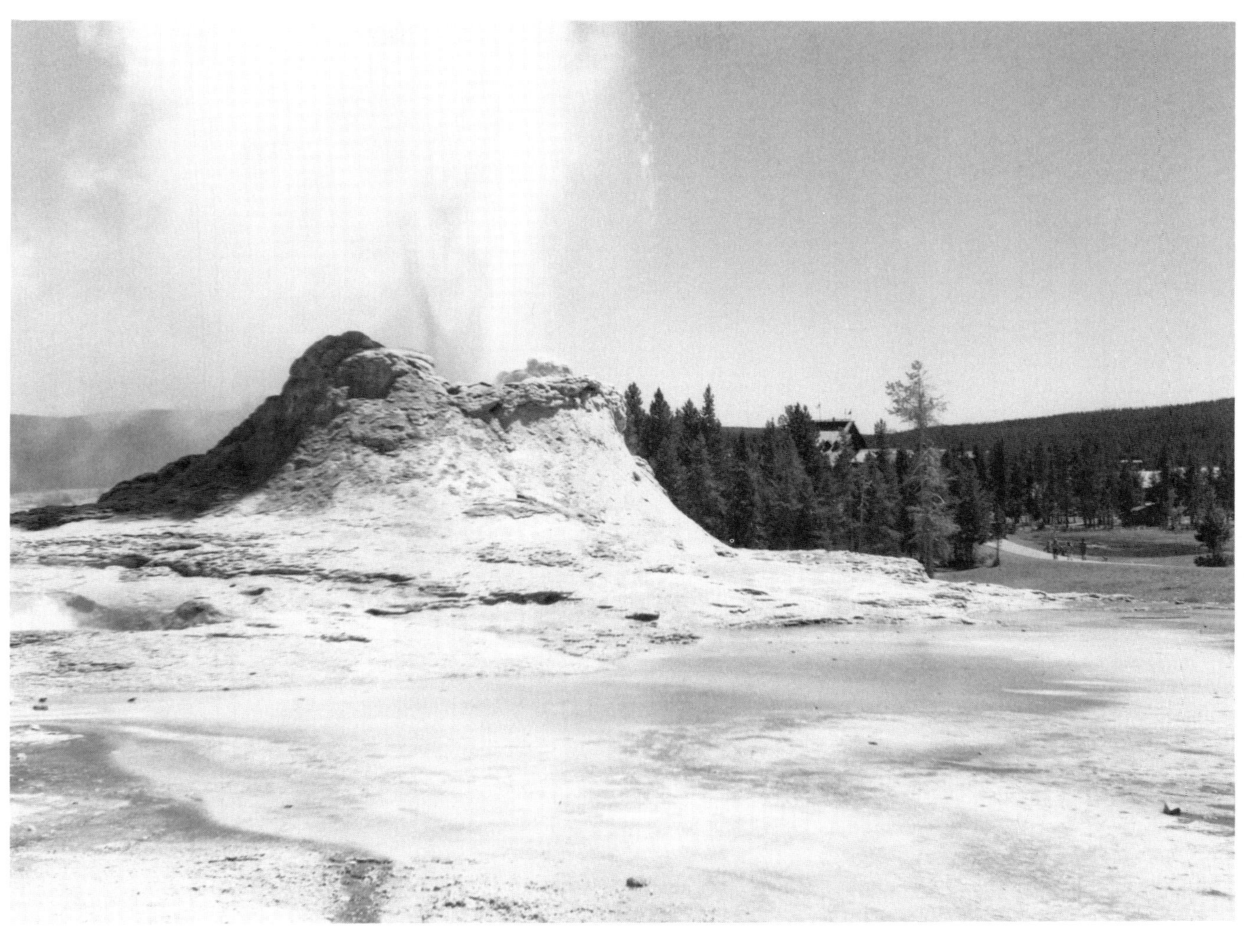

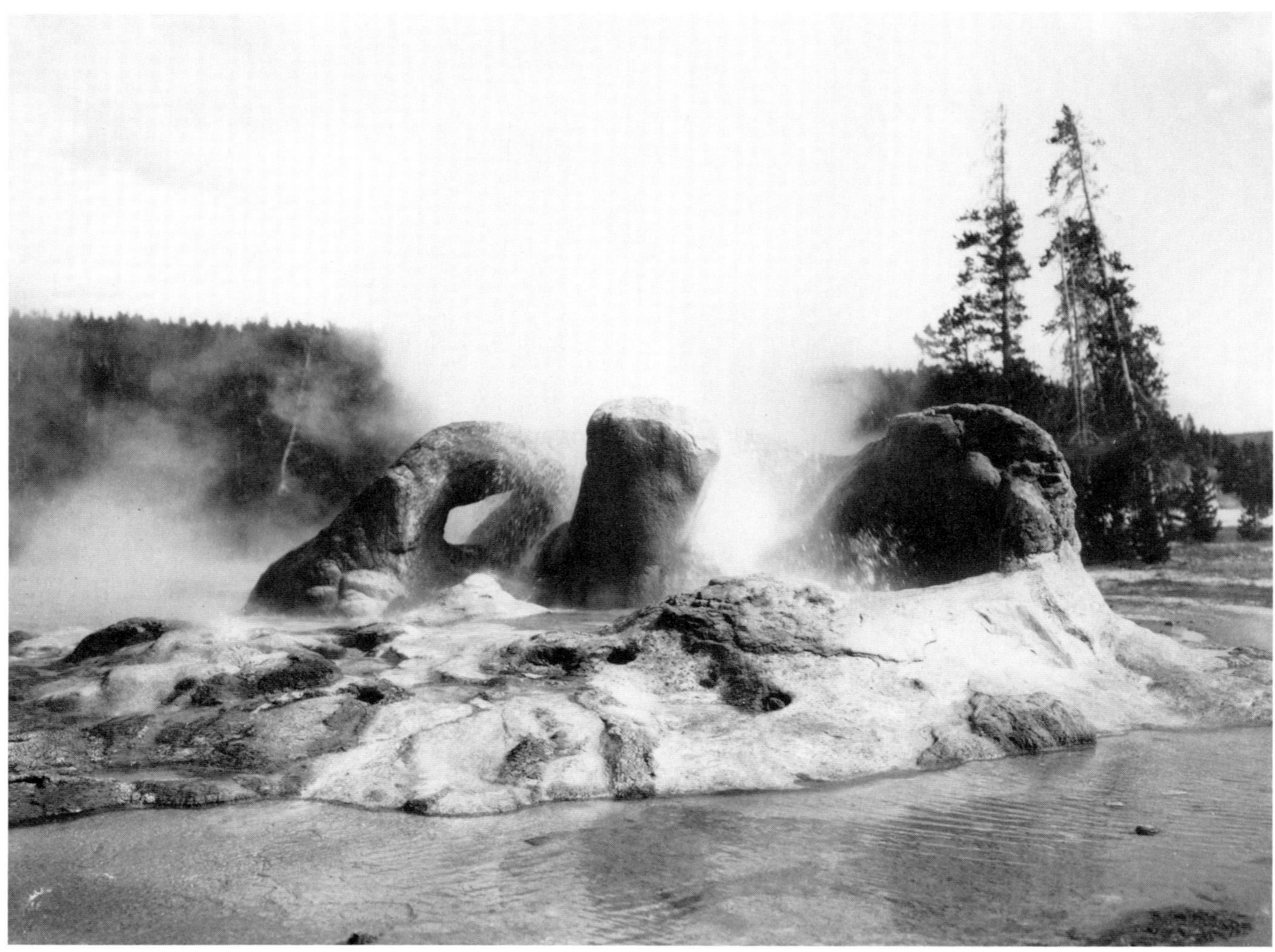

Fig. 28. Grotto Geyser, Upper Geyser Basin, 1907.

W. F. Hatfield's 1902 guidebook to Yellowstone, *Geyserland and Wonderland,* says that the Grotto Geyser "stands so close to the road and presents such an uncanny appearance with its immense dilated nostrils belching out steam, and in action water, that few animals care to pass it for the first time. This is by far the most curiously shaped formation in the Park—remarkable, not pretty." The modern view of Grotto shows that except for the background pines, little has changed over the years. Compare this lack of mineral deposit to the Thermopolis Fountain.

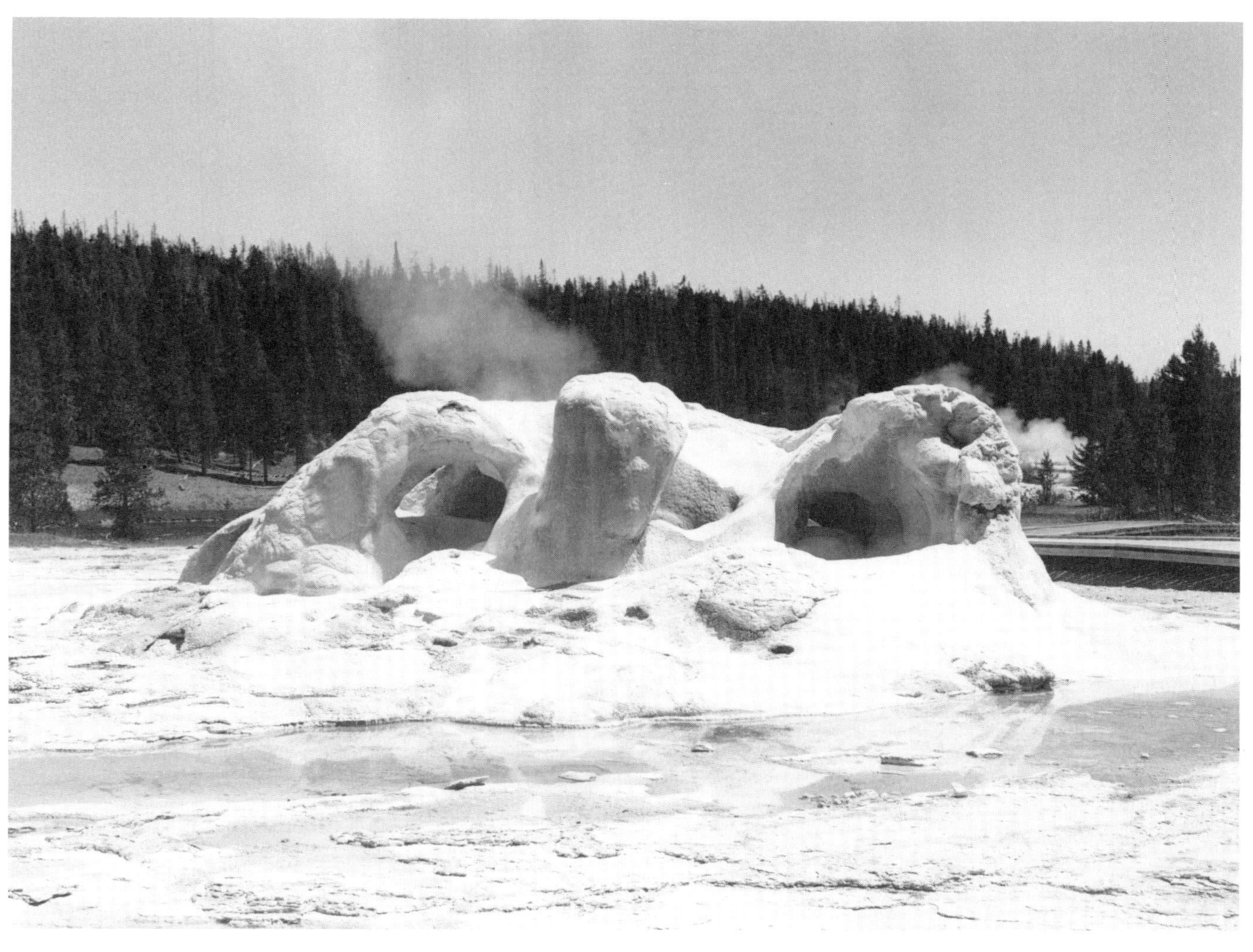

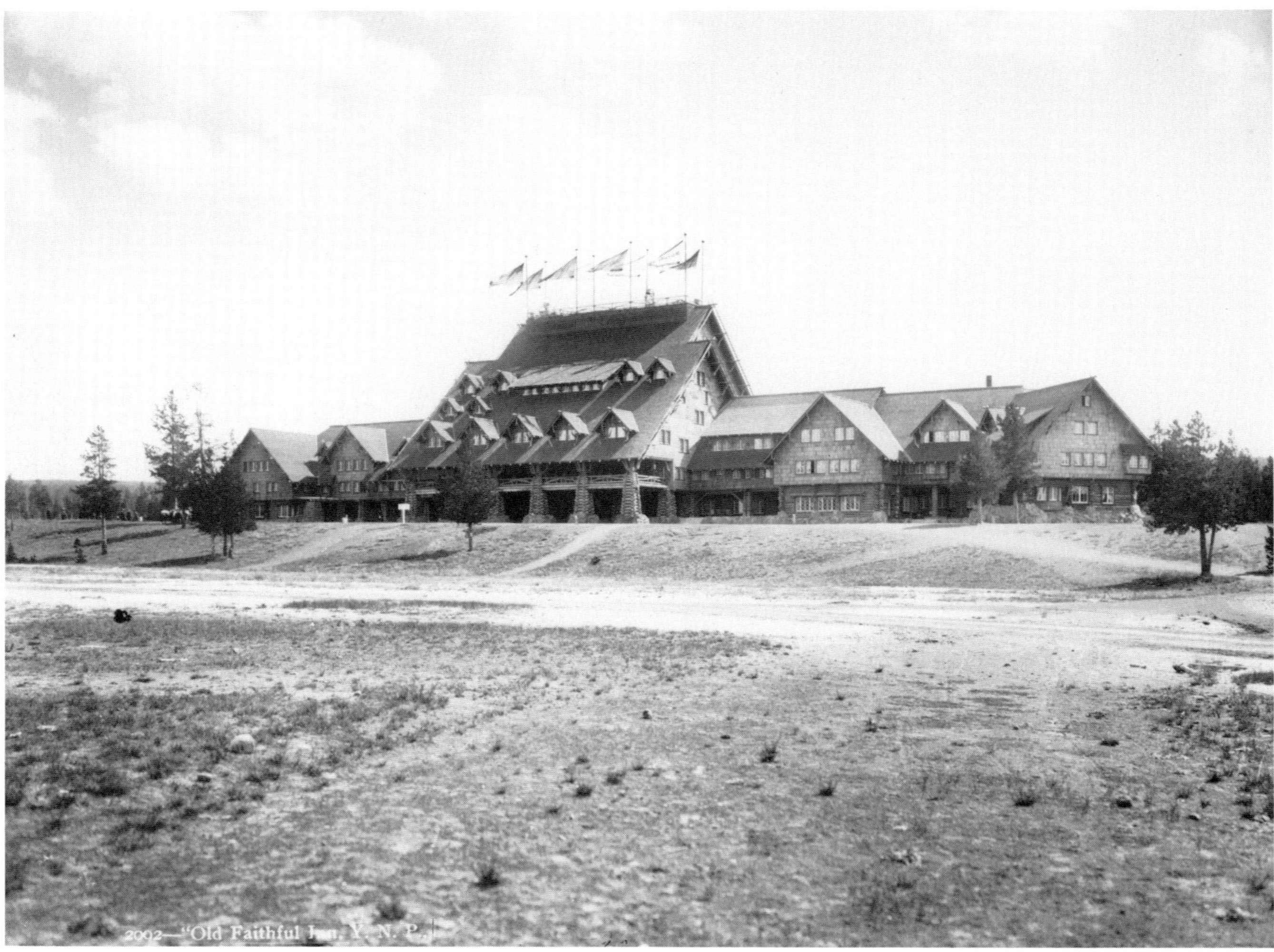

Fig. 29. Old Faithful Inn, 1907.

The largest free-standing log structure in the world, the Old Faithful Inn rises to seventy-nine feet at its highest point. Designed by Seattle architect Robert C. Reamer, the inn was built during the winter of 1903–04 at a cost of $140,000. Workers found it easier to slide the logs over ice and snow than fight the mud of summer. The original building is 350 feet long, with 140 rooms. Additional wings, constructed in 1913 and 1917, bring the total of rooms to 350 and the length to eight hundred feet. Named for the famous geyser, the inn has a special viewing porch where visitors can watch each eruption.

Stimson's view clearly shows the imbalance of dormer windows on the central section of the inn. There are five in the bottom row and four in the top row, but only two in the middle—both on the left side. Amazingly, these are both false, with no openings on the inside. Several suggestions might explain this construction. The dormers could have been a mistake. Reamer could have tried to compensate visually for the gentle slope on which the inn is built. Or the architect could have designed the building to express the idea that nothing in nature is perfectly symmetrical.

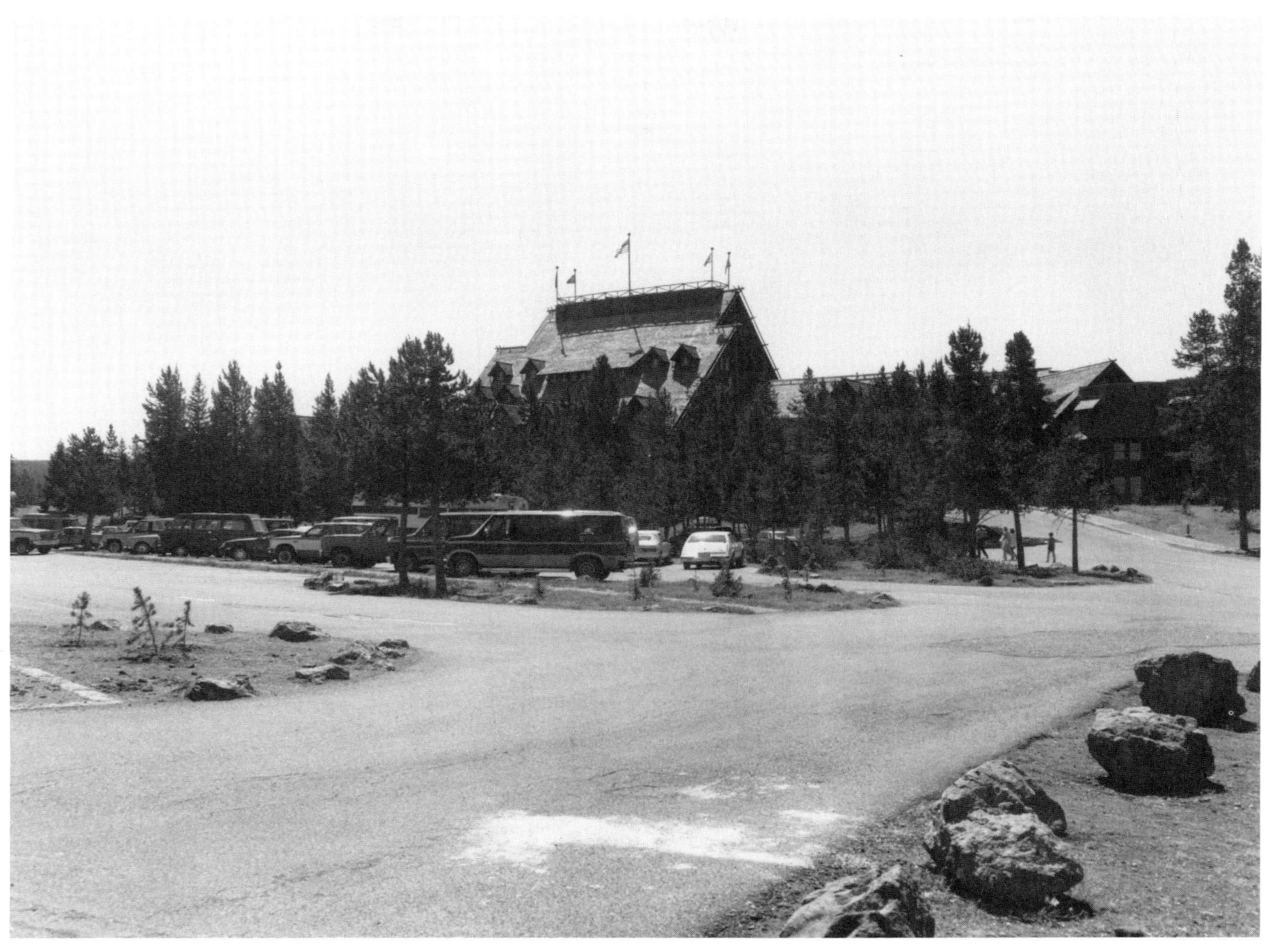

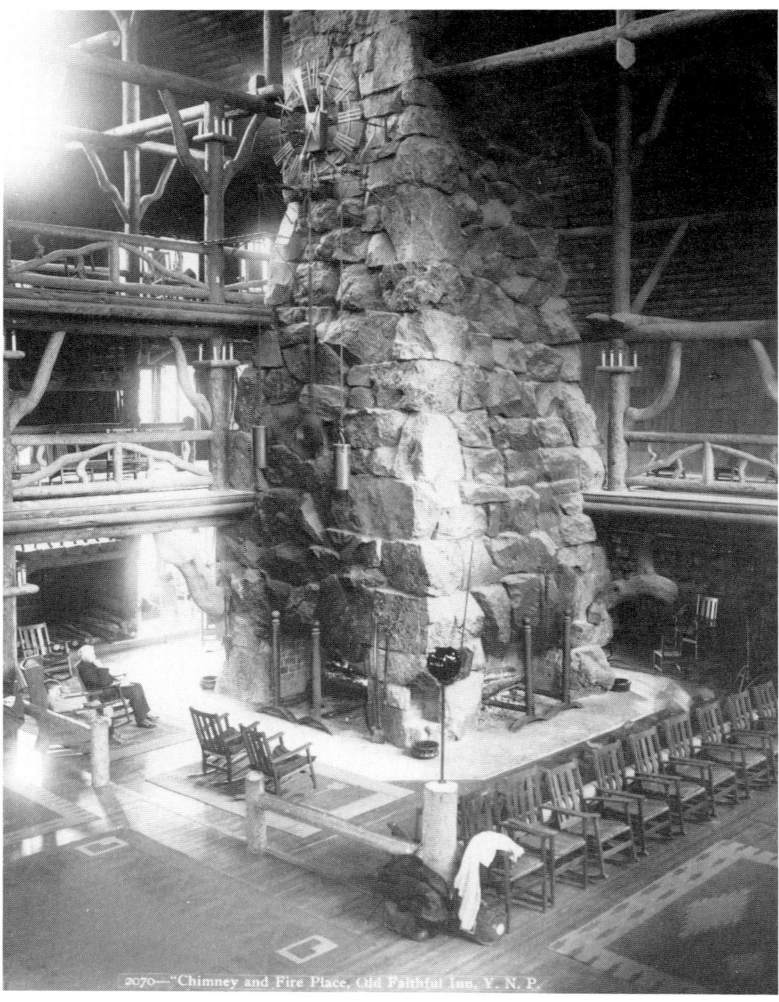

Fig. 30. Chimney and fireplace, Old Faithful Inn, 1907.

In one corner of the open, seven-story-high lobby of the Old Faithful Inn stands a fiive-ton fireplace. It is made of hand-quarried lava blocks and is fourteen feet square at its base. Eight fireplaces are located in one chimney that rises eighty feet. On the chimney can be found a gigantic popcorn popper and a clock with a fourteen-foot-long pendulum. Surrounding the fireplace are twisted lodgepole pines that form support beams for the inn.

At first glance I thought the lack of light in the lobby would pose a special problem for rephotography. Instead, this scene clearly illustrated the light sensitivity of modern film. Because most of the lighting in the lobby is natural, it is very dark and shadowy. With light meter in hand, I set up my camera and watched the crowded lobby below. I decided to open the shutter for thirty seconds. This meant, of course, that anything that moved during the exposure would be blurred. After printing the photograph I found that almost everyone in the lobby was gone, except for a ghost couple at right foreground. I also noticed that the clock's pendulum had blurred. Knowing that modern film is more light-sensitive than the glass plates that Stimson used, I looked for signs of long exposure in Stimson's photo. By carefully examining the clock, I could tell that the modern photo was made at approximately 9:48 A.M. After looking at Stimson's view, I found no sign of movement except for the minute hand of the clock. It had moved twice while the shutter of the camera was open, suggesting an exposure of about two minutes! The new support beam, center right, was added after the 1959 earthquake.

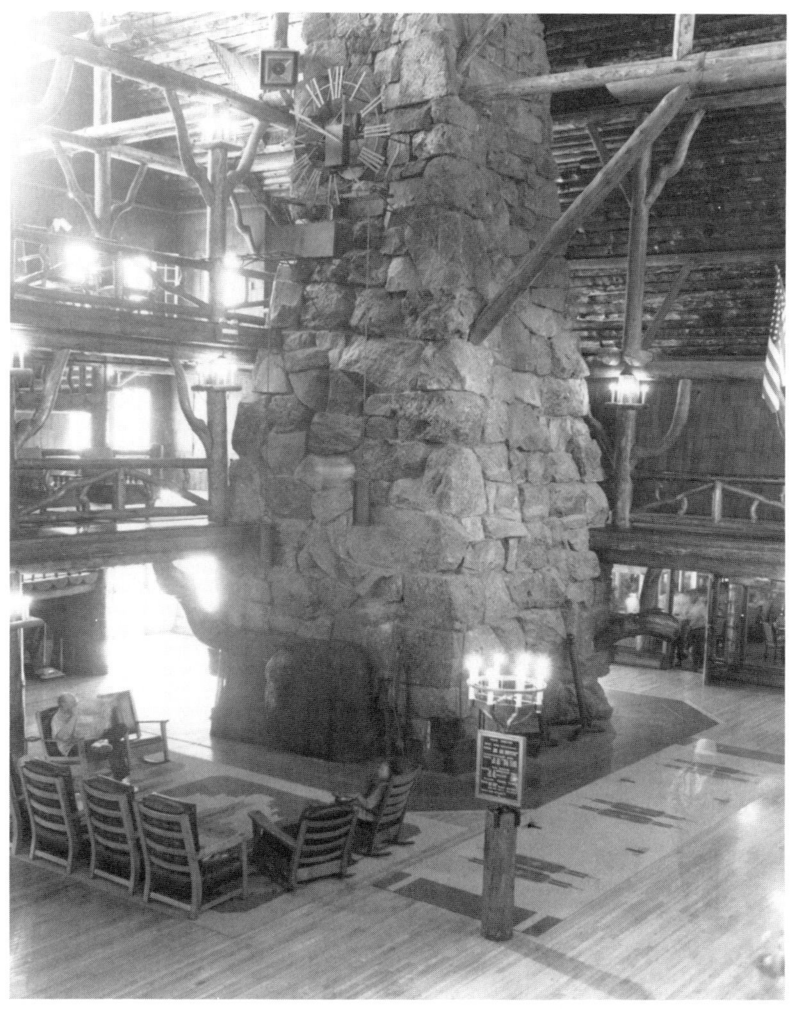

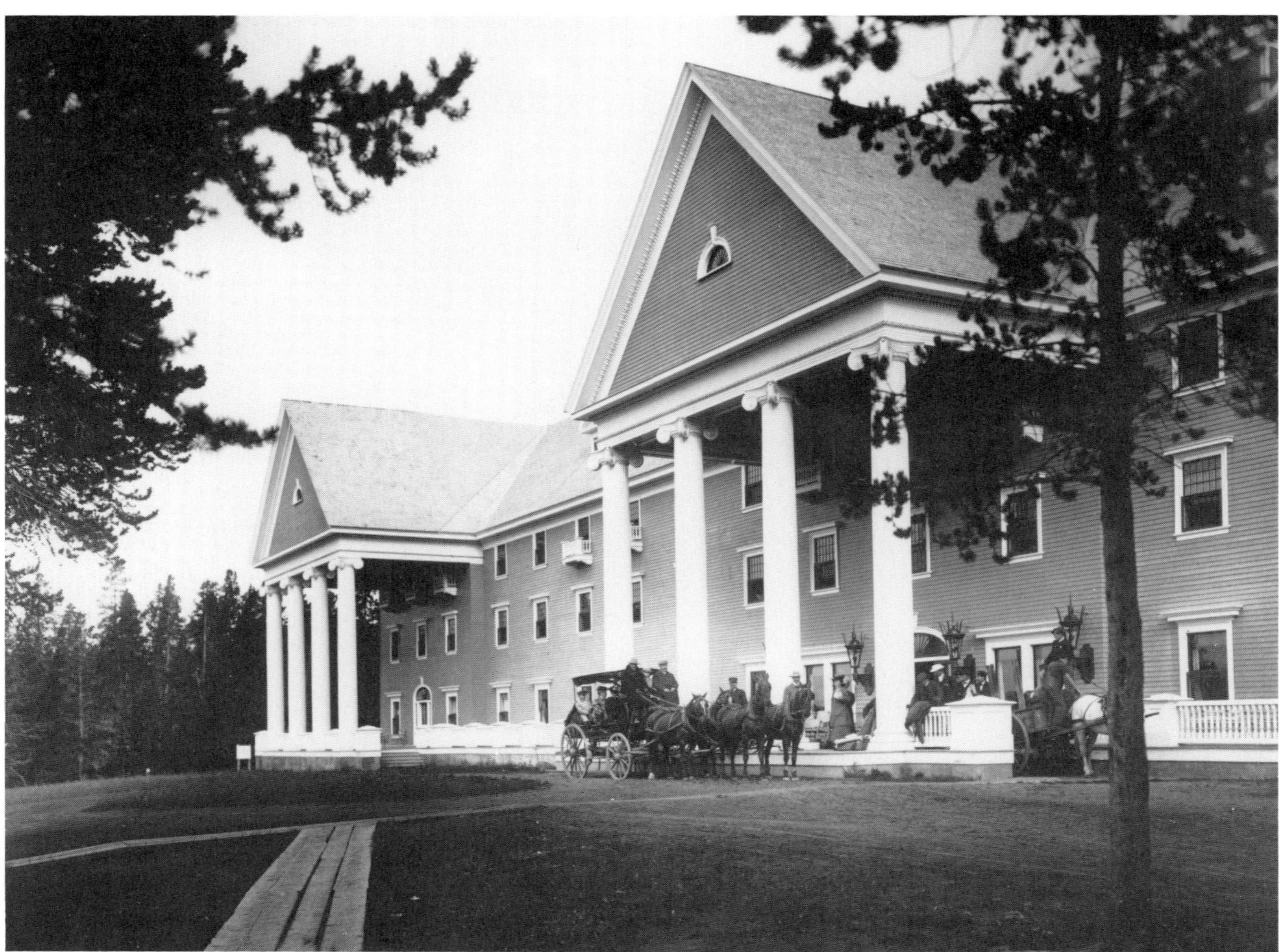

Fig. 31. Lake Hotel, 1907.

Located on the northwest edge of Yellowstone Lake, the Lake Hotel was constructed in 1889 by the Northern Pacific Railroad. It followed a traditional box design and was built of lumber cut on the site. It was redesigned between 1904 and 1905 by the same architect who built the Old Faithful Inn, Robert C. Reamer. Reamer added gables, columns, false balconies, and fanlight windows to give the boxed hotel a neoclassical look. The new design prompted suggestions that the hotel's name be changed to the Colonial, but Lake prevailed. Stimson's view shows coaches arriving at the front door in 1907.

Seventy-one years later, the Lake Hotel was in the middle of a major renovation to restore the hotel's grandeur. The same Ionic columns and fanlight window, upper center, are still visible today.

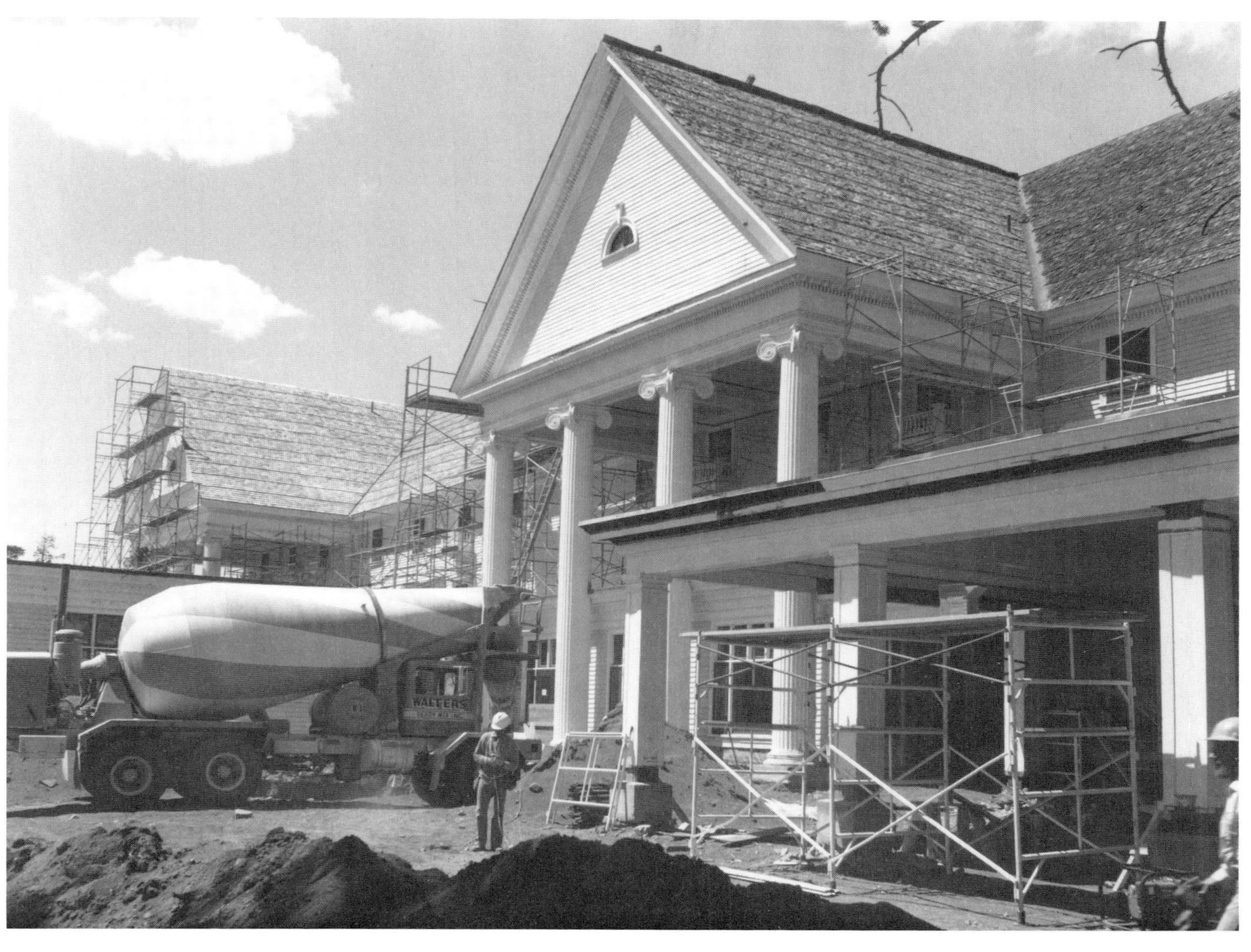
WALTERS

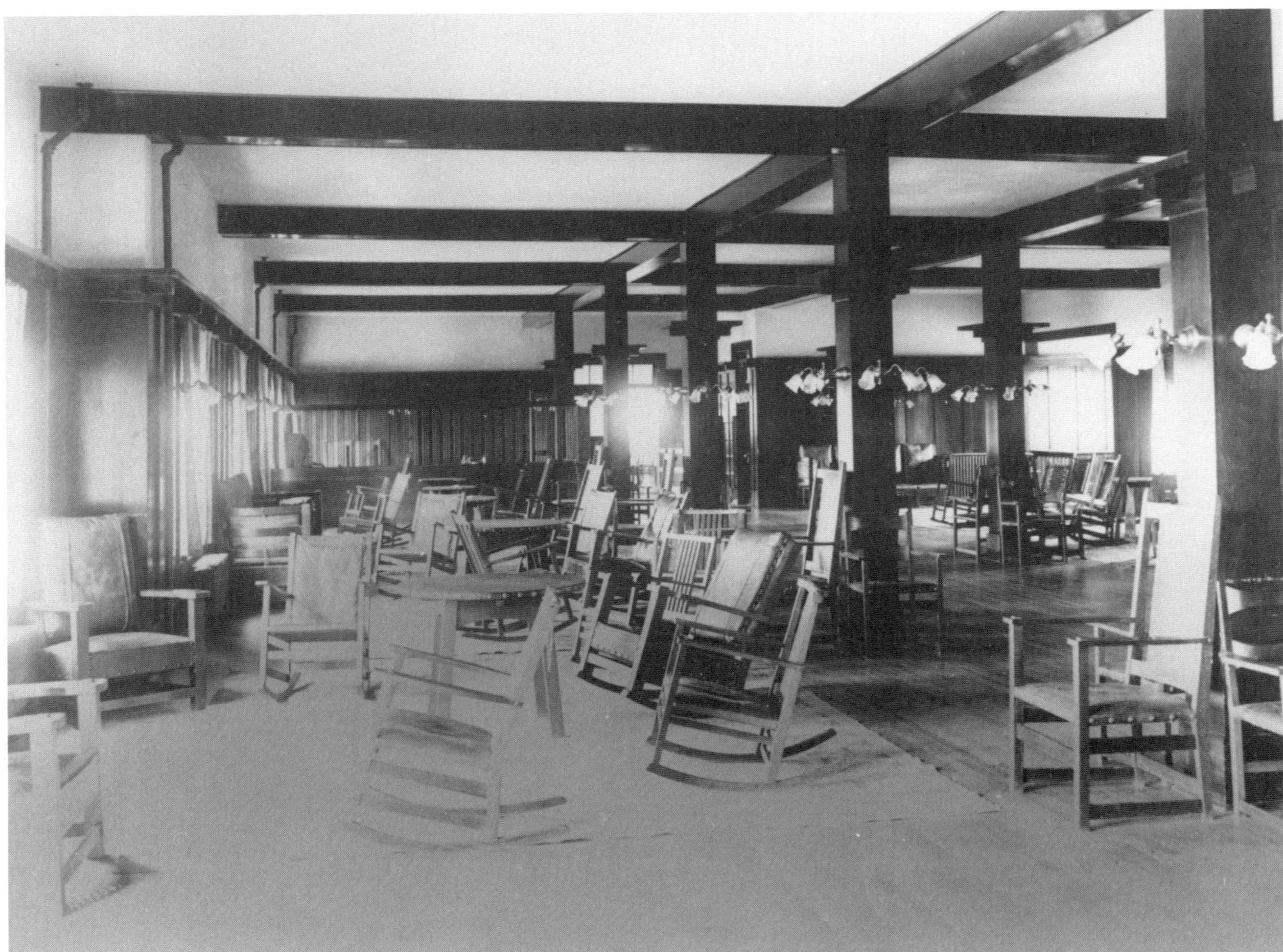

Fig. 32. Lobby, Lake Hotel, 1907.

The lobby of the Lake Hotel was first remodeled in 1923–24. The redwood paneling and posts seen in Stimson's photo were painted white, and new furniture was added. Over the next six decades, the lobby was slightly changed. Then in 1985, using authentic refinished furniture, the lobby was restored to a 1920s style.

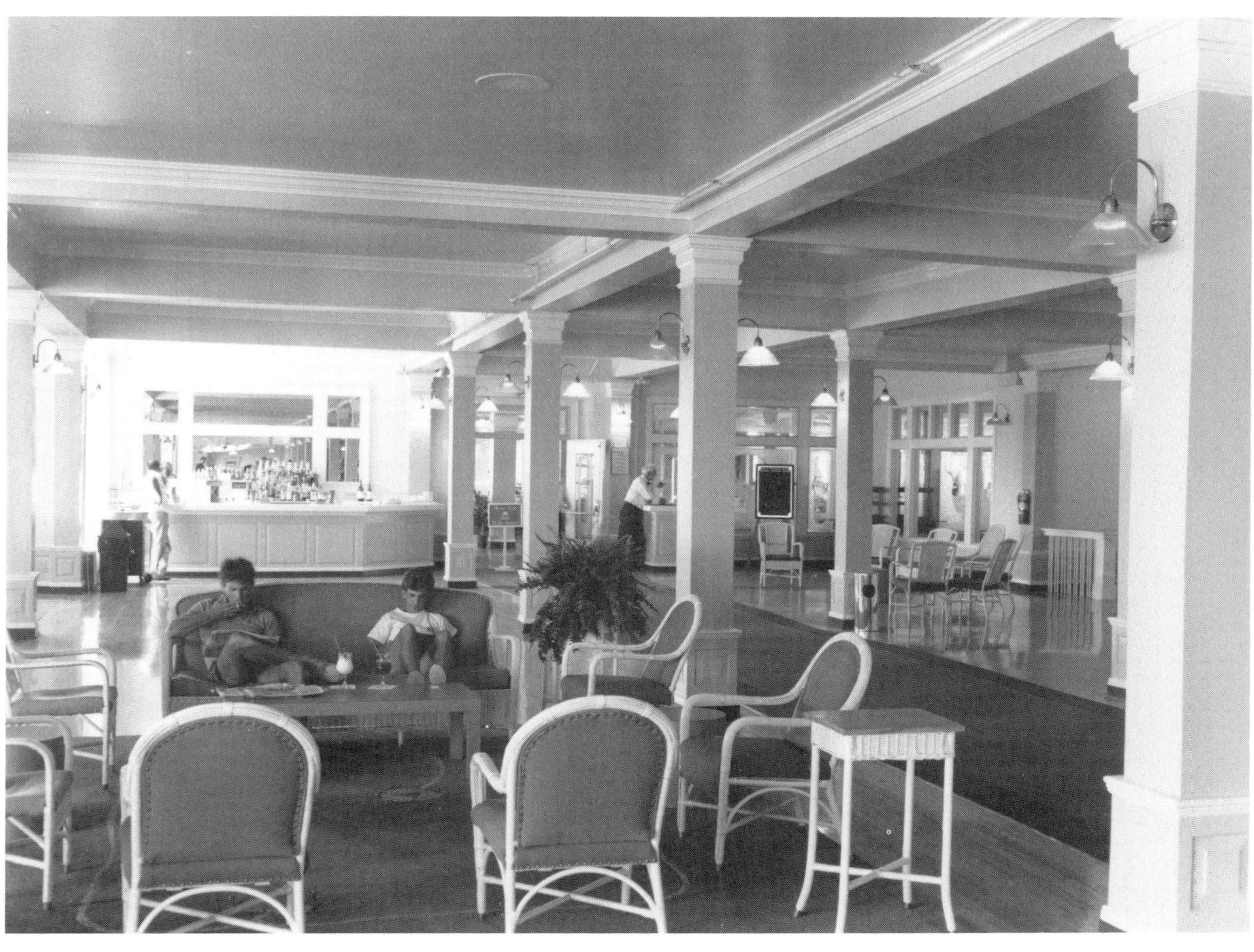

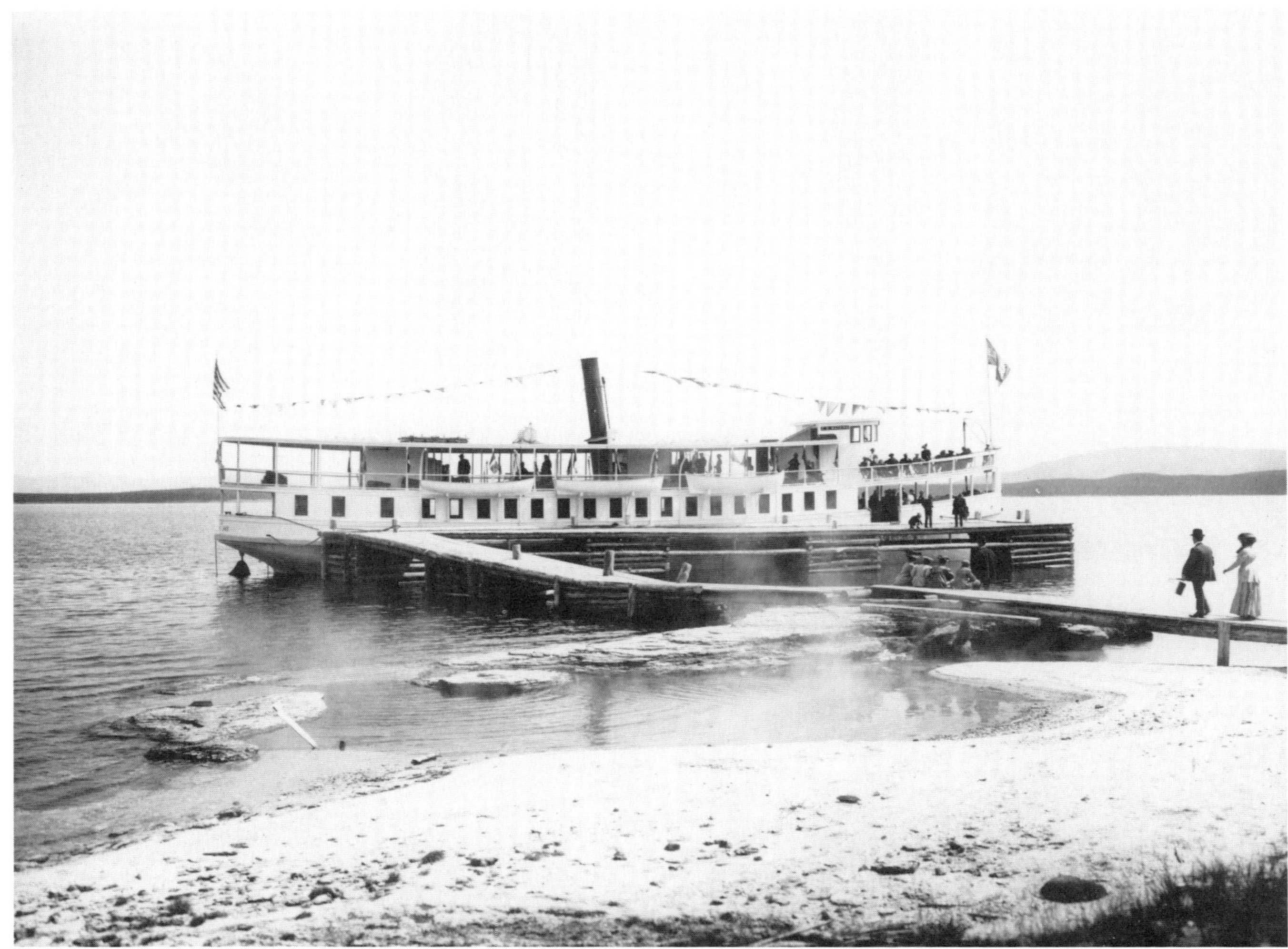

Fig. 33. Yellowstone Lake boat leaving Thumb, West Thumb, 1907.

The steamship *Zillah* had operated on the Great Lakes before being transported in pieces, via wagon, to Yellowstone Lake. The craft was reassembled and launched in the spring of 1889. Before the introduction of automobiles in the park in 1916, the *Zillah* transported up to 125 tourists at a time to various sites around the lake. The name E. C. Waters, painted on the side of the pilot house, refers to one of the park's concessionaires. After autos made the boat unnecessary in 1916, the lake cruises were stopped and the *Zillah* was scrapped. The boat's boilers were moved to the Lake Hotel to provide steam heat.

Stimson's view shows the *Zillah* at the West Thumb Dock. Nearby is the famous Fishing Cone. Today only the background of hills, right center, identifies the proper vantage point. A close look reveals that the question mark–shaped rock formation on which the boat is docked, center midground, is still present—under several feet of water.

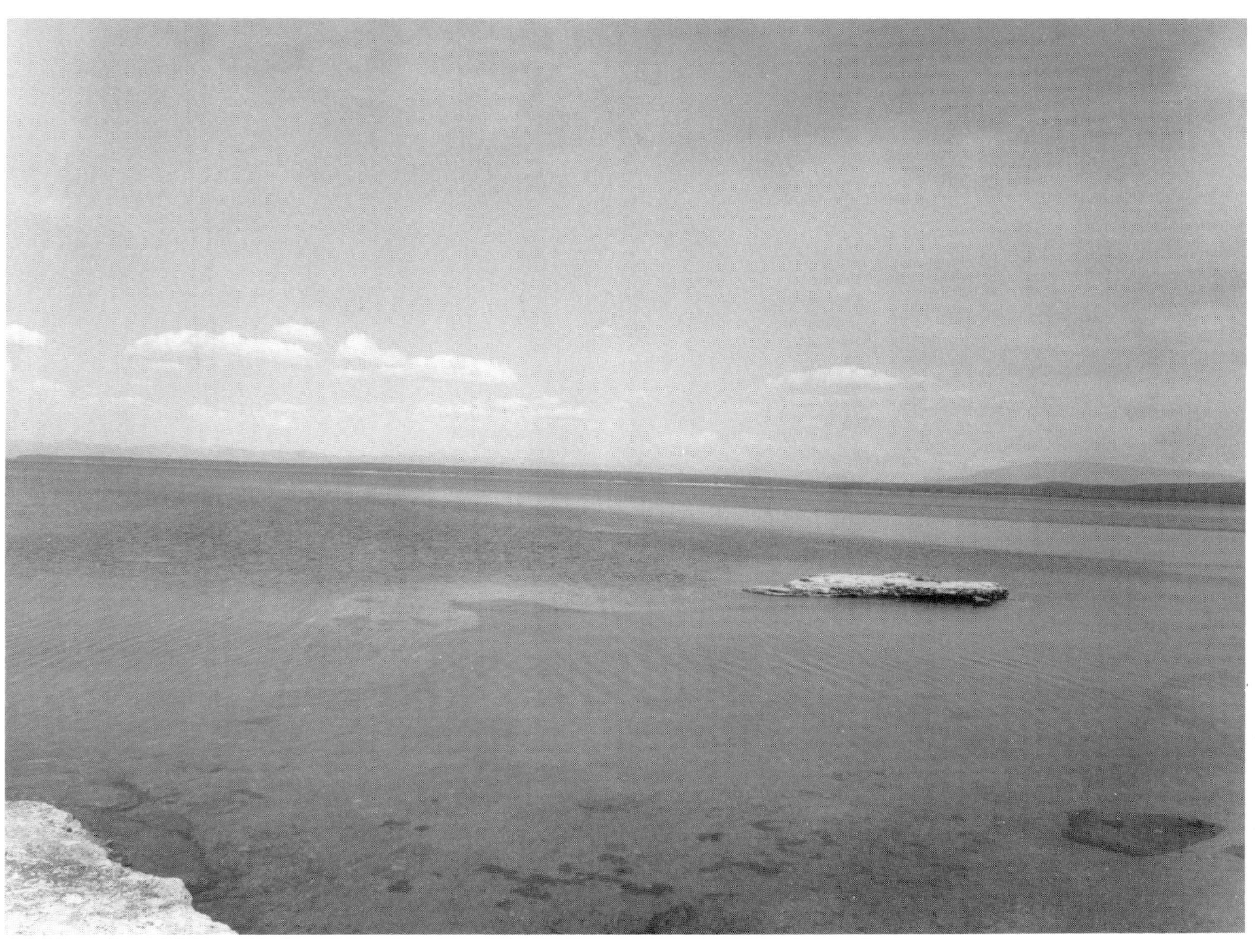

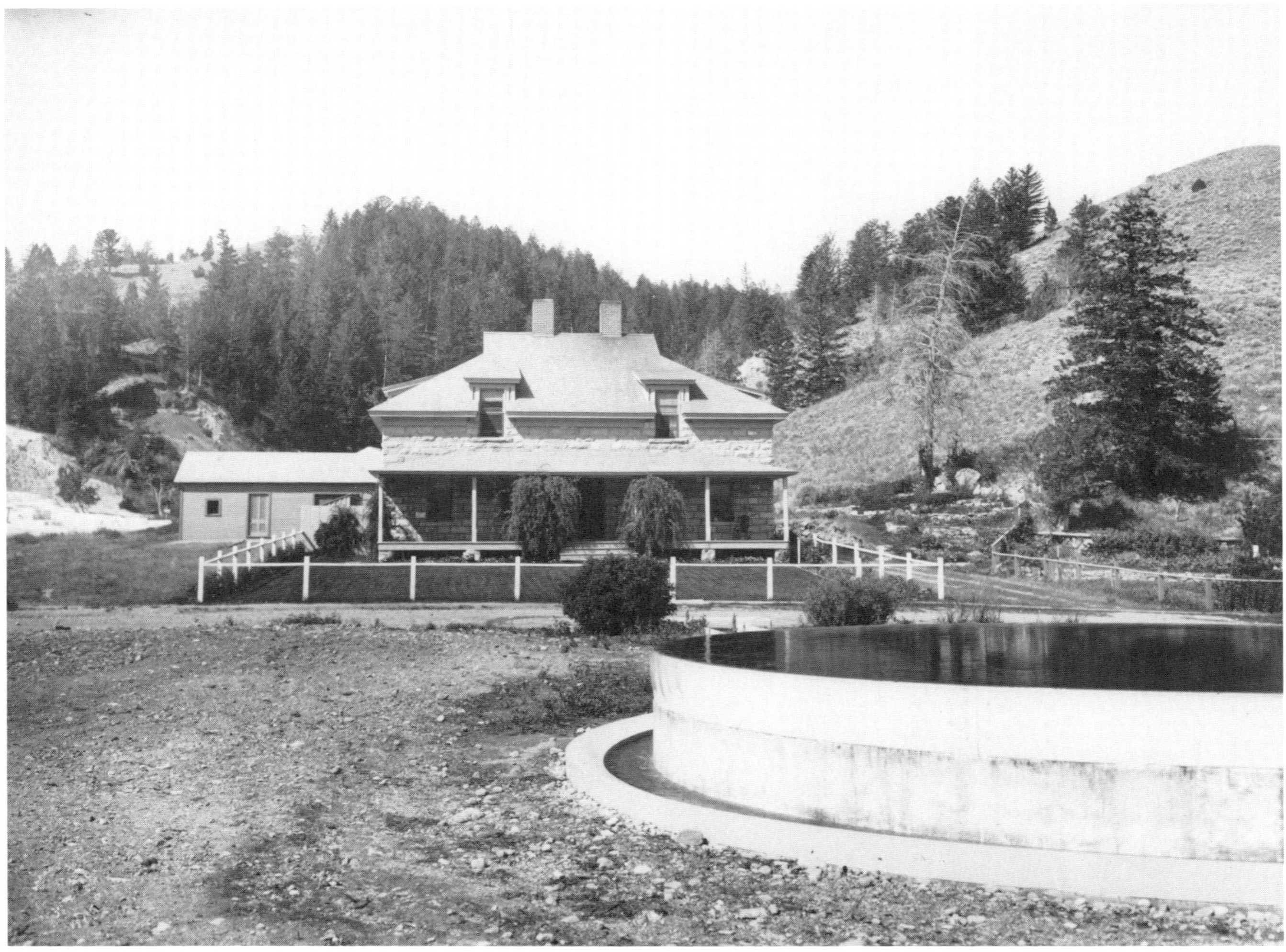

Fig. 34. Colonel Meldrum's house, Mammoth Hot Springs, 1902.

John H. Meldrum was the first Yellowstone Park commissioner and had a house at Fort Yellowstone near Mammoth Hot Springs. His duties paralleled those of a justice of the peace, except that his jurisdiction was Yellowstone. His job was created when the National Park Protective Act of 1894 directed the United States government to appoint a commissioner to reside permanently in the park. Meldrum remained in office until 1935. His house, seen in Stimson's photograph, is directly north of the Mammoth Hot Springs Terrace. It contained not only living quarters on the right half of the dwelling but also an office and jail on the left.

The army was replaced by the National Park Service in 1916, but the office of commissioner was kept. Today the house is still the home of the park's justice of the peace.

In the old photo, the trees in front of the house are much smaller. The pool, right foreground, was probably a thermal spring.

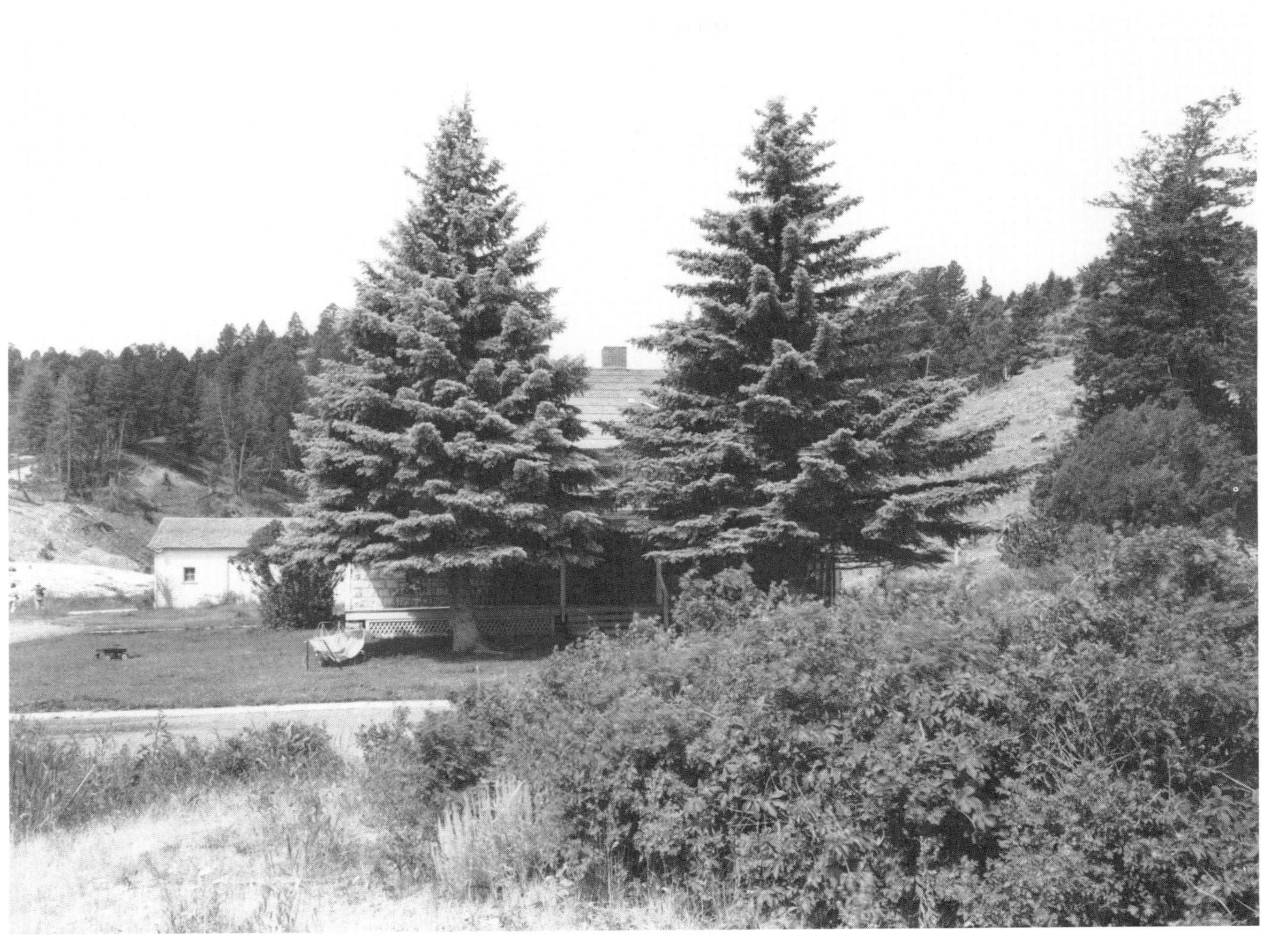

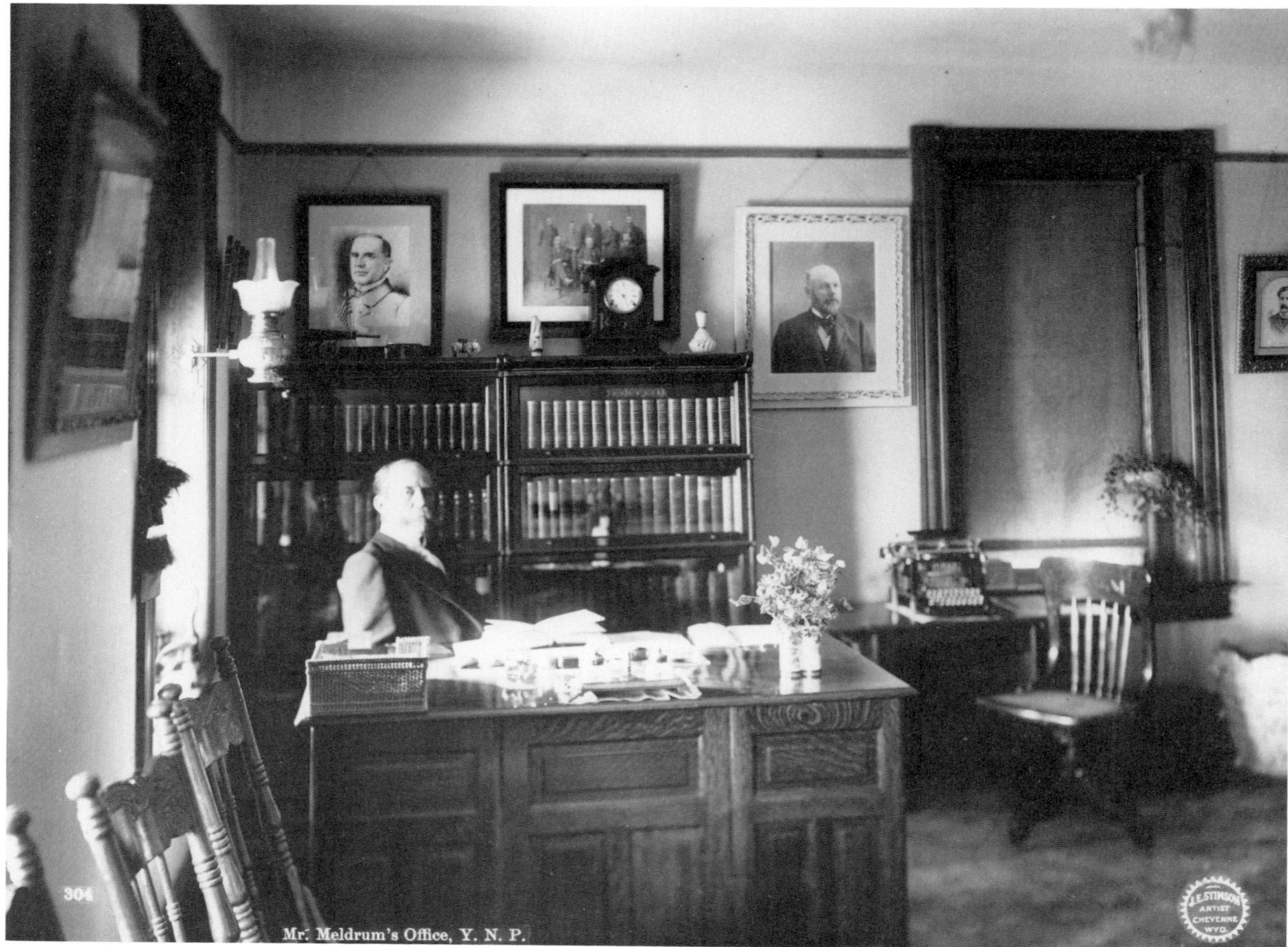

Fig. 35. Colonel Meldrum's office, 1902.

This interior view of Meldrum's office shows the front left room of the exterior photo. Behind Meldrum's desk can be found pictures of recently assassinated President William McKinley and Wyoming governor Joseph M. Carey.

Today the justice of the peace has an office in another building, and the old office has been turned into his living room. About the only feature still recognizable is the location of the two windows.

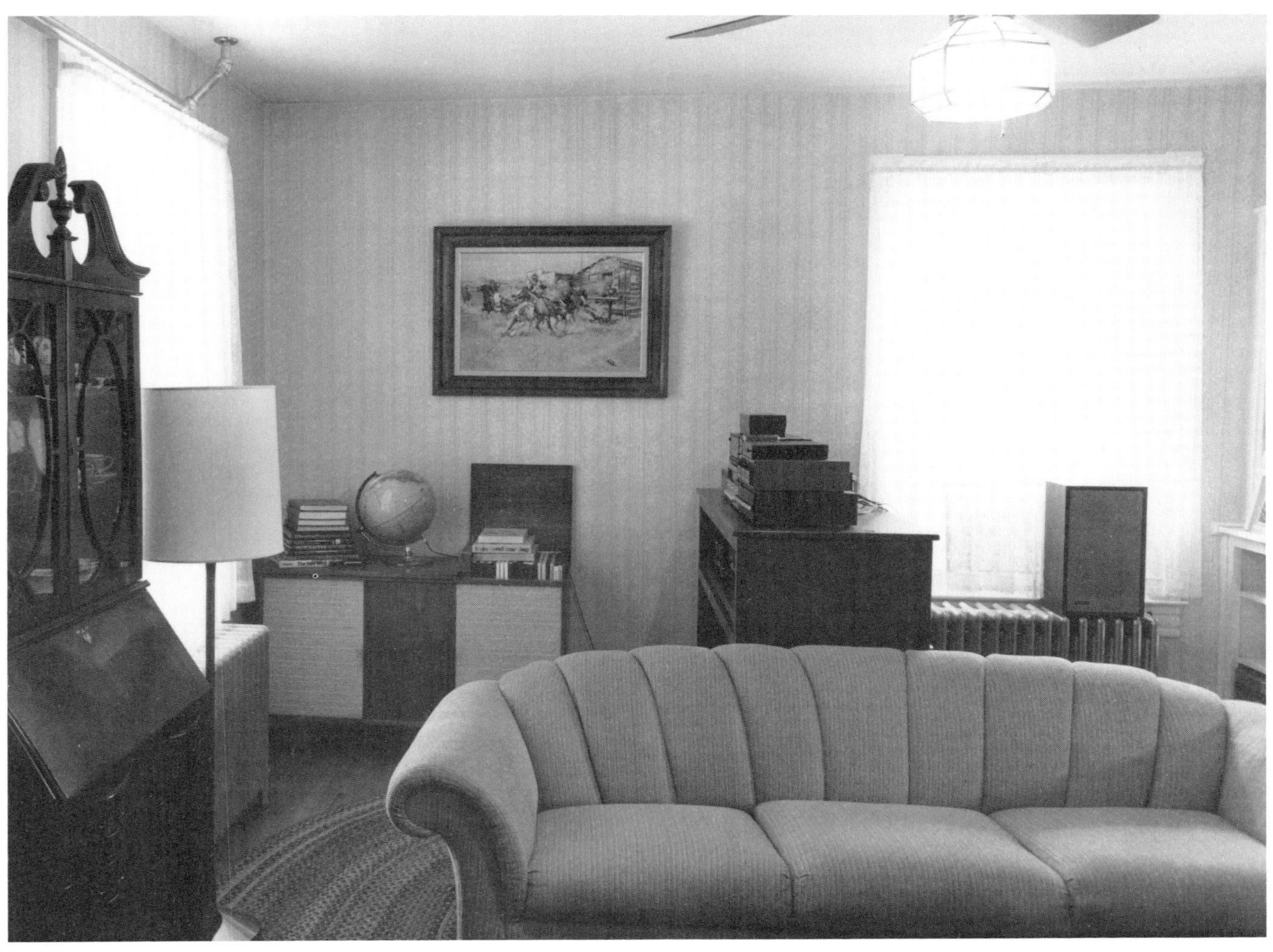

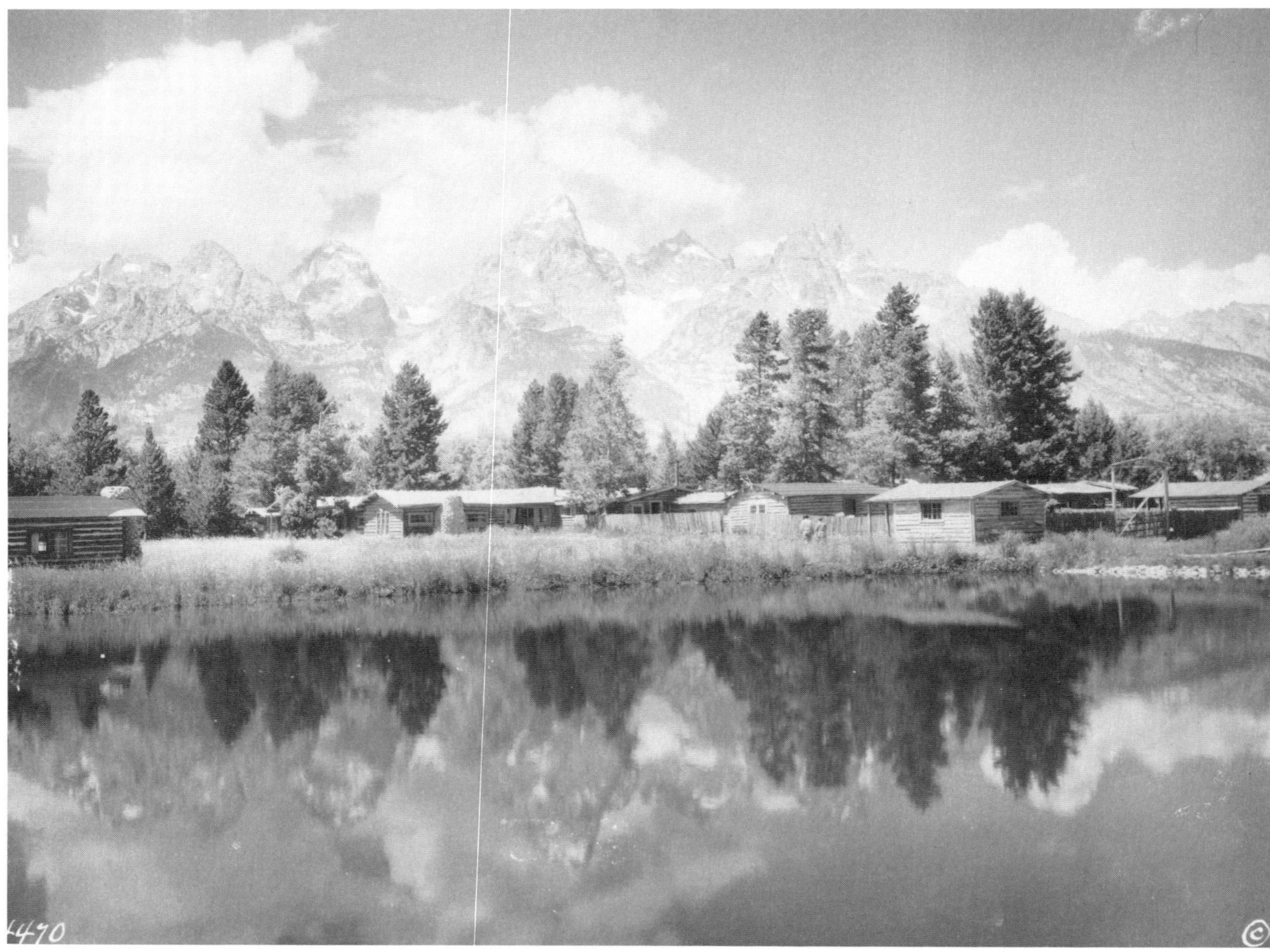

Fig. 36. Grand Tetons from Bar BC, 1924.

The Bar BC was the second dude ranch to open in the Jackson Hole country. It opened in 1912 and was operated by Struthers Burt. Burt recalled his days at the Bar BC in his book, *The Diary of a Dude Wrangler.* Today the ranch buildings are held in private ownership. The Bar BC is located just within Grand Teton National Park's southern boundary along the Snake River.

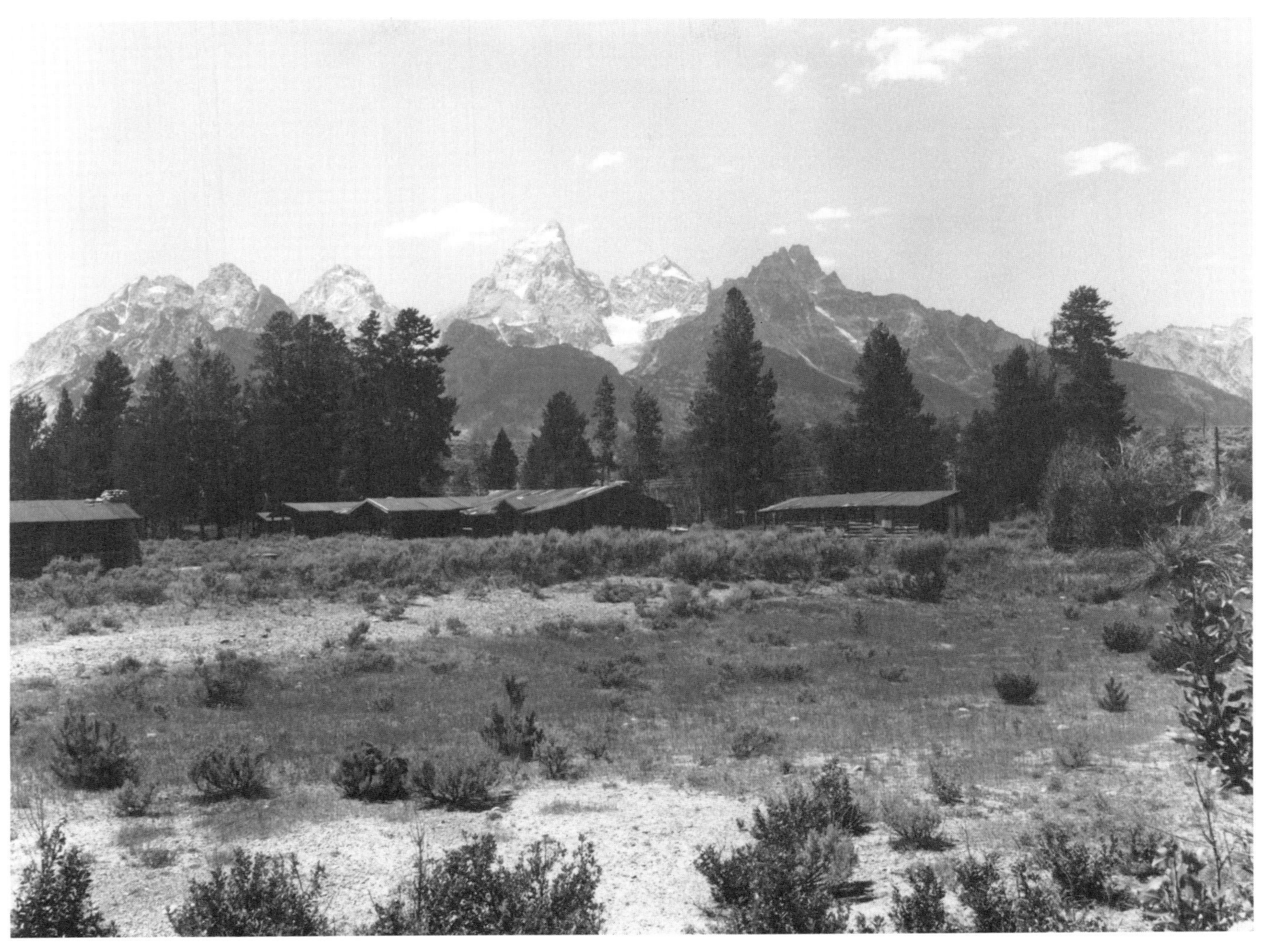

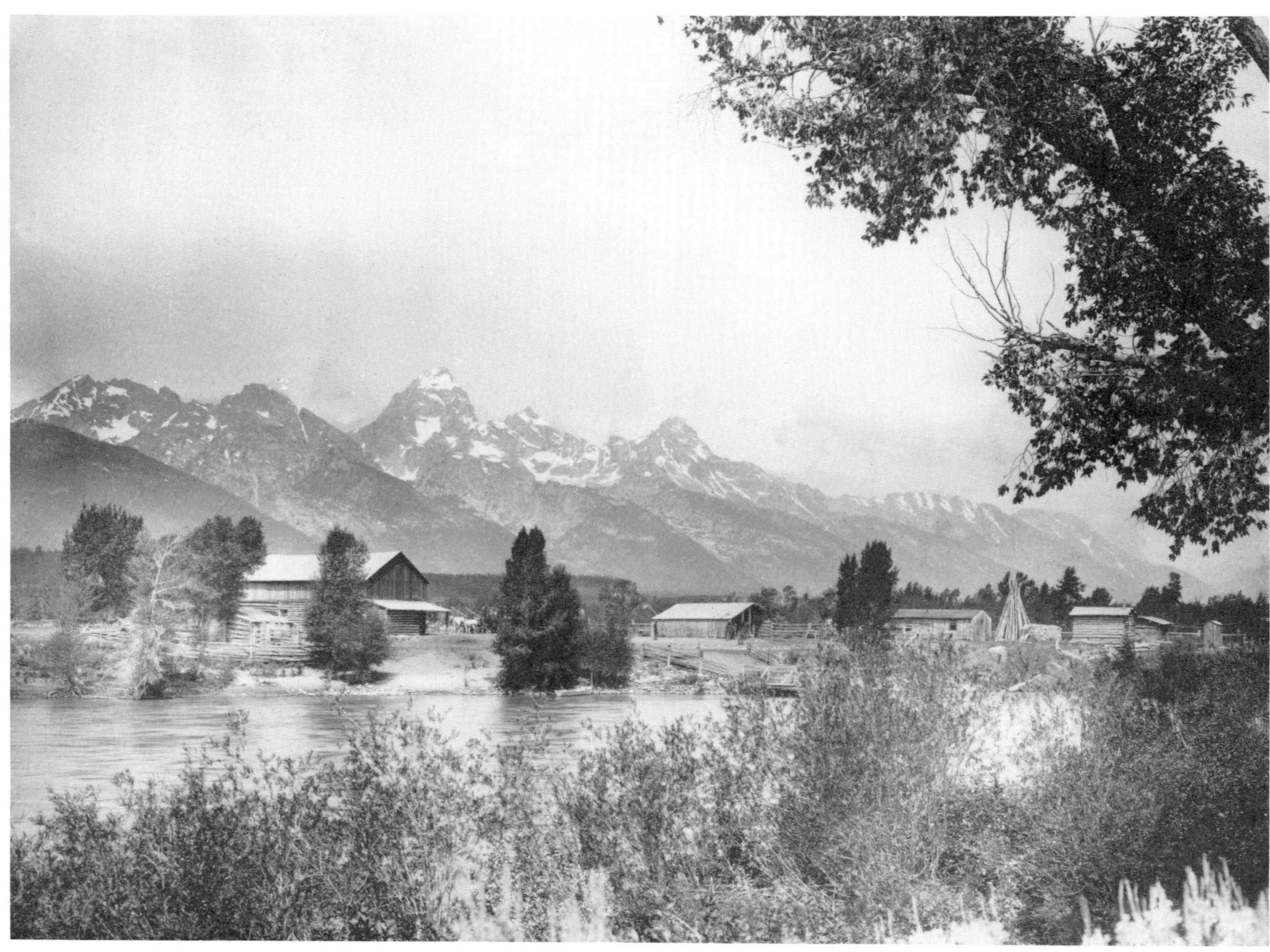

Fig. 37. Menor's Ferry on the Snake River, 1899.

Located near Moose, Menor's Ferry operated on the Snake River for over twenty-five years until the first bridge was built in 1927. The ferry boat was restored by Laurence Rockefeller in 1949. The ferry is now a historic site at the southern entrance to Grand Teton National Park. The landing steps at river's edge, center midground, can be found in both views. The large square window identifies Bill Menor's original cabin at right center.

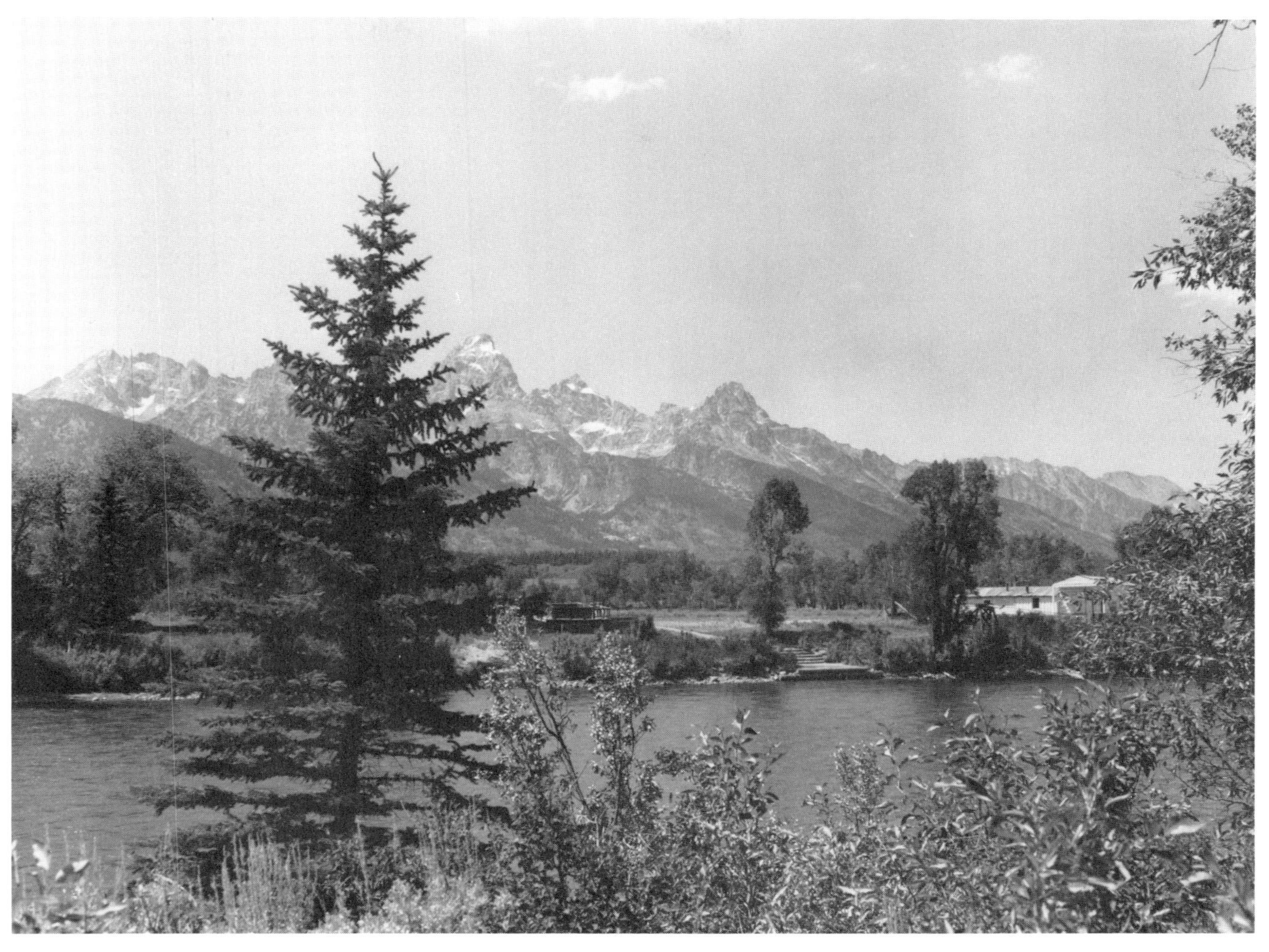

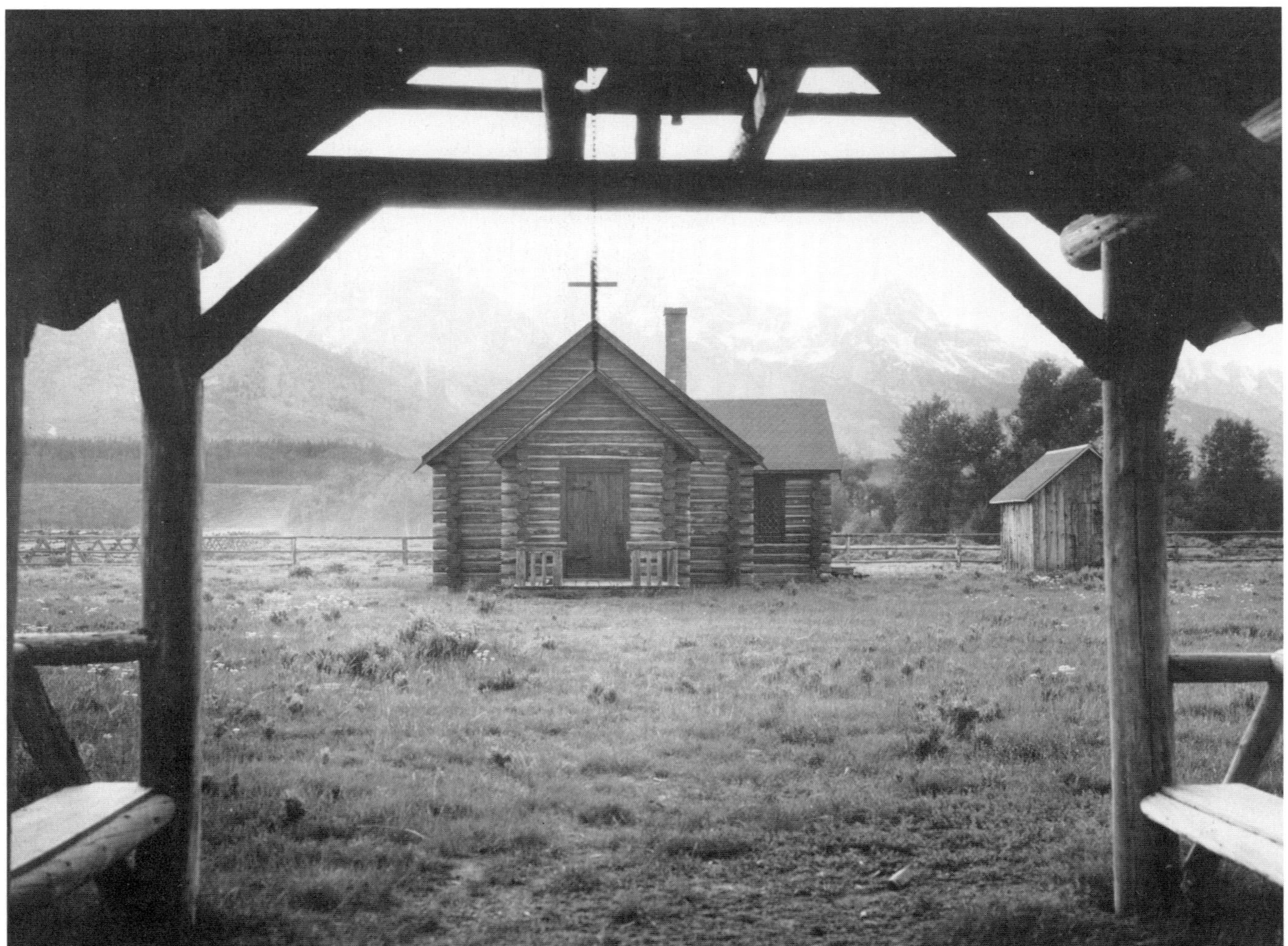

Fig. 38. Chapel of Transfiguration, 1930.

The Chapel of Transfiguration was built in 1924 for the people of Moose. It is located just inside the southern entrance to Grand Teton National Park. Behind the altar is a large picture window that frames the Tetons. Through the open door of the modern photo, a cross is visible at the back of the chapel.

After spending close to an hour setting up my tripod to rephotograph the bell from just the right vantage point (one and a half feet above the ground), I went inside and found modern color postcards of the same view.

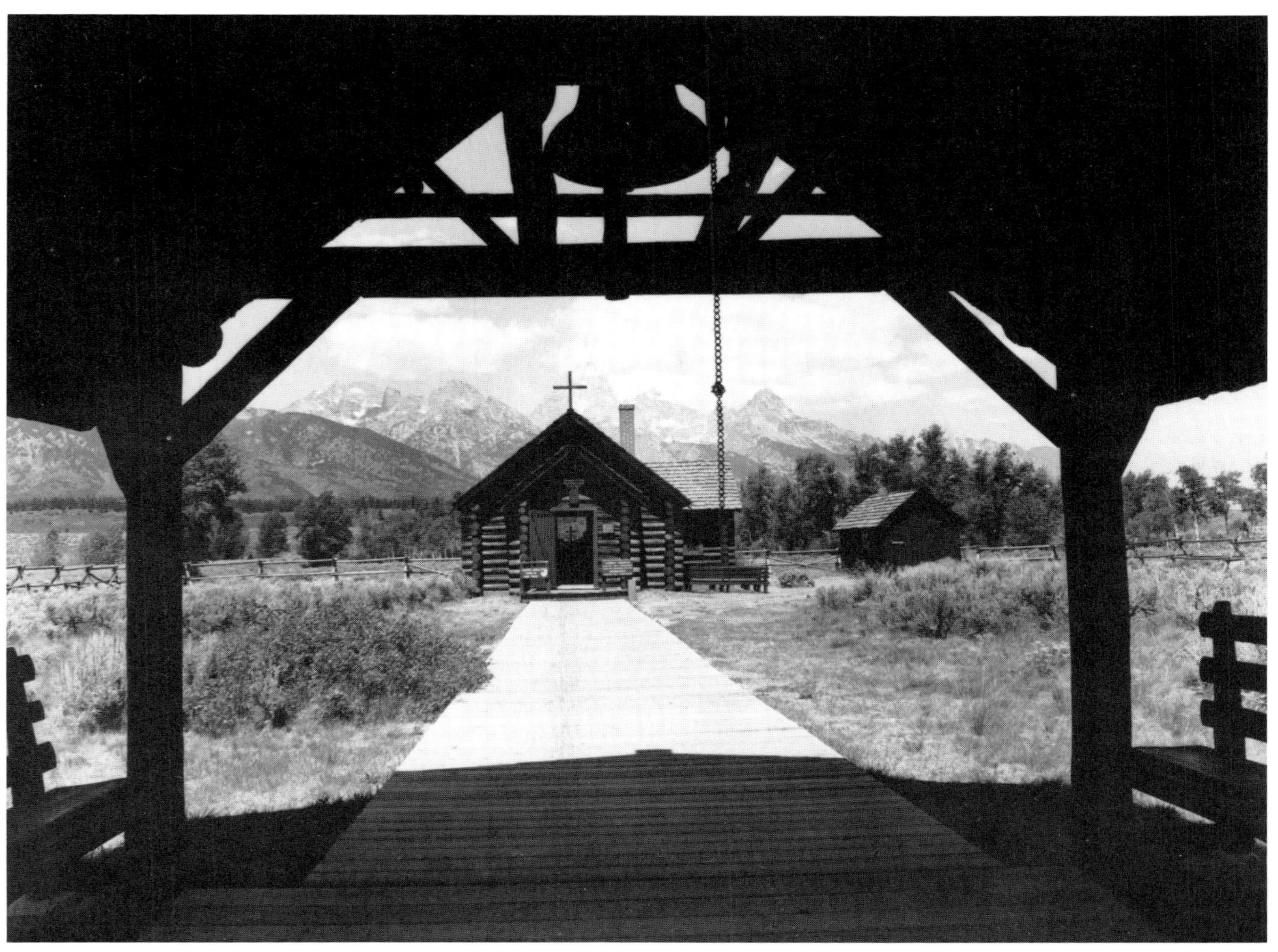

The Forgotten Past

This chapter depicts a set of places that Stimson photographed but that no longer exist. In essence this chapter shows the ghosts of Wyoming's boom and bust mining economy. Cambria, Dietz, and Kearney were coal camps that began in the late 1890s and then died out after coal prices slumped in the late 1920s. The mine at Sunrise operated for eighty years before a slump in the steel industry forced Colorado Fuel and Iron to shut it down in 1980. The Encampment smelter and Walcott Station boomed between 1903 and 1910, during the Sierra Madre copper boom. Although the Hecla mine never gained the production of these other mines, it still stands as a testimony to the dreams of the independent miner. The Dale Creek Bridge was replaced when a shorter route was constructed over Sherman Hill between Laramie and Cheyenne in 1901. The importance of these photos is that they depict both the entrepreneur's dreams and the frailty of the economy. Stimson photographed these places to show, as always, the best that Wyoming had to offer. Photos of industry would mean more investment for Wyoming and, in turn, more money for Stimson's employer, the Union Pacific. These photos, then, are not only a visual record of things past but also a visual reminder of the uncertainty of Wyoming's boom and bust economy.

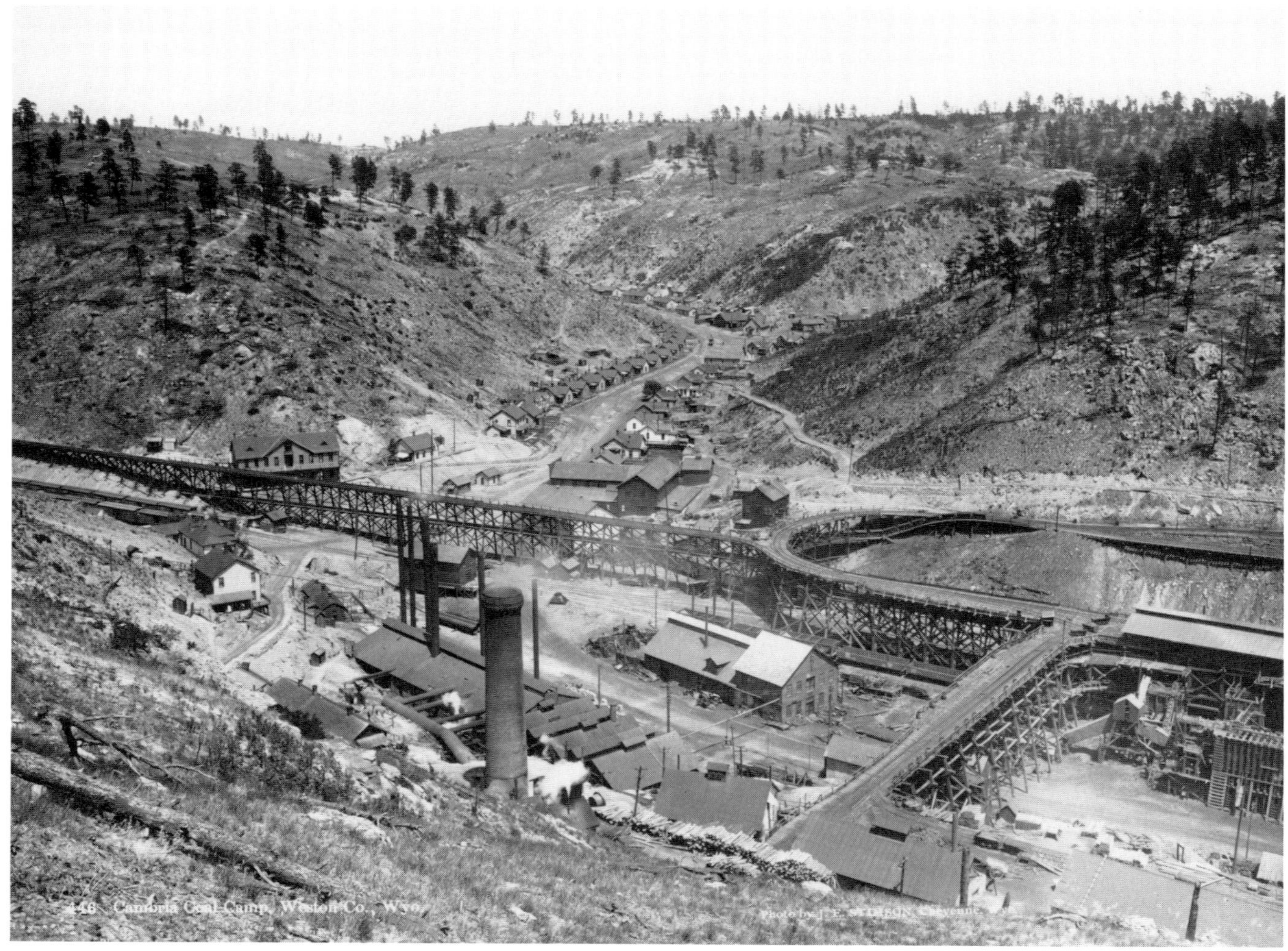

Fig. 39. Cambria coal camp, 1903.

Anthracite coal was discovered in this valley north of Newcastle by Frank Mondell in 1887. These deposits allowed the Chicago, Burlington, and Quincy Railroad to build into northeastern Wyoming. By 1915 Cambria had a cosmopolitan population of more than one thousand. It was a dry town; beer was brought by wagon from Newcastle. Houses were located throughout the floor of Coal Creek Canyon. Great staircases led up the hills to a company schoolhouse, gymnasium, and bathhouse. By 1929 the coal ran out and the town was deserted almost overnight. Stimson's view was taken above the Antelope Mine looking eastward. The remains of the tipple at lower right and the author's truck, left center, can be found in the modern view.

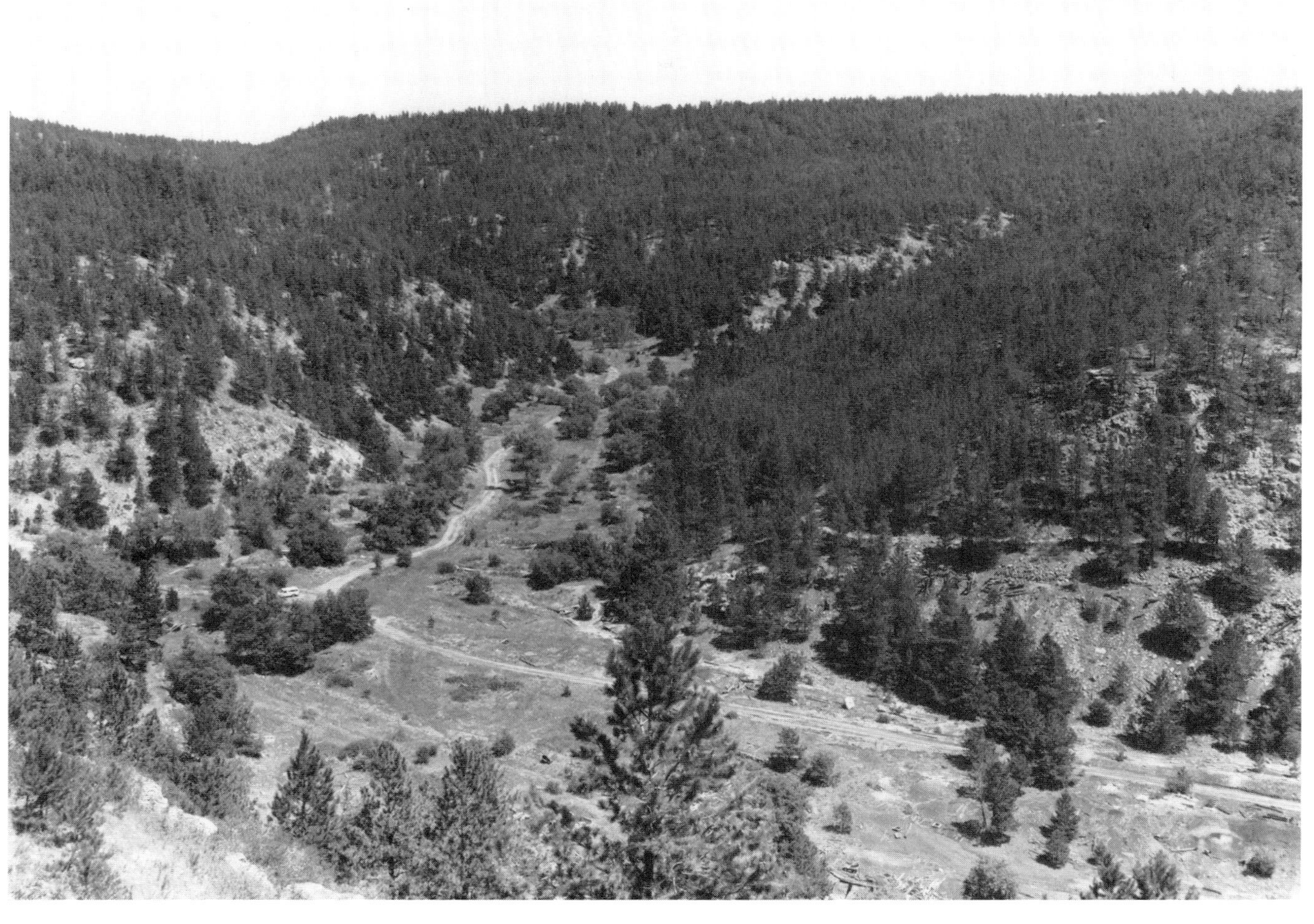

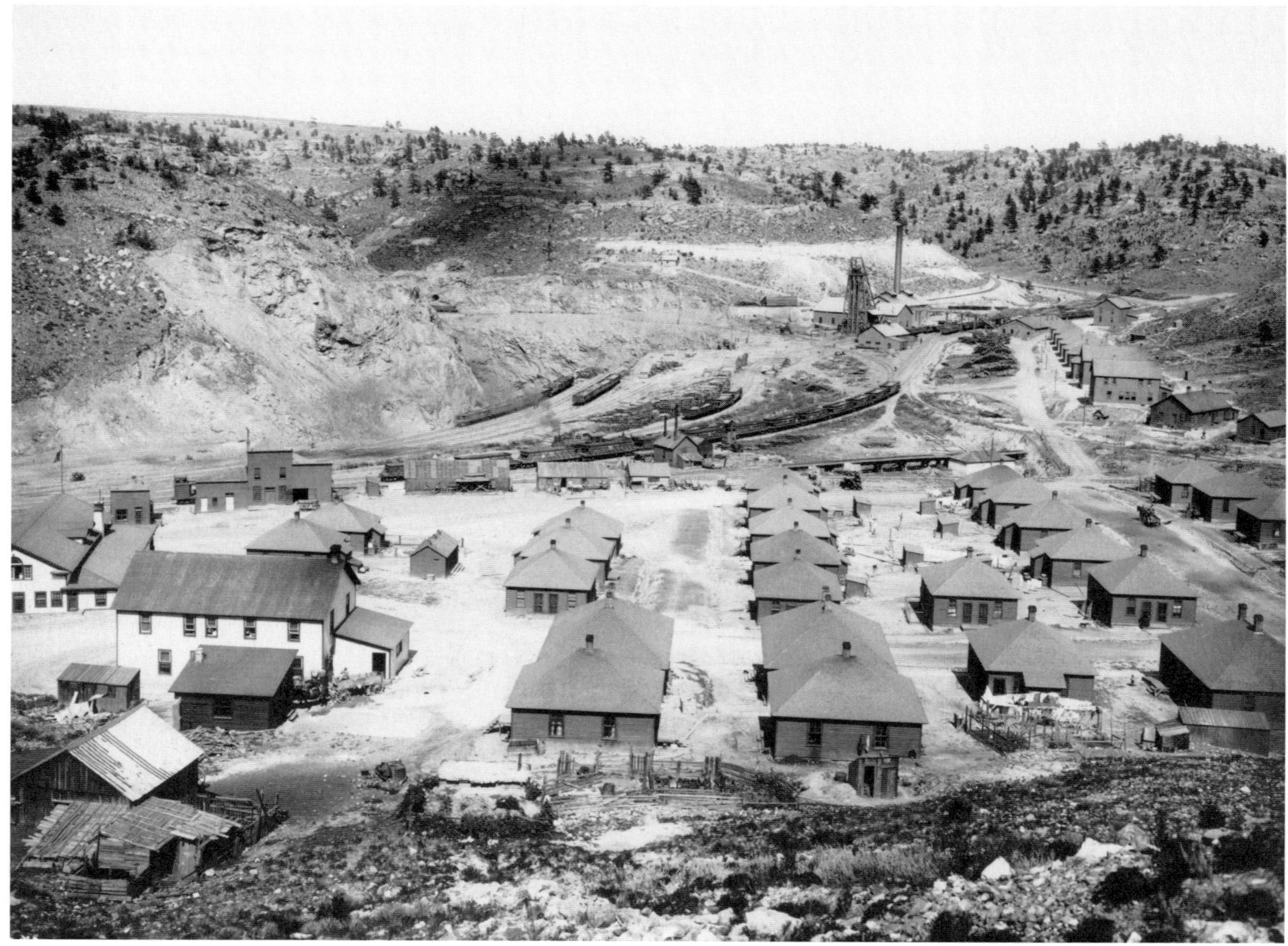

Fig. 40. View of Sunrise, looking north, 1903.

The town of Sunrise was established in 1903 as a company town of Colorado Fuel and Iron after low-grade iron ore had been discovered. The open-pit mine produced five hundred thousand tons of low-grade hematite ore each year. This ore was then shipped on the Colorado and Wyoming Railroad to Guernsey and then to Pueblo, Colorado, via the Burlington route. Because houses were so close together, common garages were built after automobiles became popular. In 1941 surface mining was discontinued. By early 1980 the steel industry dropped and the Sunrise Mine was closed.

Stimson took several views of Sunrise in 1903. This view from the city water tanks, one of the few accessible points still existing, was located by examining other photographs. After climbing to the top of a hill, two large circles proved to be the remains of the tanks. The open-pit mine, known as the Glory Hole, was carved out of the opposite hillside. The foundations in the modern photo are second generation; the wooden houses that can be seen in Stimson's photo were removed and replaced by brick buildings that have also been removed. Only two buildings remain, upper right.

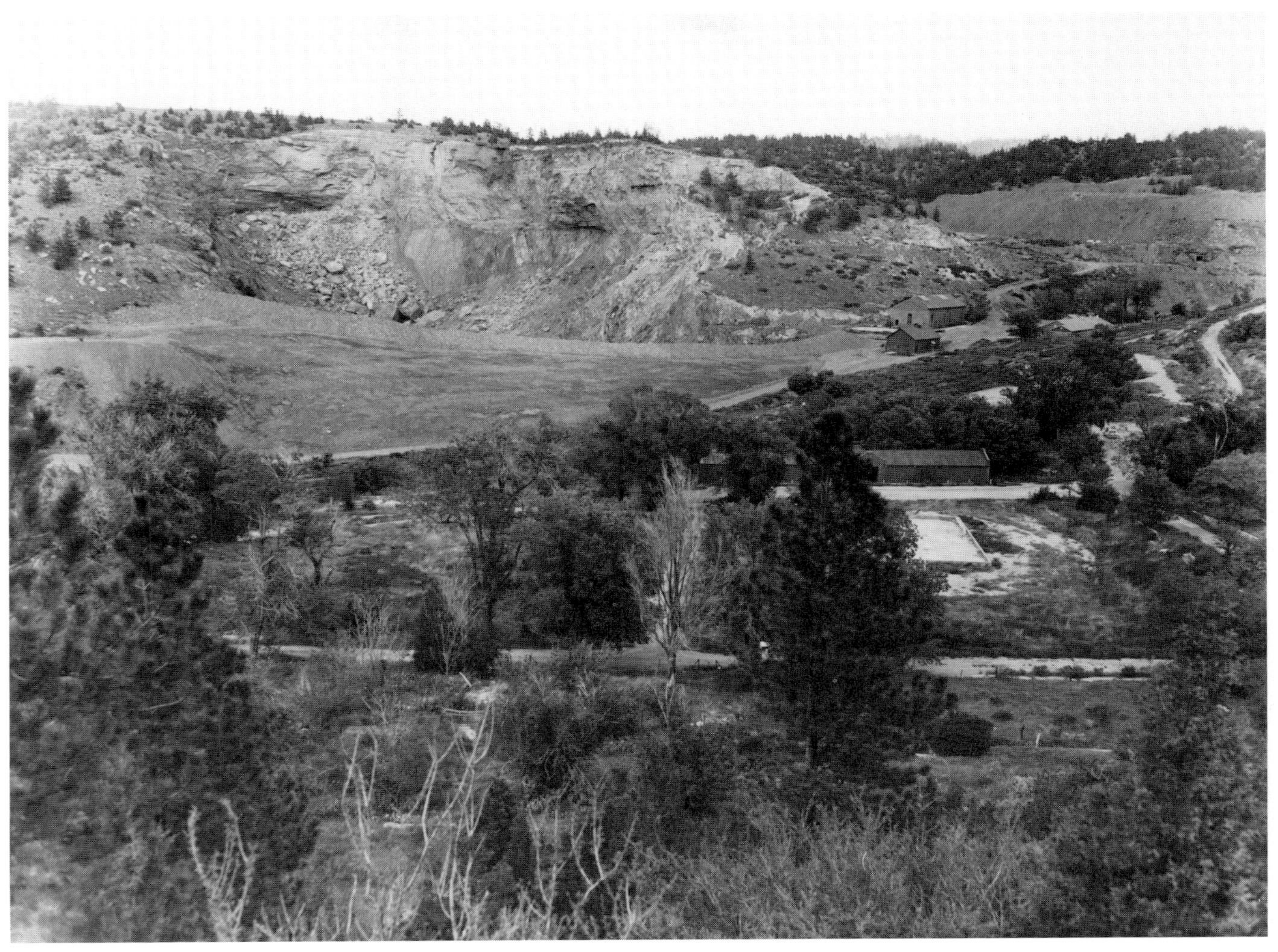

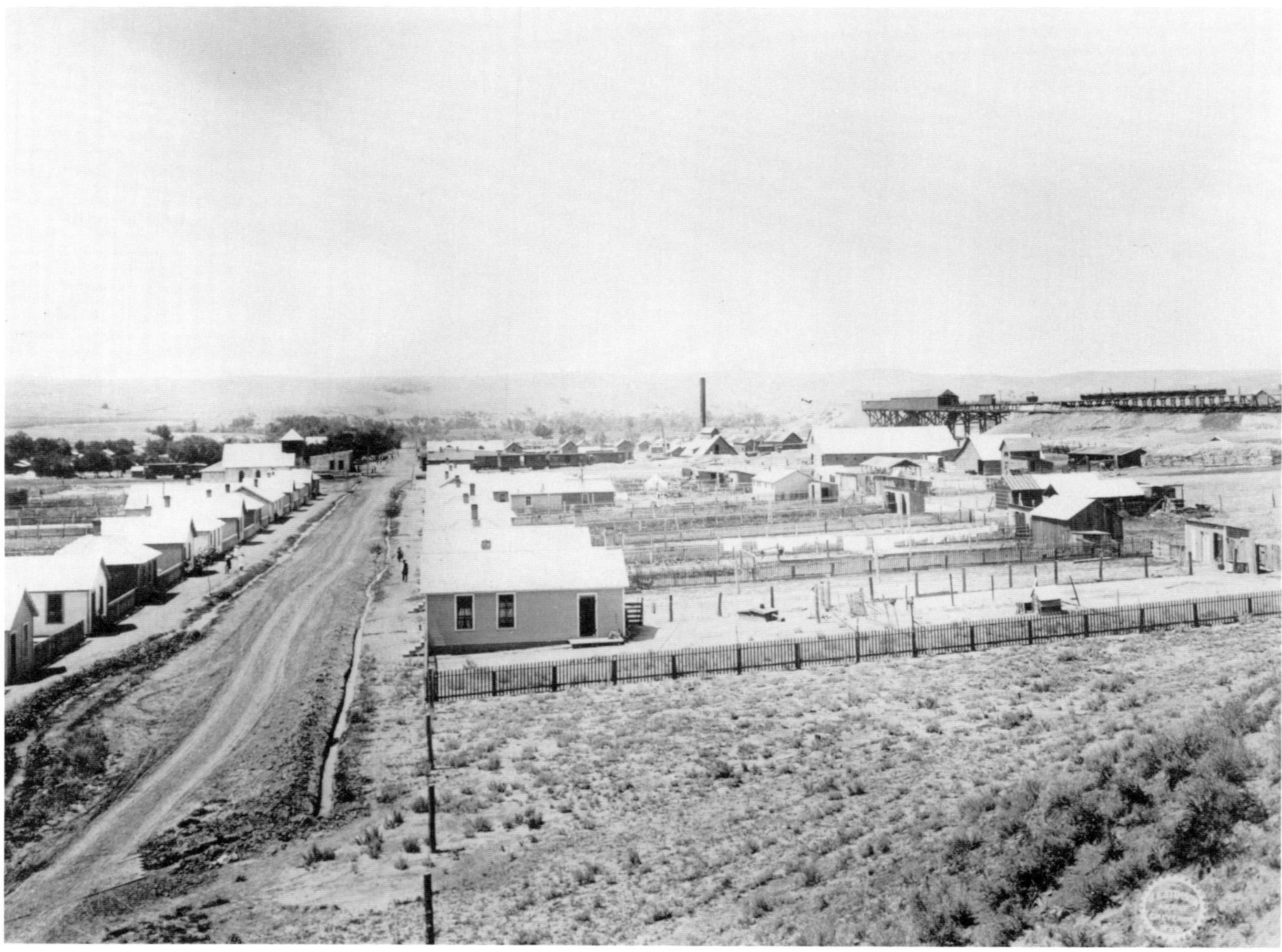

Fig. 41. Panorama of Dietz City, 1903.

The coal mining camp of Dietz was located six miles north of Sheridan. Originally called Higby when it was started in 1894, the town had a population of 306 in 1900. A year later the town's name was changed when C. N. Dietz, president of the Sheridan Coal Company and one of the founders of the Dome Lake Club, purchased interest in the mine. By 1915, the town of Dietz boasted a Catholic and a Methodist church as well as a public school and hospital. Stimson's view is from hospital hill, looking to the west. Like many of the area's coal camps, decreasing coal prices brought an end to the town in the early 1930s.

In the modern photo, only the lane and fence survive. The darkened earth of a slag pile, right, hints at the location of the mine tipple. The bridge on the horizon is on highway 338 and extensive fills show the level path of Interstate 90 in the distance.

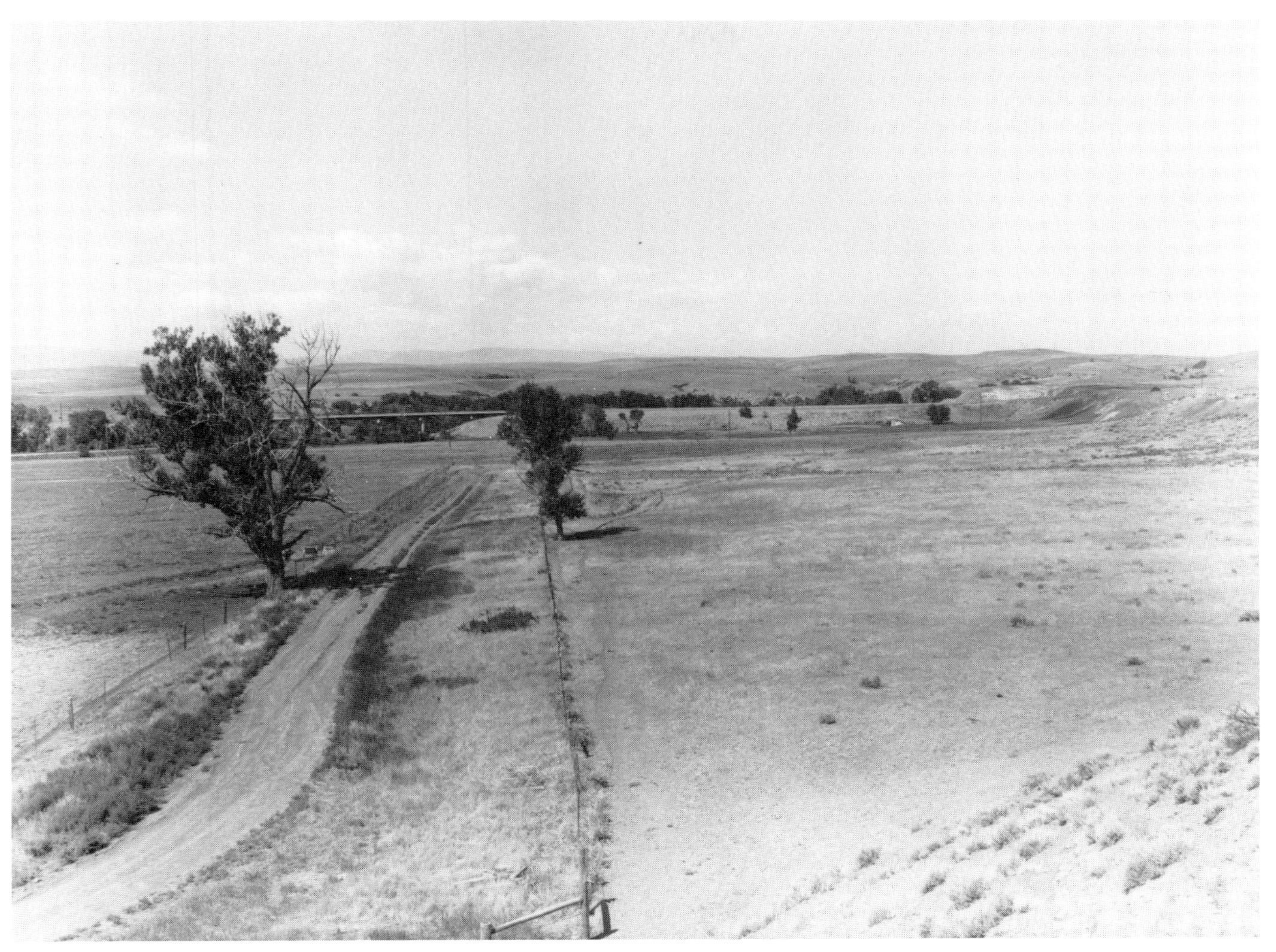

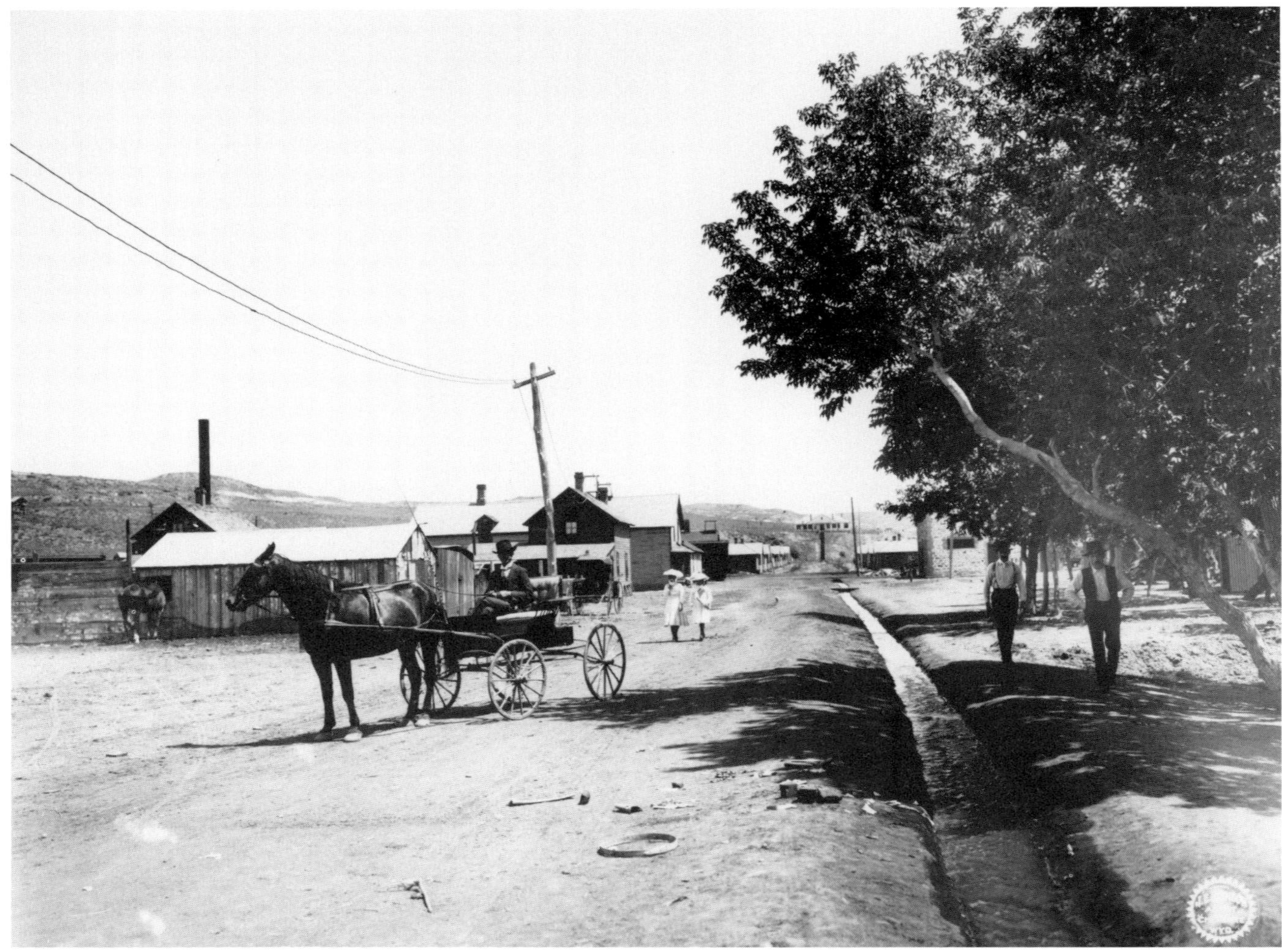

Fig. 42. Street scene, Dietz, 1903.

This view of Dietz is looking east and shows the hospital at center. A classic Stimson view, this photo shows a Wyoming boom town's variety of subjects, including two well-dressed ladies, a horse and buggy, telephone wires, and an open-canal water system. Today only the canal remains. The rise and fall of the hillside on the horizon identify the correct vantage point.

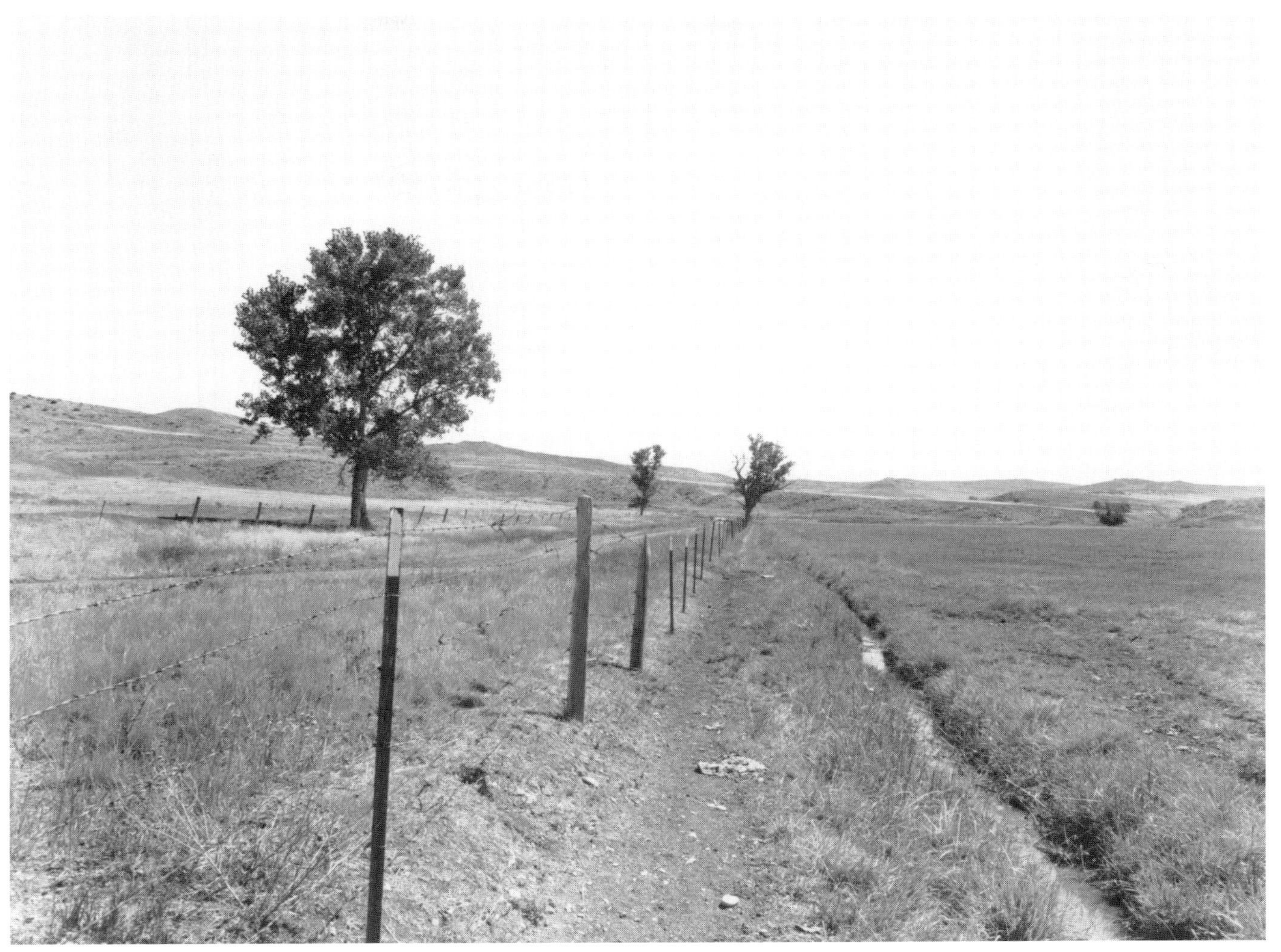

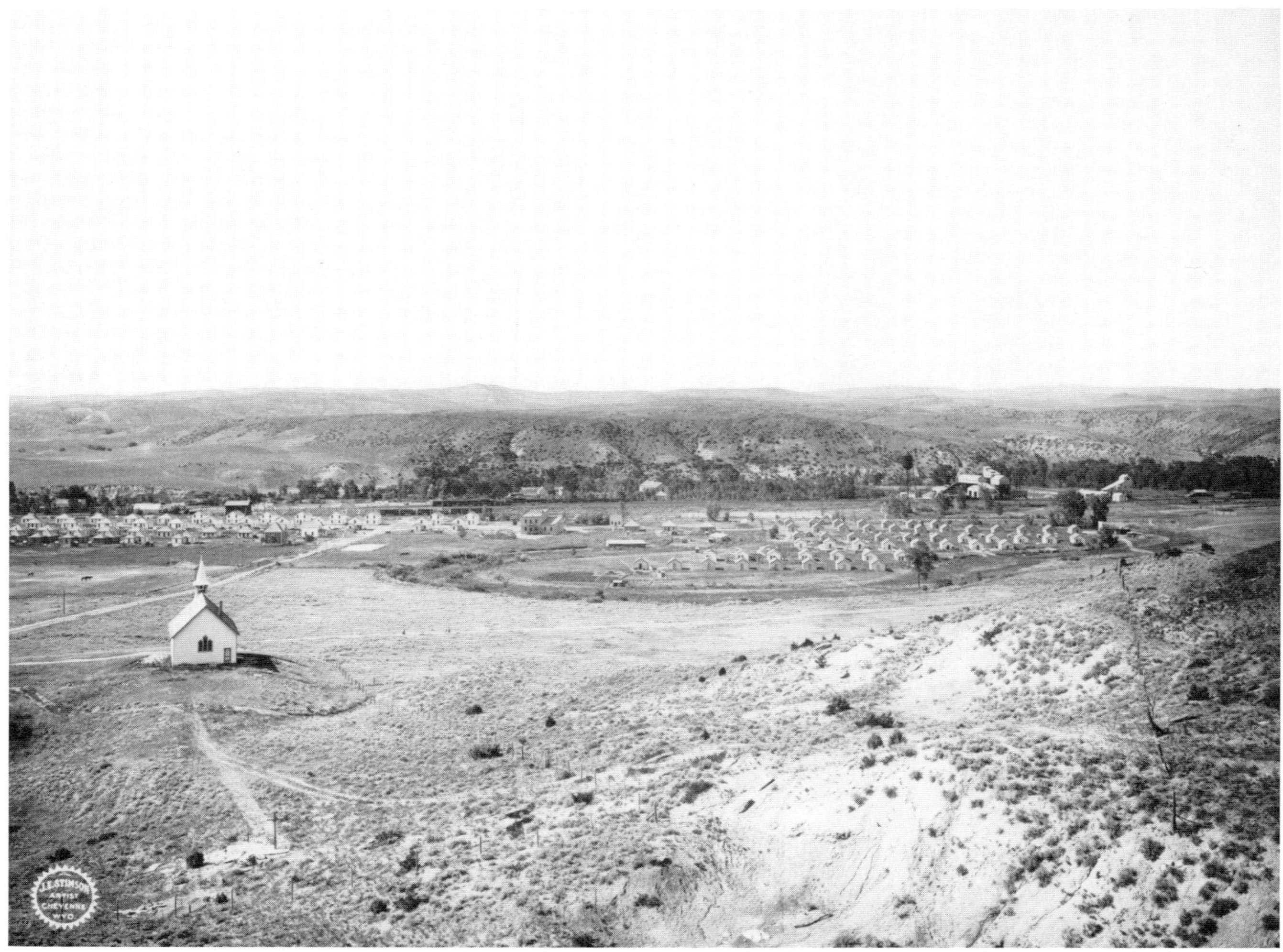

Fig. 43. View of Kearney coal camp, 1909.

The Kearney coal camp was located in the Tongue River Valley north of Sheridan. Numerous camps such as Dietz, Kooi, Monarch, Acme, and Kearney prospered and declined in the early twentieth century. The town was also known as Carneyville, and then when the mine was purchased in 1920 by a Chicago syndicate, a contest was held to give the camp a new name. Kleenburn, describing the clean-burning coal mined here, won out. The post office was closed in 1933.

Stimson's view was taken from the southern bluff of the Tongue River Valley. In the left foreground of Stimson's shot is the Kearney Catholic church and cemetery. The church burned down in 1920, but graves from the cemetery can be seen today. The edge of a fill along Interstate 90 can be seen curling along the left midground of the modern photo.

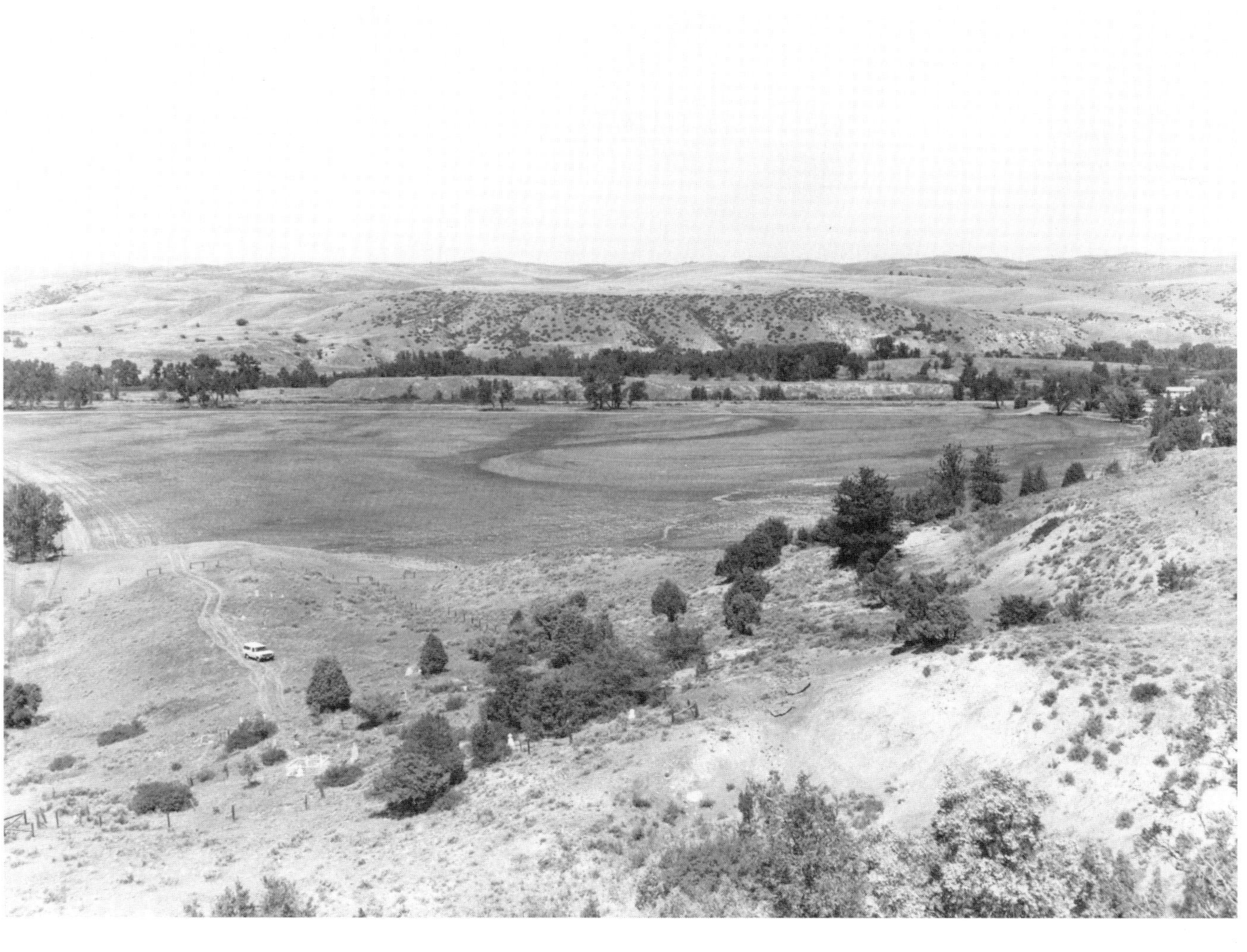

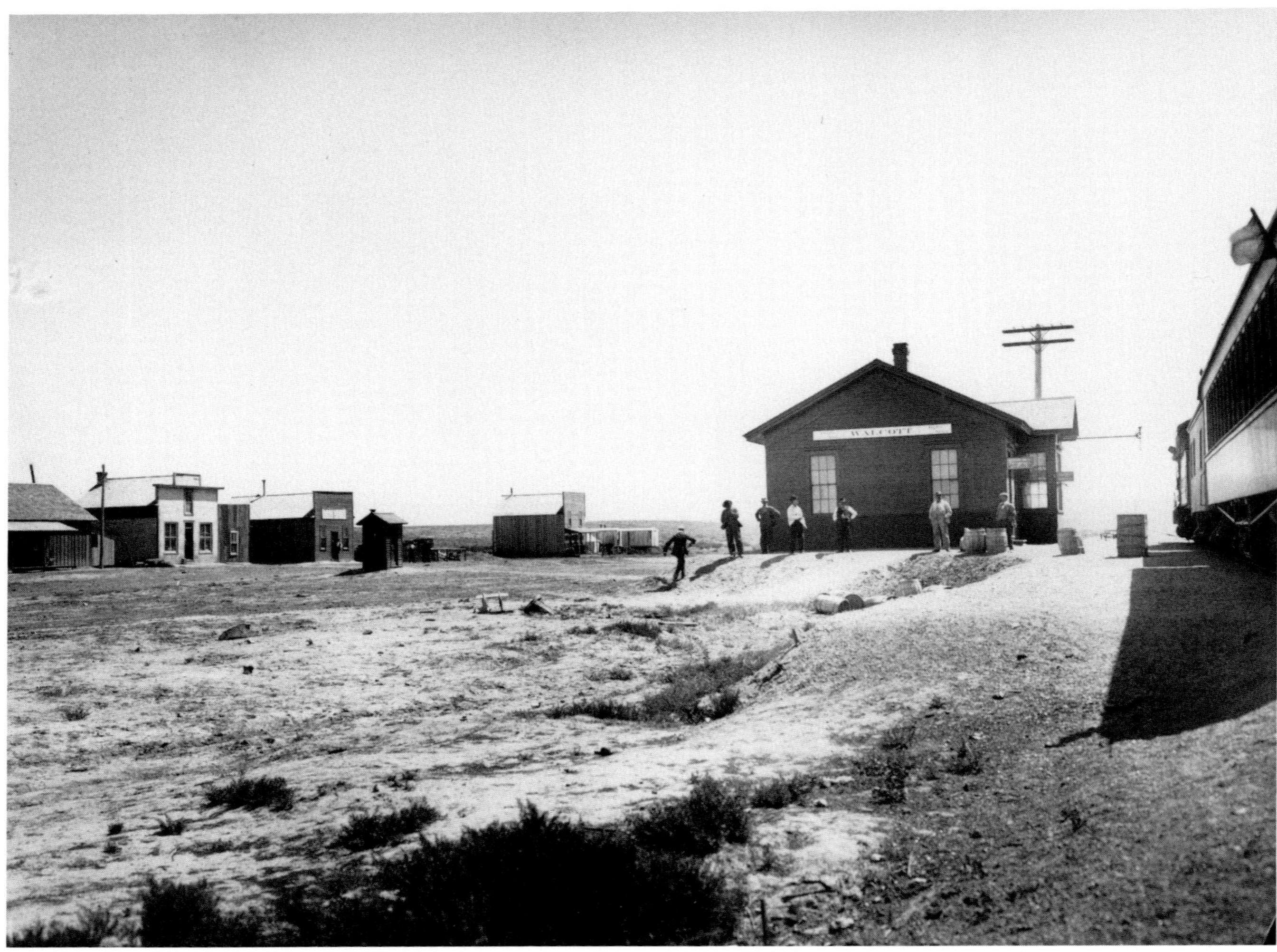

Fig. 44. Walcott Station, 1901.

Walcott is the point, east of Rawlins, where the Saratoga and Encampment branch of the Union Pacific connects with the main line. According to the WPA's guide to Wyoming, this small station handled more freight than any other Union Pacific station between Omaha and Ogden in the early 1900s. Mine and smelter machinery, coal, coke, and building materials went in and smelter products went out. There was also a large sheep shearing operation here. The foundation of the depot, center right, is all that survives. Today Walcott is best known as the meeting point for Highway 30 and Interstate 80.

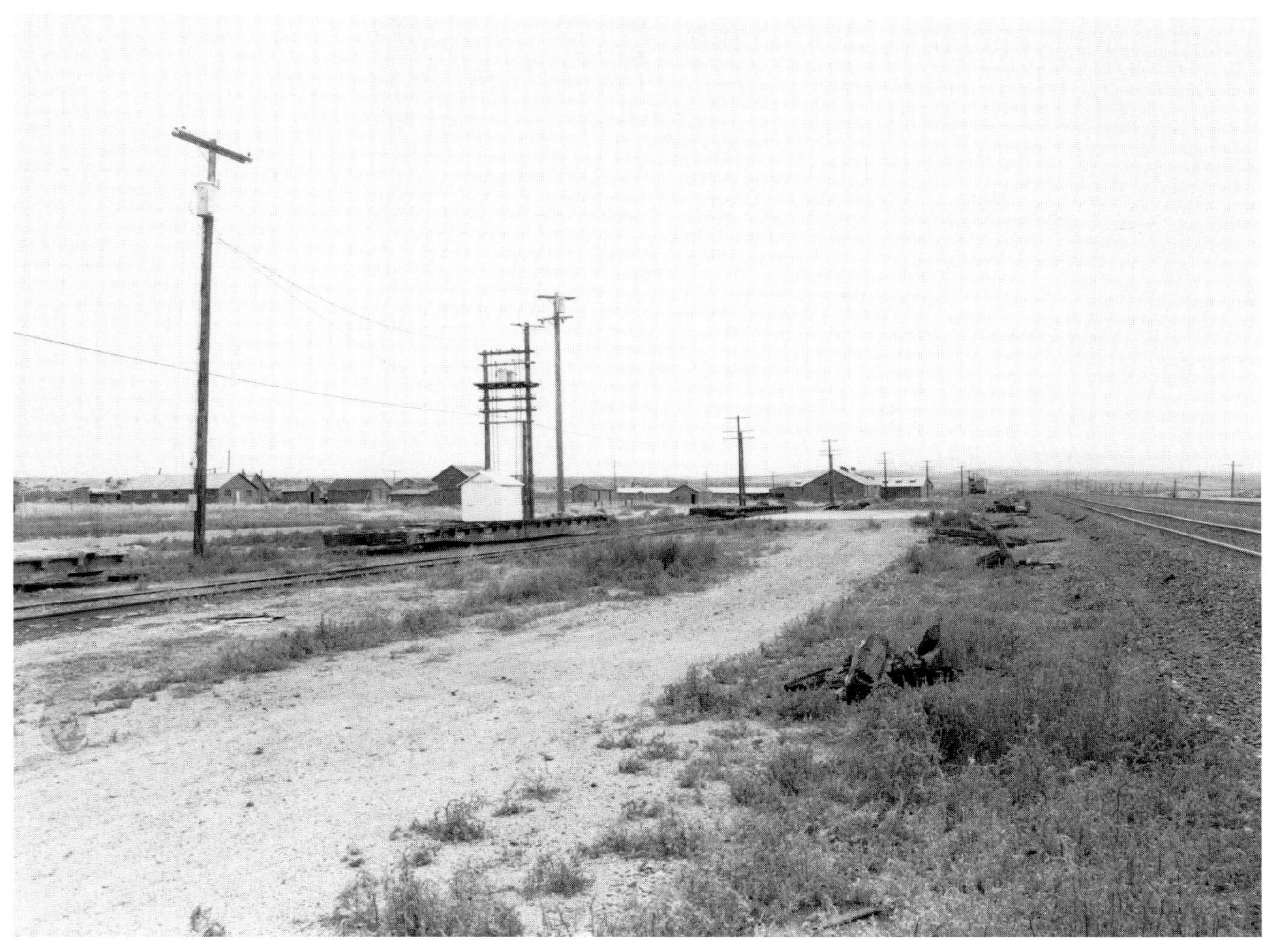

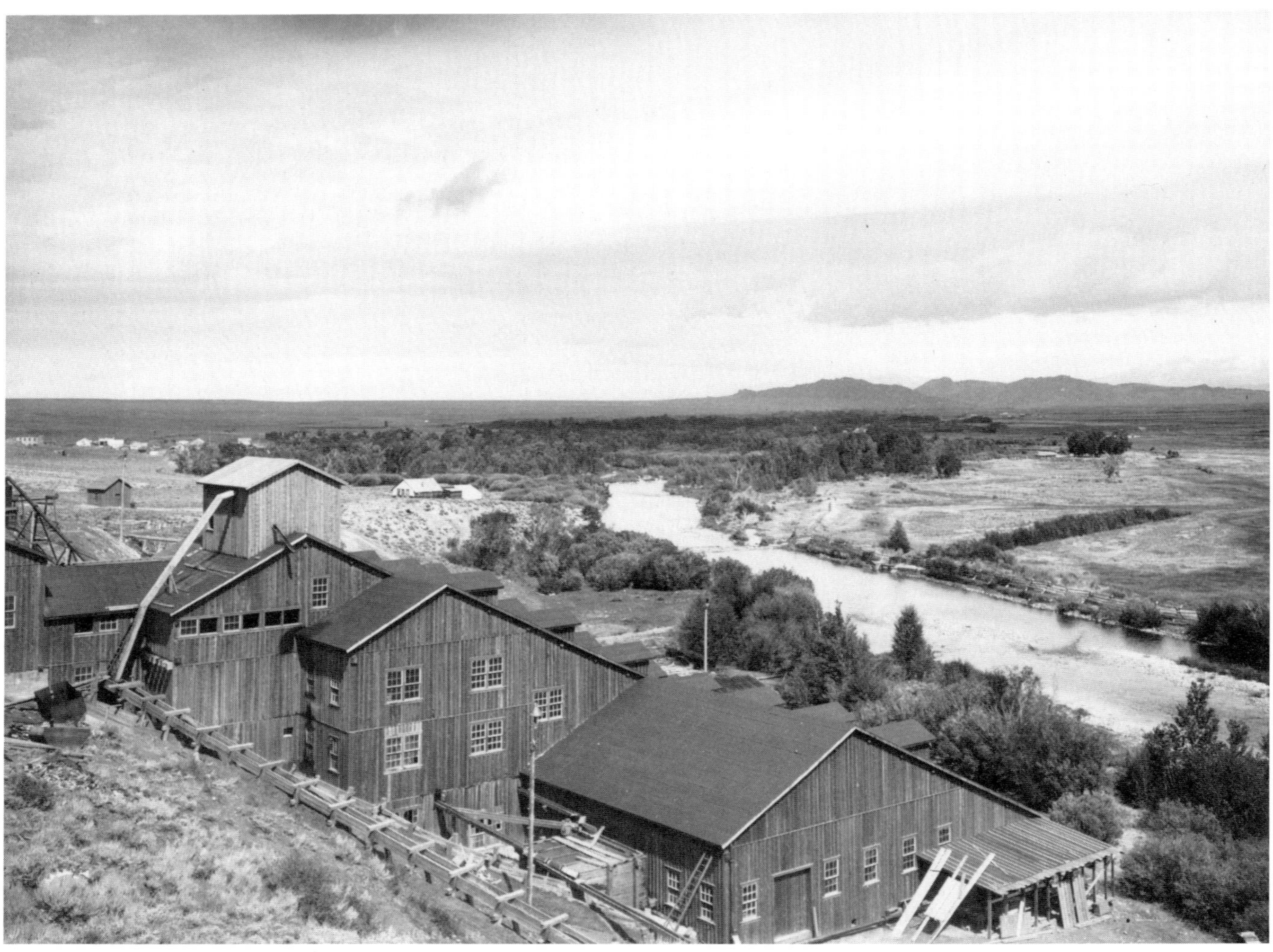

Fig. 45. Smelter, Grand Encampment, 1903.

In 1897 Ed Haggerty discovered a rich vein of copper ore high in the Sierra Madre Range along the Continental Divide. He soon filed a twenty-acre claim and named his mine Rudefeha. This unusual name is derived from the first two letters of the partners' surnames: James *Ru*msey, Robert *De*al, George *Fe*rris, and Ed *Ha*ggerty. Mine equipment, including a compressed-air locomotive, was soon freighted into the mountains. The mining towns of Copperton, Battle, Rambler, and Dillon sprang up from the forest floor. A sixteen-mile aerial tramway was then built to transport the ore back to the Encampment smelter.

Constructed in 1902 on the west bank of the Encampment River, the official name of the smelter, The Boston and Wyoming Smelter, Power and Light Company, reflected the eastern source of its capital. It daily converted an estimated three hundred to five hundred tons of ore to 99 percent pure copper ingots. When Stimson visited the area in 1903, the smelter was near its peak production year. By 1904 more than $1 million of copper had been mined, but the boom would not last. That same year the smelter changed ownership to the Penn-Wyoming Copper Company. The new company was overcapitalized and stockholders had a difficult time showing a profit on their investment. Severe weather wreaked havoc in the high altitude mines, and between 1906 and 1907 two fires destroyed much of the smelter. By the time it was rebuilt, falling prices made further production prohibitive. In 1913 the owners of the mines were bankrupt, and the property was salvaged by a Denver machinery company.

Today a few foundations, as well as the background hills, provide the only glimpse into the smelter's past.

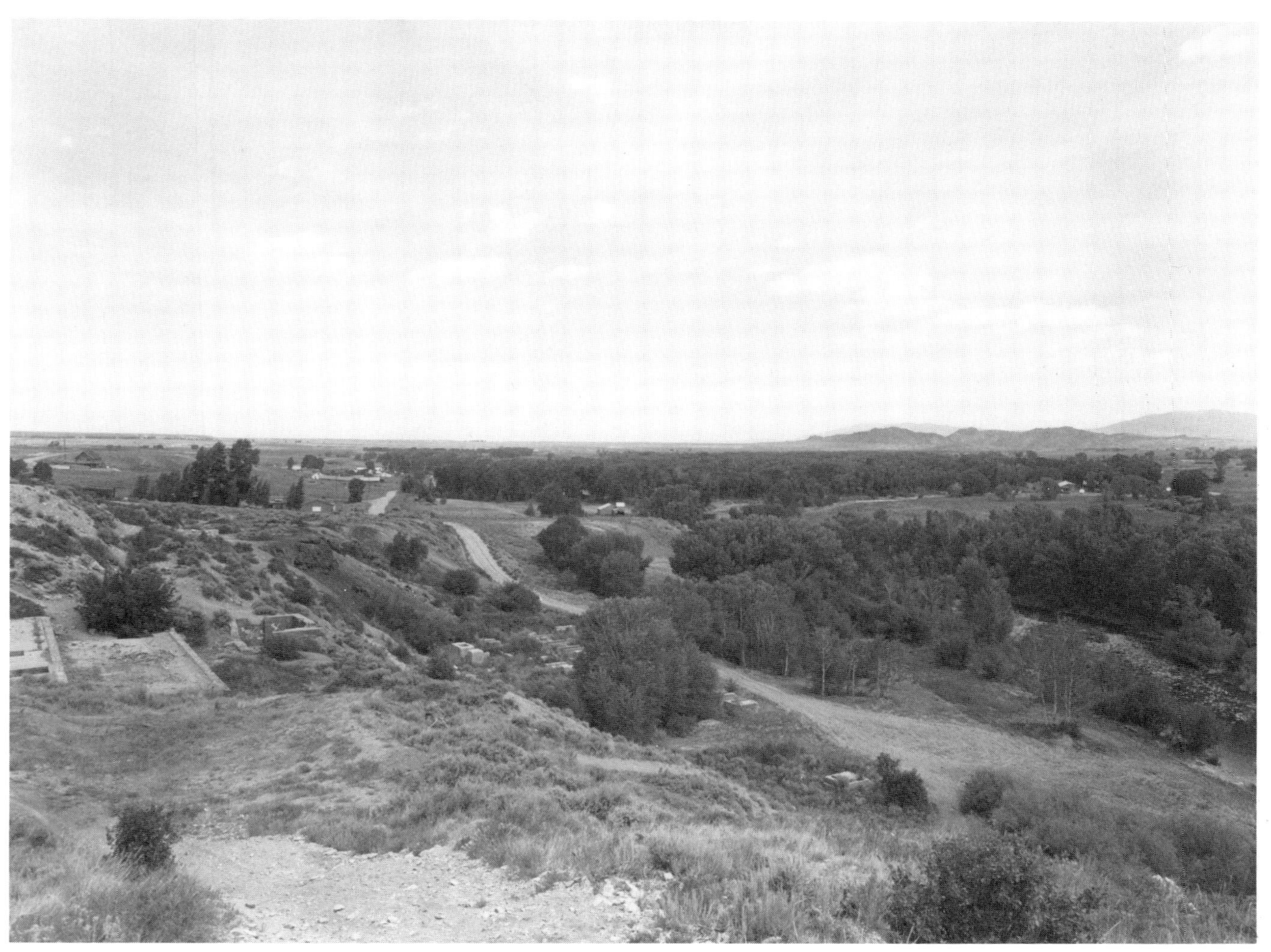

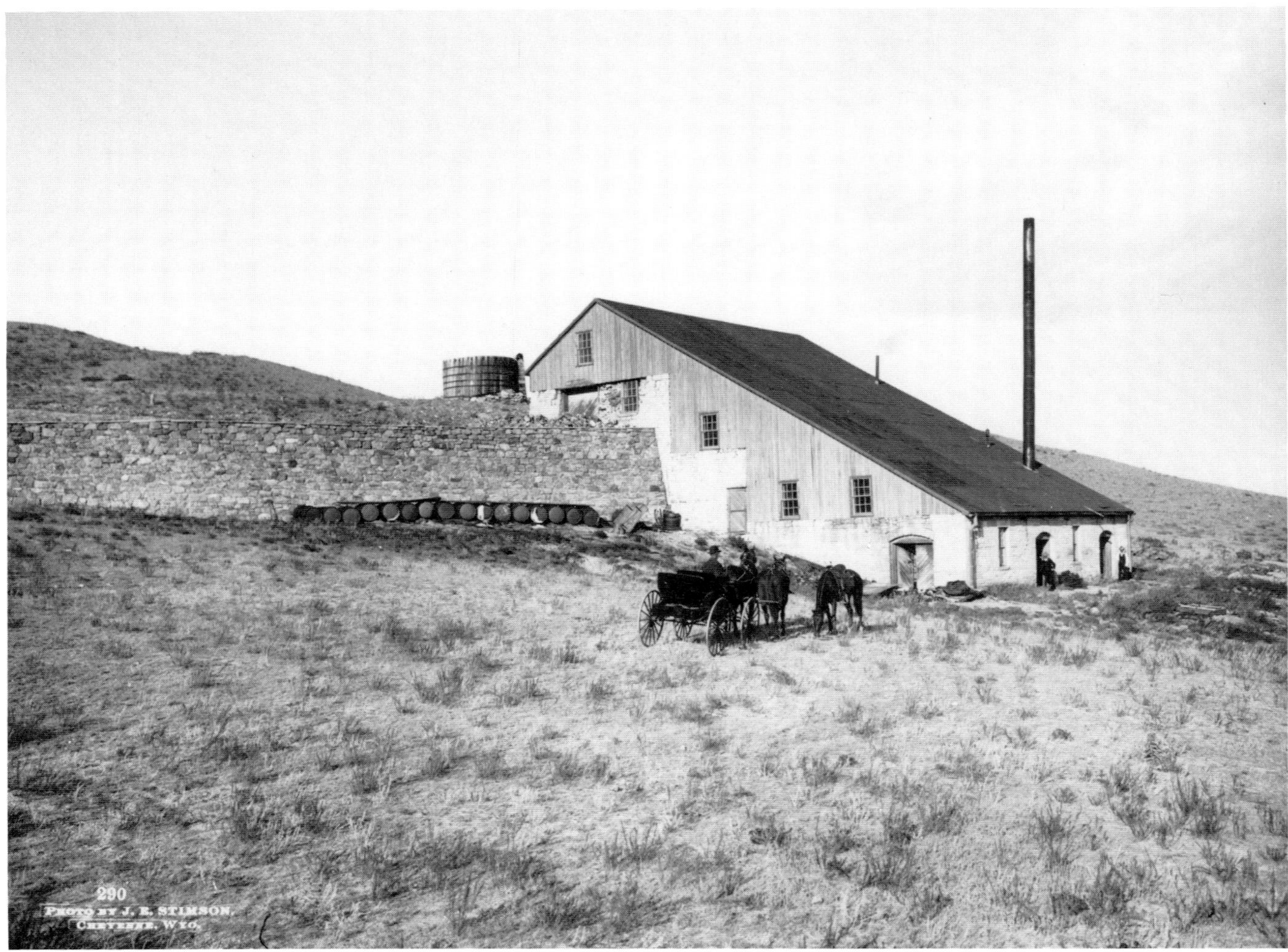

Fig. 46. Mill at Hecla Mine, 1902.

The Hecla and Silver Crown mines were located about twenty miles west of Cheyenne near the southern edge of what is now Crystal Reservoir. Deposits of gold, copper, and silver were discovered here in the 1880s, and a small rush occurred in 1886. When Stimson visited in 1902, another operation had built this large ore-crushing plant. Ore was brought along the top of the rock wall and then dumped into a bin inside the building. Steam-powered machines then crushed the rocks. Today the stone wall, center, and a steam engine and boiler are all that remain.

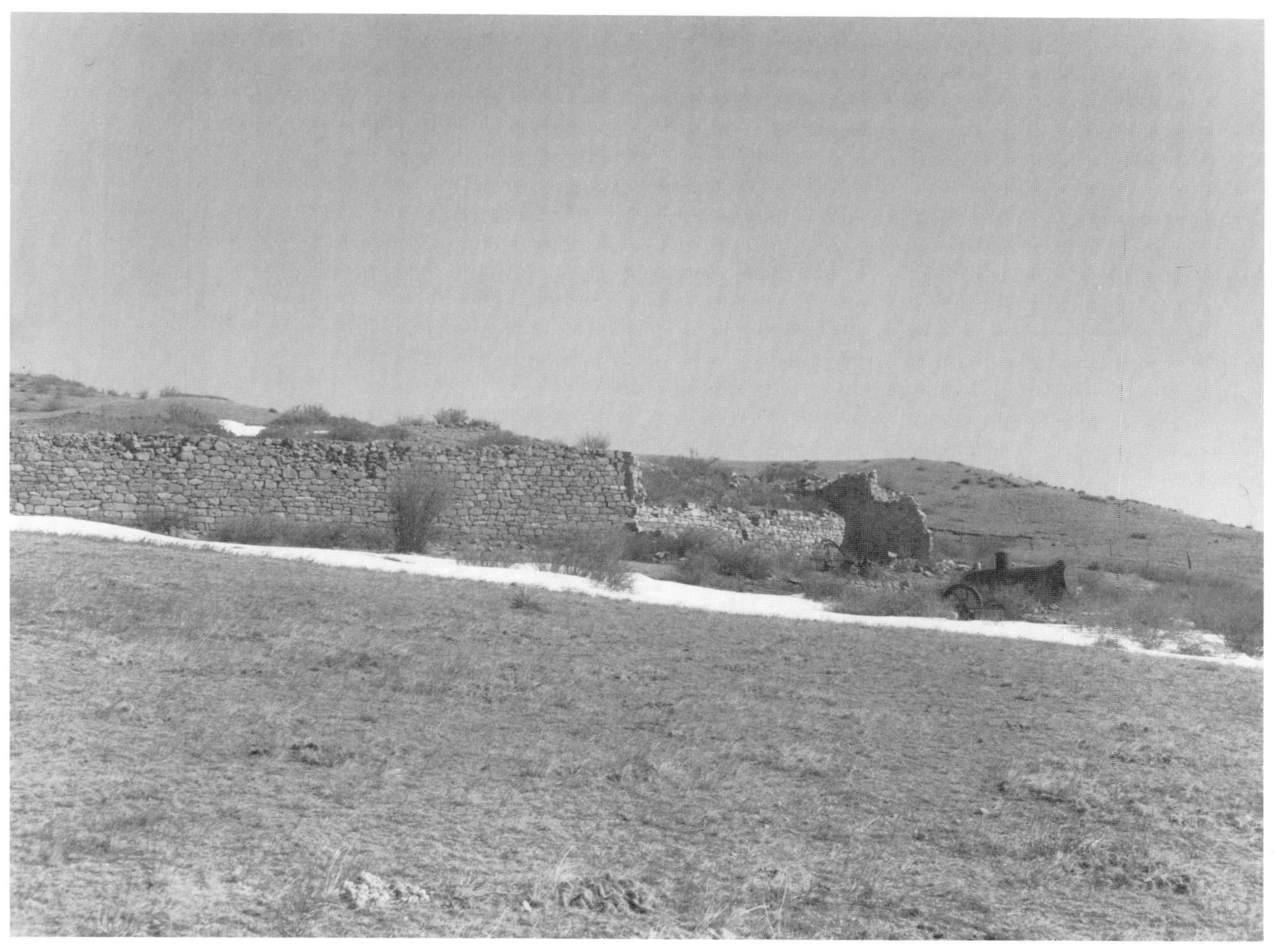

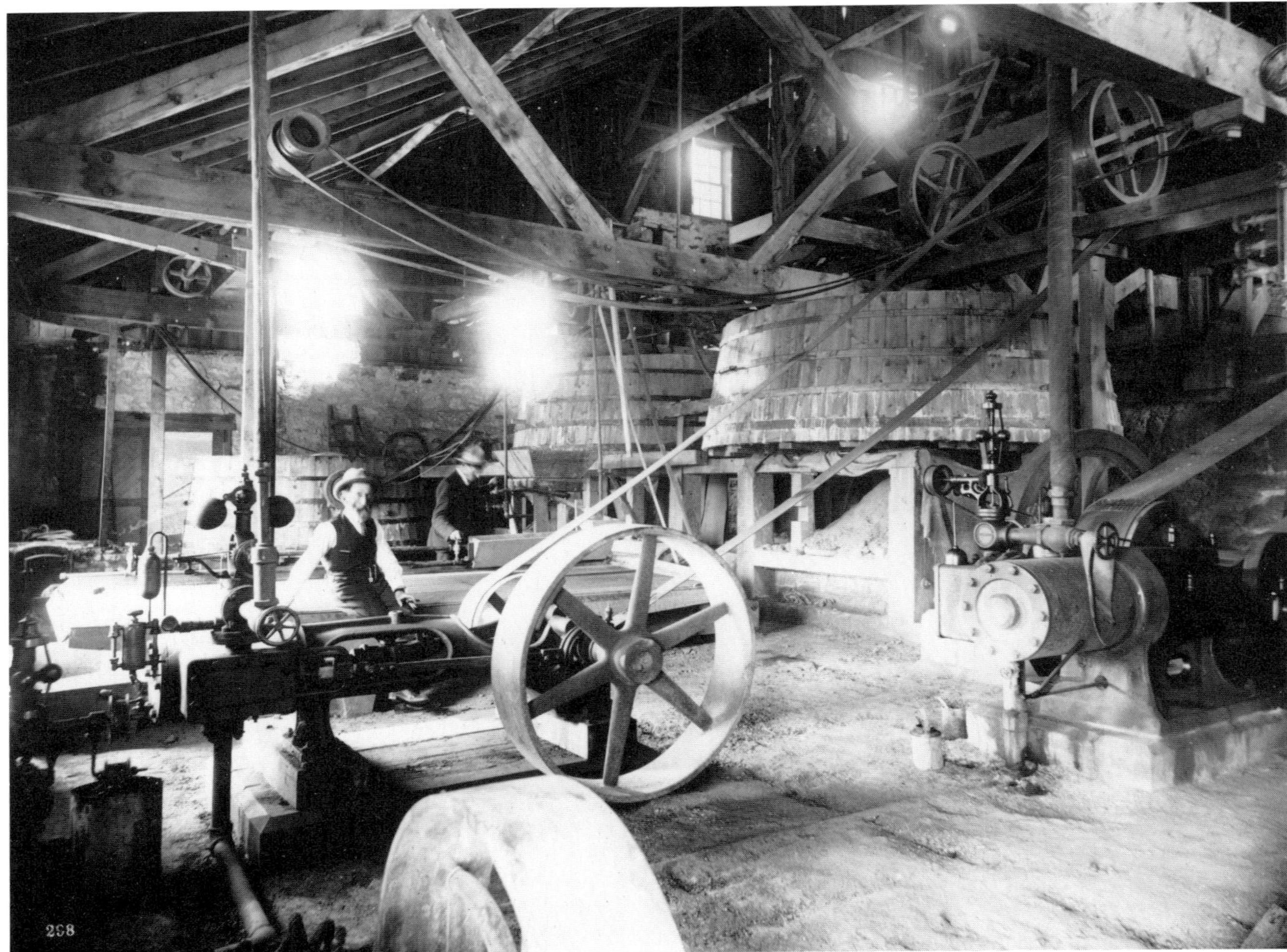

Fig. 47. Interior of mill at Hecla Mine, 1902.

This interior view of the Hecla mill shows various steam-driven, rock-crushing machines. The support for the large machine, center, remains today, as does the steam engine at right center. Although one bolt is gone, the large flywheel has survived.

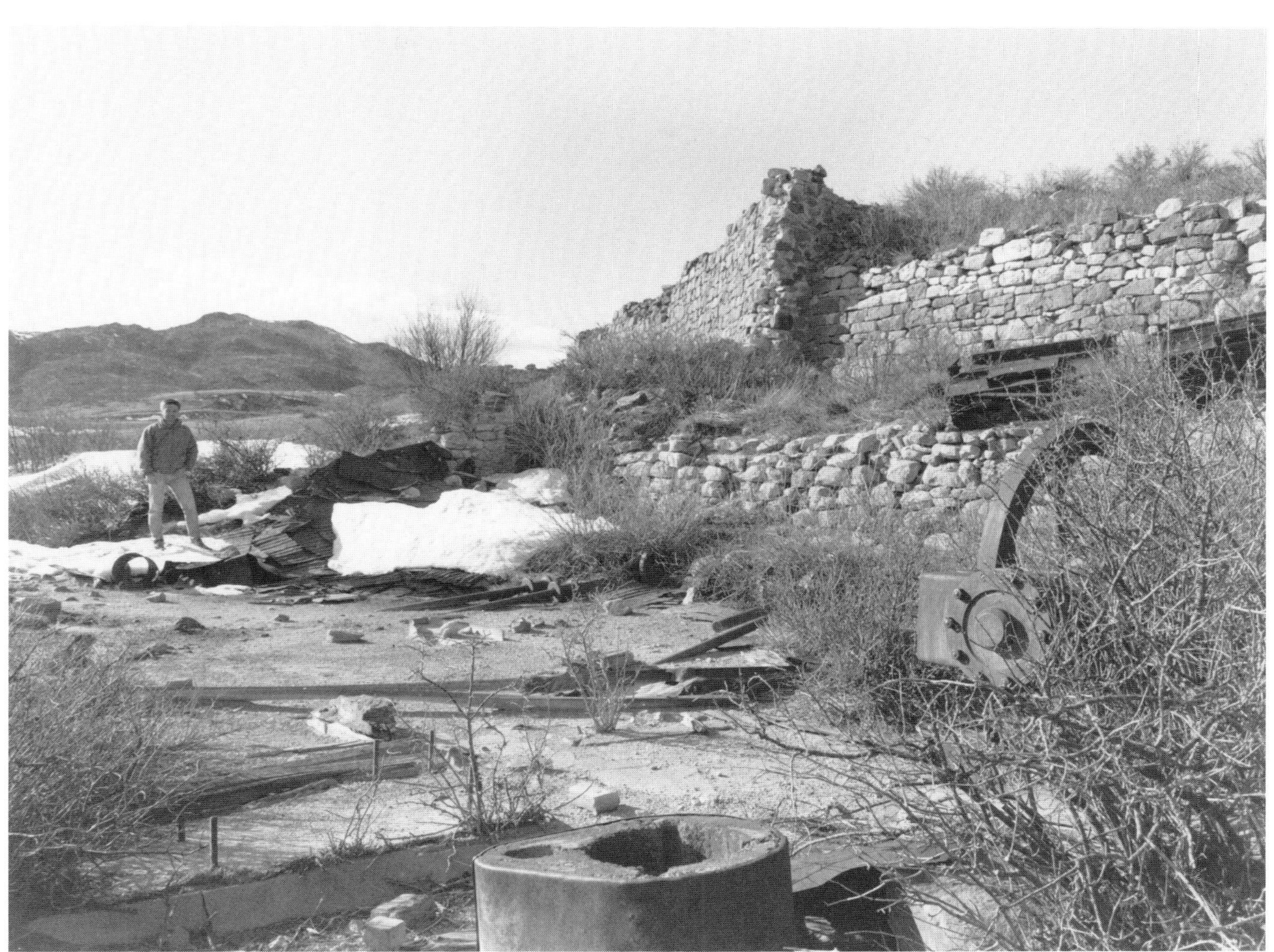

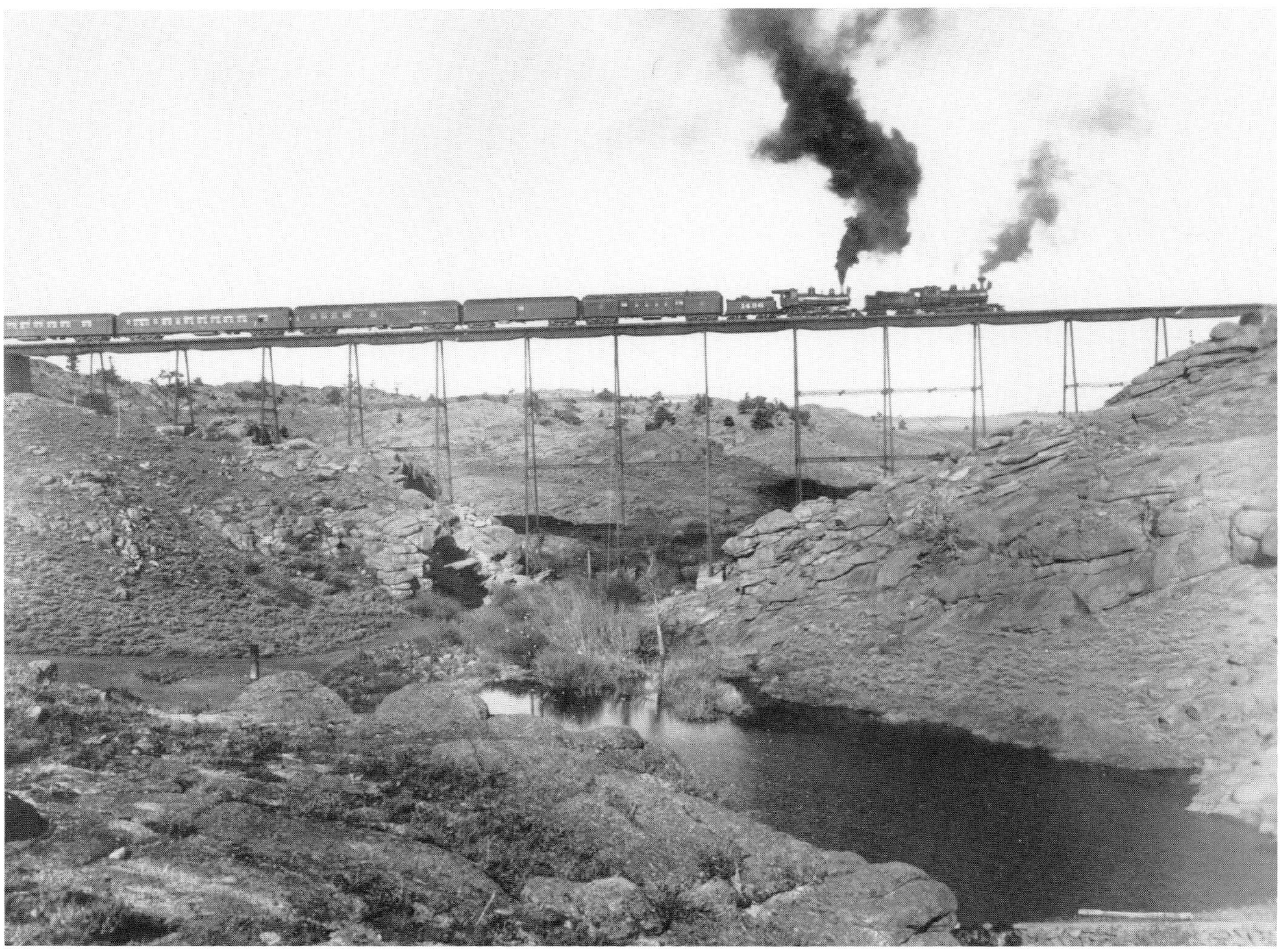

Fig. 48. Train passing over Dale Creek Bridge, 1901.

Reported to be the world's highest railroad bridge when it was built on the transcontinental railroad in 1868, the Dale Creek Bridge was originally of hand-cut wooden construction. Located southeast of Laramie between Tie Siding and Sherman, the bridge had a colorful but short life. In late 1884, rock and earth fills replaced burned out trestlework on each end. The following year, the wooden bridge was replaced by a more substantial steel girder bridge. High winds in the area forced the UP to maintain a watchman nearby. The chimney from the watchman's house, left center, can be seen just above the rocks in Stimson's photo. The bridge was finally dismantled in 1901 when the tracks were relocated a mile south. Today the original supports from the 1868 bridge can be found in the valley as well as the 1885 abutment, left horizon, on the west side of the canyon.

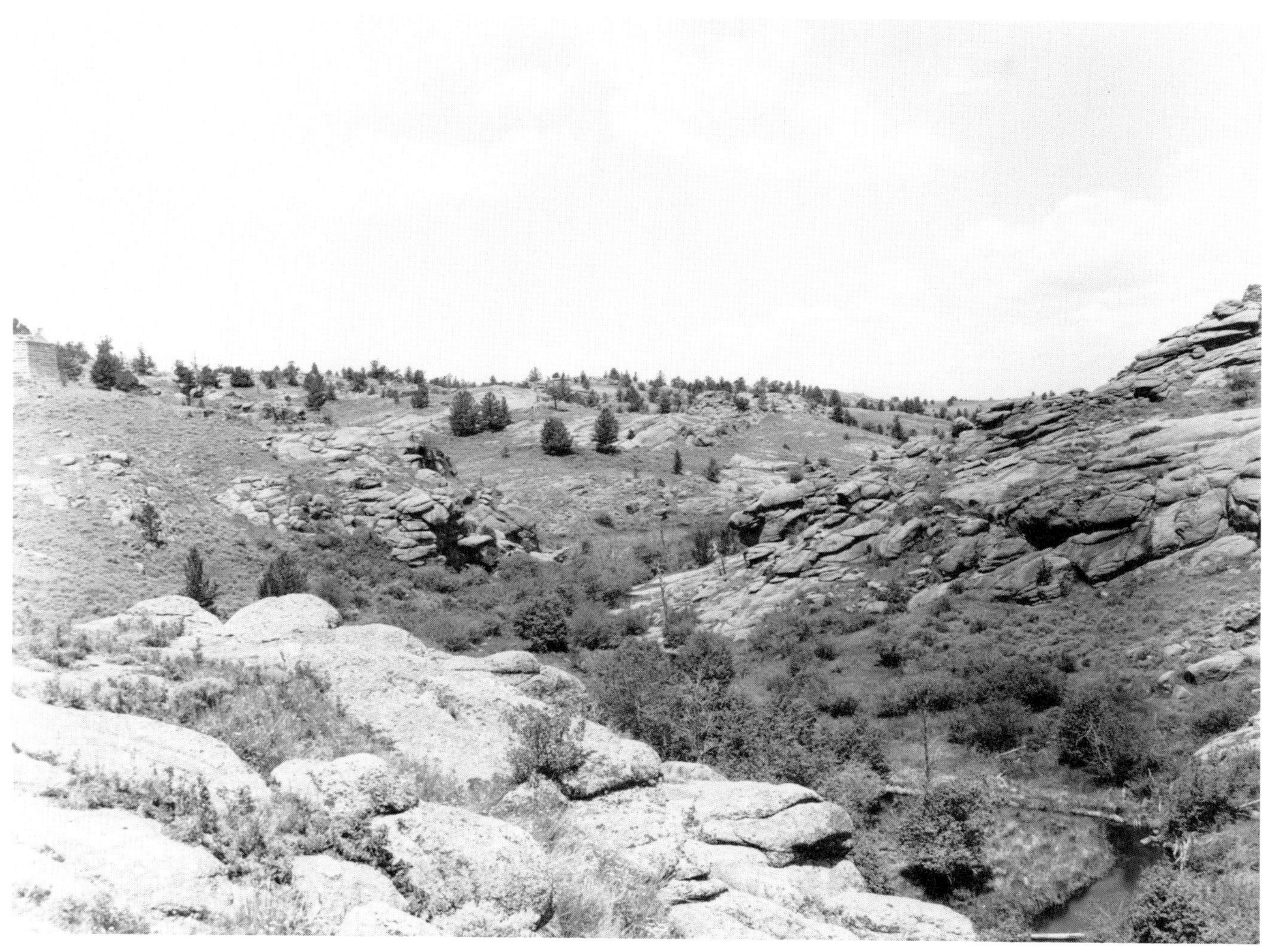

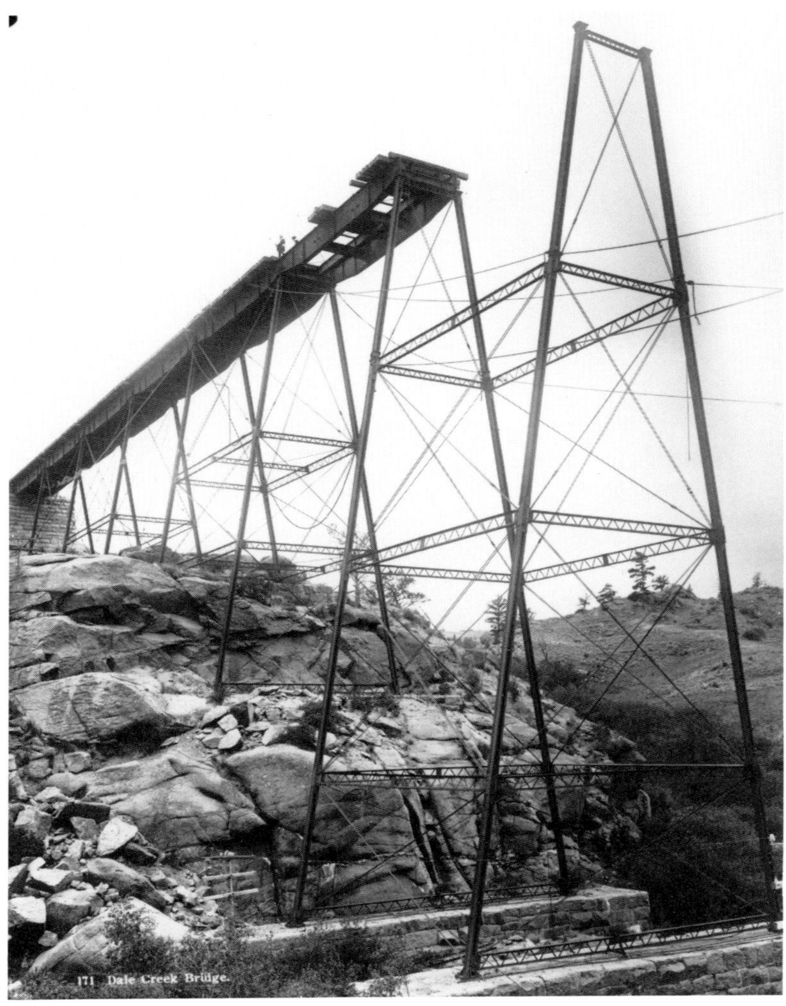

Fig. 49. Dismantling Dale Creek Bridge, 1901.

This view shows the west end of the bridge from the floor of the valley. The original 1868 stone supports, center foreground, as well as the 1884 stone trestle, left center, can still be seen. A close examination of the photo reveals that many of the same trees, upper right, can also be found from Stimson's shot. Looking at the rocks in the center of the photo reveals something interesting. Find the large, pie-section shaped boulder behind the left leg of the second support in Stimson's view. Sitting on this rock are five smaller boulders, including a square-shaped boulder sitting on an arrowhead-shaped boulder. By finding this same pie section-shaped boulder in the modern photo, one can quickly find the square-ended rock as well. A quick look shows that the arrowhead-shaped boulder below has fallen onto one of the 1868 supports on the canyon floor.

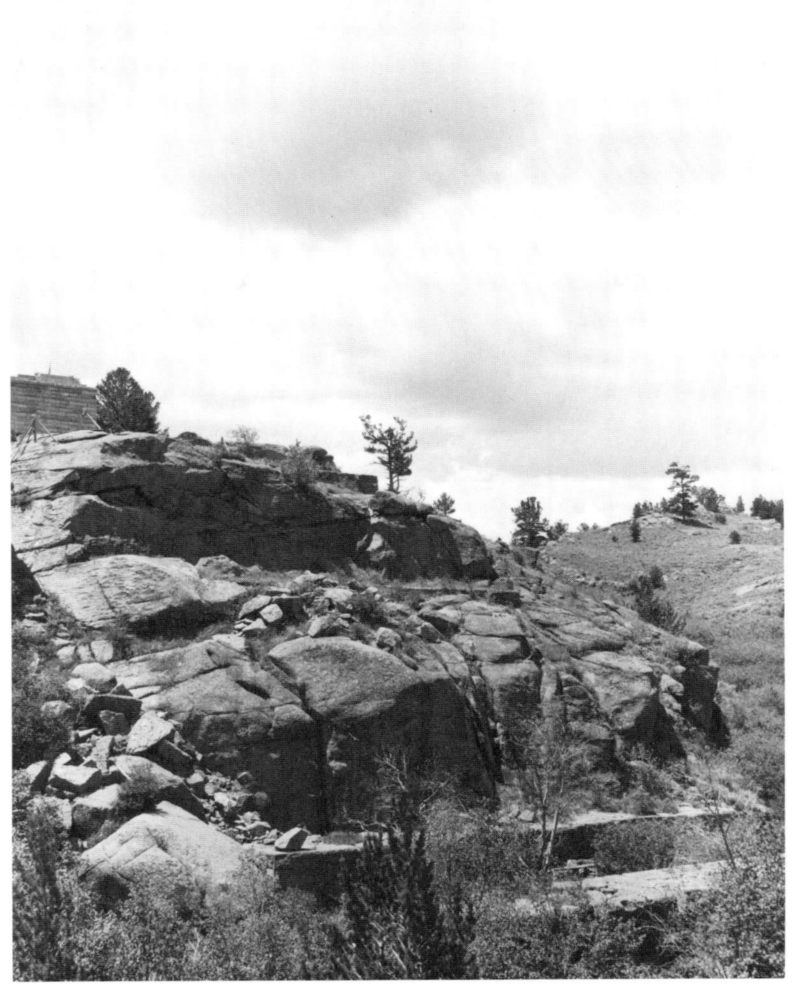

The Dynamic Townscape

In 1910, during the height of Stimson's career, the population of Wyoming was 145,965. Spread over the state's large area of 97,914 square miles, the population density was approximately 1.5 people per square mile. But the population was not evenly distributed; instead, the people of Wyoming were huddled around small towns throughout the state. The largest city, Cheyenne, had a population of only 11,320. No other town had a population greater than ten thousand, but there were over three hundred post offices. Although the image of the Cowboy State suggests a rural disposition, Wyoming has always been a state of small urban outposts.

Most of these towns were started to serve a nearby industry. In the south, the Union Pacific built the towns of Cheyenne, Laramie, Rawlins, Green River, and Evanston. Elsewhere, mining and agriculture helped build the towns of Kemmerer, Diamondville, Newcastle, Sheridan, and Worland. Two health resorts were founded around the mineral springs of Saratoga and Thermopolis. Tourism has prolonged the lives of many of these towns.

"The Dynamic Townscape" traces Wyoming urban sites that look, at first glance, not to have changed since Stimson's photograph. Street scenes, homes, business blocks, hotels, state buildings, fraternal lodges, and panoramas can all be found in this section. A closer look, however, reveals subtle differences that suggest changes in the urban scene. This chapter will look first at Stimson's base of operations, Cheyenne, then trace the Union Pacific westward before turning clockwise around the state.

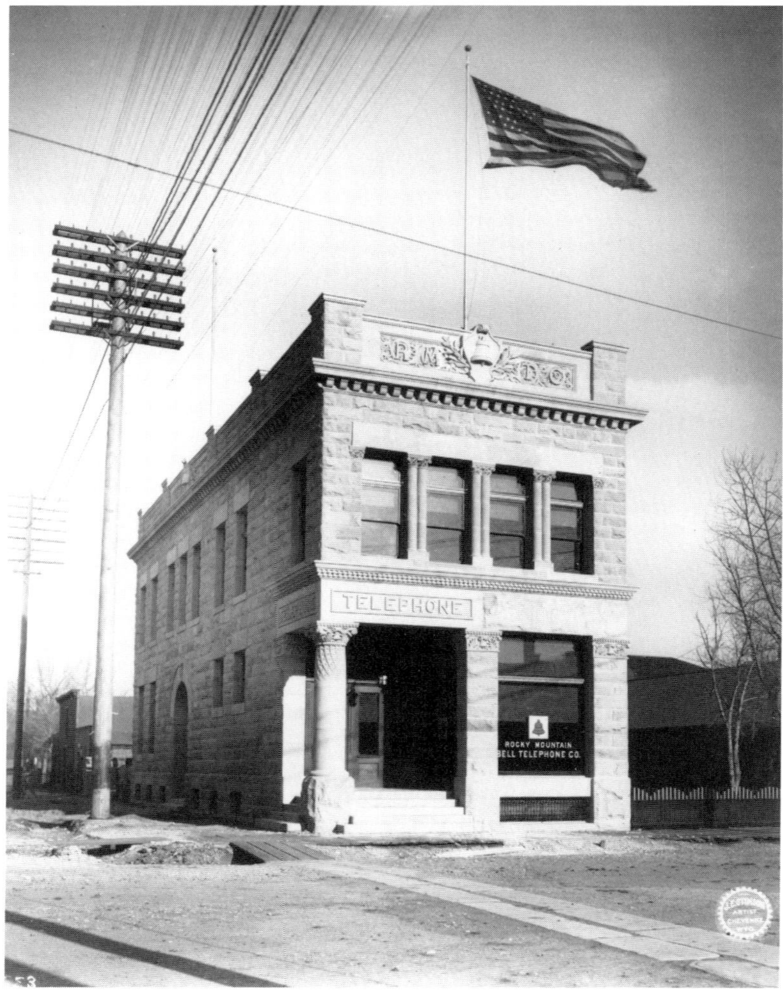

Fig. 50. Rocky Mountain Bell Telephone Company, Cheyenne, 1906.

The telephone building, located on the southeast corner of Eighteenth Street and Capitol Avenue, was opened in 1906. It remained the company's home until the late 1920s. The third floor was added later when the building was converted to a hotel. The abundance of wires on the telephone pole in Stimson's photo and the sculpted sign above the main door are both gone. Stimson's view reads "Telephone," but the modern shot reads "Capitol."

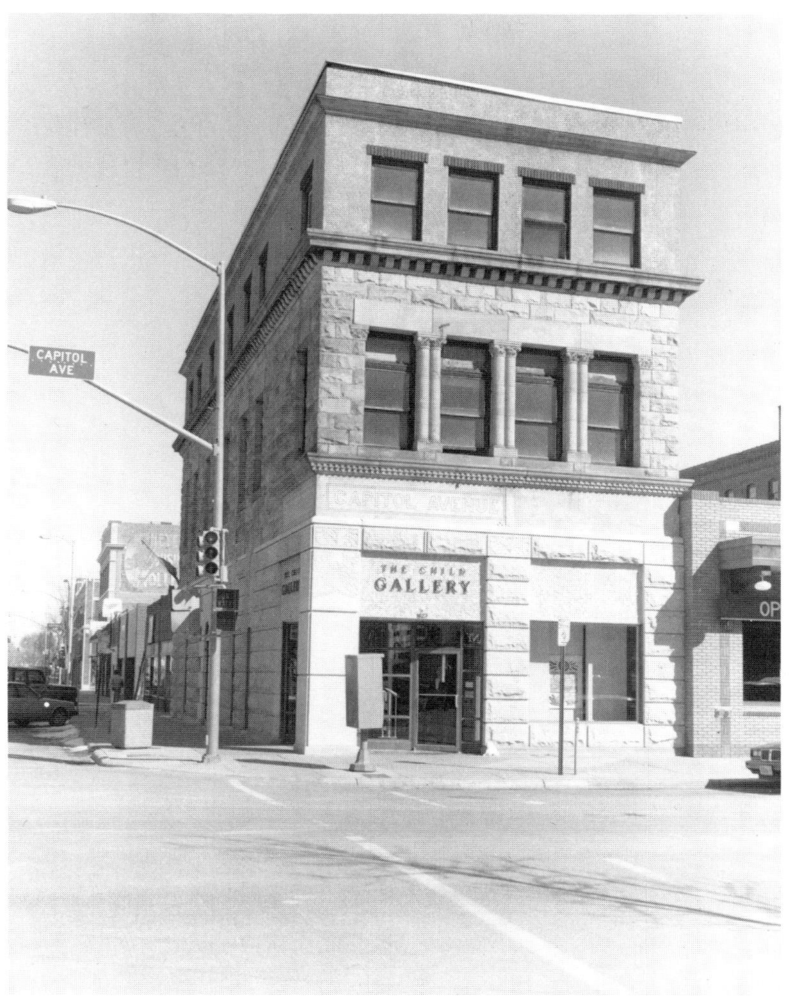
CAPITOL
AVE
THE CHILD
GALLERY

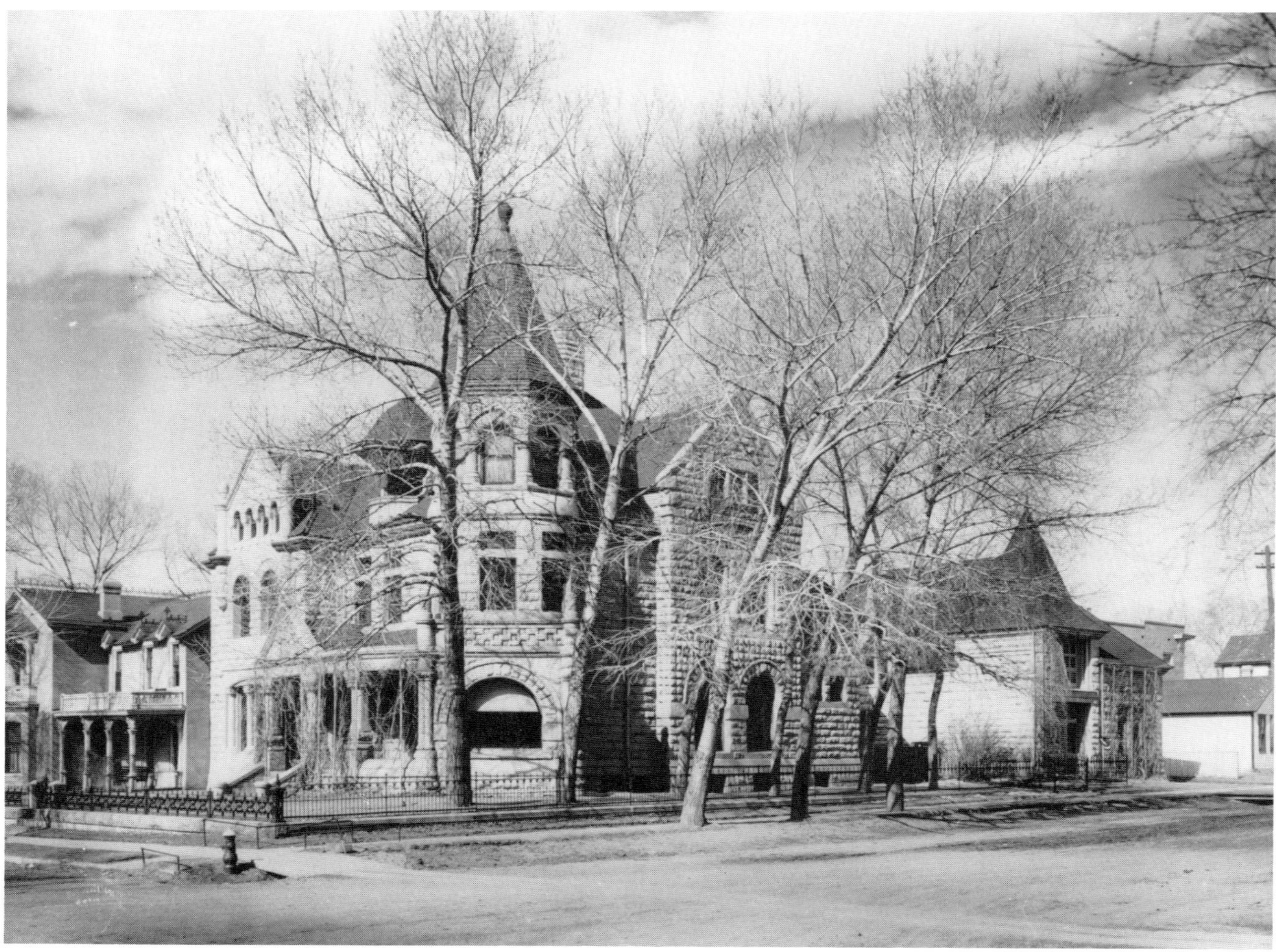

Fig. 51. Nagle residence, Cheyenne, no date.

Erasmus Nagle, chairman of the first Capitol Building Commission, constructed this residence in 1888 at a cost of fifty thousand dollars with stone that had been rejected for use in the State Capitol building. Hindsight showed the state to be right: in the 1950s the stone started to crack and chip and had to be reinforced with concrete. Only the carriage house, right center, remains with its original stone intact. Also intact are both original iron fences, the front cross hatch and the side picket. The neighboring house, left center, has a new porch. Finally, the fire hydrant has moved from the left side of the sidewalk in Stimson's photo to the right side in the modern view.

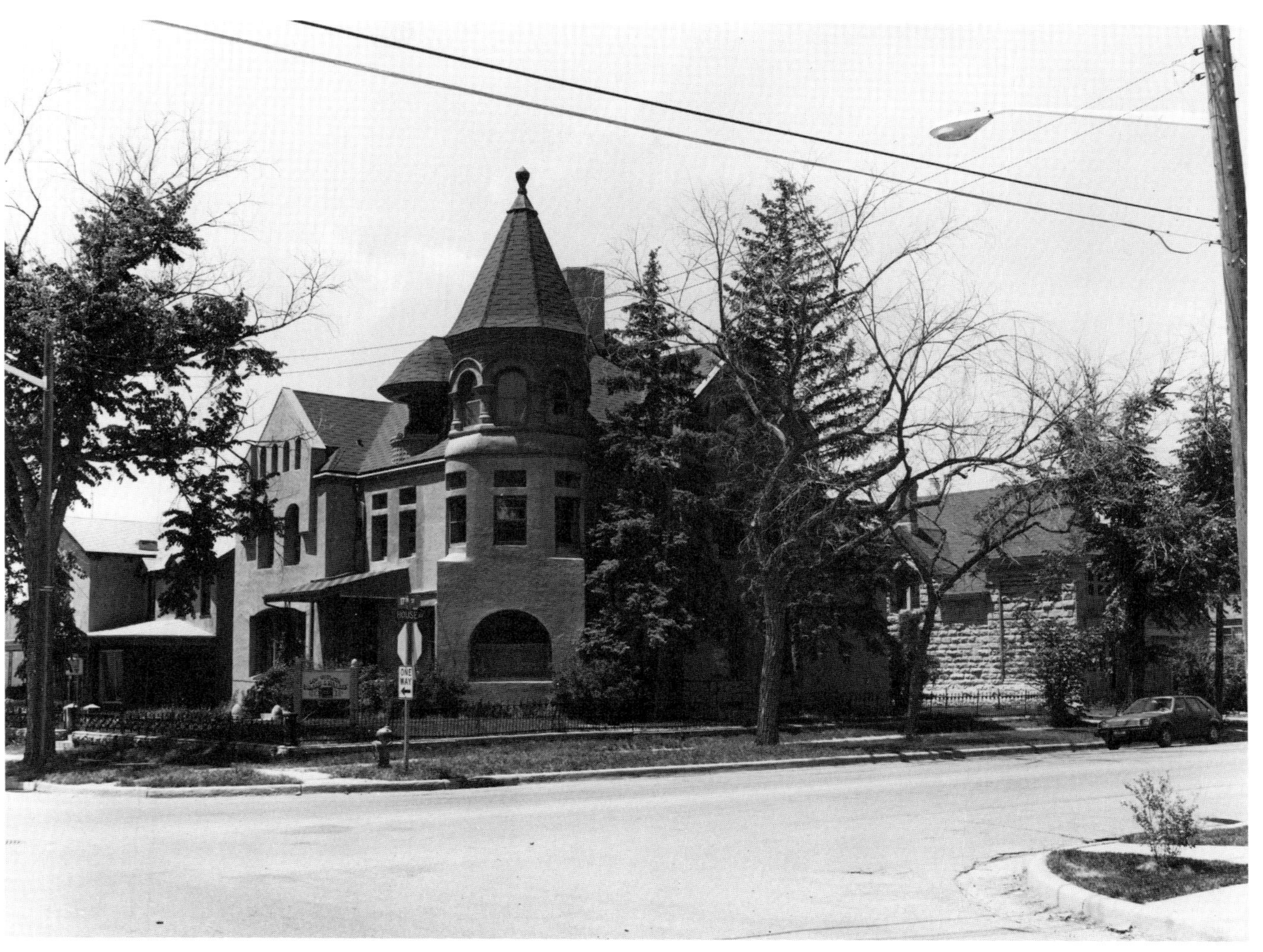
ONE WAY

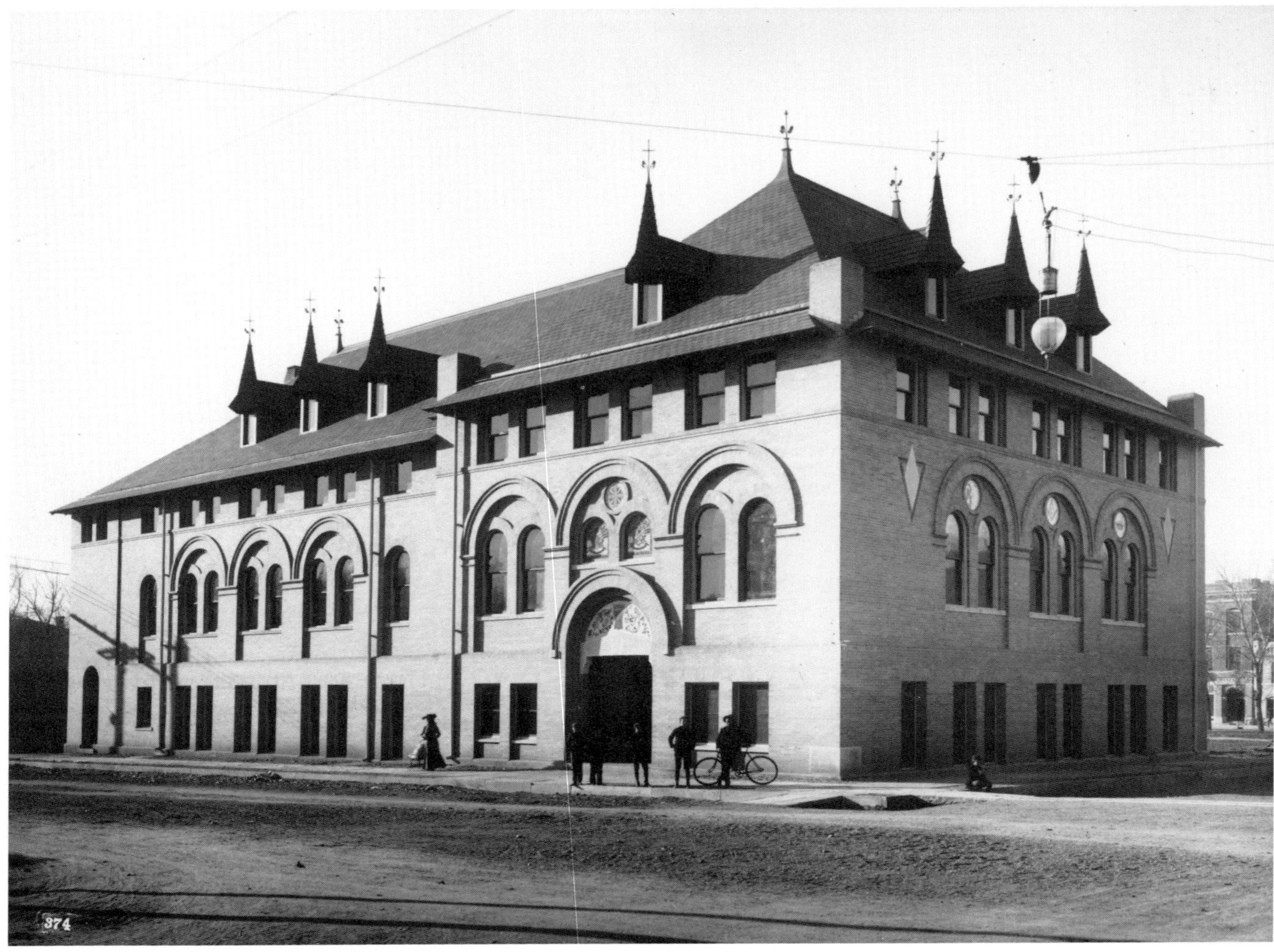

Fig. 52. Masonic Temple, Cheyenne, 1903.

Cheyenne Lodge Number One of the Masonic Order received its charter in 1868 and built a temple on Sixteenth Street. The Masons then moved to this structure at the turn of the century. The cornerstone for the Masonic Temple was placed in June of 1901, and the building had only been completed for about a year when it was gutted by fire in 1903. When the structure was rebuilt around the original shell, the Gothic architectural style was gone. The spired dormers were taken off the roof. The west wing, center right, was added in 1911.

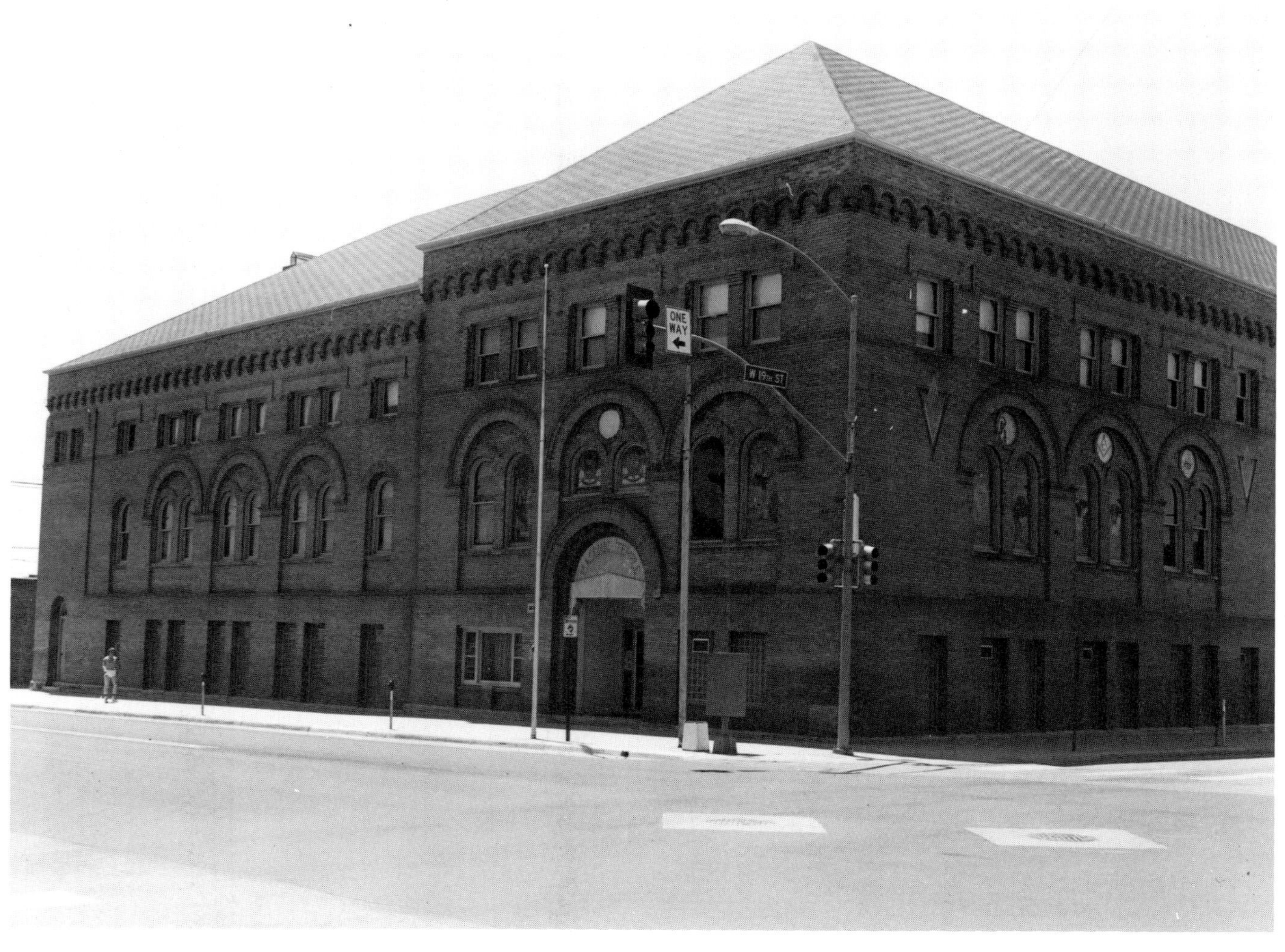
ONE
WAY
W 19TH ST

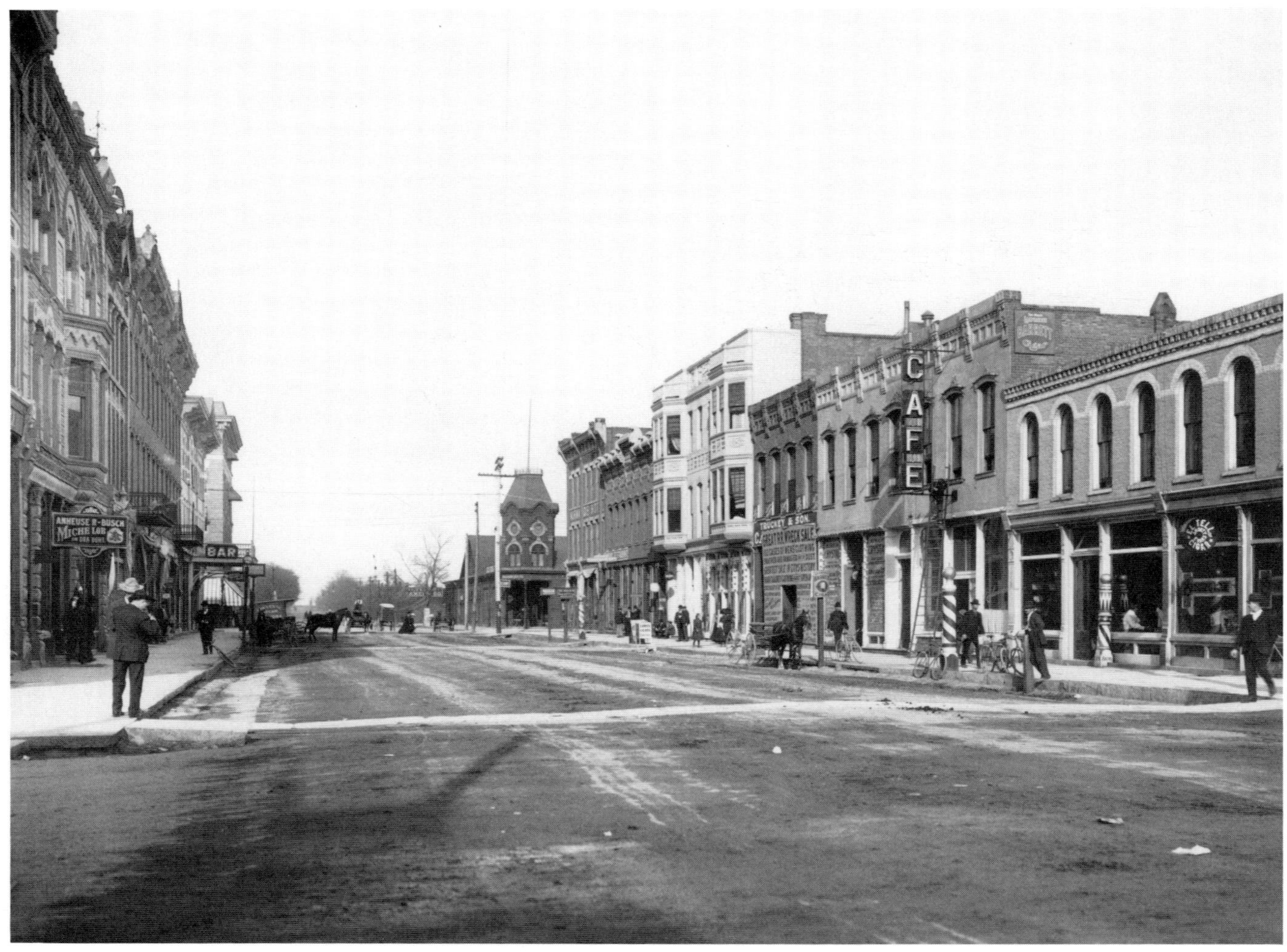

Fig. 53. Sixteenth Street, looking east, Cheyenne, 1908.

This classic view shows that the pace of traffic has increased since Stimson made his shot in 1908. Many historic buildings have survived on the southern, right, side of the street. The Atlas Theatre, with its second-story bay windows, was built in 1887 and first housed a tea and confectionery shop. It was remodeled in 1907 as a theater. Several other businesses have operated over the years, and it is now the summer home of the Cheyenne Little Theatre Players. On the corner is the Phoenix Block. Built in 1882 at a cost of $35,000, it once housed five stores, seventeen offices, and twenty-seven family rooms throughout its three fioors. Today, with a galloping horse in front, it is the home of Wrangler Western Wear. At the right center of Stimson's photo is the Burlington Northern Depot. It was built in 1882 and demolished in 1928.

Signs can also tell much about a photo. A study of the signs in Stimson's photo produces an interesting advertisement for a men's clothing sale. Located immediately right of the Atlas, it reads, "Great R.R. Wreck Sale—Greatest Sale in City's History."

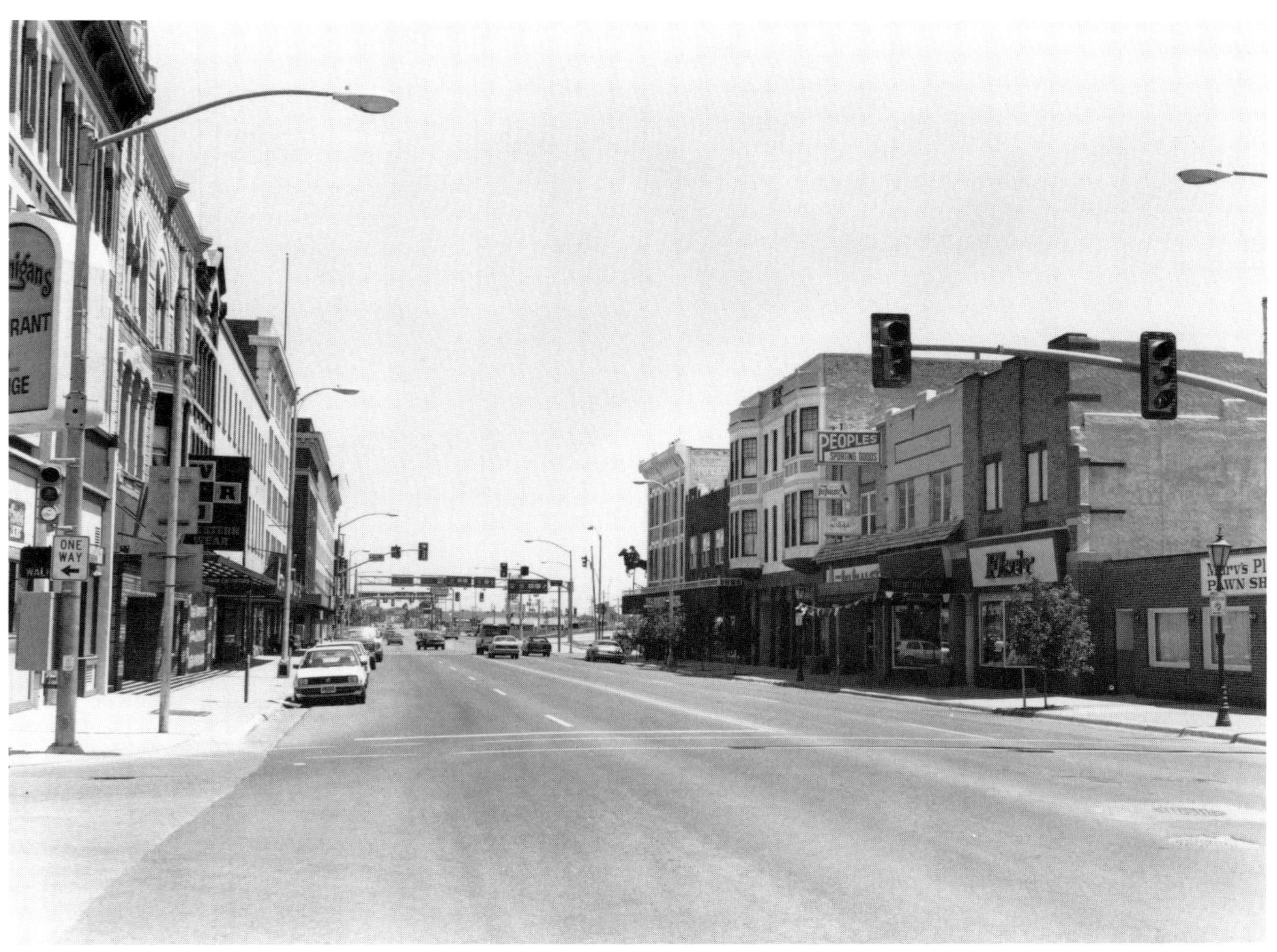
ONE
WAY
WALK
PEOPLES
SPORTING GOODS

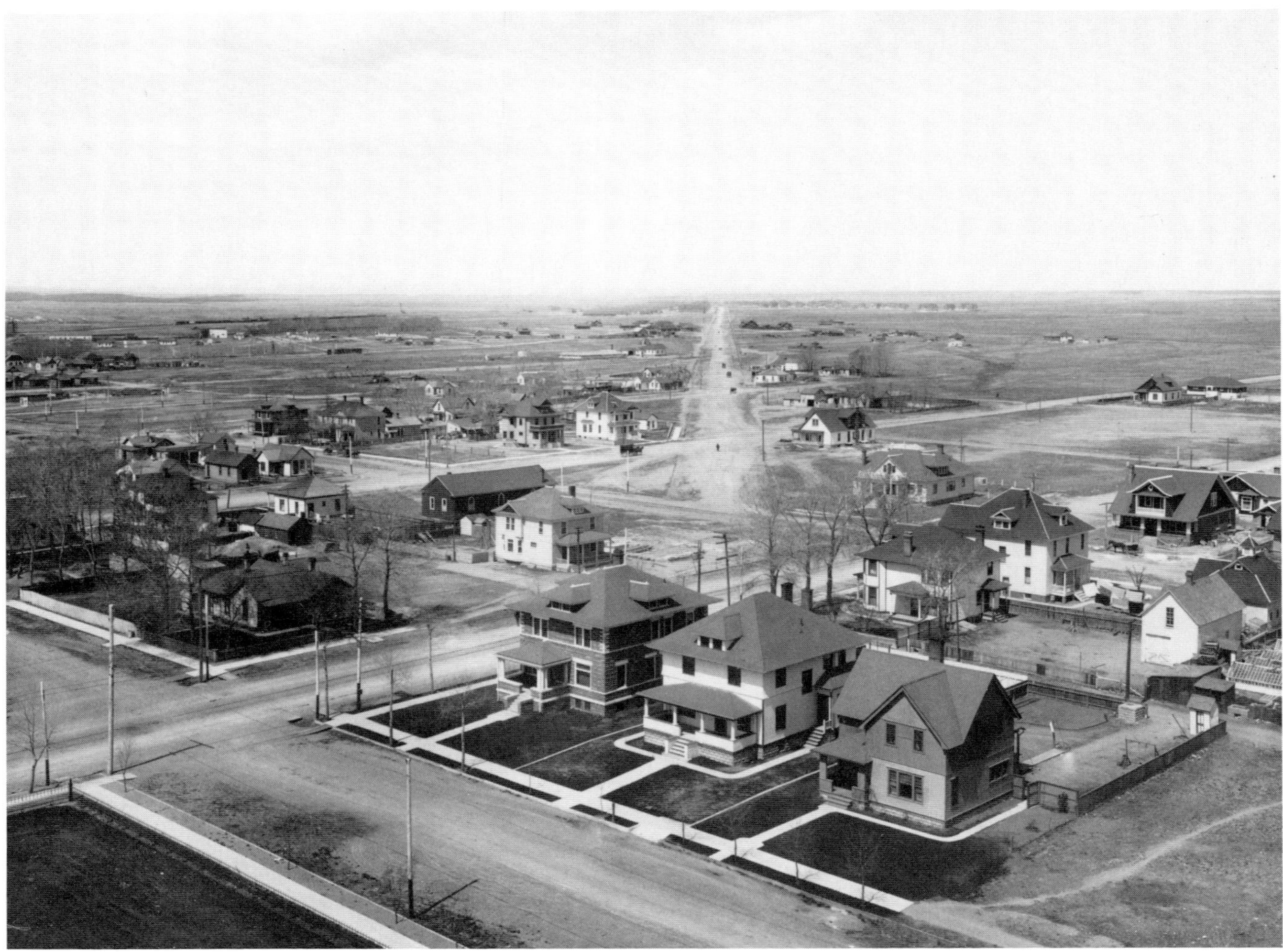

Fig. 54. Cheyenne, looking up Randall Avenue, 1910.

Stimson's view of Randall Avenue, the street heading northwest toward Warren Air Force Base, was taken from a window in the dome of the Capitol. Stimson's house is at the lower right of the old photo. In the modern view, the Herschler Building, named for former Governor Ed Herschler, encompasses the entire block. This building was constructed in 1976.

A close inspection of the modern photograph shows that it was not taken from the same place as Stimson's shot. The new view is from a lower vantage point. After gaining access to the dome from a security guard, I found that a satellite dish blocked the correct window. The guard suggested I try the roof, which we walked around until we were directly below the right window. I shot the photo from there.

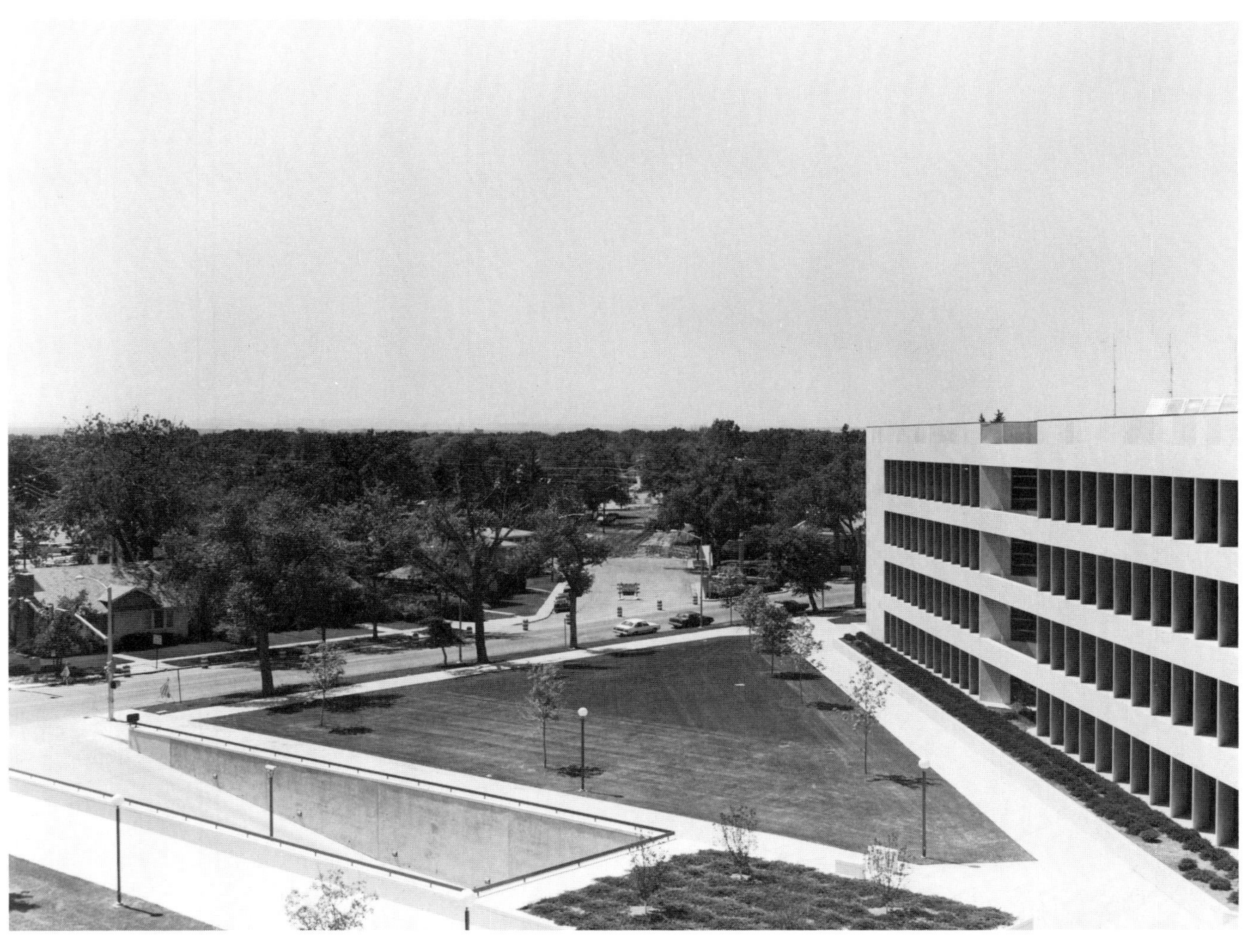

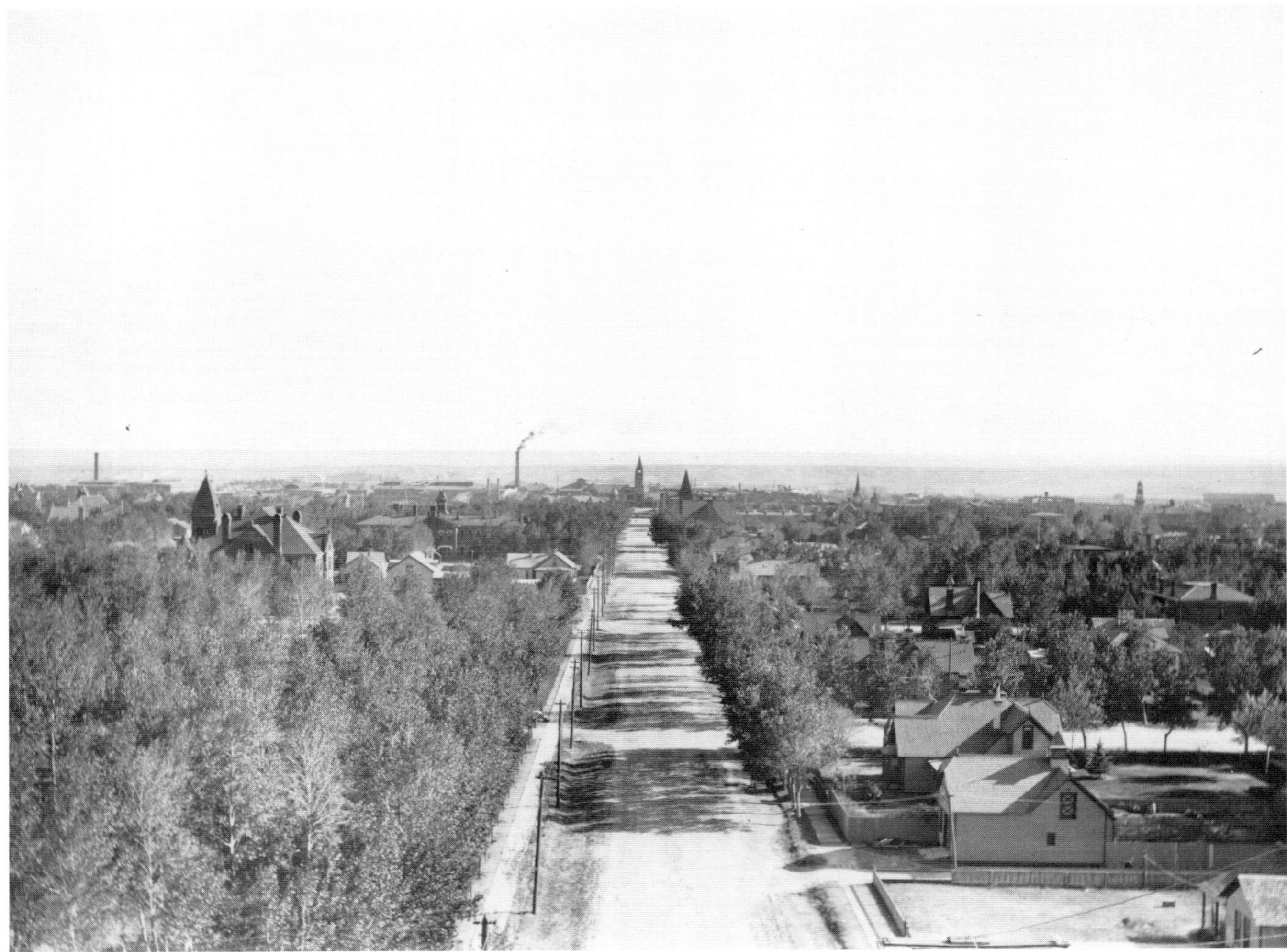

Fig. 55. Capitol Avenue, looking south, 1898.

This view was also taken from a window in the Capitol. The Union Pacific Depot tower can be seen at the opposite end of Capitol Avenue. The city skyline in this early photo was dominated by smokestacks and church spires. At left center is the original Cheyenne High School. The presence of many trees as well as the absence of St. Mary's Cathedral, built fourteen years later, are noteworthy.

In the modern photo, the Hathaway and American National Bank buildings dominate the landscape. At left center can also be seen St. Mary's Cathedral. The Union Pacific Depot tower almost goes unnoticed. The spots in the picture were on the outside of the immovable dome window.

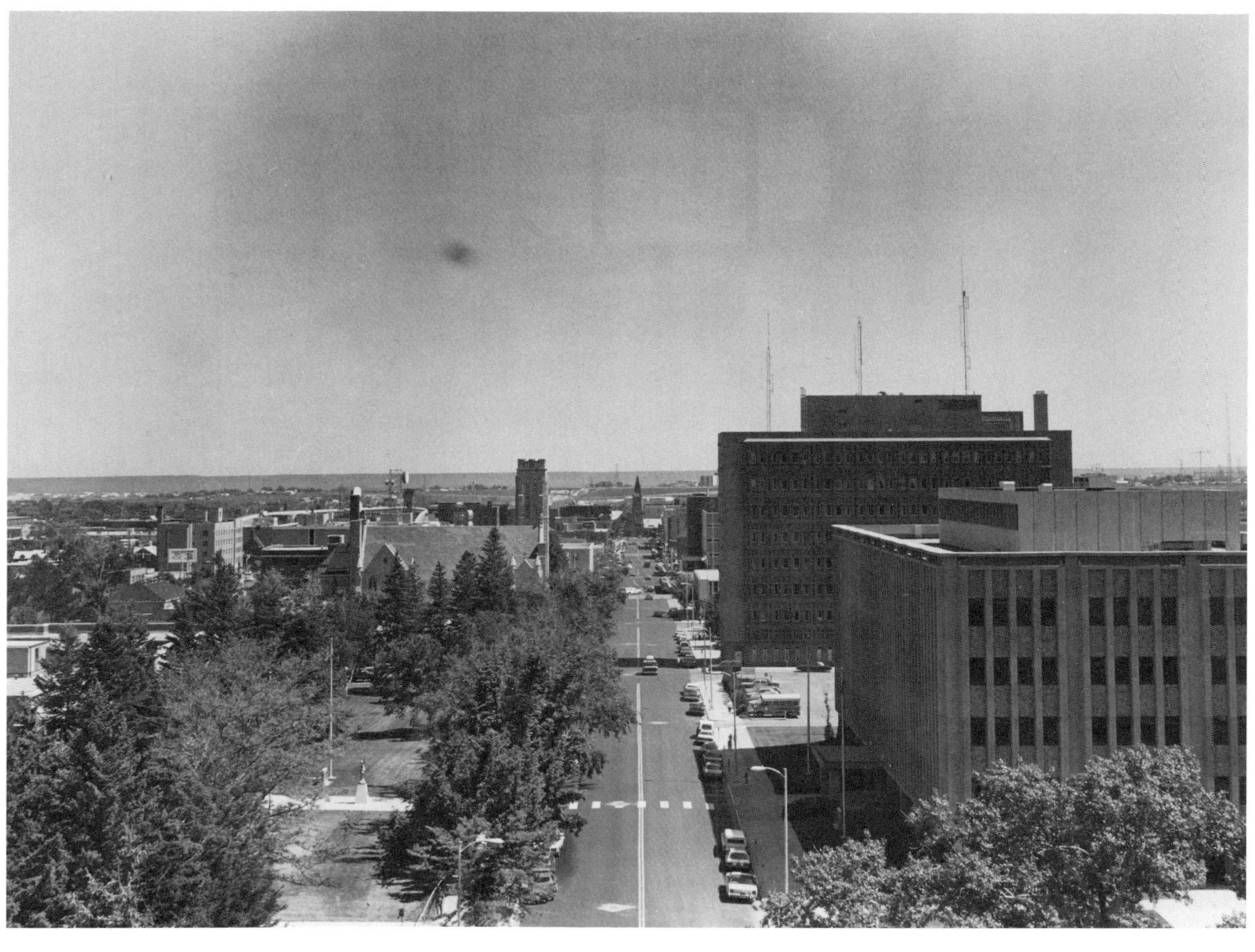

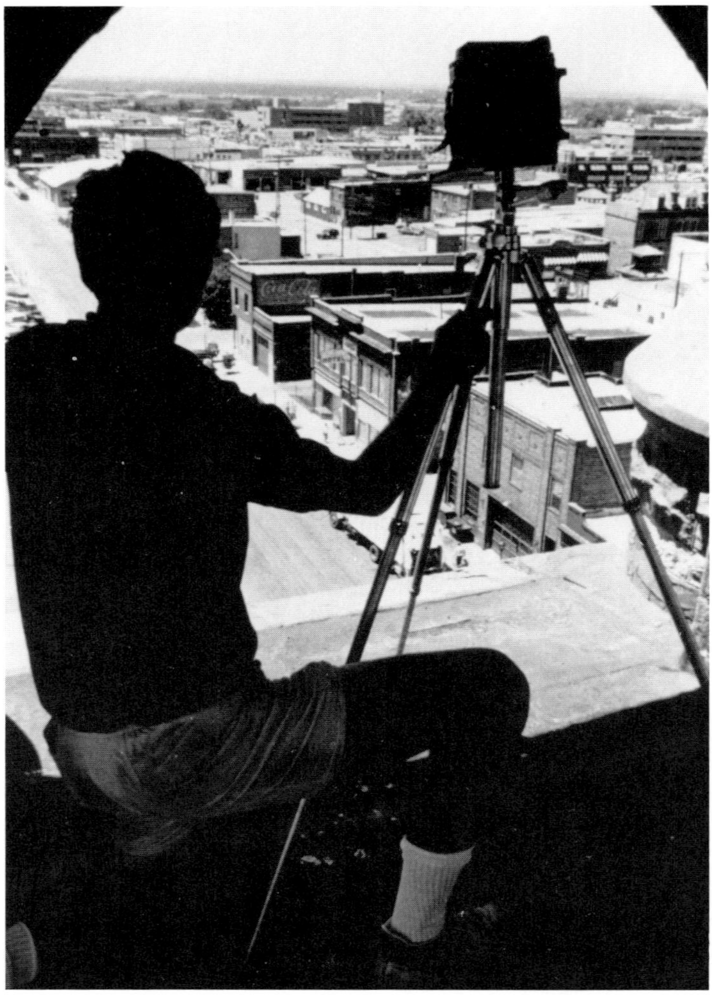

The next three pairs of photos were taken from the tower of the Union Pacific Depot in Cheyenne. The vantage point is a small archway that can be seen in the photograph above. The tower was constructed in 1886–87, and since then a number of photographers have captured the growth of Cheyenne from this location, including Stimson in 1910.

I discovered that it was very difficult to gain access to the 118-foot-high red sandstone tower. With the help of Stimson biographer Mark Junge, I signed a waiver for the Union Pacific stating that if I fell, I would not blame the company. We then started through a trap door located in an office. We climbed five stories of ladders, with equipment in hand, to the level of the clock. Every week a workman climbs to this spot and cranks up a two-and-one-half-pound weight that keeps the clock going. Through the roof of this room was another trap door that led to the archway. The six-foot-high stone archway enclosed an area of aluminum sheeting, ten feet by ten feet. There was no rail to catch me if I slipped.

With Mark's help, I set up my 4 × 5-inch camera on its tripod and shot the pictures. Luckily the wind that day was calm, but I still clung to the archway. By the end of the hour, the job was done. The modern photos not only provide an unusual perspective on Cheyenne today but also give the rephotographer a bird's-eye view of the changing city landscape.

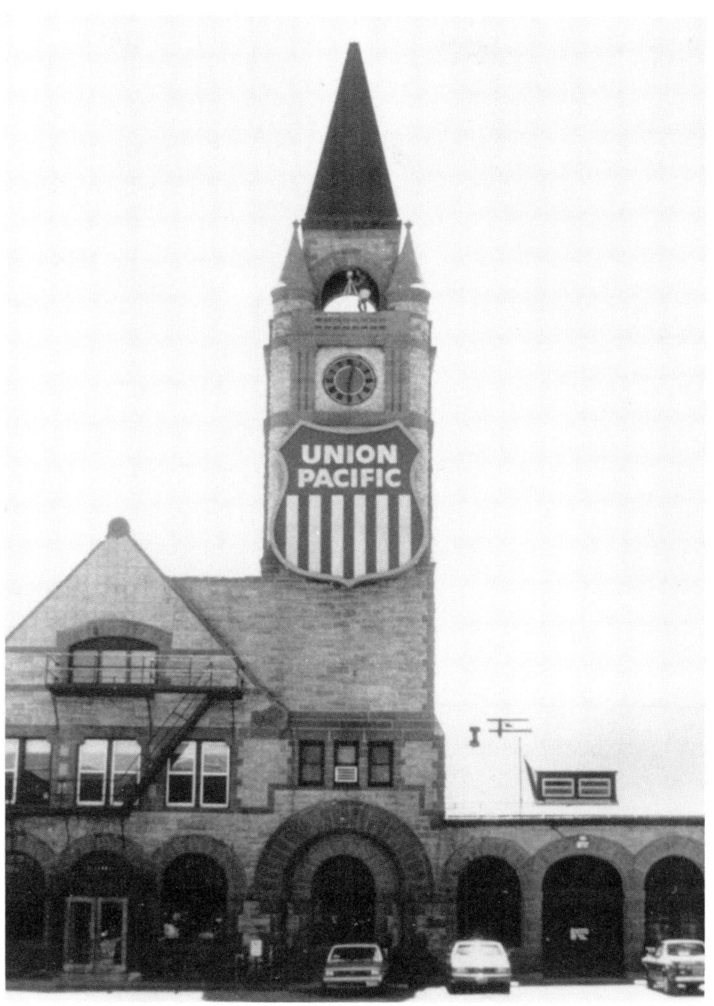
UNION
PACIFIC

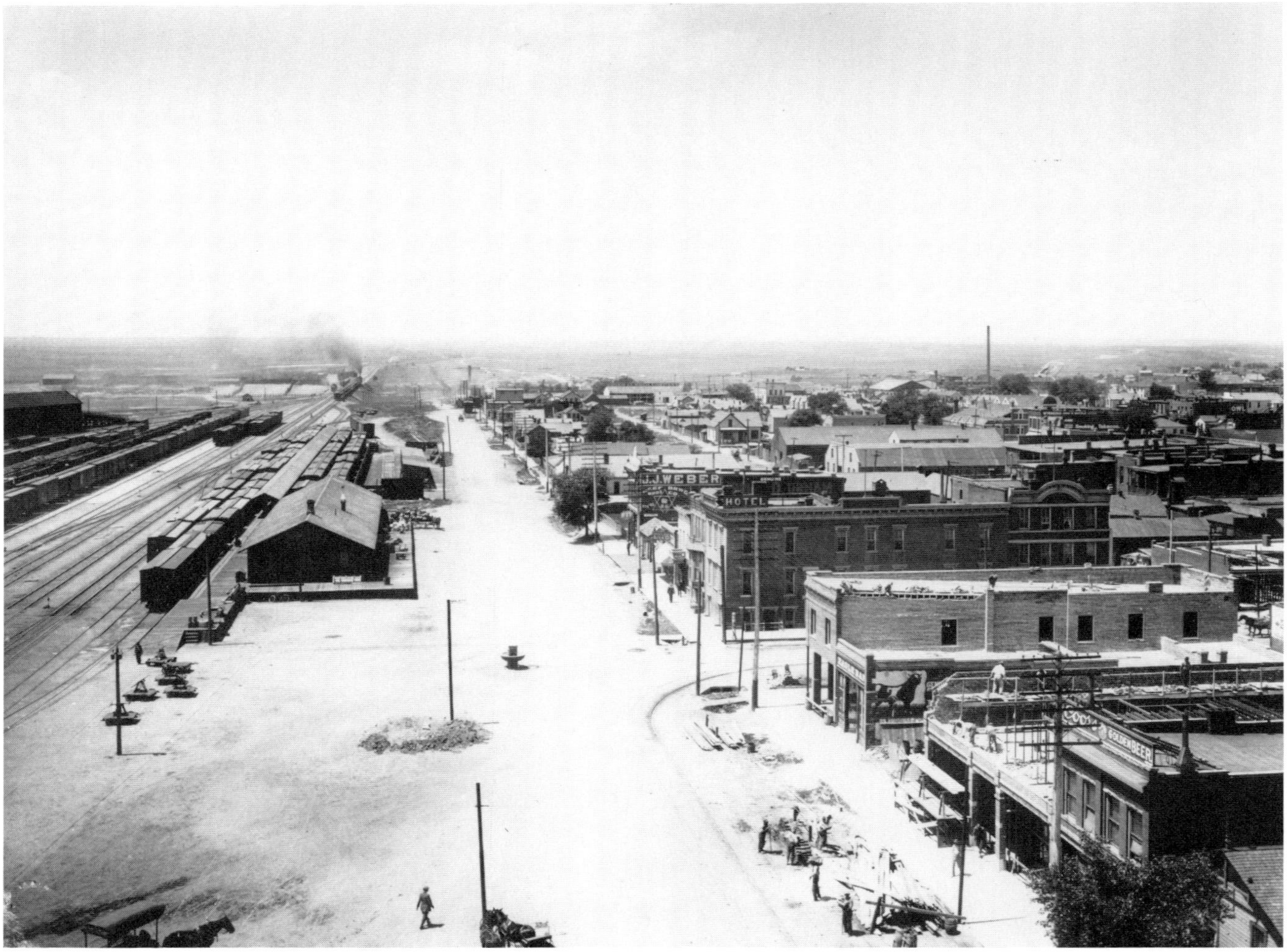

Fig. 56. Cheyenne west from Union Pacific Depot, 1910.

This view shows the Union Pacific freight yards and the construction of buildings on Fifteenth Street. The object at the center of Stimson's photo was a combination drinking fountain and horse trough placed there by the Society for the Prevention of Cruelty to Animals. After the city removed it, local rancher Earl Vandehai purchased the fountain as an ornament for his lawn. It seems that Vandehai, while riding in the Frontier Days parade, had often stopped at the fountain to water his horse. The trough remained in his yard until his death in 1962, when it was moved to the Lakeview Cemetery and placed over Vandehai's grave as a tombstone. It is still there (see photo at right).

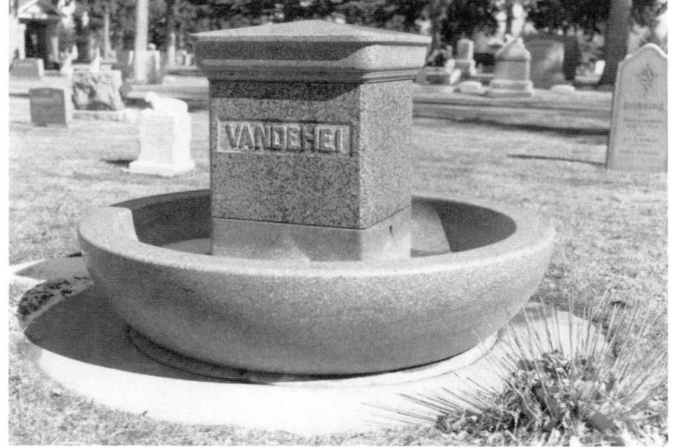

The modern photo also shows the absence of the building labeled "Hotel" in Stimson's photo. Old Town Mall now occupies that space. The buildings under construction in Stimson's photo, lower right, are now run-down hotels. Many of the Union Pacific tracks have also been removed from the freight yard at left center.

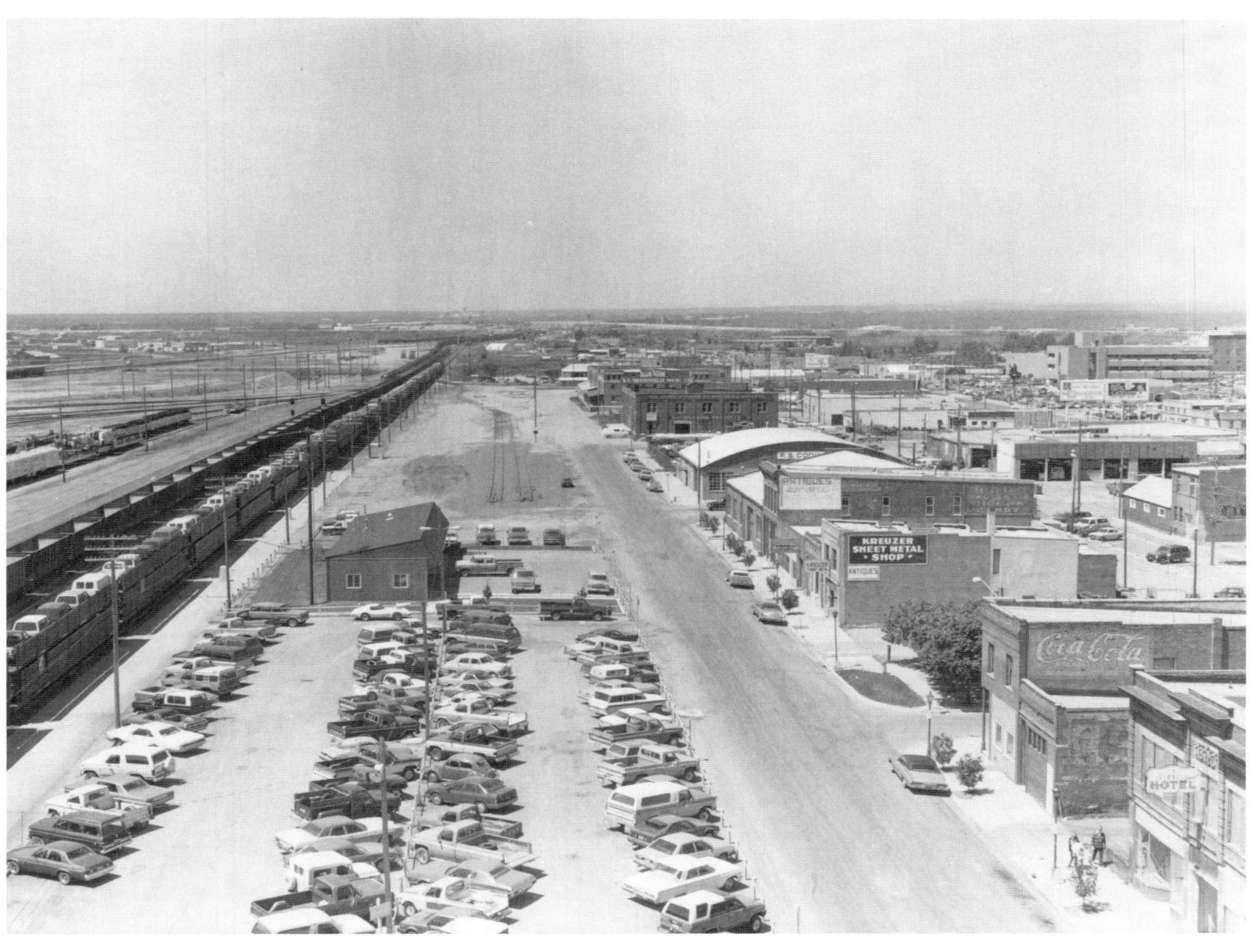
KREUZER
SHEET METAL
SHOP
ANTIQUES
ANTIQUES
Coca-Cola
HOTEL

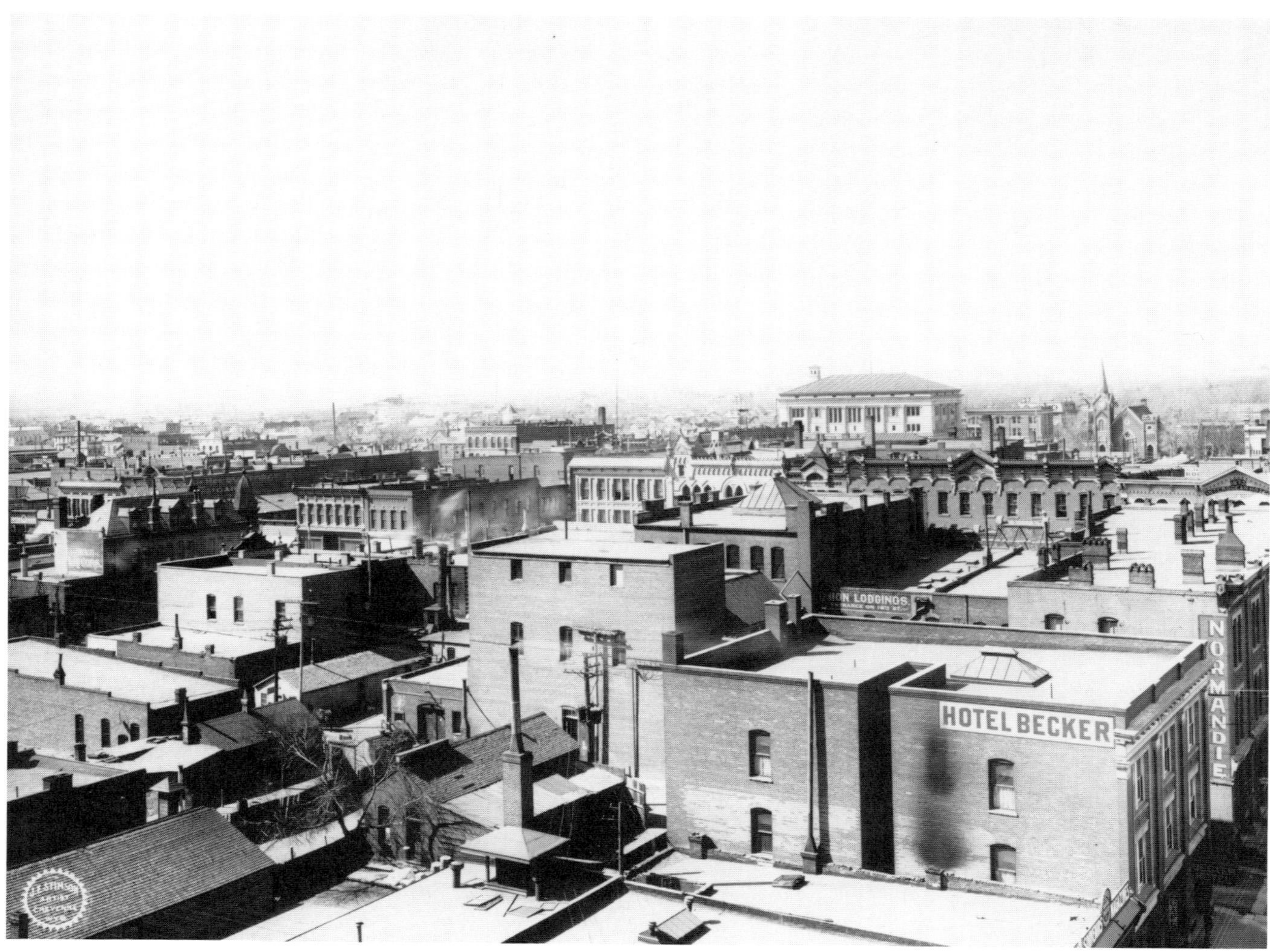

Fig. 57. Panorama of Cheyenne from Union Pacific Depot, 1910.

This view shows the roofs of buildings along Capitol Avenue and Sixteenth Street. At left center can still be seen the turrets of the Tivoli Building, although those directly across the street have since been torn down. The sign for the Hotel Becker has been painted over.

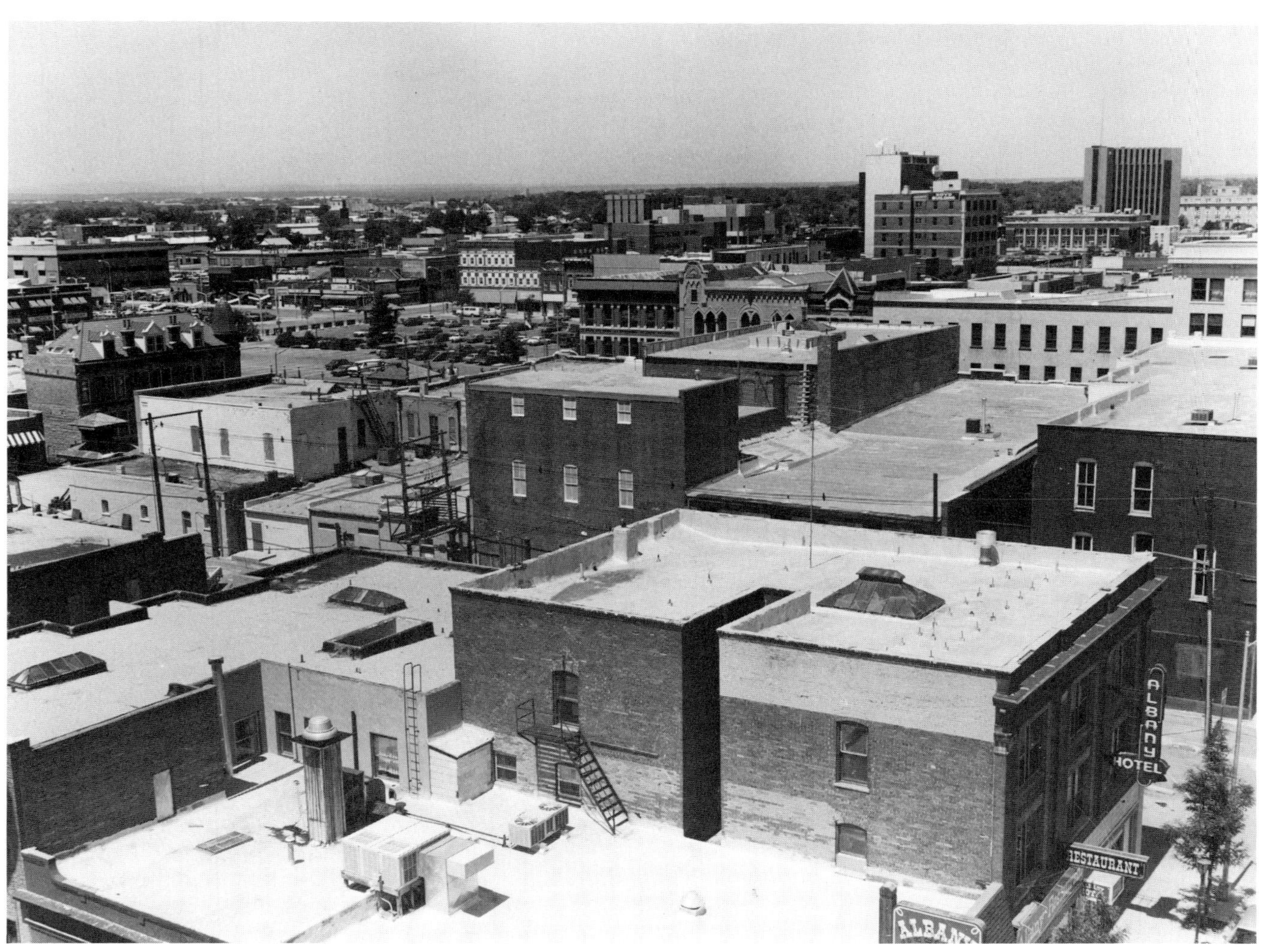
ALBANY
HOTEL
RESTAURANT

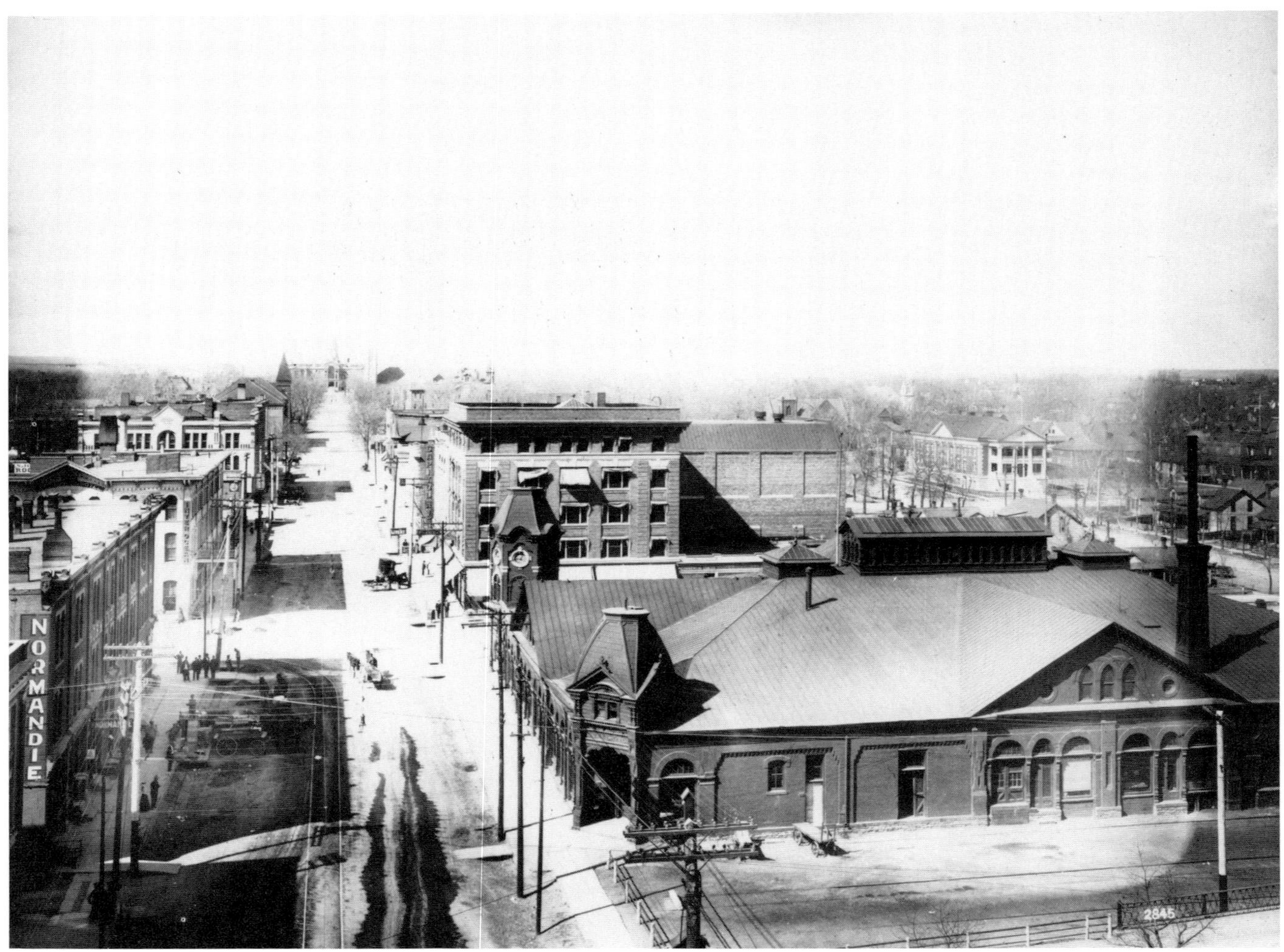

Fig. 58. Panorama of Cheyenne from Union Pacific Depot, 1910.

This view, looking north up Capitol Avenue to the State Capitol, shows the large Burlington Depot at right, with the First National Bank building directly behind it. Constructed as the Warren Mercantile in 1882, Burlington took over the building when the railroad built into Cheyenne in 1887. This depot was razed in 1928 and replaced by another depot that lasted until 1956 when it was razed too. Tracks for the city streetcar can be found in the middle of Capitol Avenue. The Plains Hotel was not built until 1911.

Today the Burlington Depot has been replaced by a parking lot, and the Plains Hotel has been expanded to connect with the First National Bank building. Across the street to the left, the Hynds Building replaced the Inter-Ocean Hotel in 1923.

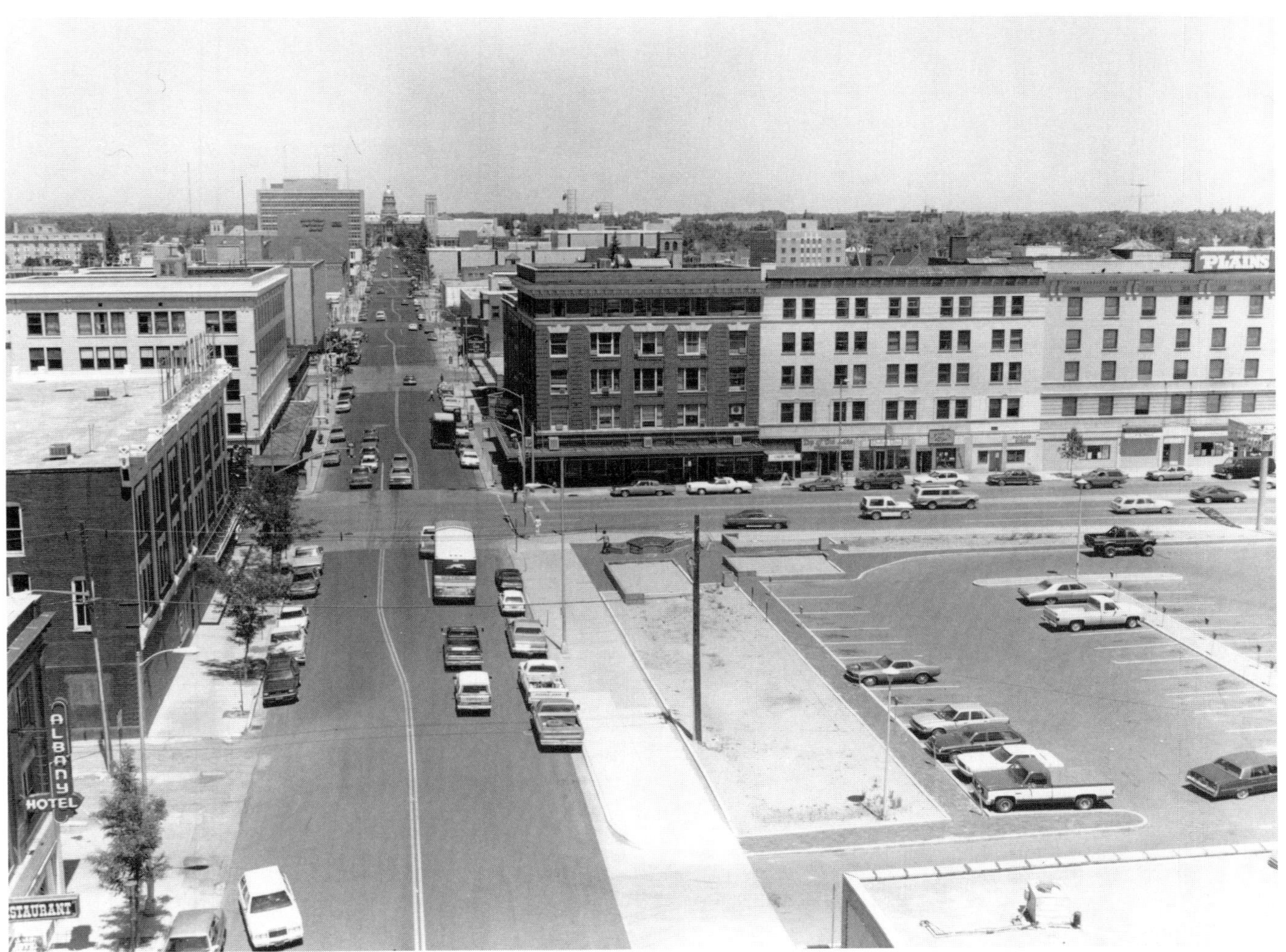
PLAINS
ALBANY
HOTEL
STAURANT

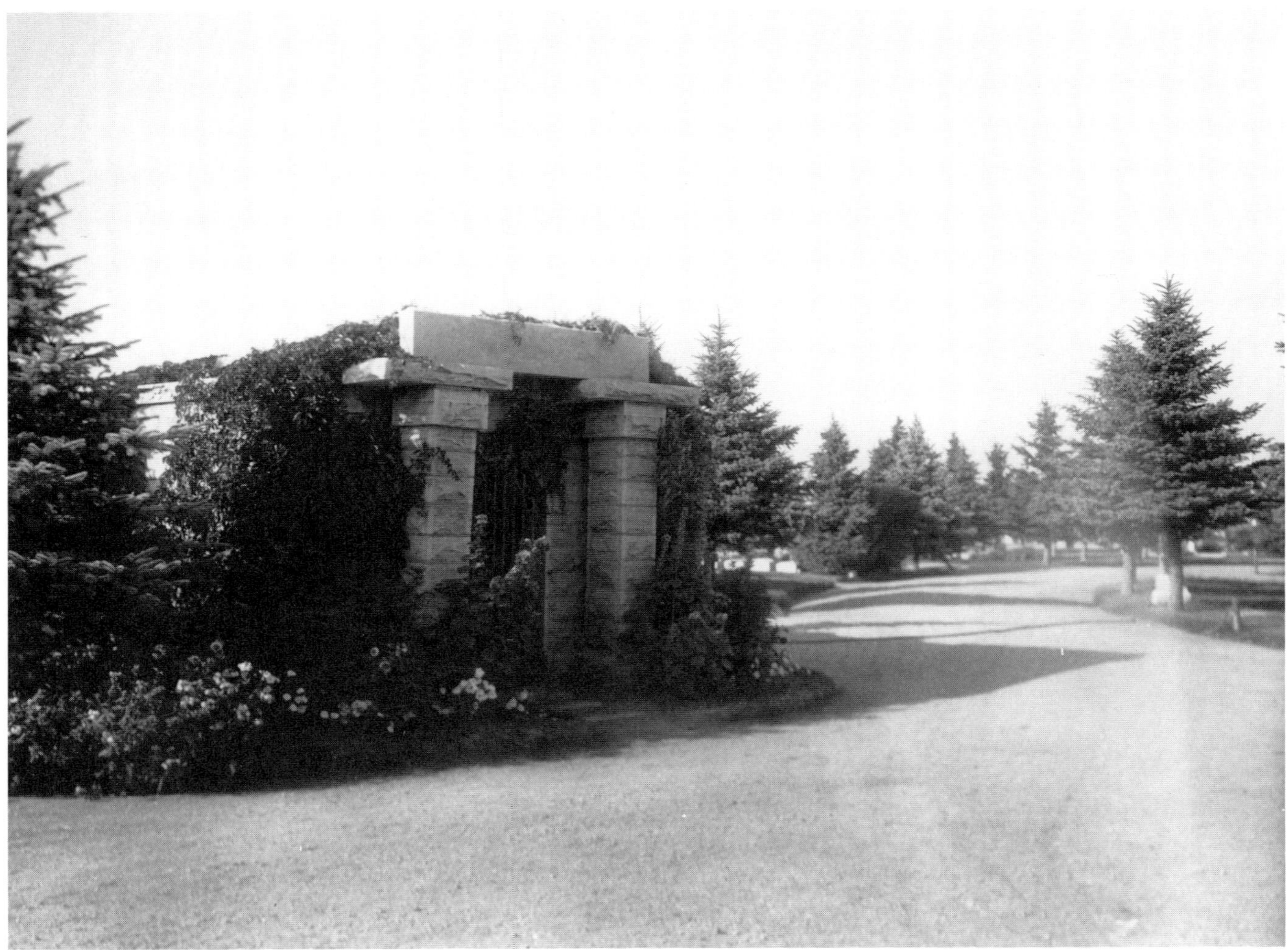

Fig. 59. Lakeview Cemetery, Cheyenne, 1911.

As the city of Cheyenne grew from an end-of-tracks town into a municipality, certain civic necessities such as water, fire, and police operations were needed. Another of these necessities, a city cemetery, was established in 1872. Through the 1880s, as prosperity came to Cheyenne, the city conducted campaigns to sell plots to the members of fraternal, labor, military, and ethnic groups. These owners were then encouraged to beautify their lots until a city maintenance crew could be established. In 1893 the stone "receiving vault" shown in Stimson's view was built. This building could hold three to four coffins during the winter until the ground thawed and they could be interred. The back office room and gabled roof were added at a later date. Today the city morgue provides this service and the vault is used for equipment storage.

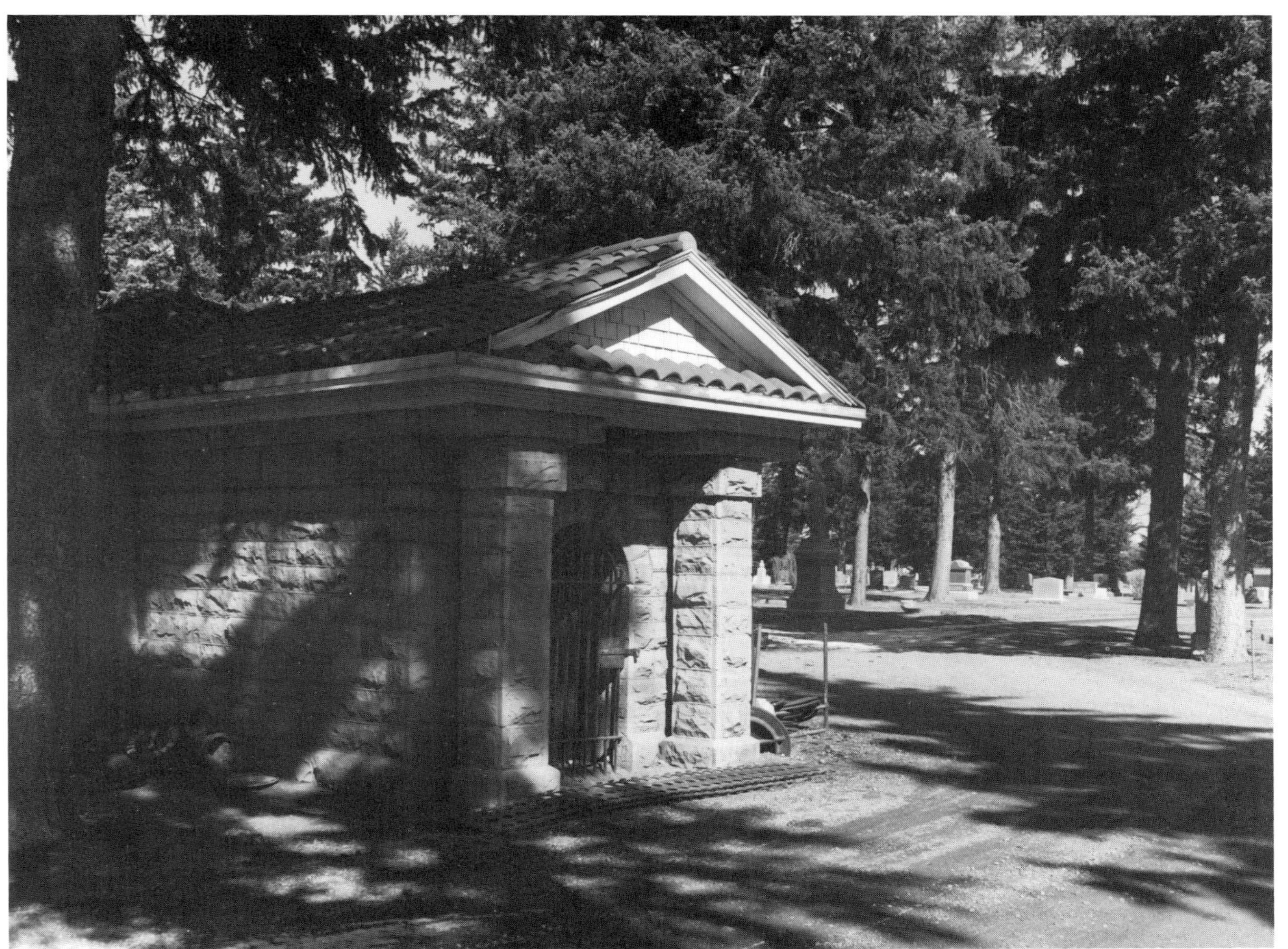

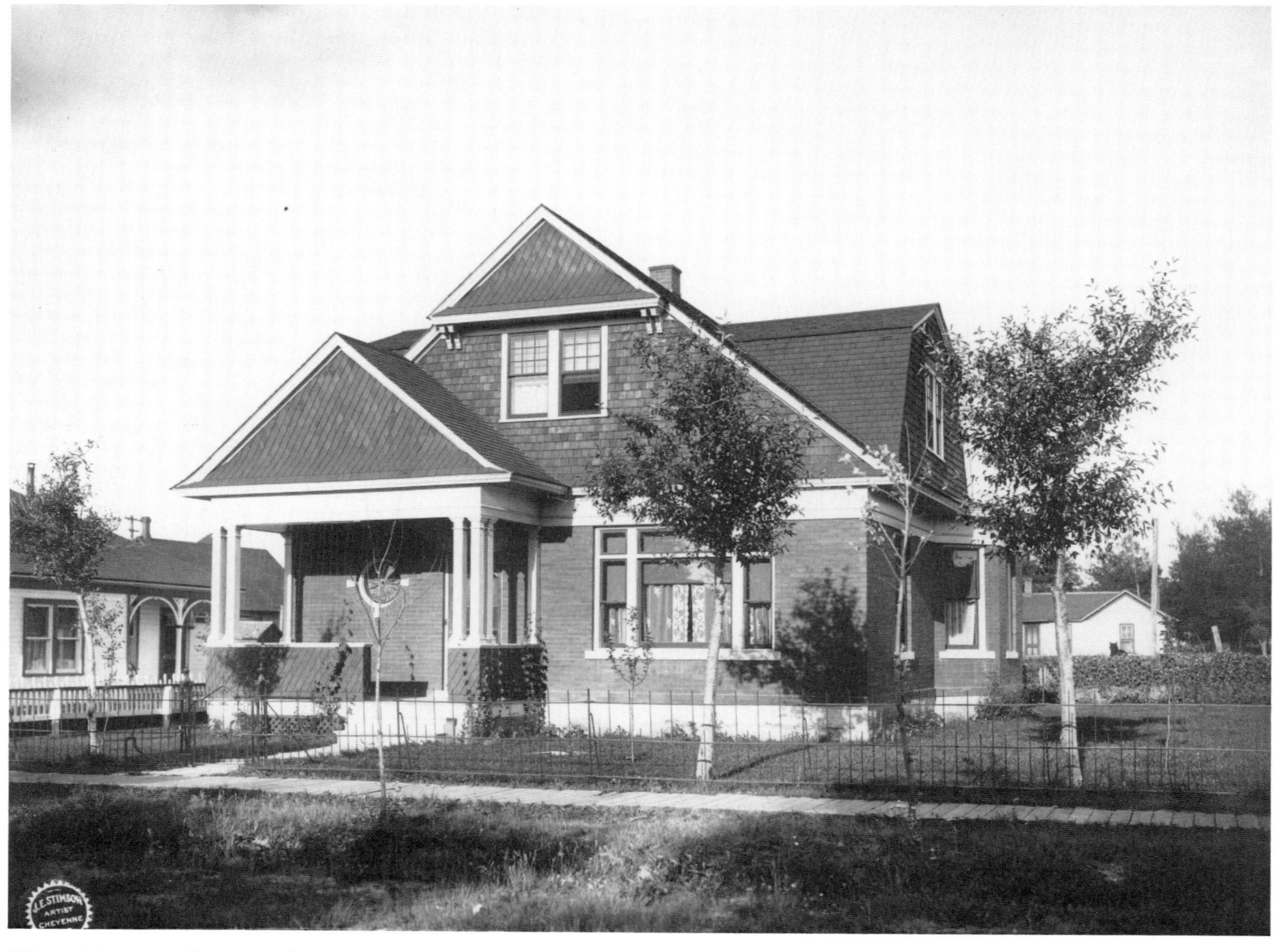

Fig. 60. Residence of James Mathison, Laramie, 1905.

When I decided to rephotograph this scene, I had no idea where, in Laramie, this house might be located. I knew that Stimson's photograph was taken around 1905, so I thought a quick survey of the older sections of Laramie would enable me to find this house with its distinctive round porch window. Then someone suggested an old city of Laramie directory. I found one in the University of Wyoming library and looked up James Mathison. The directory not only gave his address, 419 South Sixth Street, but also his telephone number and place of work. Mathison was a vice-president for one of the local newspapers, the *Republican.* Through more research, I discovered that Mathison was Anna Stimson's cousin, and that was probably the reason that the photo was taken. While I was taking the rephotograph, the present owners of the house produced a small painting that they had found in the attic. Written on back was "J. Mathison, 1906."

Besides the enclosed porch, the most interesting changes in this scene are trees. The tall evergreen at right center cannot even be found in the Stimson photo, and the deciduous trees are gone. The neighbor's house at left center also has gone through some changes. Finally, it is nice to see that although the round window of Stimson's photo has been covered (it is still there), a small window was placed above the porch to maintain the house's style.

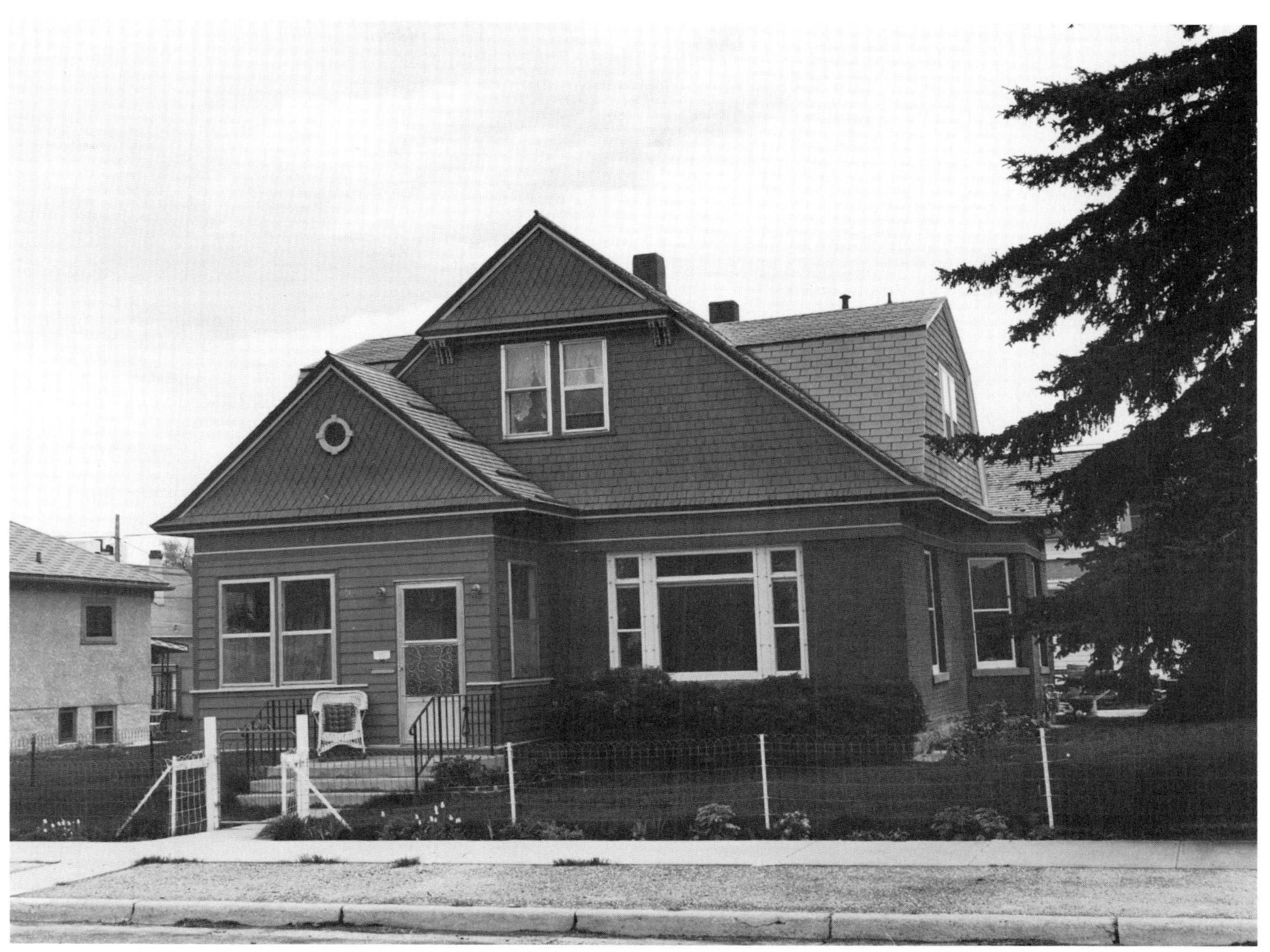

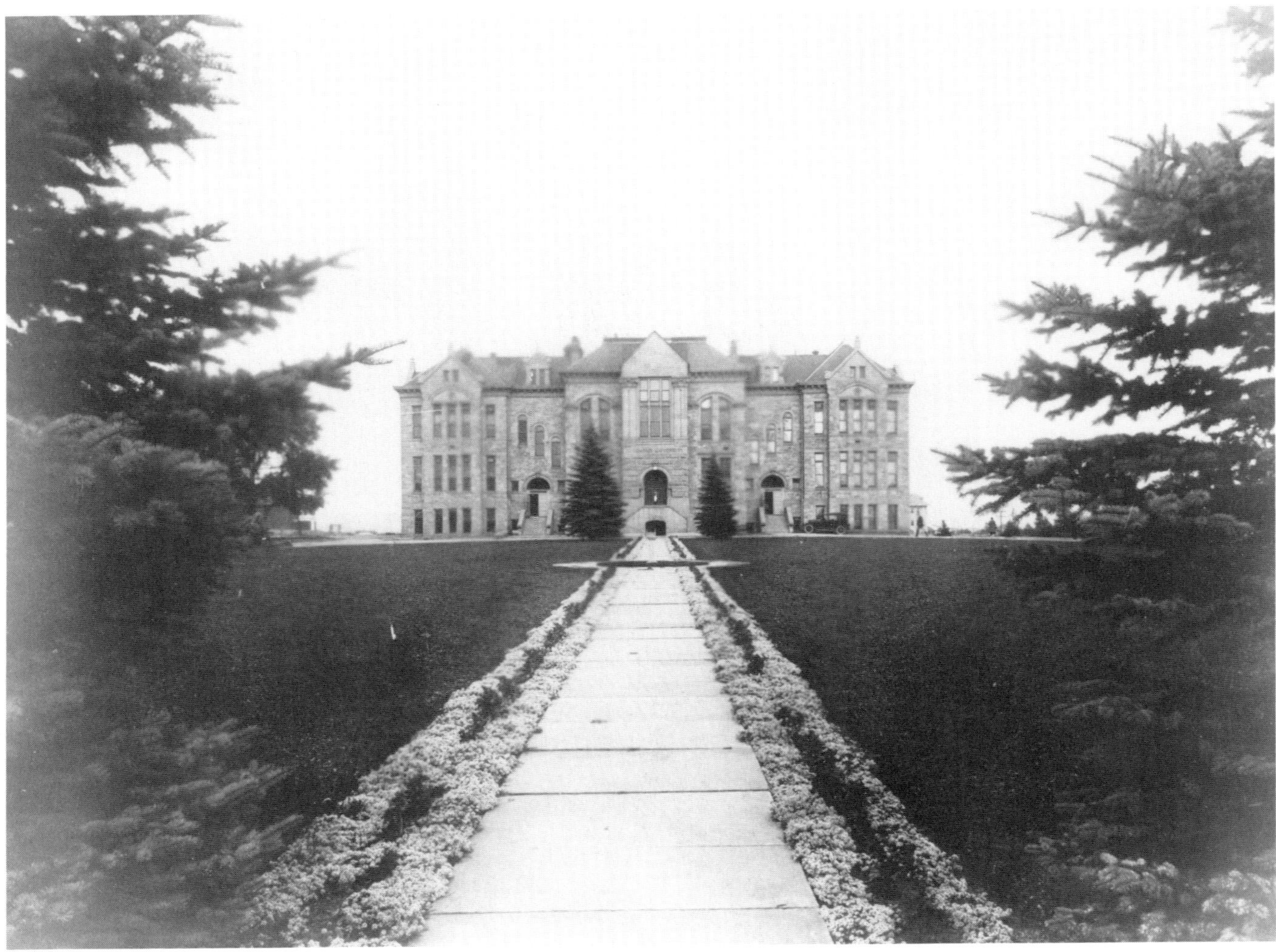

Fig. 61. Old Main, University of Wyoming, Laramie, 1922.

This view of Old Main, the original home of the University of Wyoming, was taken under two large evergreen trees near the Ninth Street campus entrance. Old Main was built in 1886 and originally had a large tower rising from the center of its roof. The tower was torn down in 1917 for structural reasons, and the building remained basically intact until 1949. At that time the building was gutted and converted from classrooms to offices.

The most obvious detail about this pair of photographs is the landscaping of the grounds around Old Main in both photos. Trees, flowers, and even sprinklers can be found. The original stone sidewalk remains from Stimson's photo, as do the two evergreens in front of Old Main—with the exception that the right tree is now taller than the left! Changes can also be found in the front entryways. The two side entryways shown in Stimson's view have been closed. Also, the original main entrance, which allowed direct access to both the first and second floors, has been altered. The modern photo shows that the new main entrance leads to the first floor. These changes were all made in 1949.

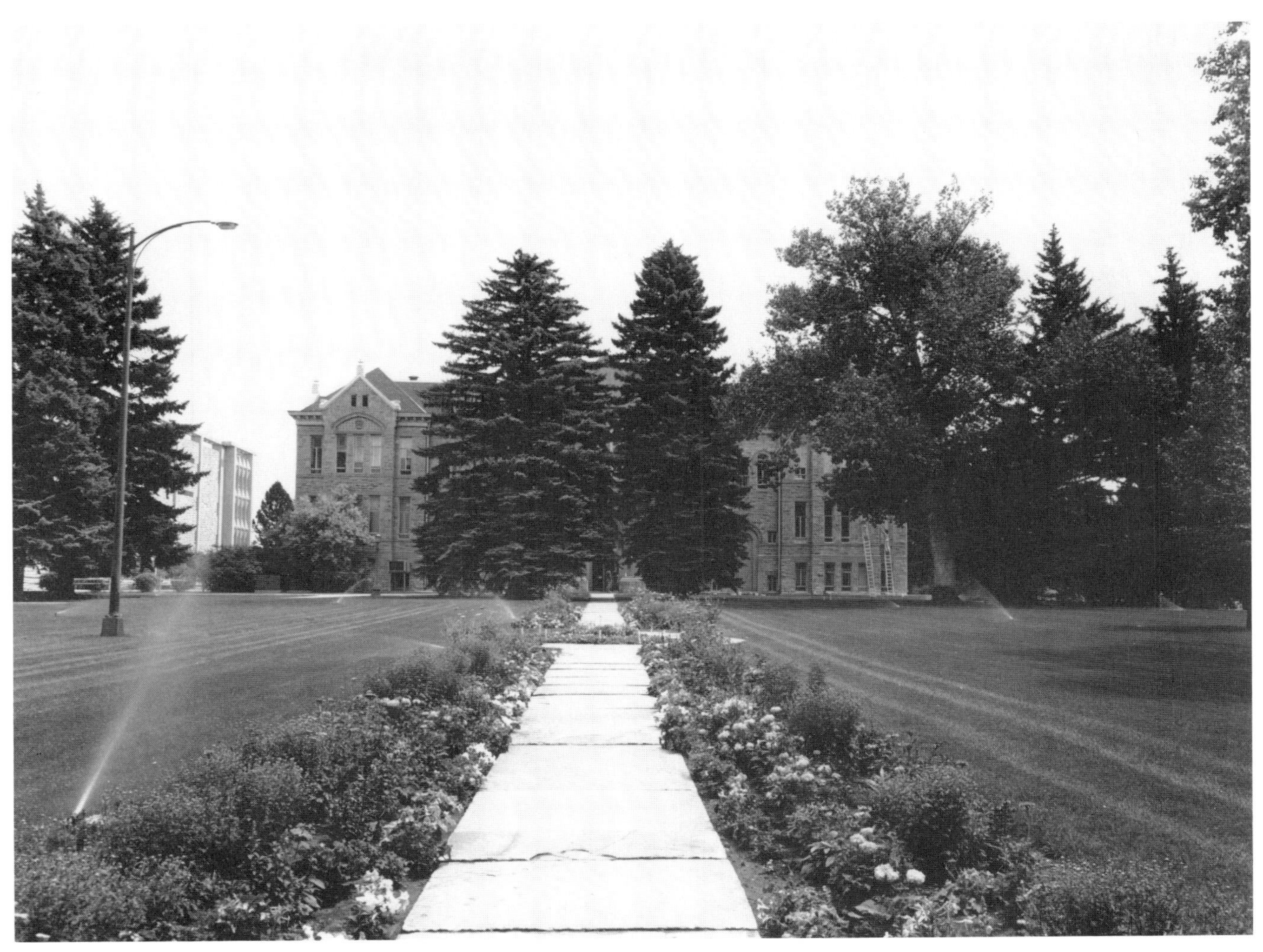

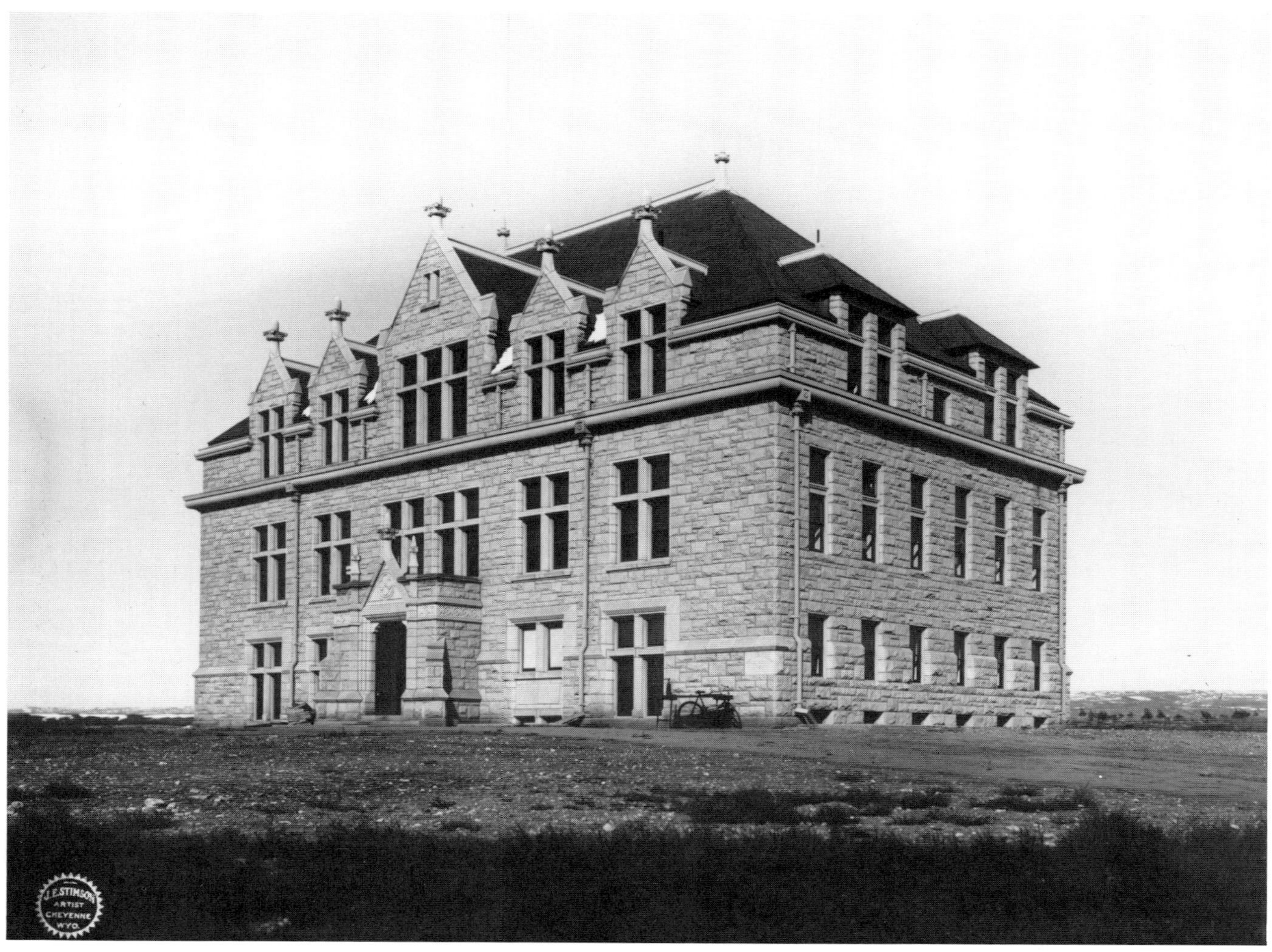

Fig. 62. Science Hall, University of Wyoming, Laramie, 1903.

The Science Hall was opened in 1903 and is the second oldest building still standing on campus. It is now the home of the Department of Geology. The elaborate stonework and spires still remain from Stimson's view.

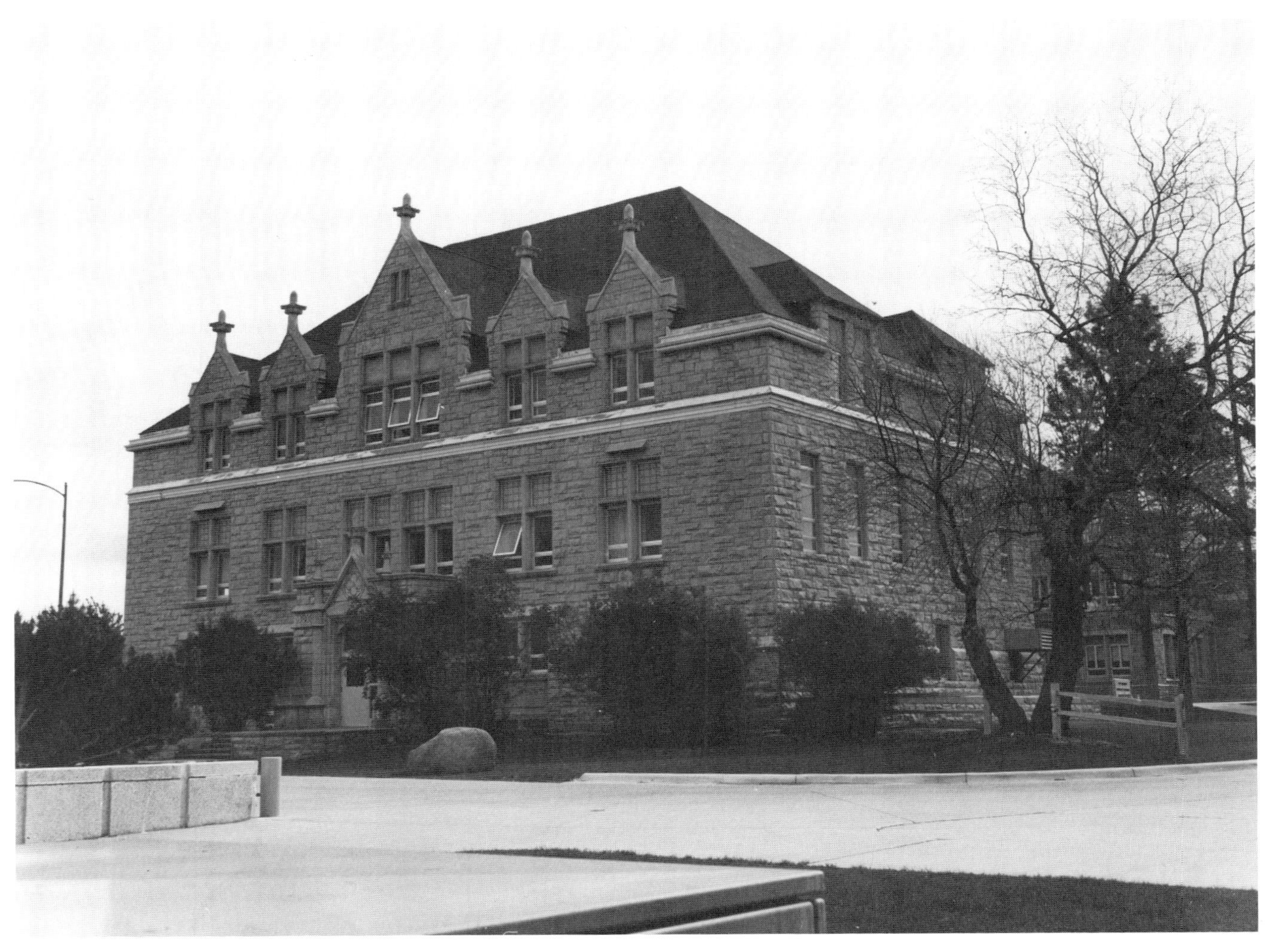

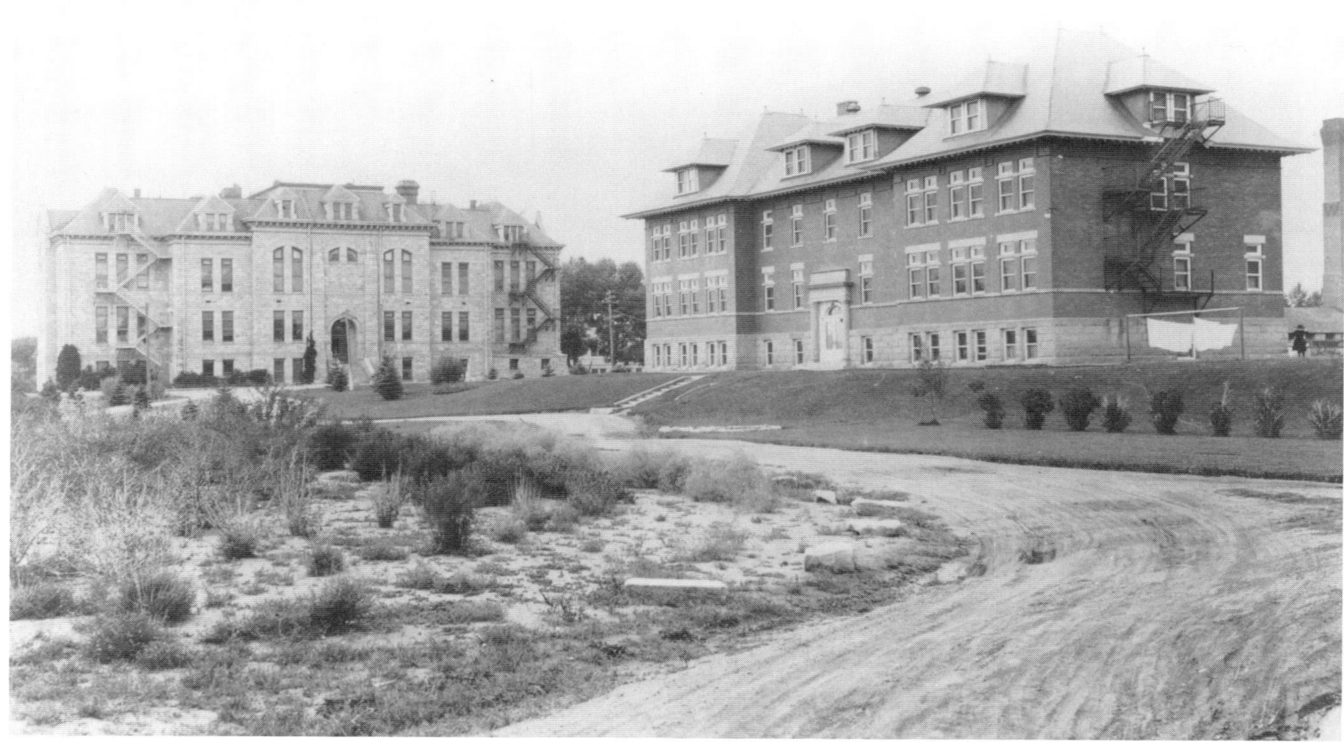

Fig. 63. Merica Hall, University of Wyoming, Laramie, 1922.

Merica Hall, the university's first women's dormitory, can be seen, right center, with the back of Old Main, center. Opened in 1915, Merica was named for early university president Charles Merica. The sheets on the line attest to its use as a dorm. From the back steps of Old Main, President Teddy Roosevelt spoke to a large Laramie audience in 1903 before riding horseback to Cheyenne. The ground at left foreground is called the campus "green" although it was not very green in Stimson's photo. Trees dominate the two buildings that are now offices.

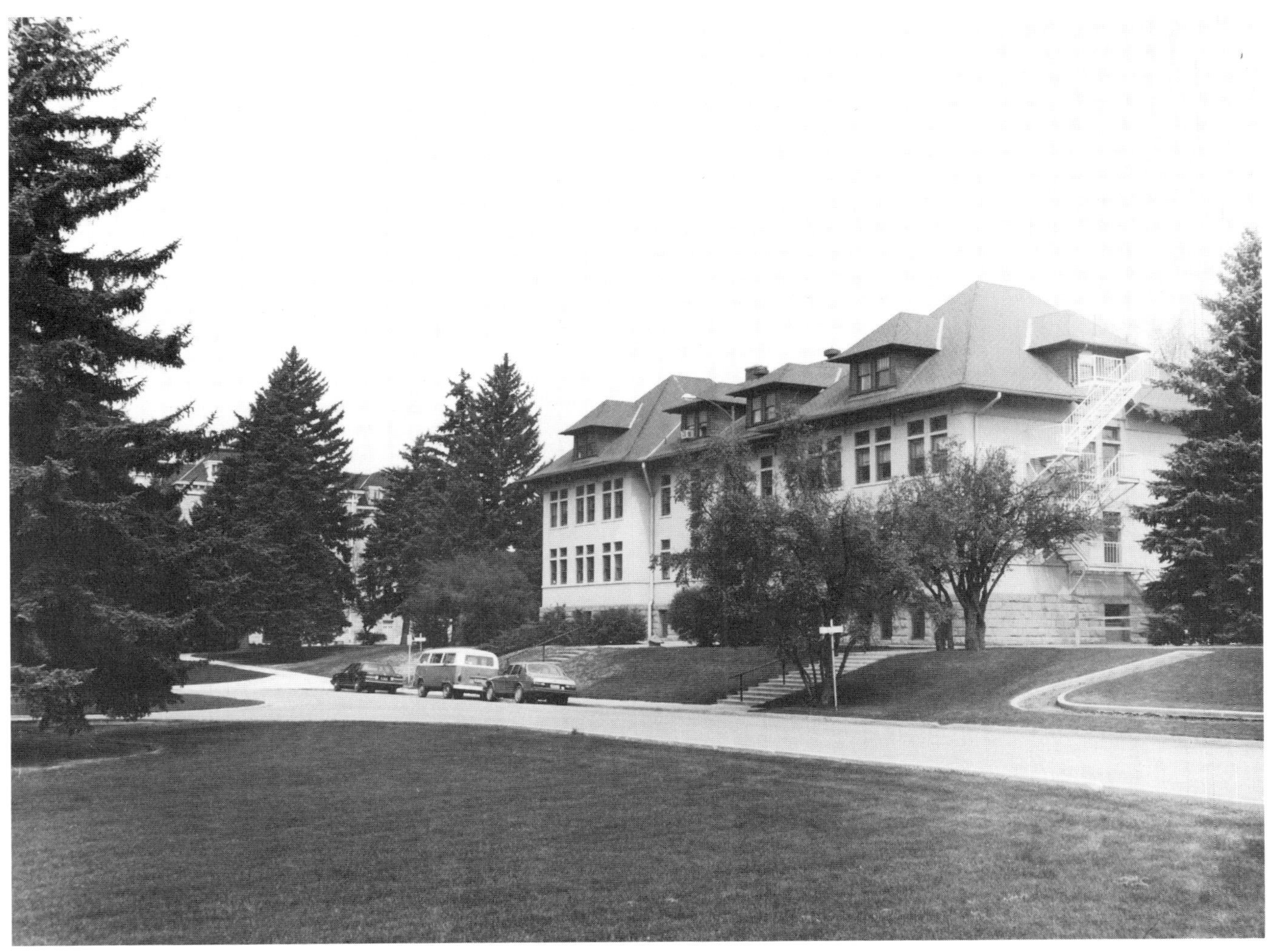

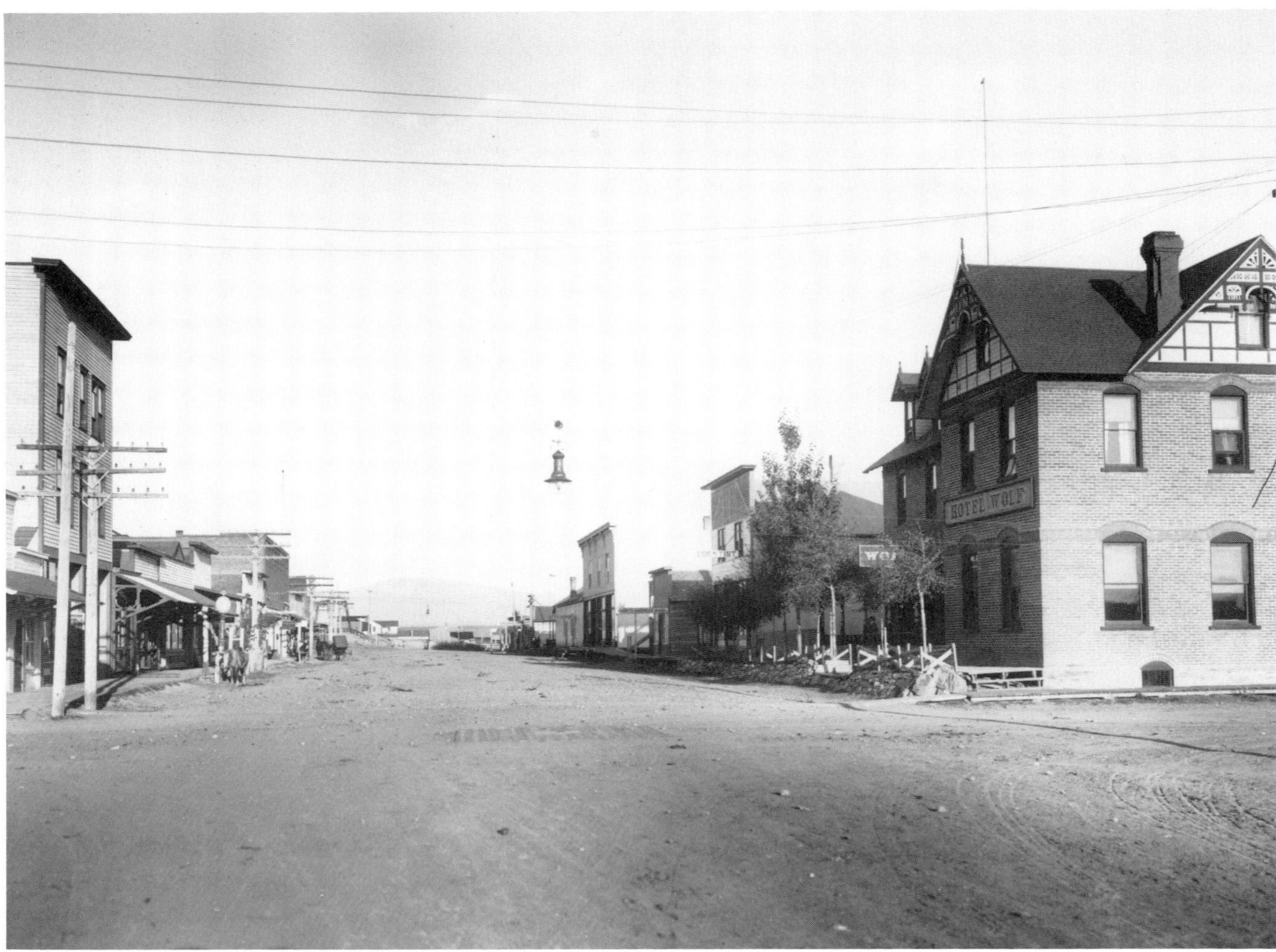

Fig. 64. Street scene, Saratoga, 1907.

With the exception of a few cars and a street lamp that has moved from a wire to a post, the town of Saratoga looks much the same as when Stimson visited in 1907. That same year the Saratoga and Encampment Railroad reached the town. The town was started in 1878 and named for another health spa, Saratoga Hot Springs, New York. The town's spring remains a popular spot with mineral bathers. The Hotel Wolf, built in 1894, remains in business today (at right).

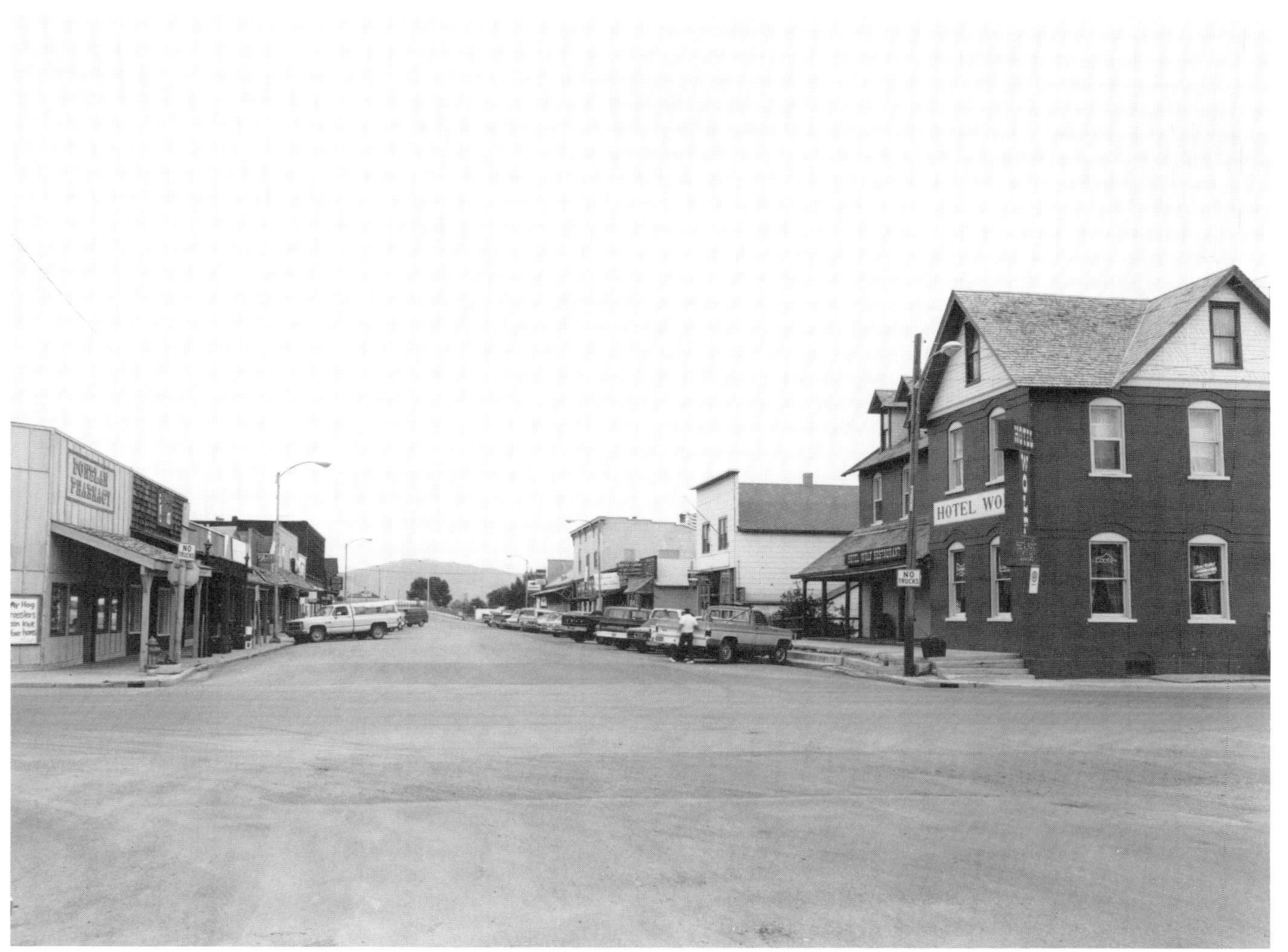
PHARMACY
HOTEL WO
NO TRUCKS

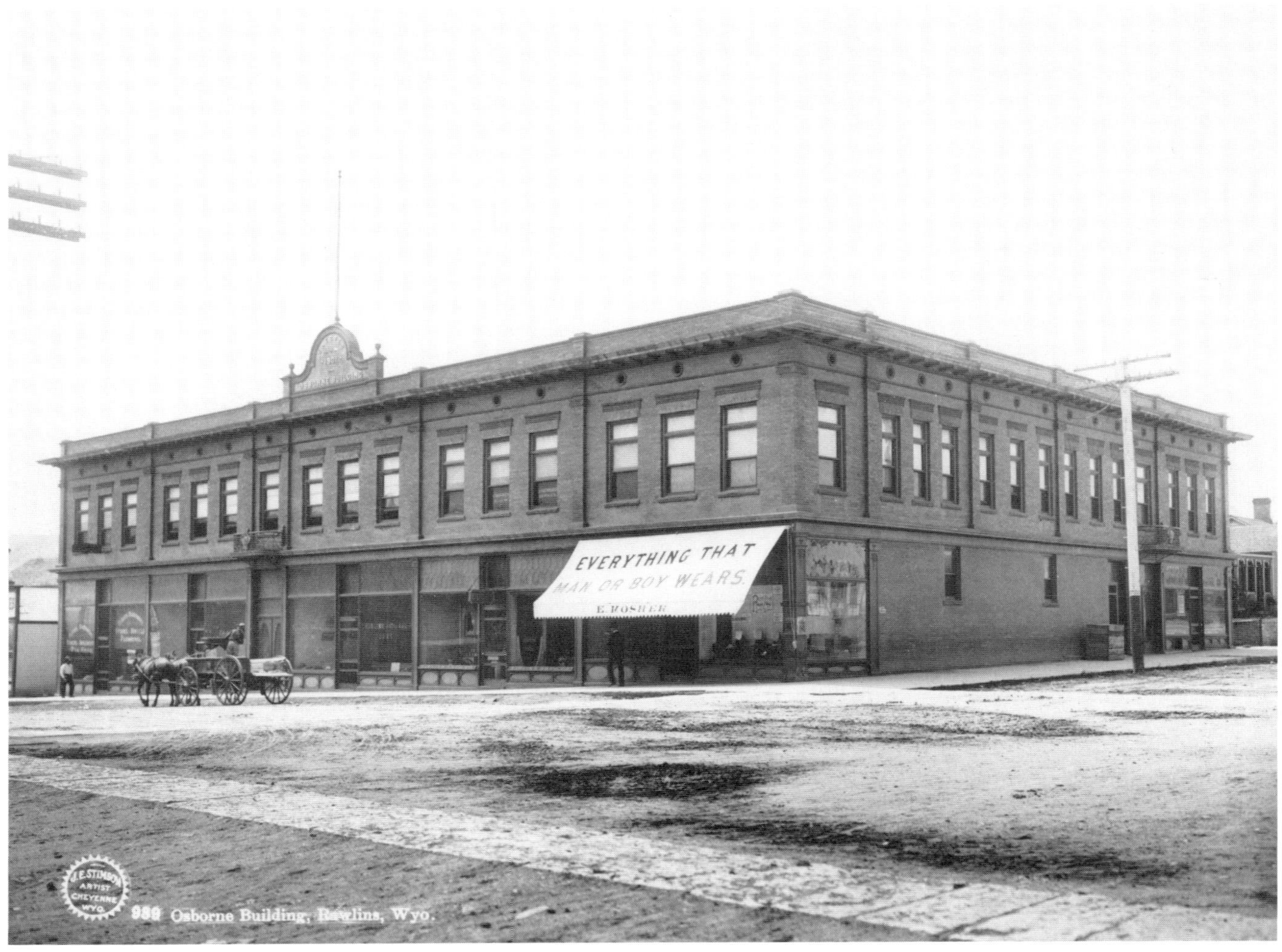

Fig. 65. Osborne Building, Rawlins, 1905.

This commercial block in downtown Rawlins was built in 1901 and named for prominent doctor John E. Osborne. Osborne was governor of Wyoming from 1892 to 1895. The flag pole seen in Stimson's photo remains.

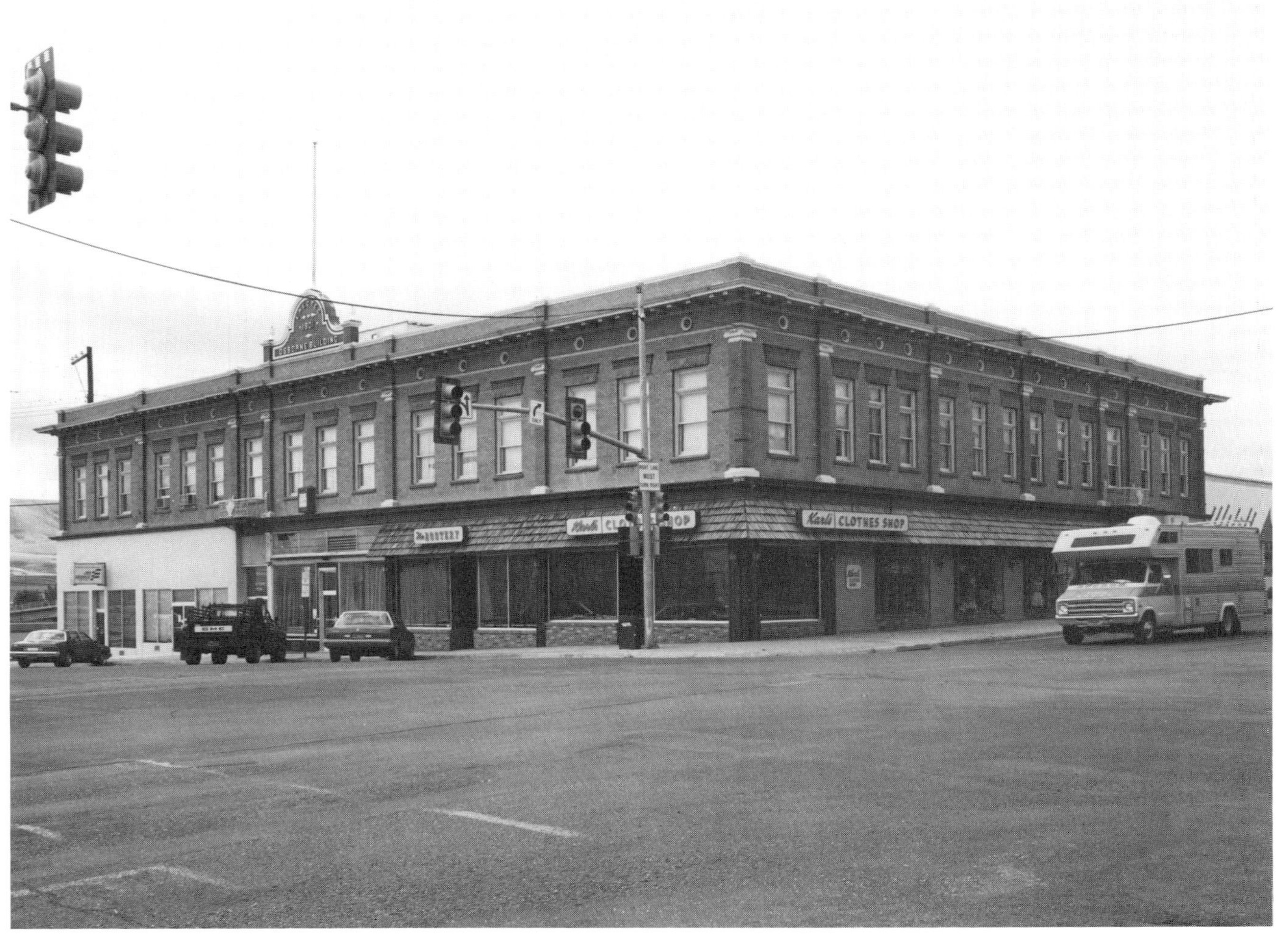
CLOTHES SHOP

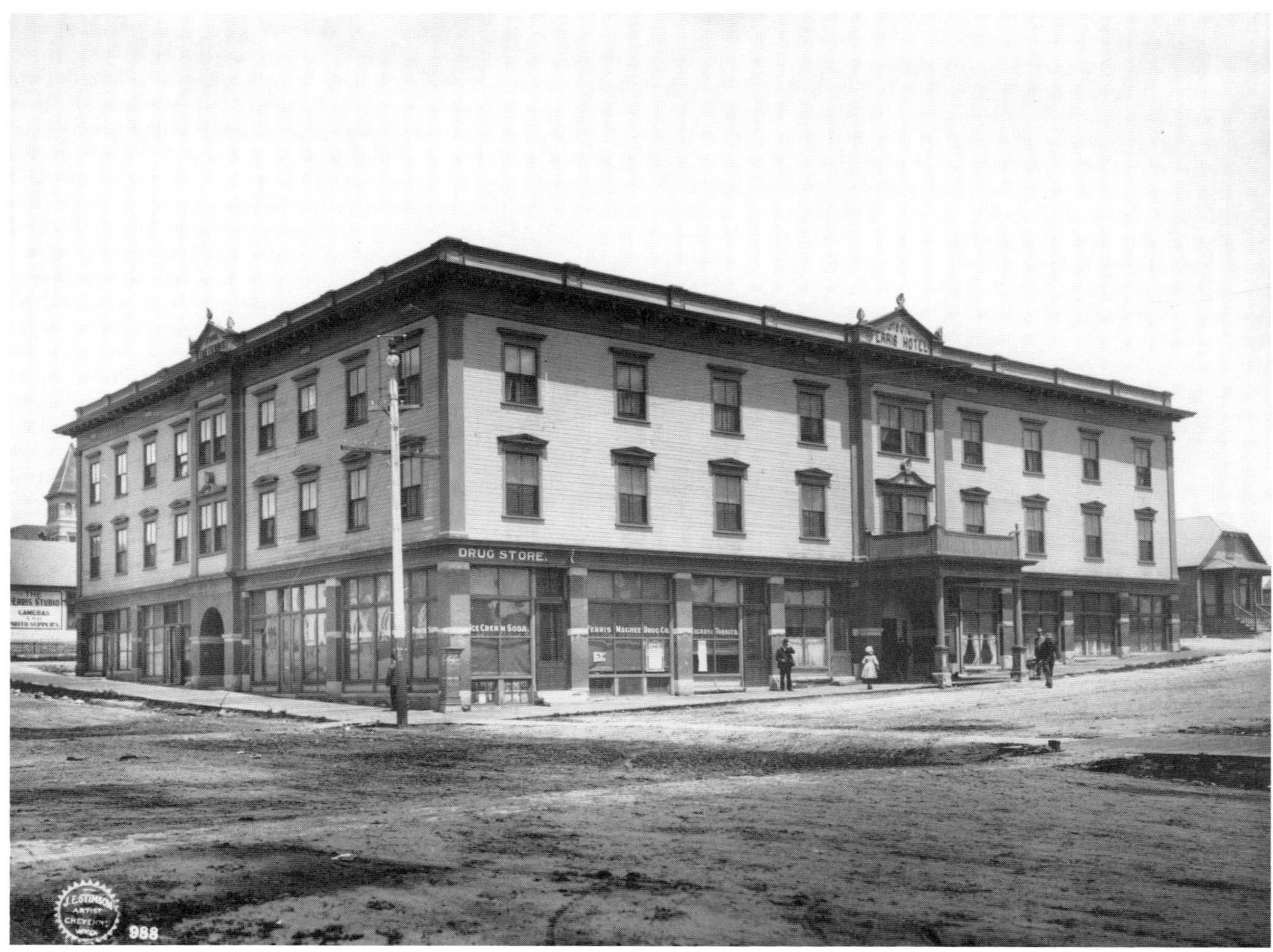

Fig. 66. The Ferris Hotel, Rawlins, 1905.

Named for the late copper-boomer George Ferris, this hotel was built in 1902. With its elaborate woodwork and shops, the Ferris first served as a railroad hotel. When the Lincoln Highway was routed through Rawlins, the Ferris became a popular stopover for motorists as well. In 1956 the entire exterior was remodeled with stucco. A large neon sign was placed on top of the hotel, and the second story porches were removed. The Ferris finally closed its doors in 1983.

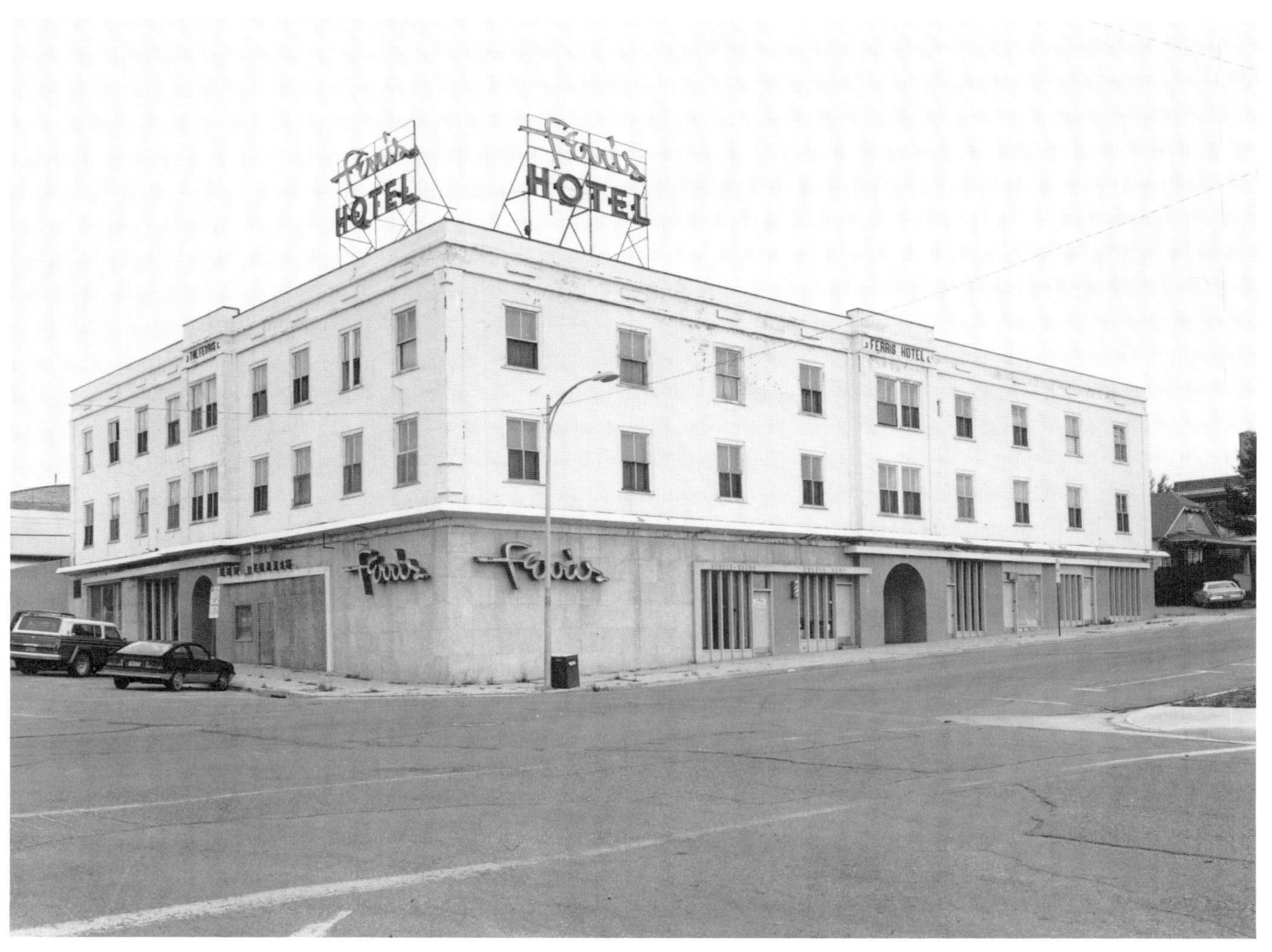
Ferris
HOTEL
Ferris
HOTEL
THE FERRIS
FERRIS HOTEL
Ferris
Ferris

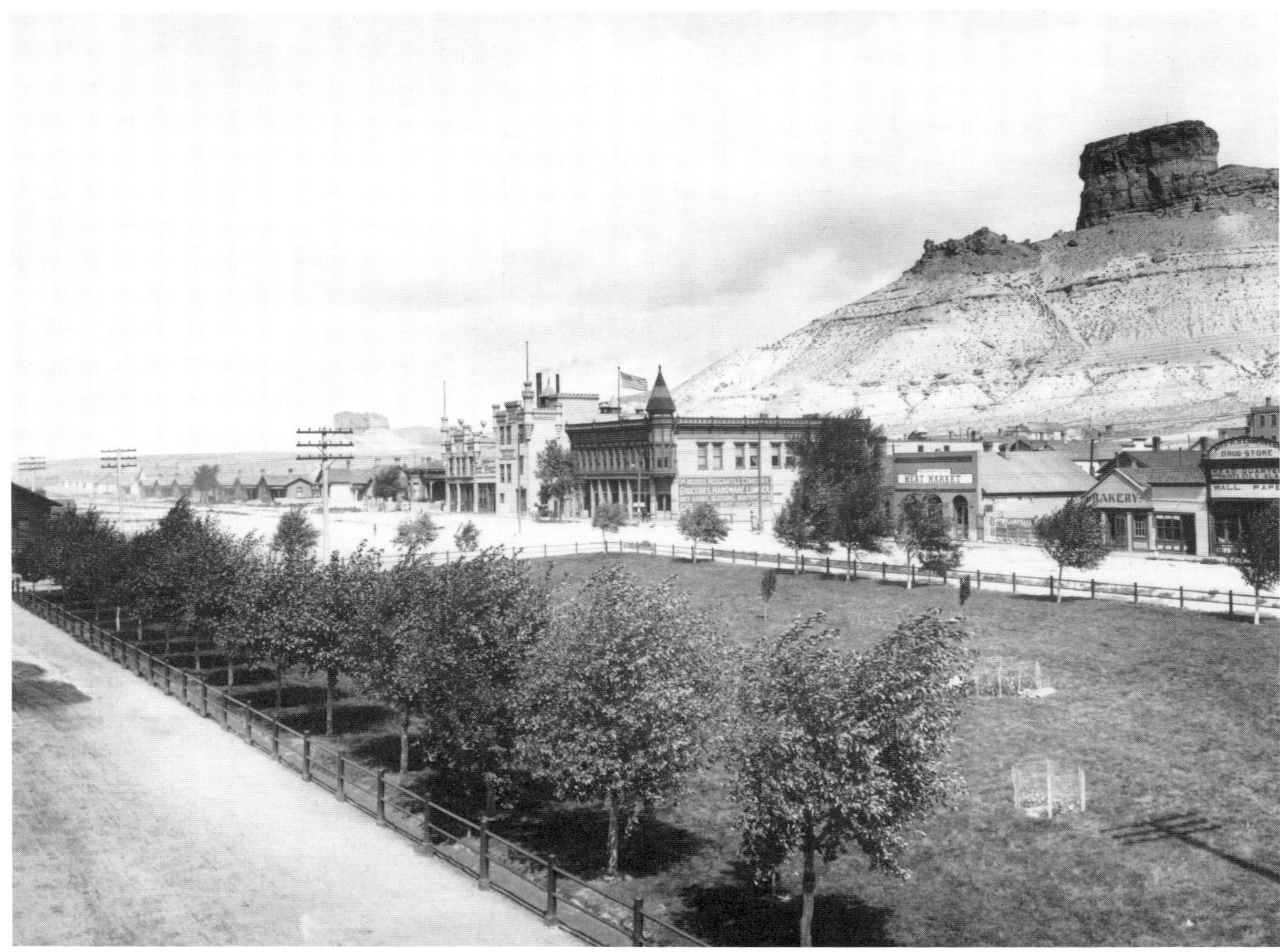

Fig. 67. Green River, from Union Pacific gate tower, 1903.

Castle Rock, rising one thousand feet above the town, dominates this view of the Union Pacific Depot park at Green River. Taken from a gate tower near the depot, Stimson's shot includes the spires and flag poles of the Sweetwater Brewery and the shops along Railroad Street. Because the gate tower no longer exists, the modern view was taken from a foot bridge near the old vantage point. The building in the center of the old photo burned down in the 1920s. Interstate 80 can be found along the base of Castle Rock.

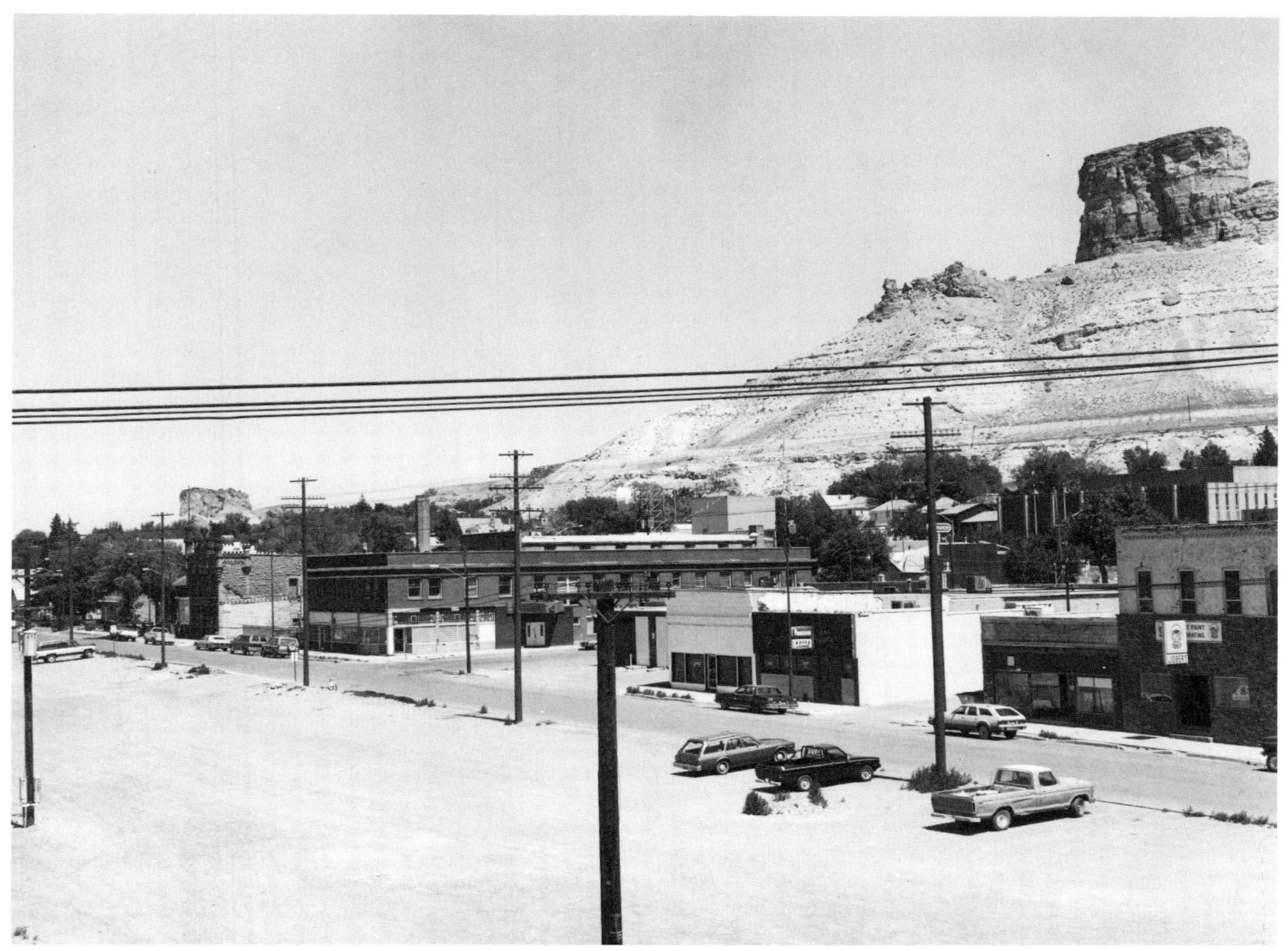

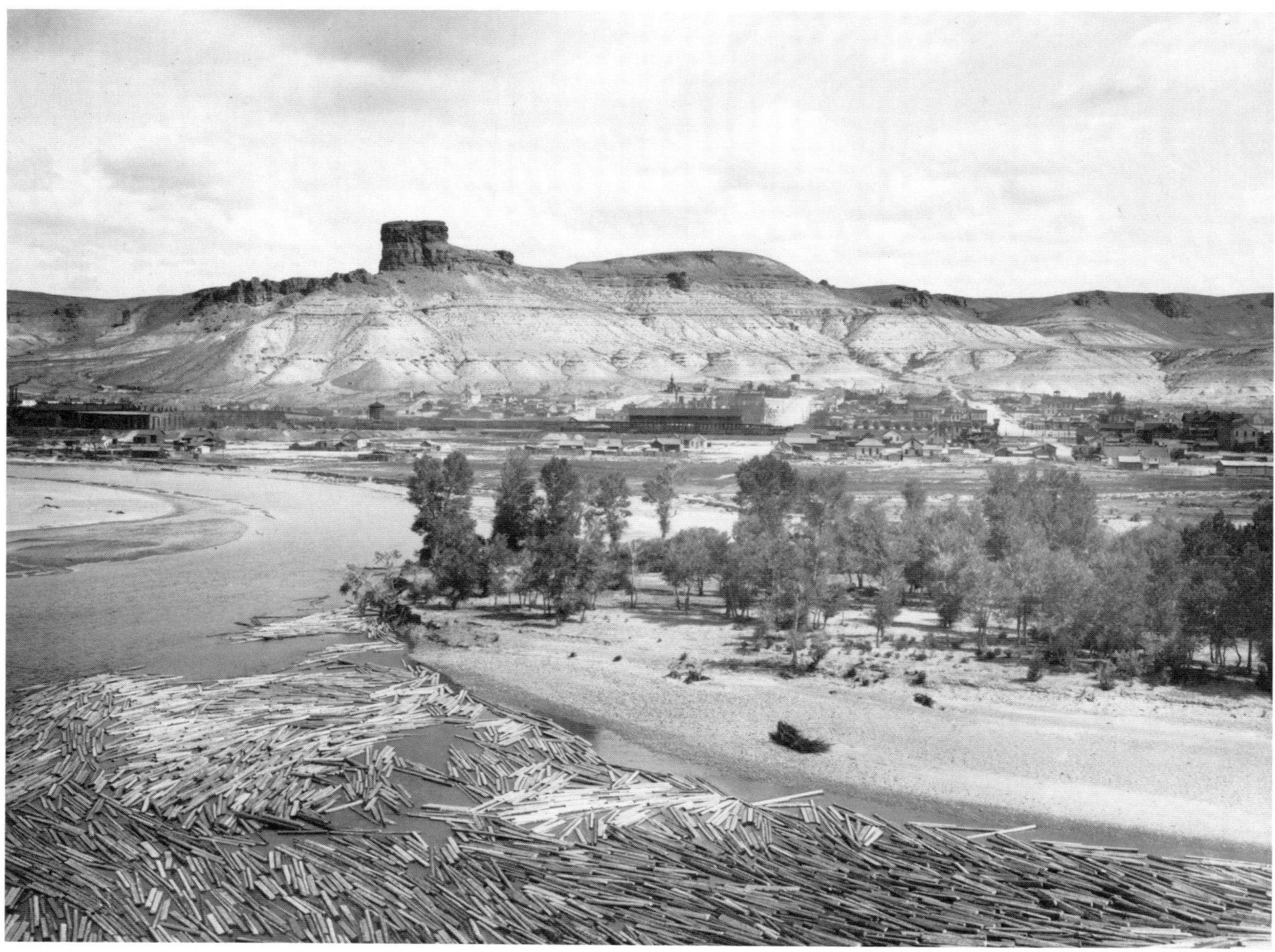

Fig. 68. Green River, 1903.

Overland Stage and Pony Express stations had both operated nearby in the early 1860s. When the Union Pacific built through in 1868, the town of Green River City was platted. In 1869 and 1871, Major John Wesley Powell departed from Expedition Island, foreground, to explore the Green and Colorado rivers.

Stimson's 1903 photograph shows a tie boom on the river. Ties were cut in the foothills of the Upper Green and then floated down the river in the spring. The ties were collected and treated before being used by the railroad.

The John Wesley Powell marker can be found on Expedition Island in the modern view. Interstate 80, along the base of Castle Rock, is visible in the modern photo. The patch of green on the hillside at right center is the Green River Cemetery.

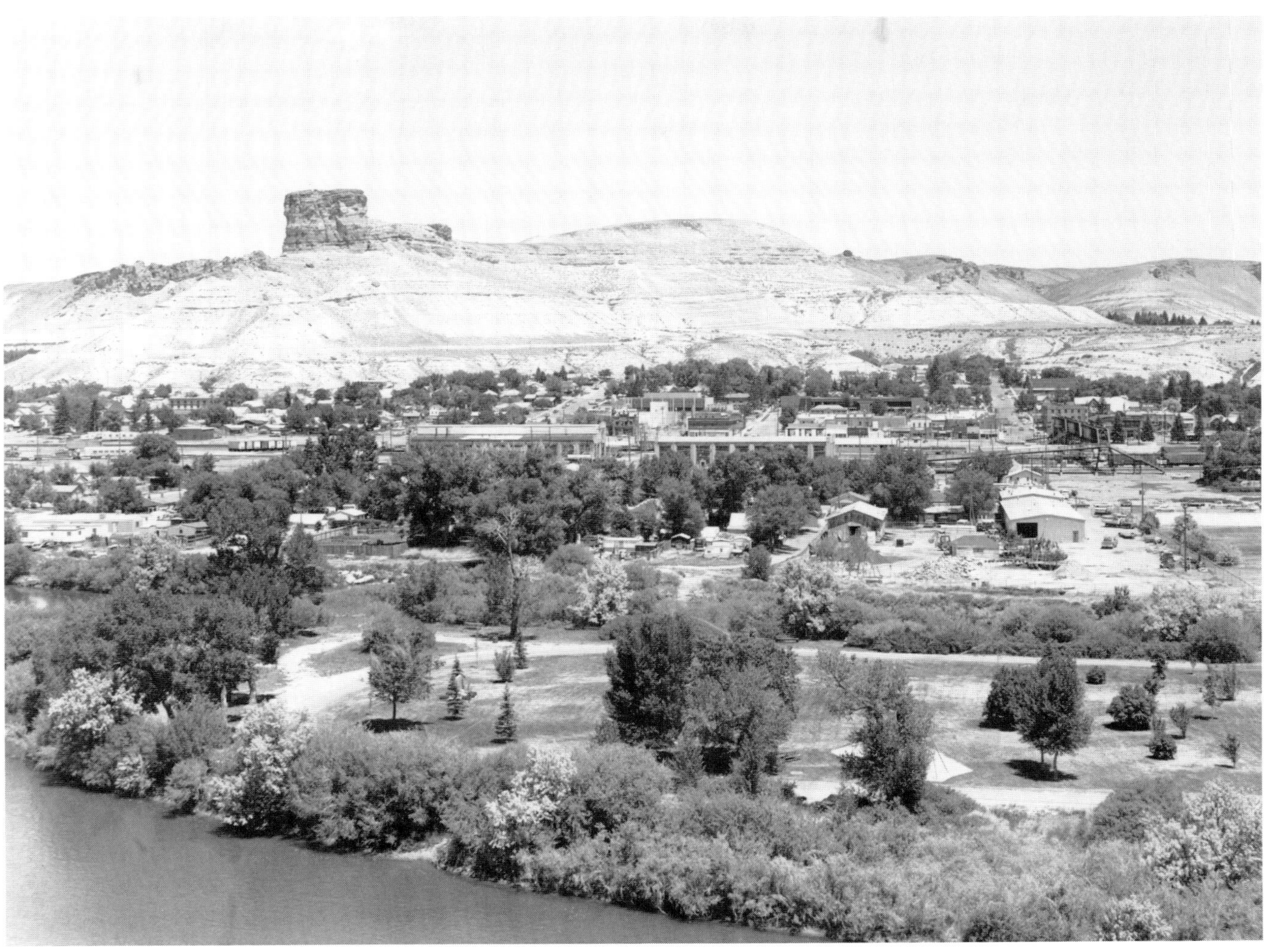

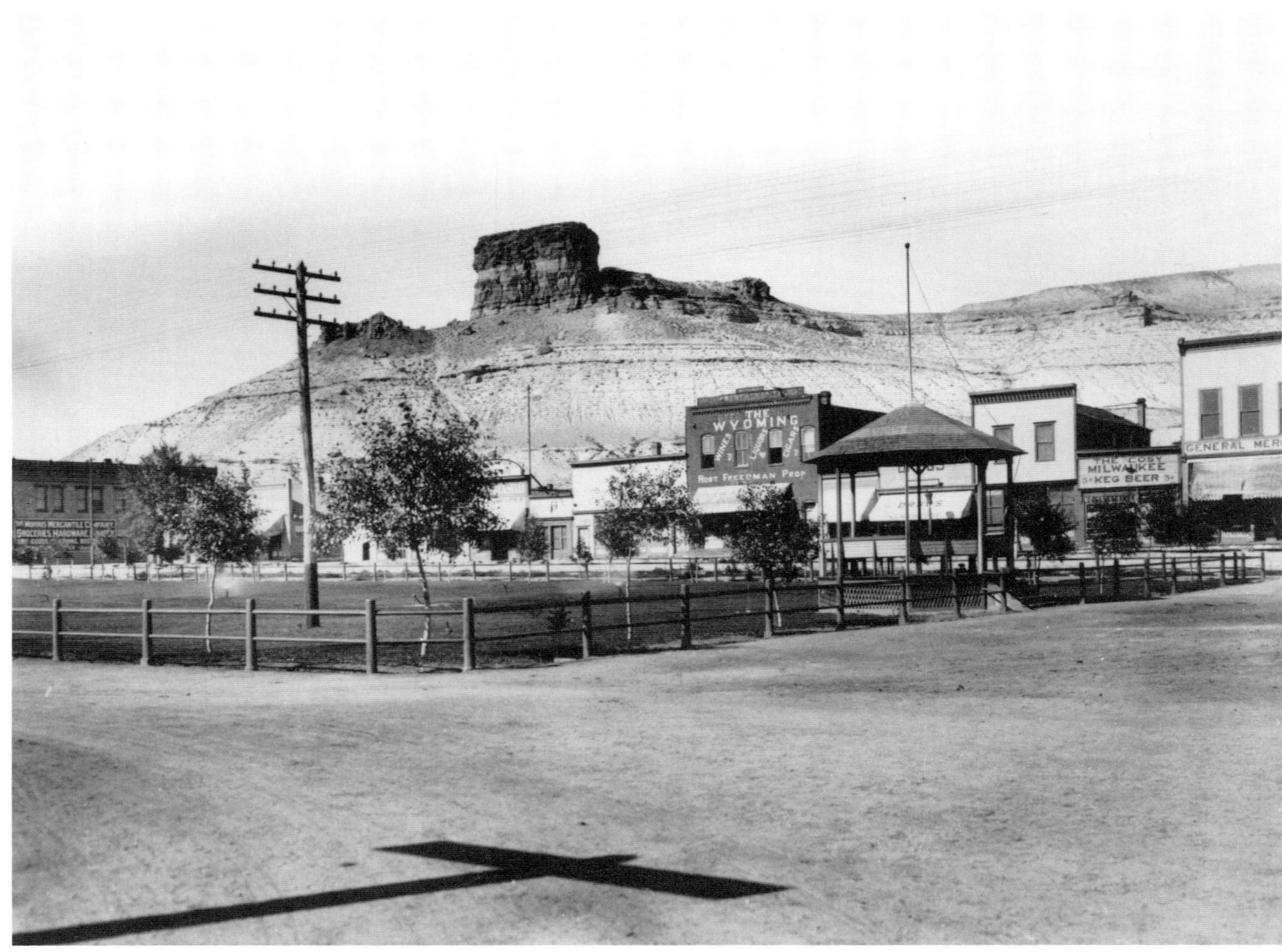

Fig. 69. Pilot Rock, Green River, 1903.

This early view of Green River City shows the depot park with its gazebo. The four-windowed "Wyoming" store and three-windowed "General Merchandise" store can still be seen in the modern view. The depot park, like most along the Union Pacific, is now a dusty parking lot.

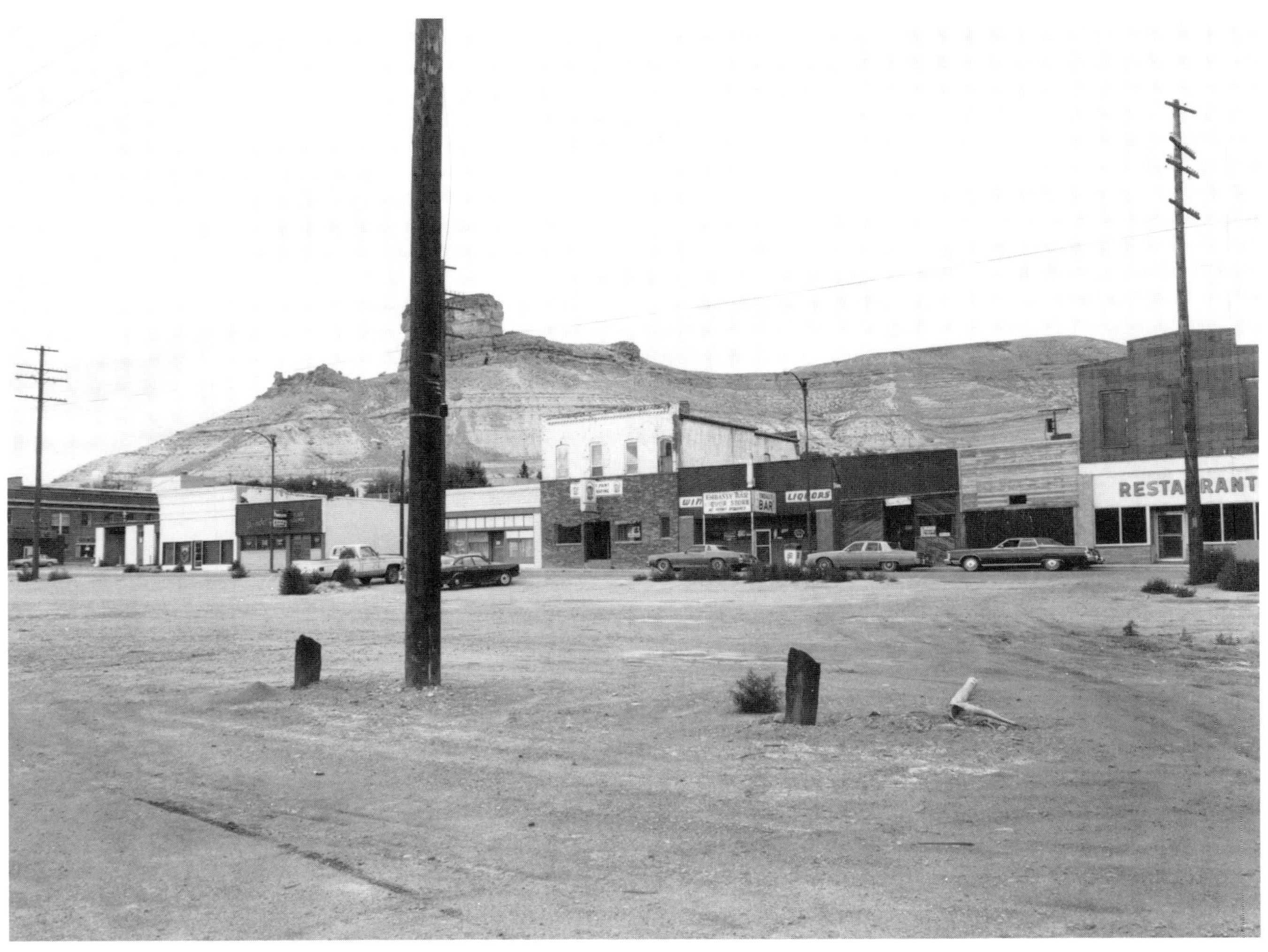
BAR
LIQUORS

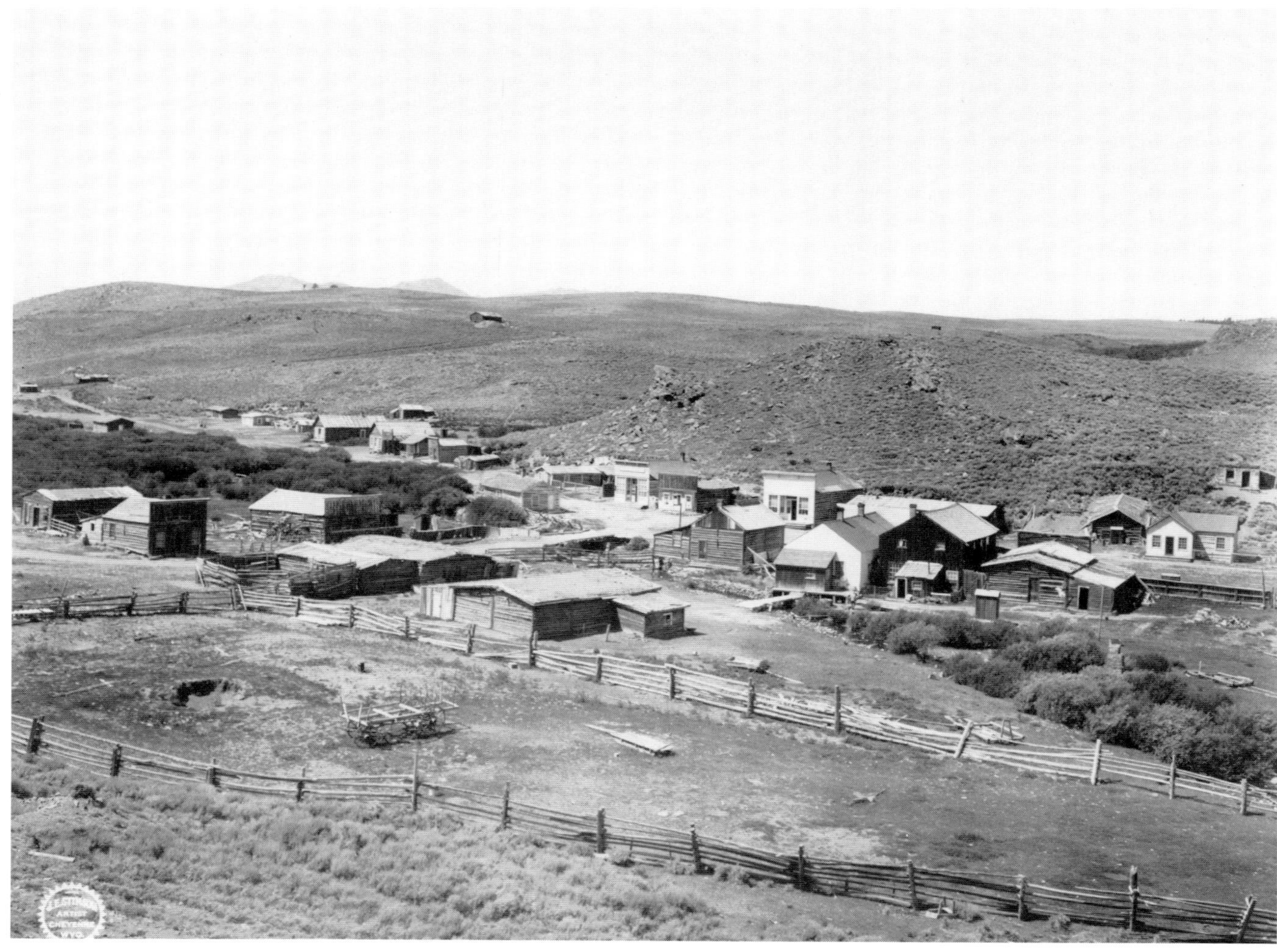

Fig. 70. South Pass City, 1903.

In the spring of 1867, a small party of discharged soldiers discovered paying quantities of gold in the South Pass region. The following year, the largest gold rush in Wyoming history brought several thousand prospectors, freighters, businessmen, and women to the community of South Pass City. In 1869 William Bright, a saloon keeper, mine owner, and representative from South Pass City, introduced a women's suffrage bill to the territorial legislature. The next year Esther Hobart Morris was appointed by county commissioners as the town's justice of the peace. She was the first female judge in the nation. In 1872 bust hit the Sweetwater mining district, and by 1875 less than one hundred people remained in the area. Successive, although smaller, booms have hit the area in the 1880s, 1890s, 1930s, and 1940s. In 1967 the Wyoming state government took over the care of the city as a state historic site.

Many of the town's oldest buildings survive from Stimson's view. At left foreground, the white false front of the Miner's Exchange Saloon, built in the 1880s, stands in front of the city jail, built in 1870. The livery stable, center foreground, was constructed in the 1890s. At center midground, the white face of the famous Carissa Saloon, built in the 1890s, can be seen. Across the street, the back of the two-story Sherlock Hotel, erected in 1868, also survives.

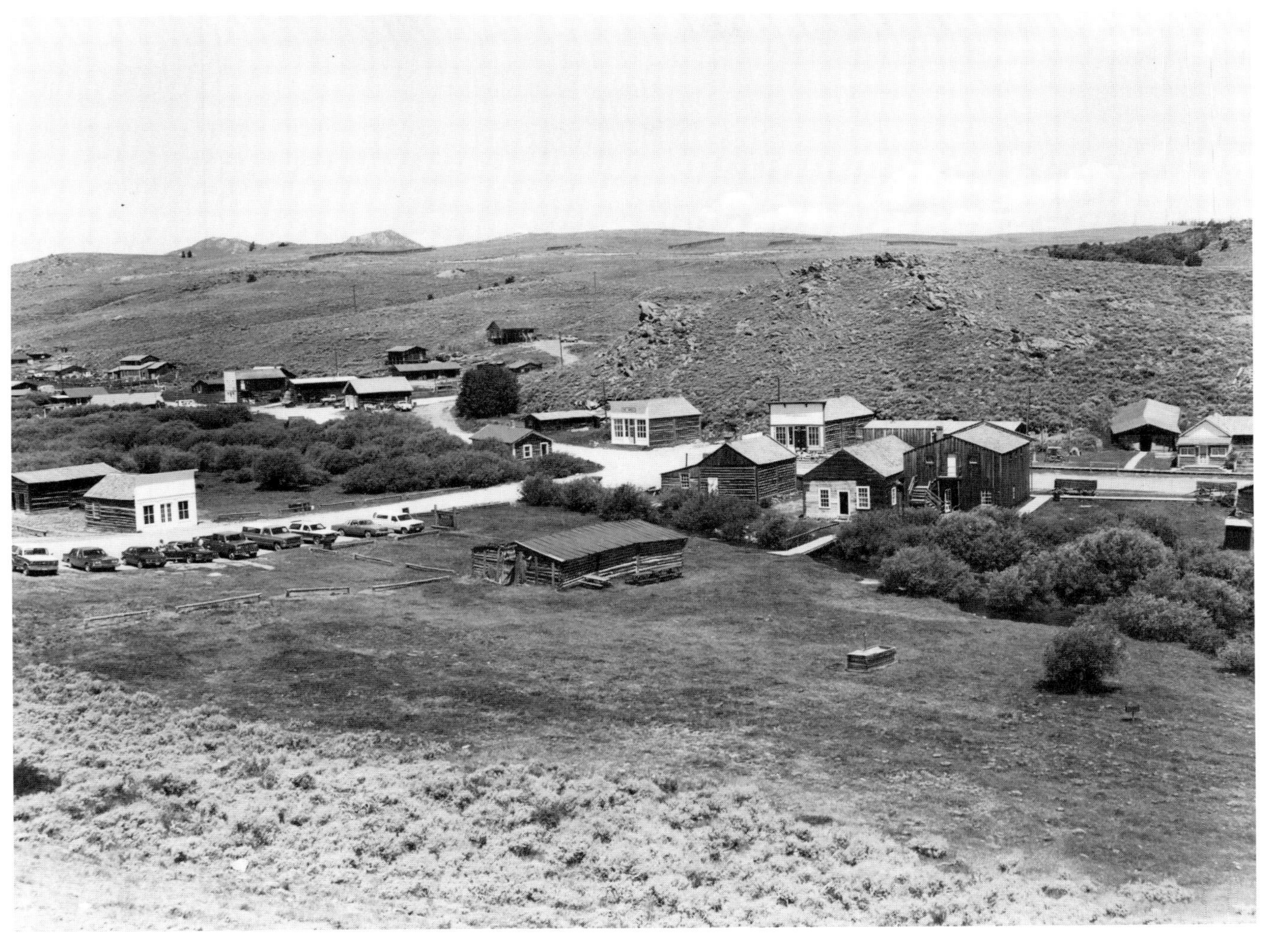

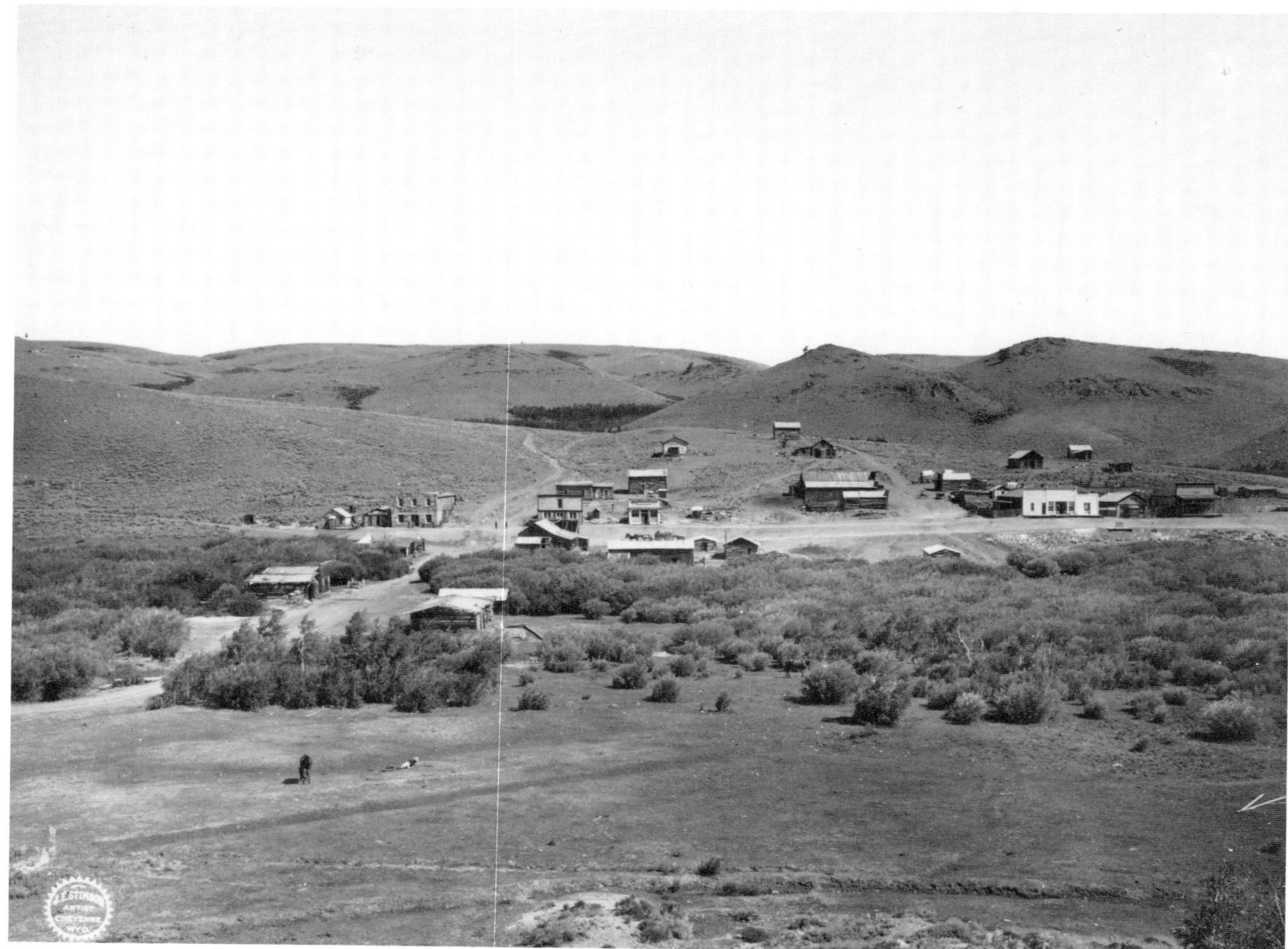

Fig. 71. Atlantic City, 1903.

Atlantic City was founded in 1868 by miners from South Pass City, four miles to the west. Its name is derived from the town's location on the Atlantic side of South Pass. In the 1870s the town had a population of more than two thousand, as well as an opera house and Wyoming's first brewery. The Atlantic City Mercantile, right center, opened in 1893 and is still in operation. At center left, the stone McCauley store remains, although without its top story.

A similar rephotograph of Stimson's view of Atlantic City can be found in Robert Redford's book, *The Outlaw Trail.* After completing my photograph and comparing it to Redford's view, I was puzzled. I knew that the old photo was Stimson's because of the man and horse in the foreground, but the modern views did not match. In Redford's view, the steepled church is to the right of the mercantile, but my view shows the church to the left of the mercantile. By pinpointing other buildings, I was able to determine that his photo had been printed backwards!

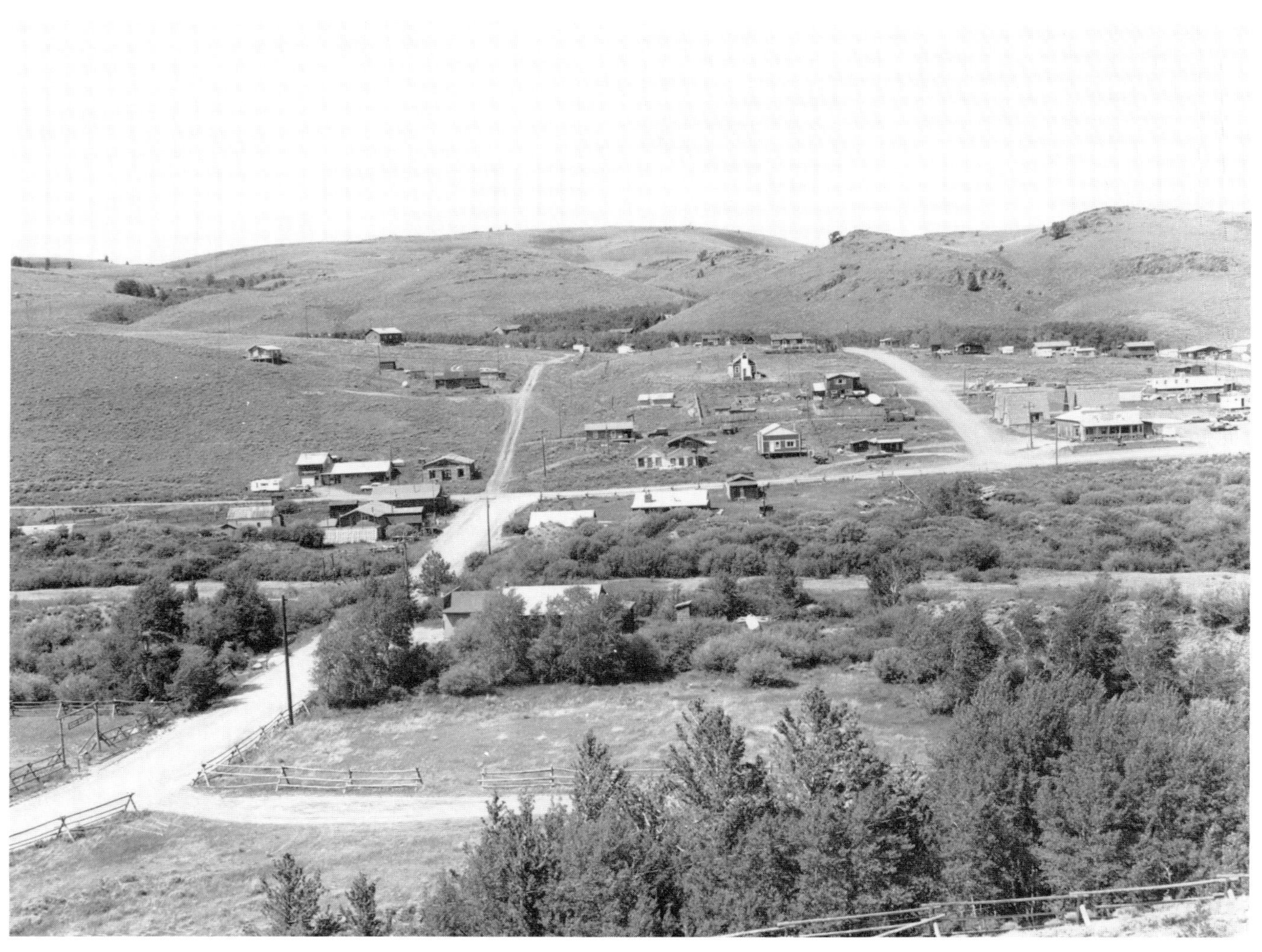

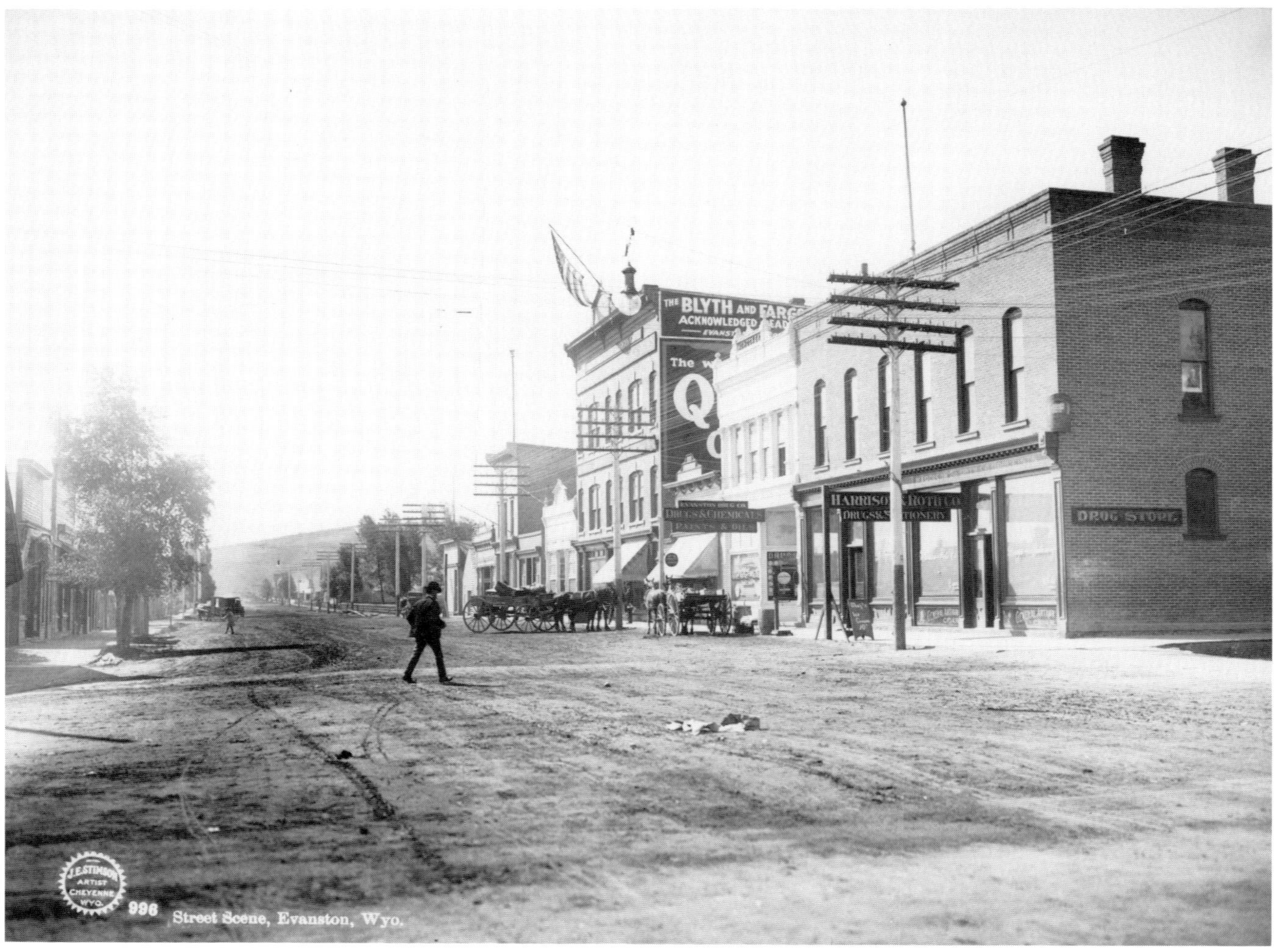

Fig. 72. Street scene, Evanston, 1905.

Signs dominate this view of Main Street in Evanston. Established in 1869 by the Union Pacific, Evanston was once home to a large Chinese population. The Blyth and Fargo Co., right center, advertises itself as dealers in drygoods, clothing, boots and shoes, furniture, hardware, stoves, and groceries. The two buildings to the right of the Blyth and Fargo were torn down in 1986.

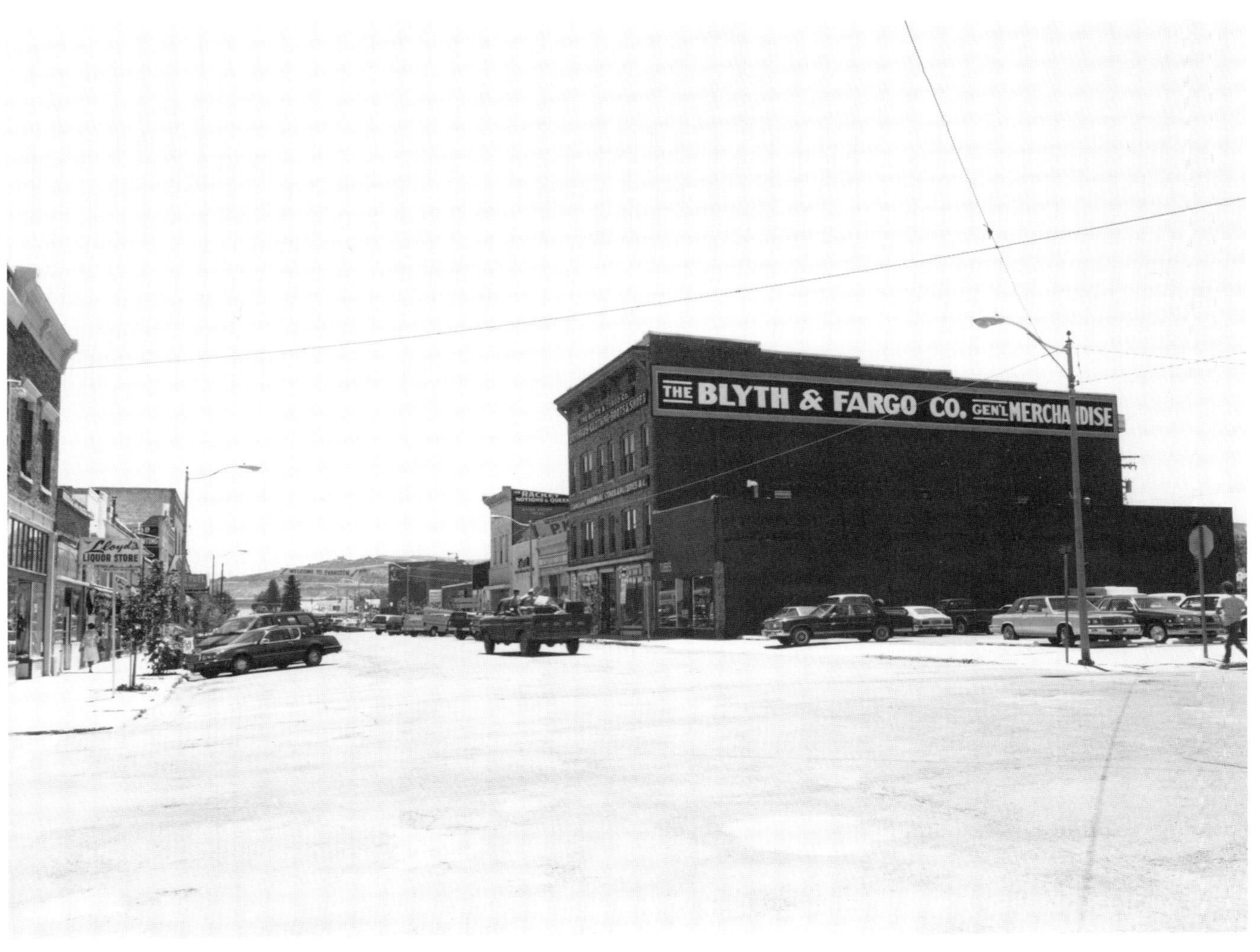
THE BLYTH & FARGO CO. GEN'L MERCHANDISE
Lloyd's
LIQUOR STORE

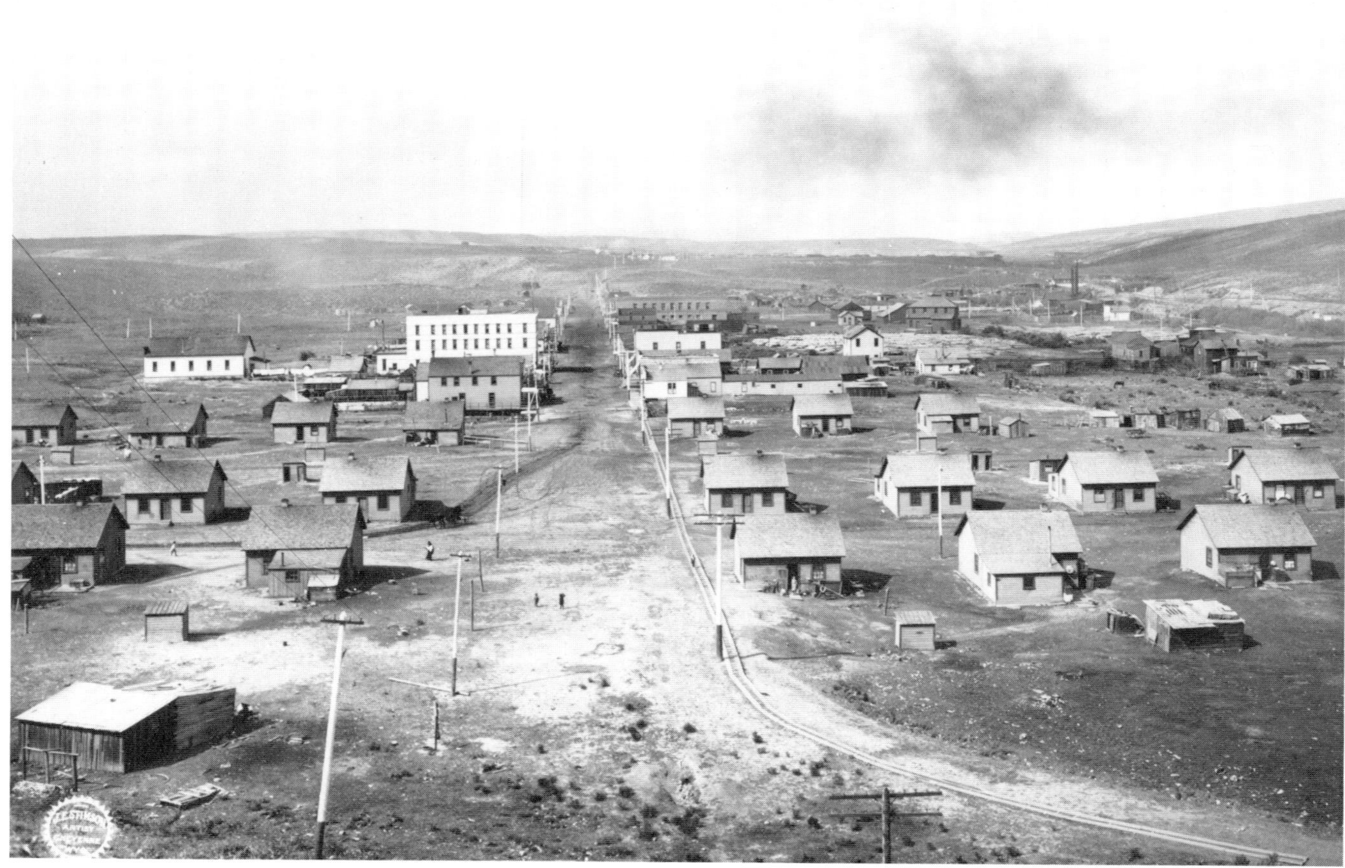

Fig. 73. Diamondville, 1903.

The steeply sloped roofs of miners' cabins can still be seen, amid additions and new siding, in this view of Diamondville. Owned by the Diamond Coal and Coke Company, the mines were first opened here in 1894 and by 1915 employed three thousand men. The Mountain Trading Company, one of the largest mercantile outfits in southwest Wyoming, was located in the large brick building on the right side of the street at center. Traces of the wooden sidewalk are visible at lower right, and the growth of Kemmerer can be seen on the horizon.

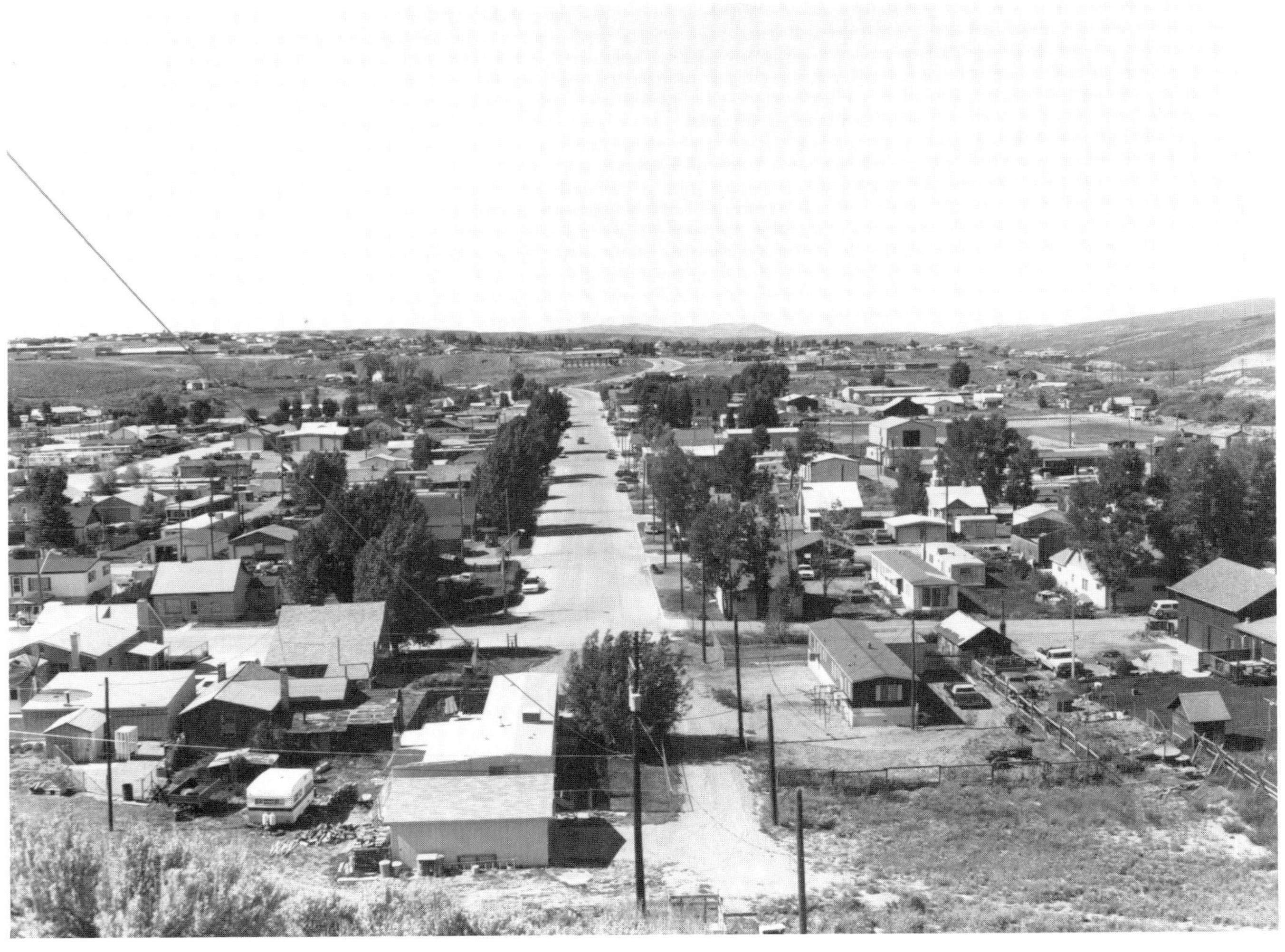

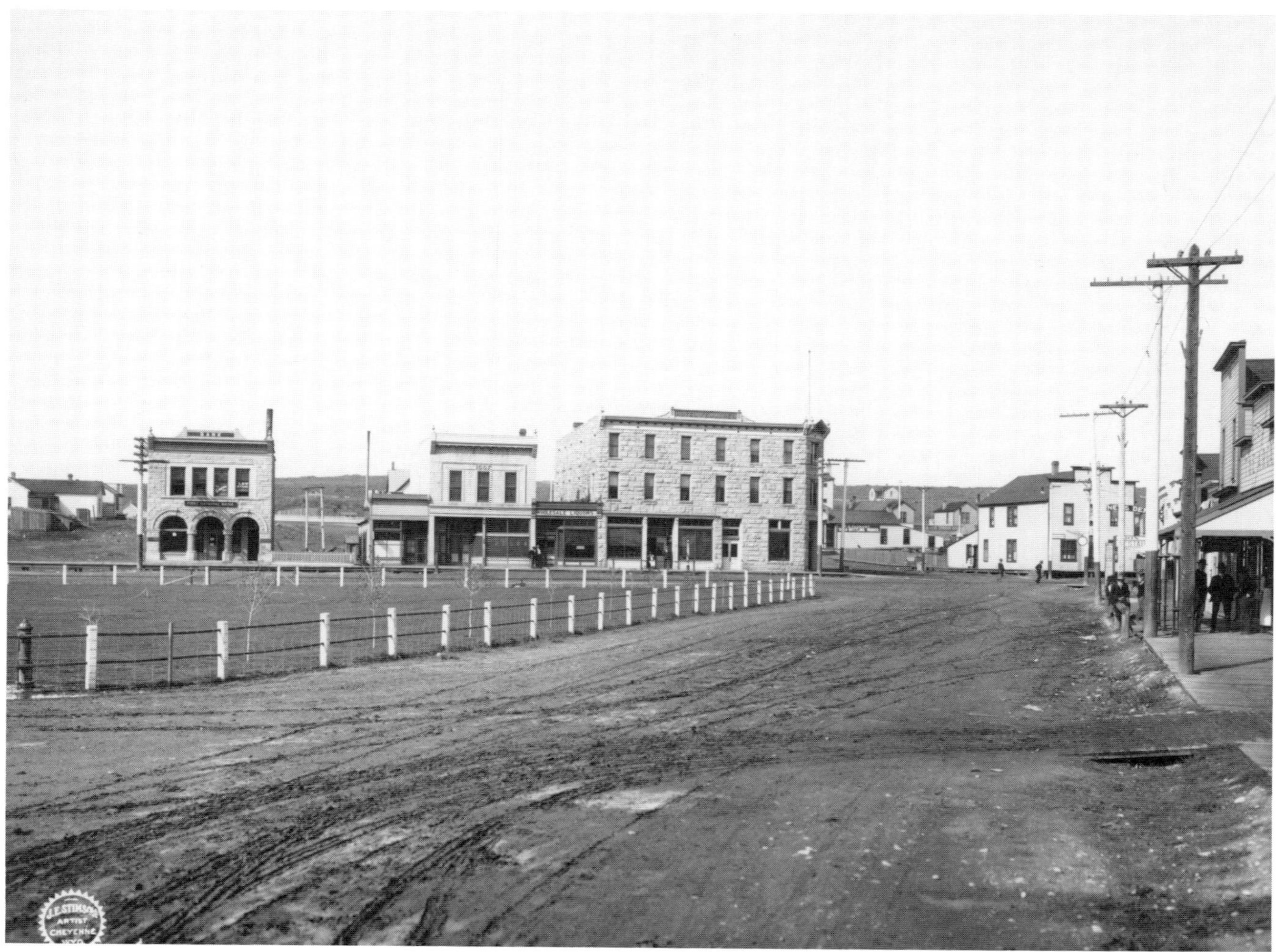

Fig. 74. Street scene, Kemmerer, 1903.

The Kemmerer Hotel, on the triangle in downtown Kemmerer, is one of the few surviving structures from Stimson's view of 1903. Kemmerer was established as an independent coal town by Patrick J. Quealy in 1897. Five years later J. C. Penney opened his first store, The Golden Rule, on a cash-only basis. The trees at left have grown substantially since Stimson's photo was taken.

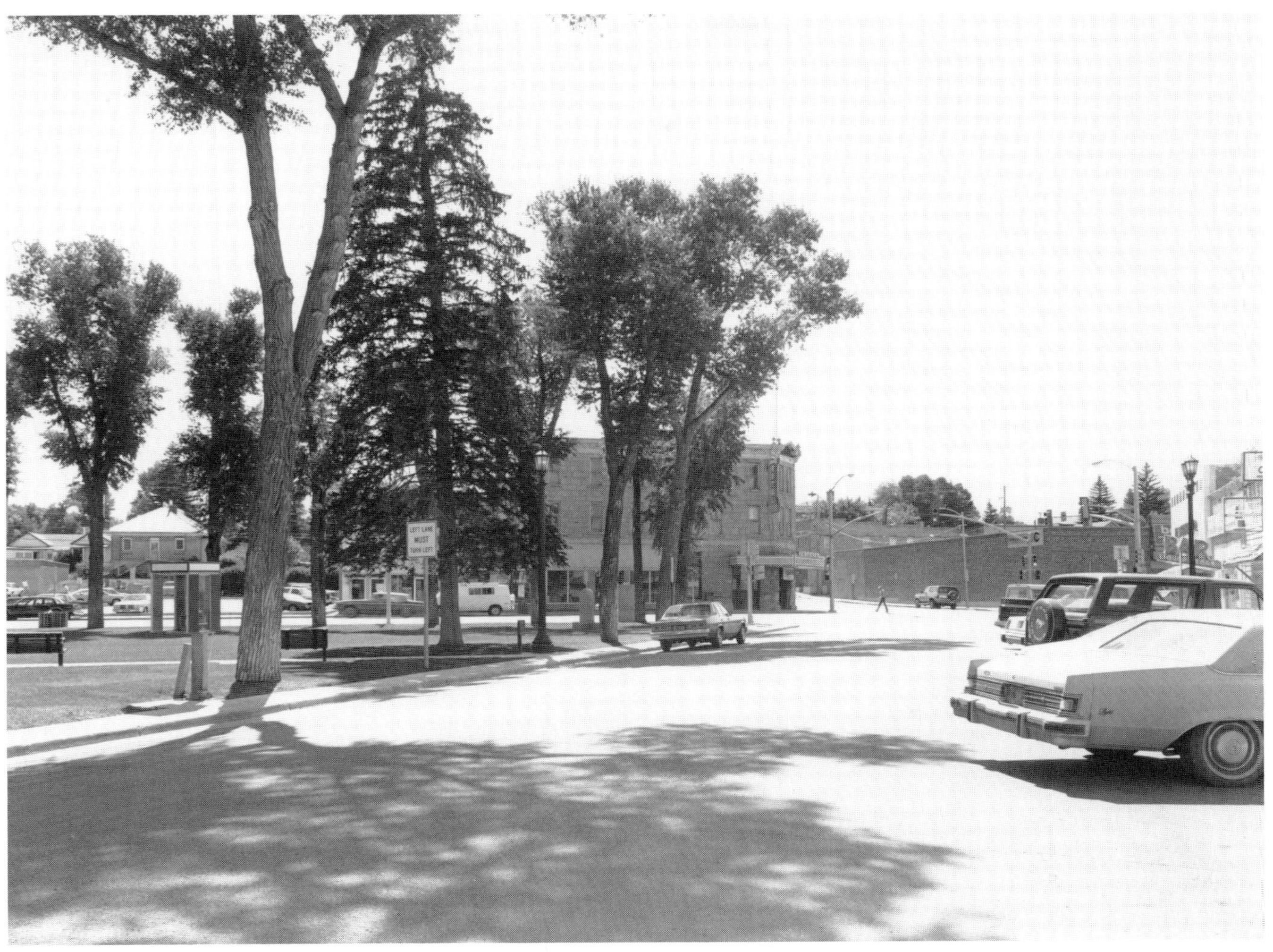
LEFT LANE
MUST
TURN LEFT

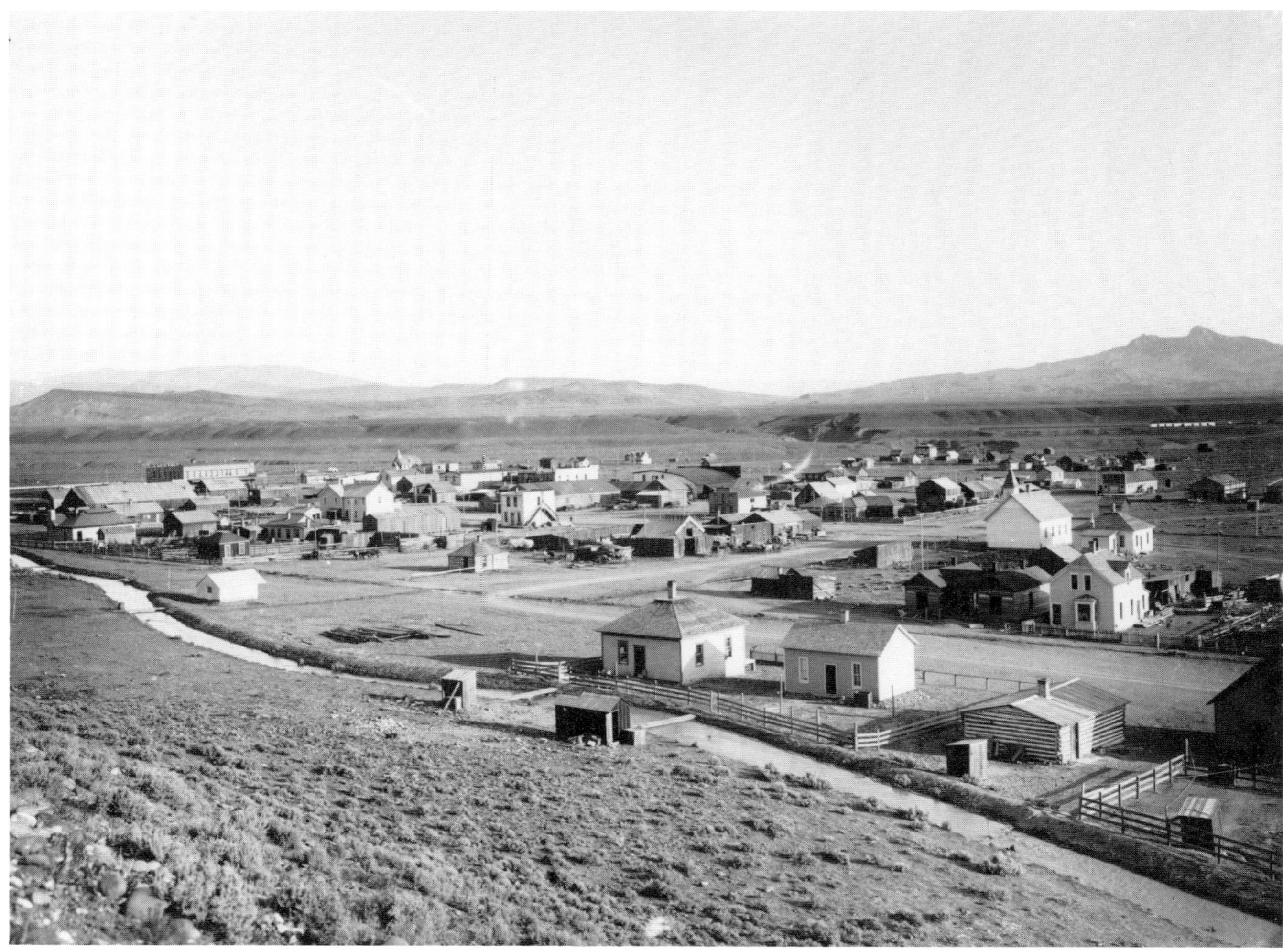

Fig. 75. Bird's-eye view of Cody, 1903.

The town of Cody, named for its famous promoter, William F. "Buffalo Bill" Cody, was platted by George T. Beck in 1895 and incorporated six years later. The Burlington Railroad reached the town in 1901. Eight years later Cody was named the seat of newly created Park County.

Through the years Cody has served as a shipping point for a local irrigation project as well as the east gateway for Yellowstone National Park. Today it is also the home of the Buffalo Bill Museum and Whitney Gallery of Western Art.

This view, looking north toward Heart Mountain (right horizon), shows that several houses, right center, survive from Stimson's photo.

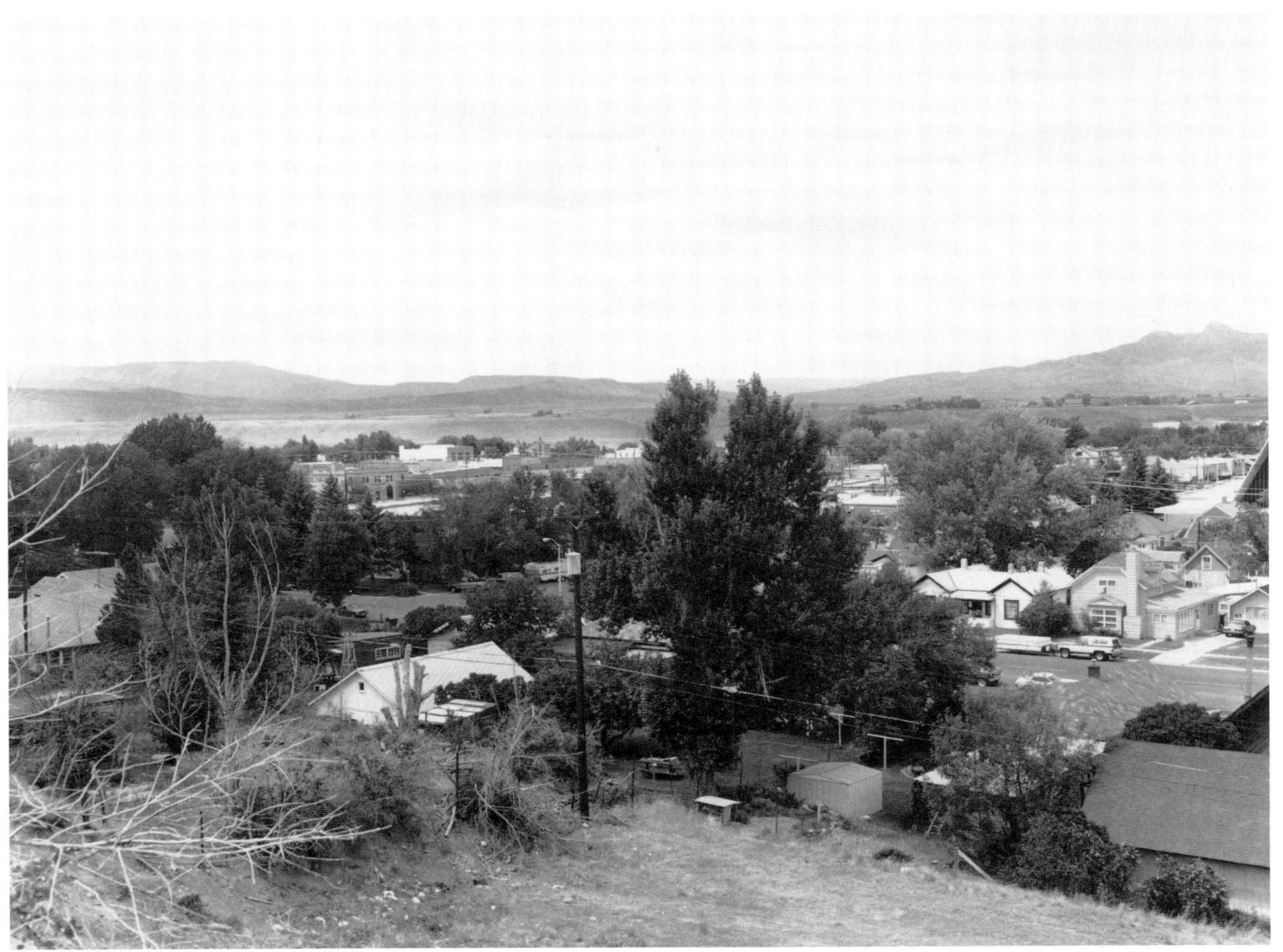

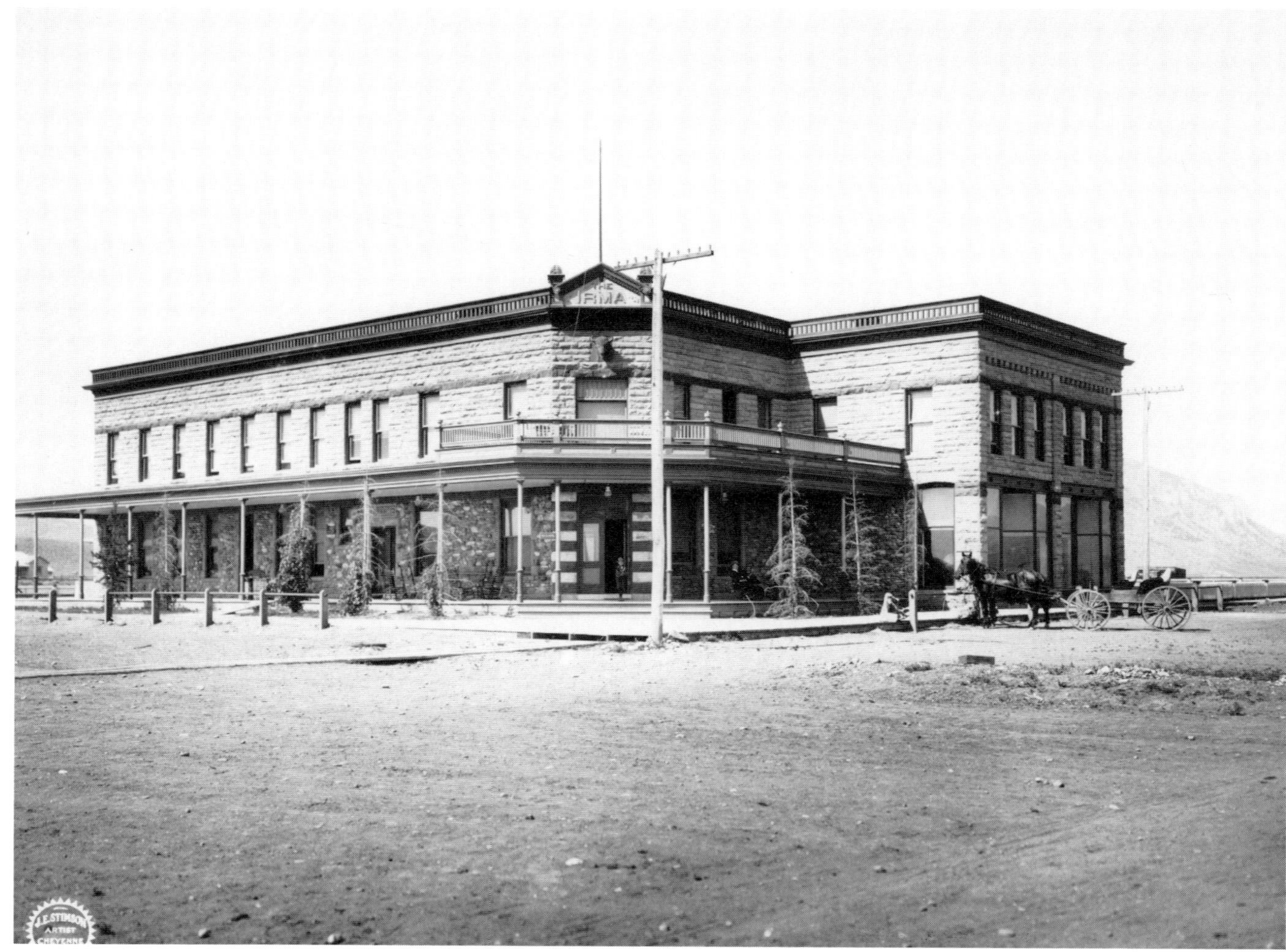

Fig. 76. Irma Hotel, Cody, 1903.

The Irma Hotel, named for Buffalo Bill's daughter Irma Cody Garlow, was built in 1902. The Irma was one of four businesses that Cody built near the town of Cody to promote it as a stopover for travelers on their way to Yellowstone National Park.

The Irma looks much the same as it did in 1903. The buffalo head below the flag pole remains, as does the porch. A small addition at right center and a few signs are also visible.

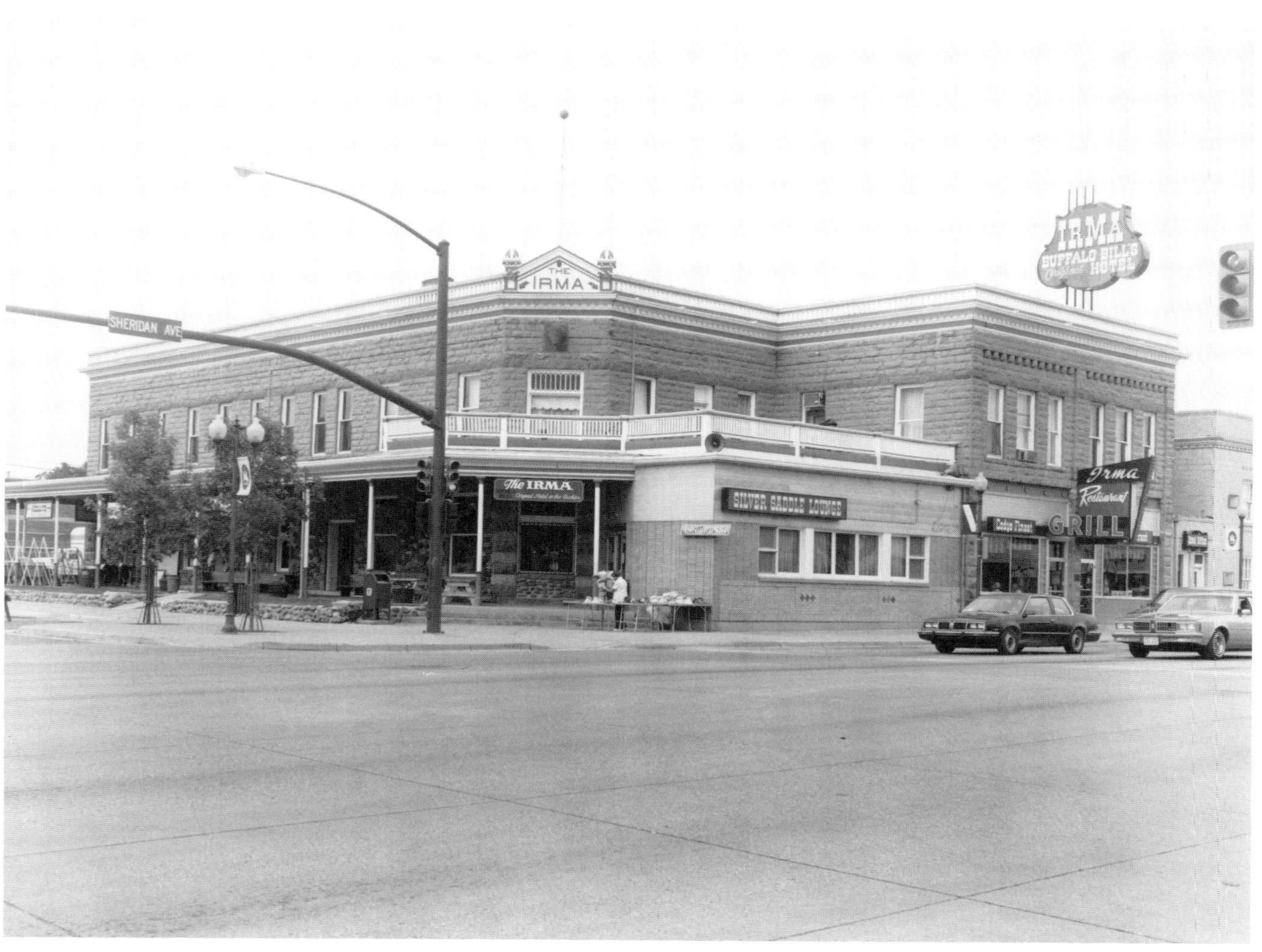
IRMA
BUFFALO BILL'S
HOTEL
THE
IRMA
SHERIDAN AVE
The IRMA
SILVER SADDLE LOUNGE
Irma
Restaurant
GRILL

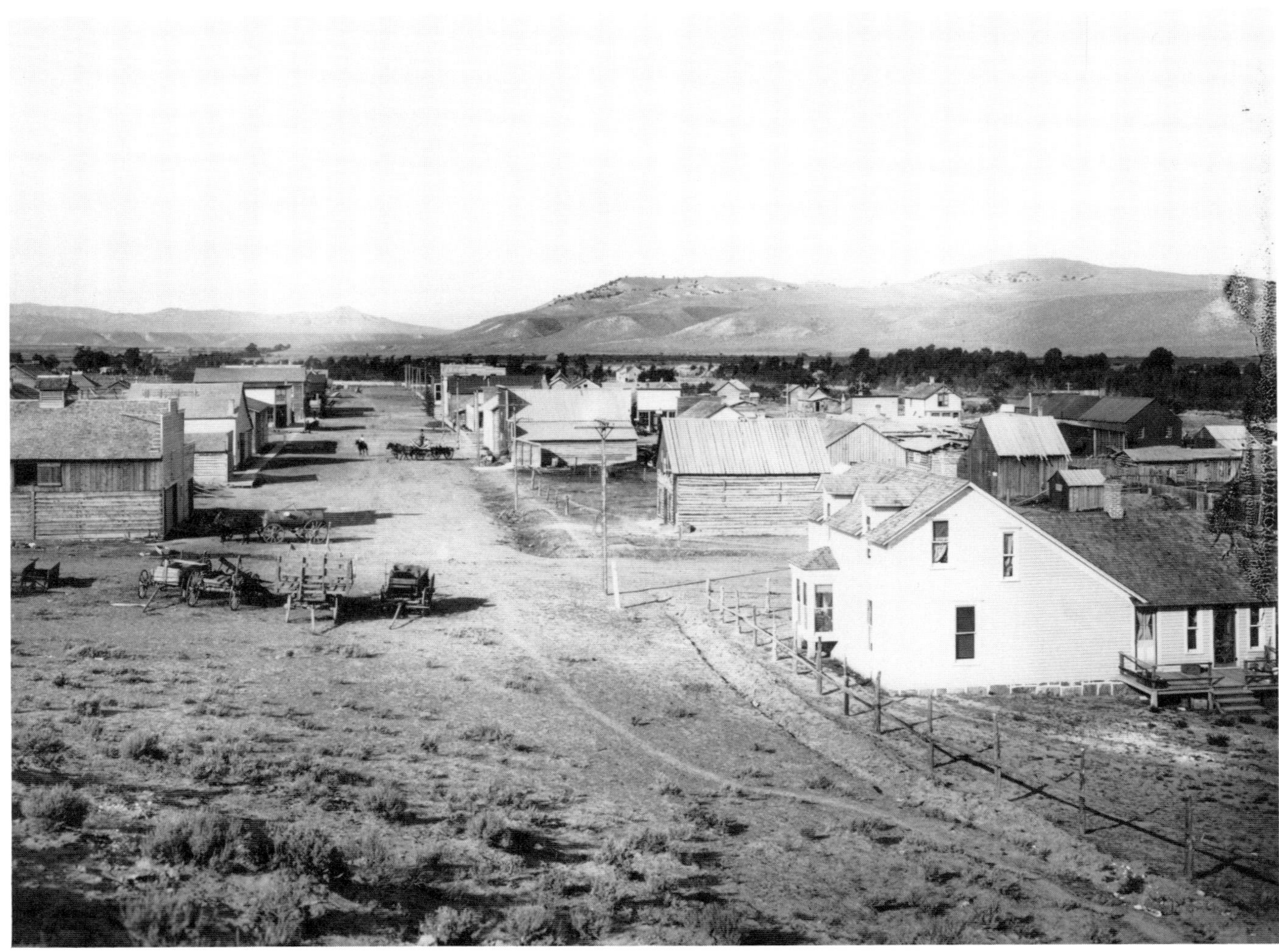

Fig. 77. Meeteetse City, 1903.

Today Meeteetse City has dropped the "City" from its name and is best known as the last home of the black-footed ferret. The town was started in 1881 on the banks of Meeteetse Creek but then moved in 1893 to its present site on the Greybull River. This view is looking west, with Wyoming Highway 120 running left to right one block to the west.

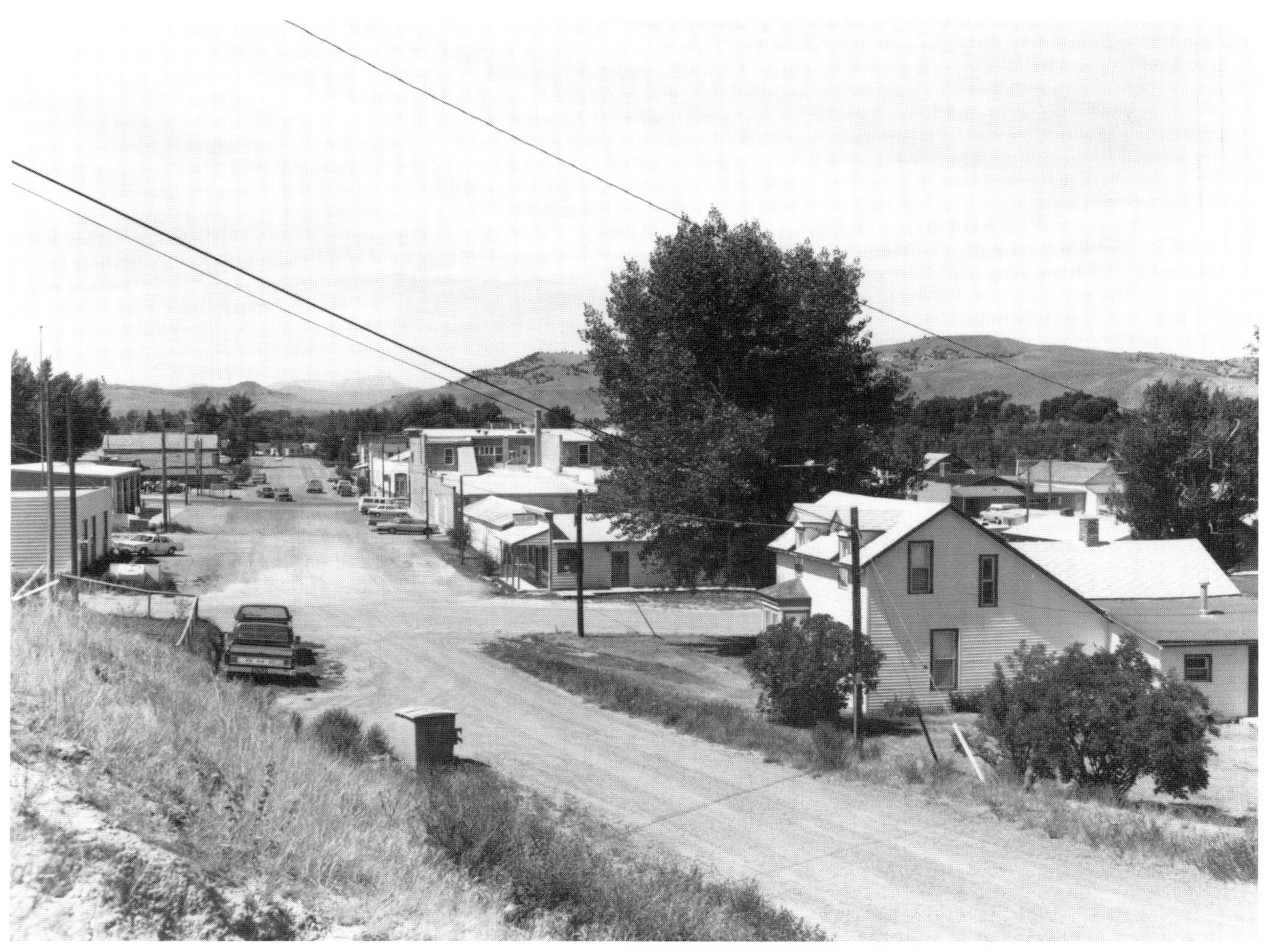

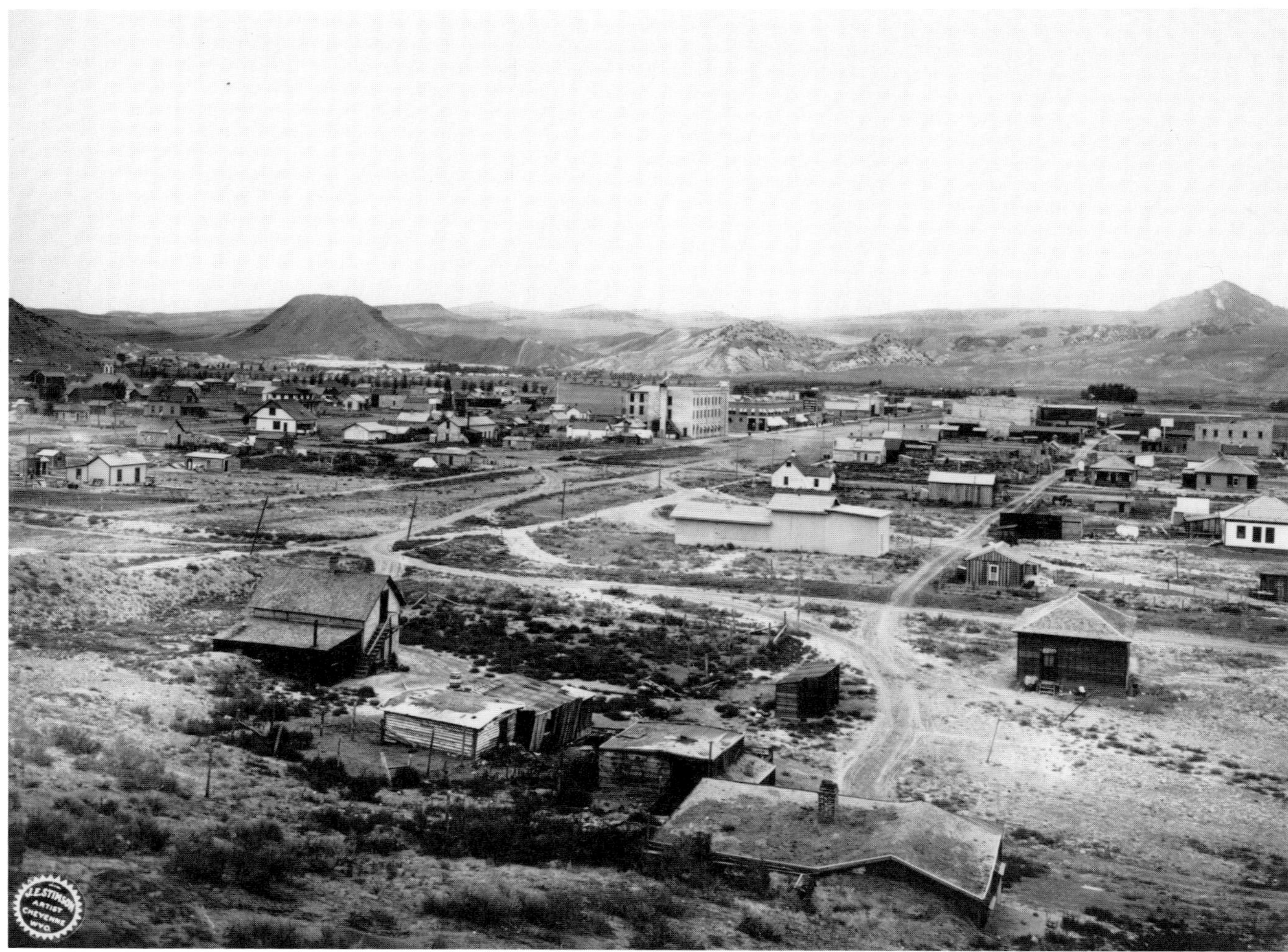

Fig. 78. Bird's-eye view of Thermopolis, 1910.

Located at the base of the world's largest hot spring, the town of Thermopolis was platted in 1897, after a treaty with the Indians of the nearby Wind River Reservation ceded the land to Wyoming. The name Thermopolis is a combination of the Latin word *thermae* (hot bath or spring) and the Greek word *polis* (city). In 1913 the town became the seat of newly created Hot Springs County.

The Shoshone name for the hot spring is *Bah-Bui-Wana,* or "smoking water." A special pageant, "Gift of the Waters," is enacted annually in the town.

Several buildings can still be found from Stimson's view, including two cabins, lower right, as well as a city block, center.

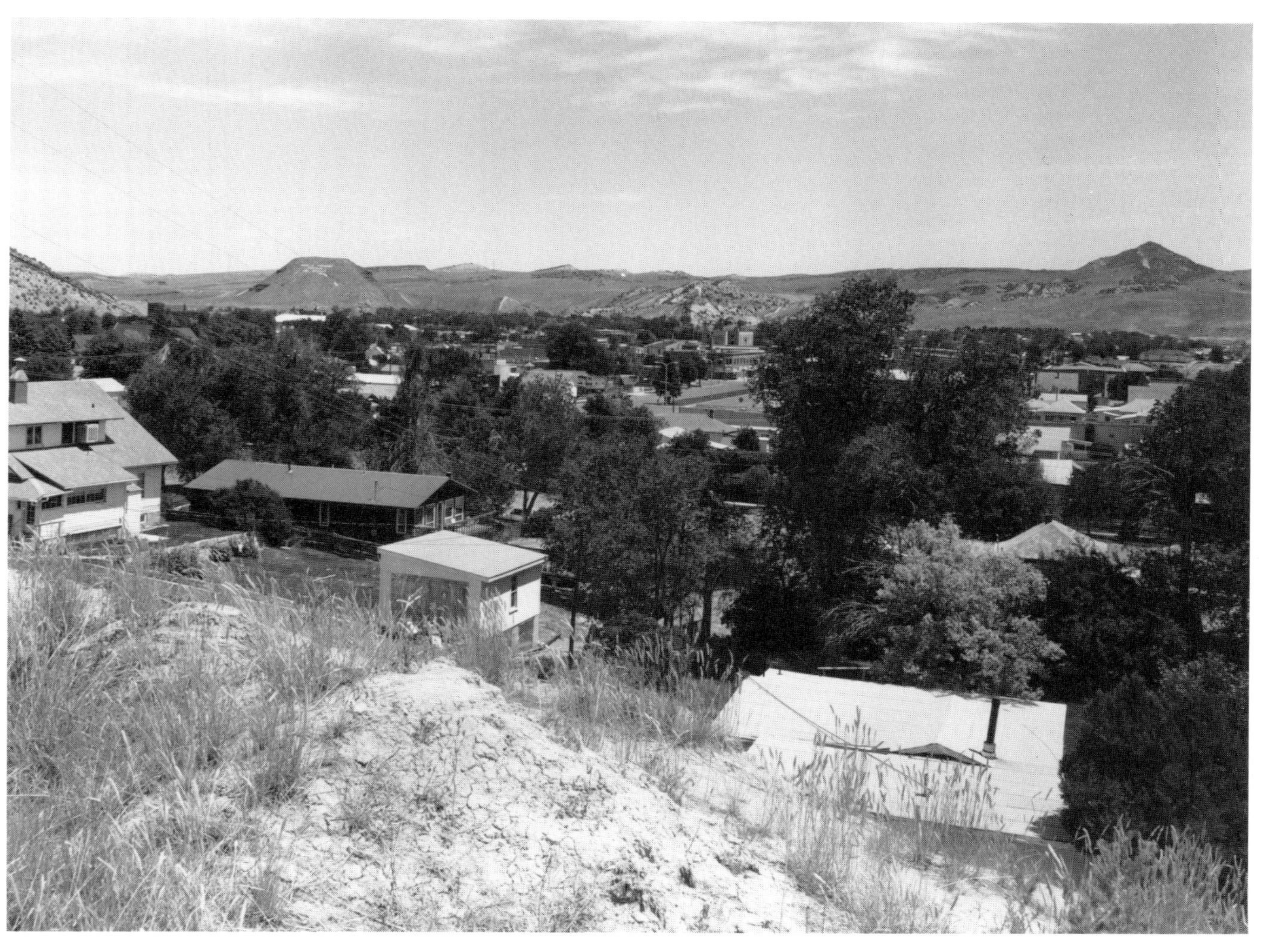

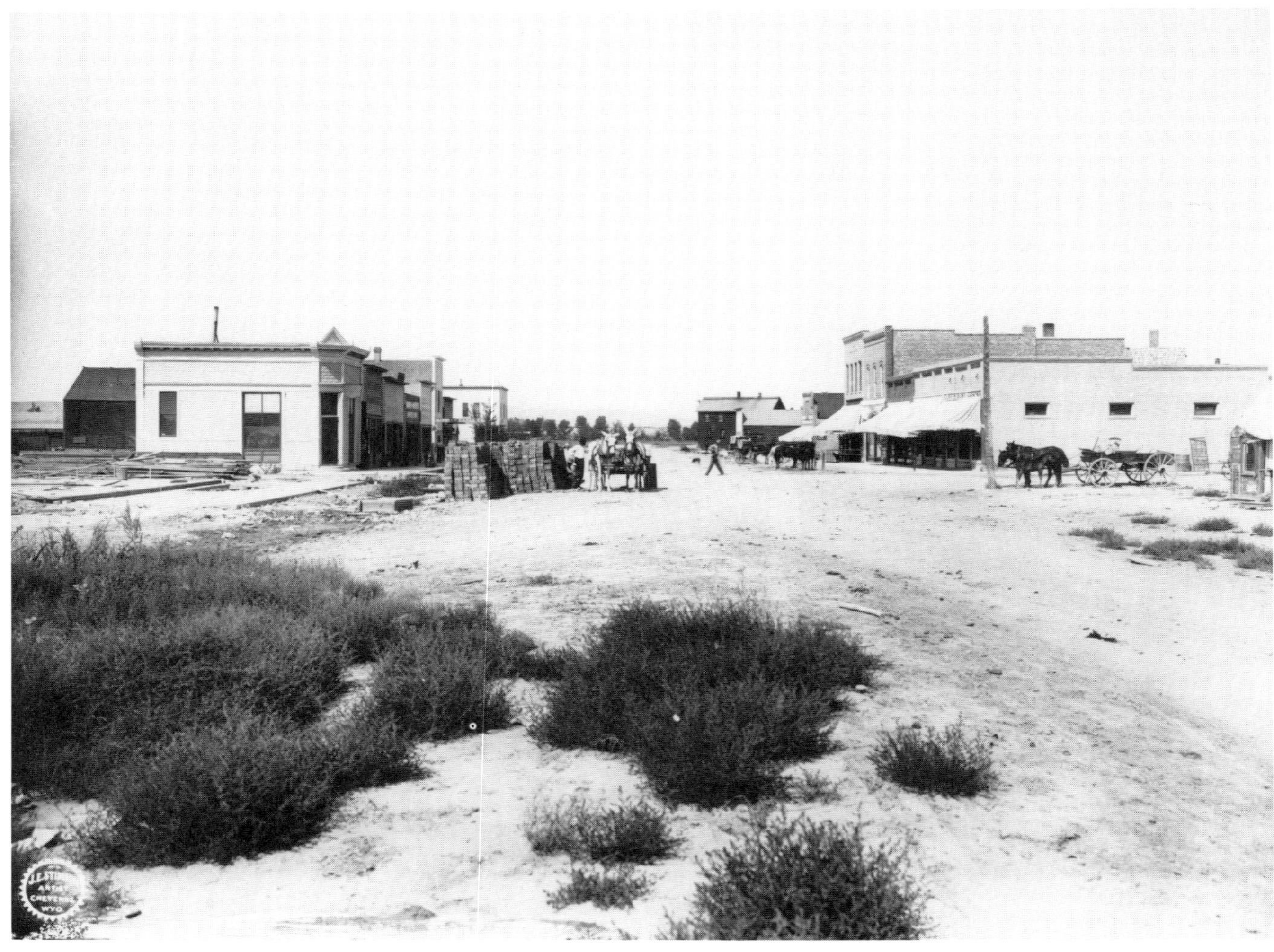

Fig. 79. Street scene, Worland, 1910.

The town of Worland was named for C. H. "Dad" Worland, its first settler. By 1903 a small trading center for local farmers had begun around his ranch, after several irrigation canals were dug to bring water from the Bighorn River. In 1906 the Burlington Railroad built through, and the camp was moved across the river to a new townsite. When Washakie County was created in 1911, Worland was named the county seat. In 1917 industry came to town when a sugar beet plant was built.

Although the sagebrush is gone from Bighorn Avenue, a few buildings on the right side of the street remain from Stimson's early view of Worland.

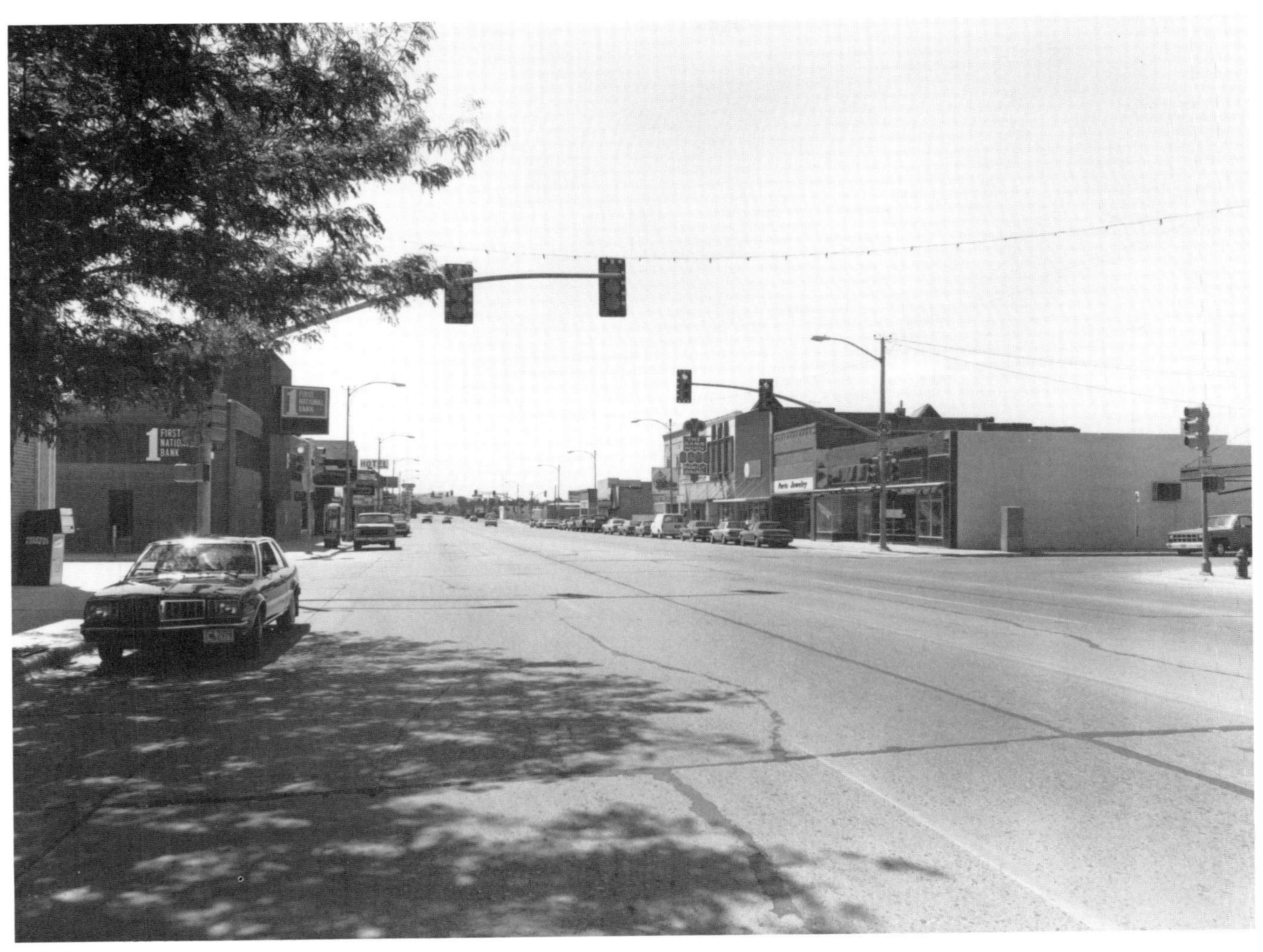
1 FIRST NATIONAL BANK
1 FIRST NATIONAL BANK
HOTEL

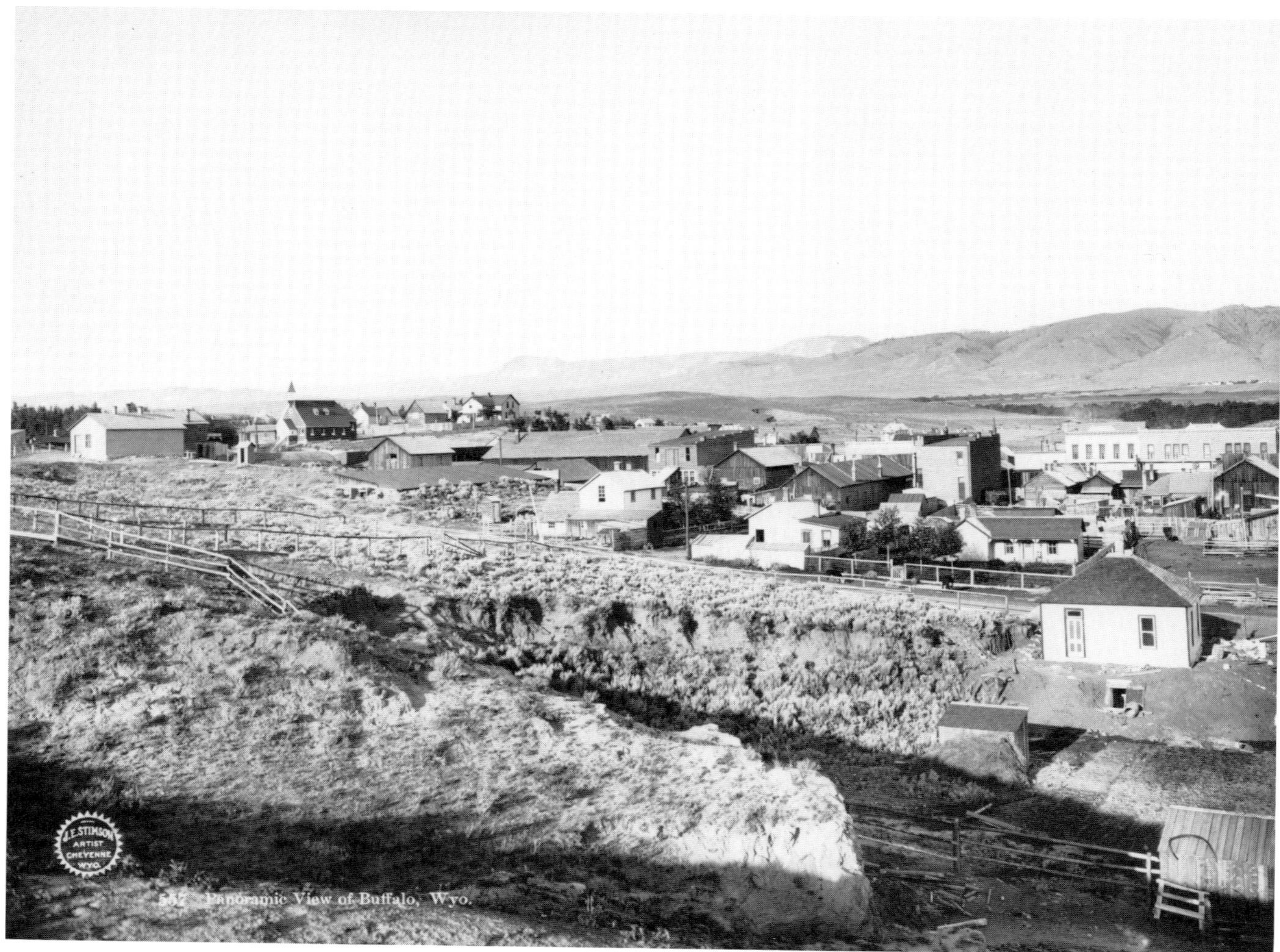

Fig. 80. Panoramic view of Buffalo, 1903.

After the Sioux Wars of the 1870s cleared the Powder River country of northern Wyoming, the town of Buffalo was established in 1879 near Fort McKinney on the banks of Clear Creek. It was named not for the American bison but for Buffalo, New York, the hometown of one of its pioneers.

This panorama is looking to the west and shows the slow winding main street and its intersection with Clear Creek. On the horizon can be found the front range of the Big Horn Mountains.

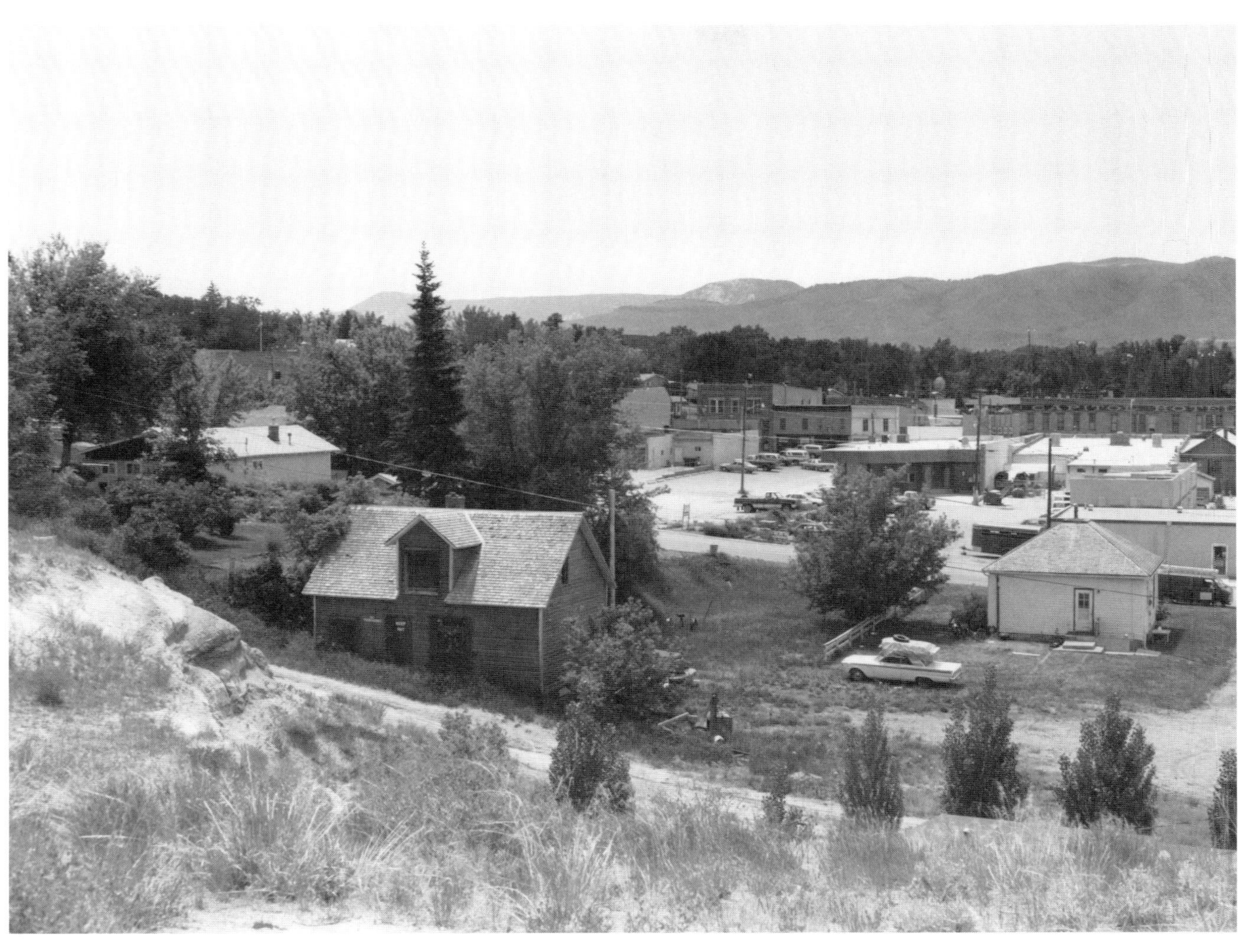

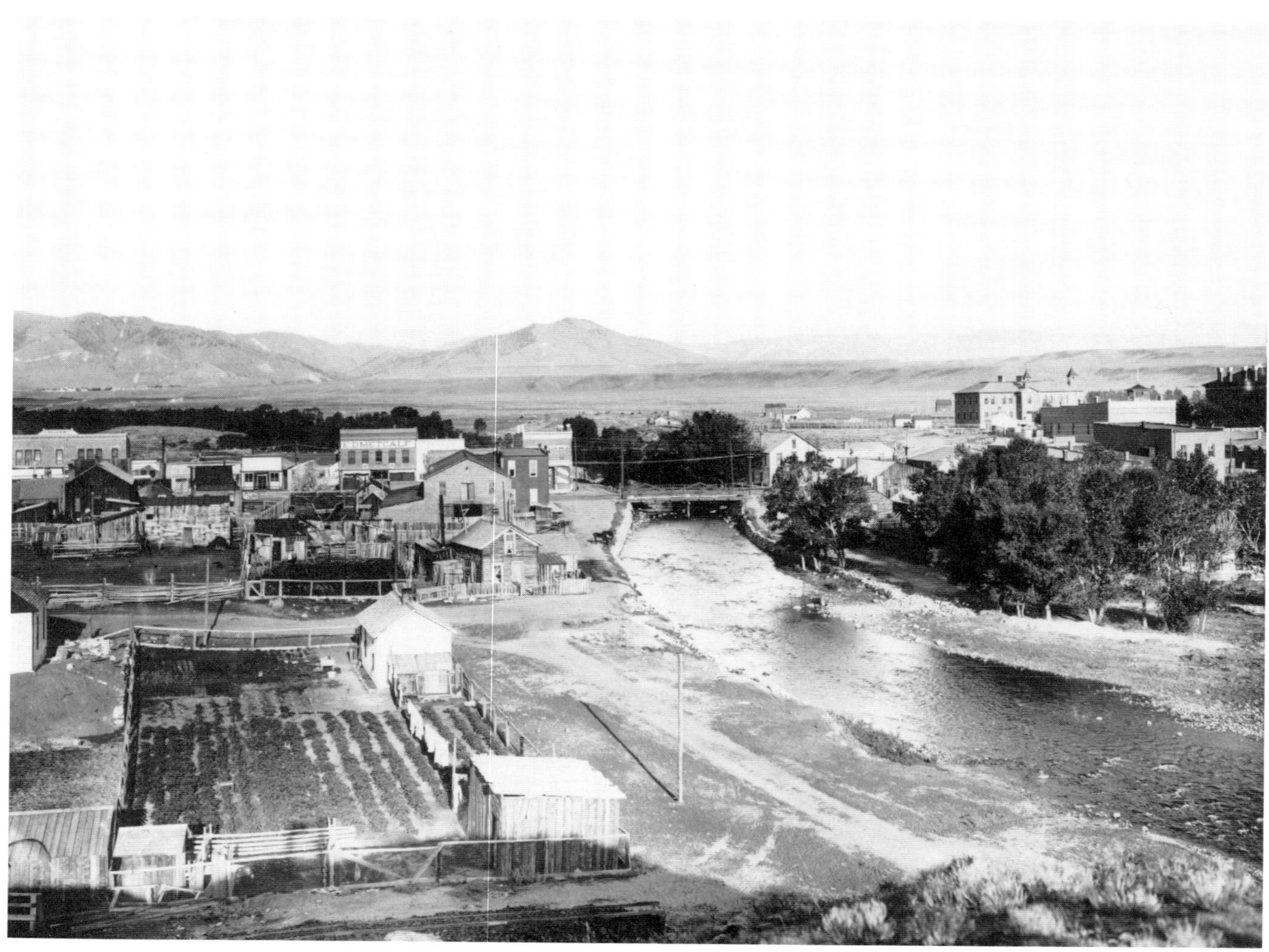

Fig. 81. Panoramic view of Buffalo, 1903.

This view of Buffalo, the right side of the previous panorama, shows Clear Creek as it winds through the center of Buffalo. Main Street can be seen running across the photos from the Capitol Hotel at left to the Johnson County Courthouse at right. Across the background can be found the front range of the Big Horn Mountains. Also notice the early vegetable garden in the Stimson photograph and the presence of another bridge in the modern view.

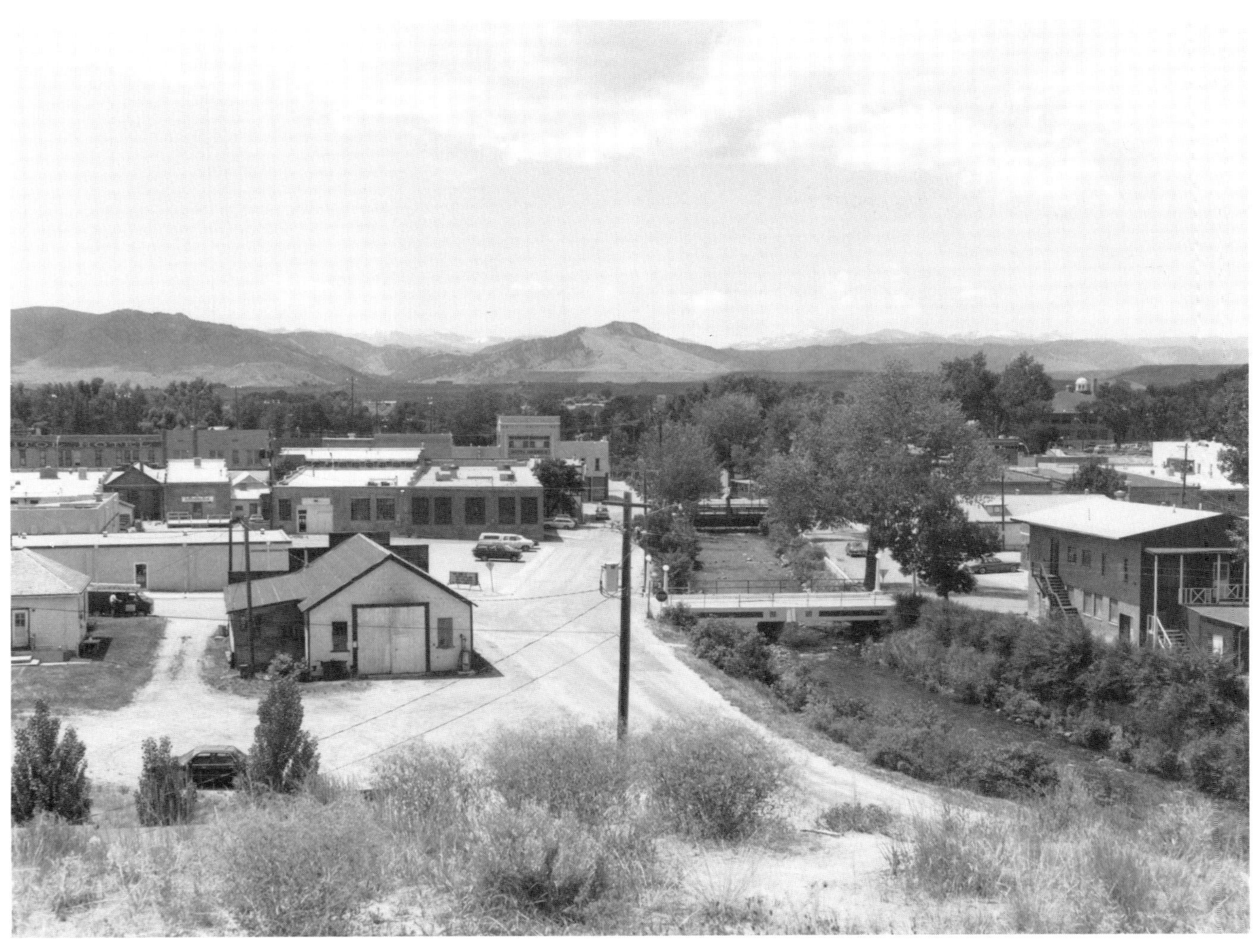

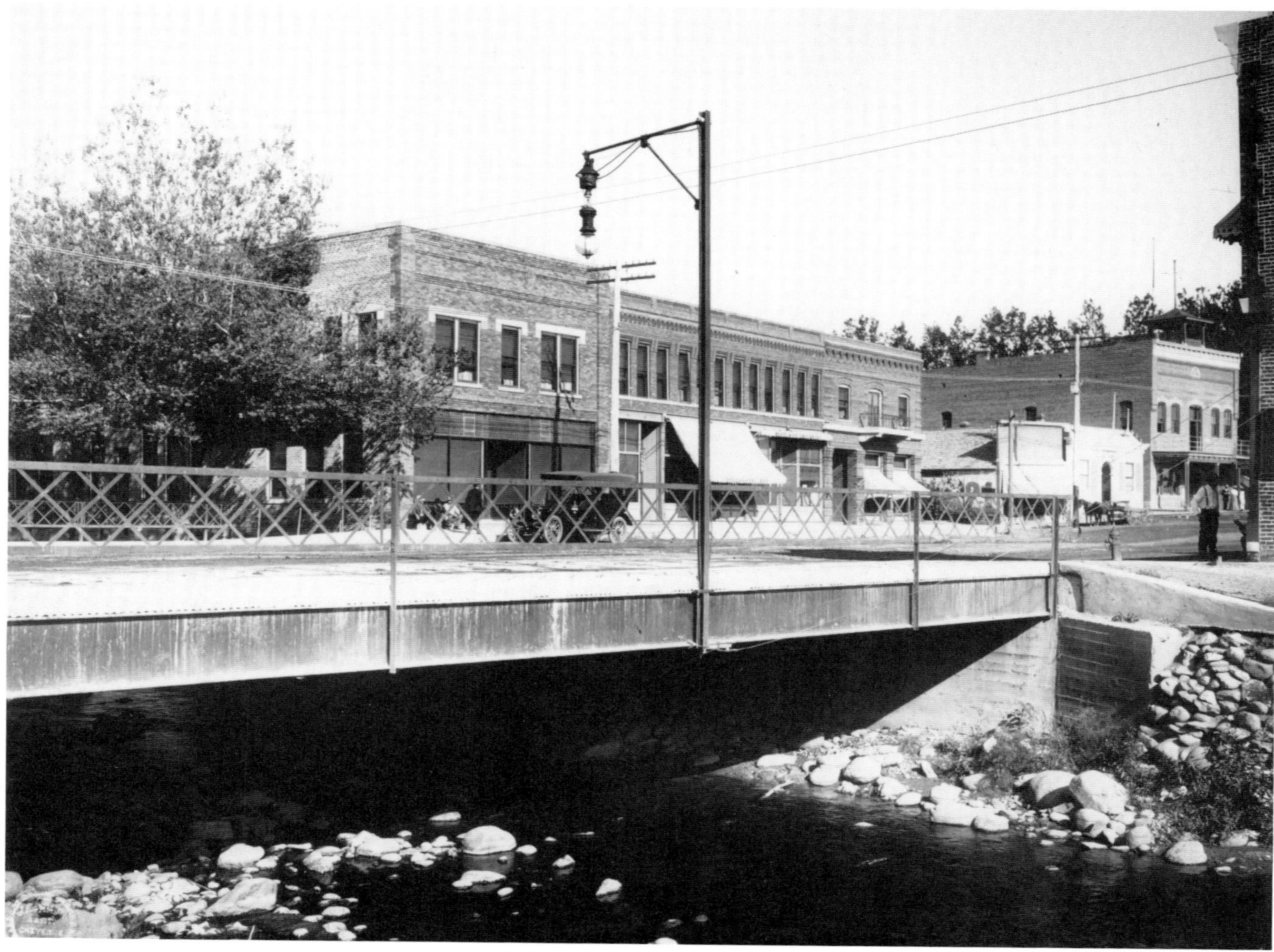

Fig. 82. The Occidental Hotel, Buffalo, 1910.

The original Occidental Hotel, constructed in 1879, was one of the first buildings in Buffalo. The brick hotel was finished in 1900. In Owen Wister's book *The Virginian,* the Occidental Hotel was the site where the Virginian captured his man.

The modern view shows a new tourist bridge over Clear Creek, as well as the Busy Bee Lunch counter to the left of the Occidental.

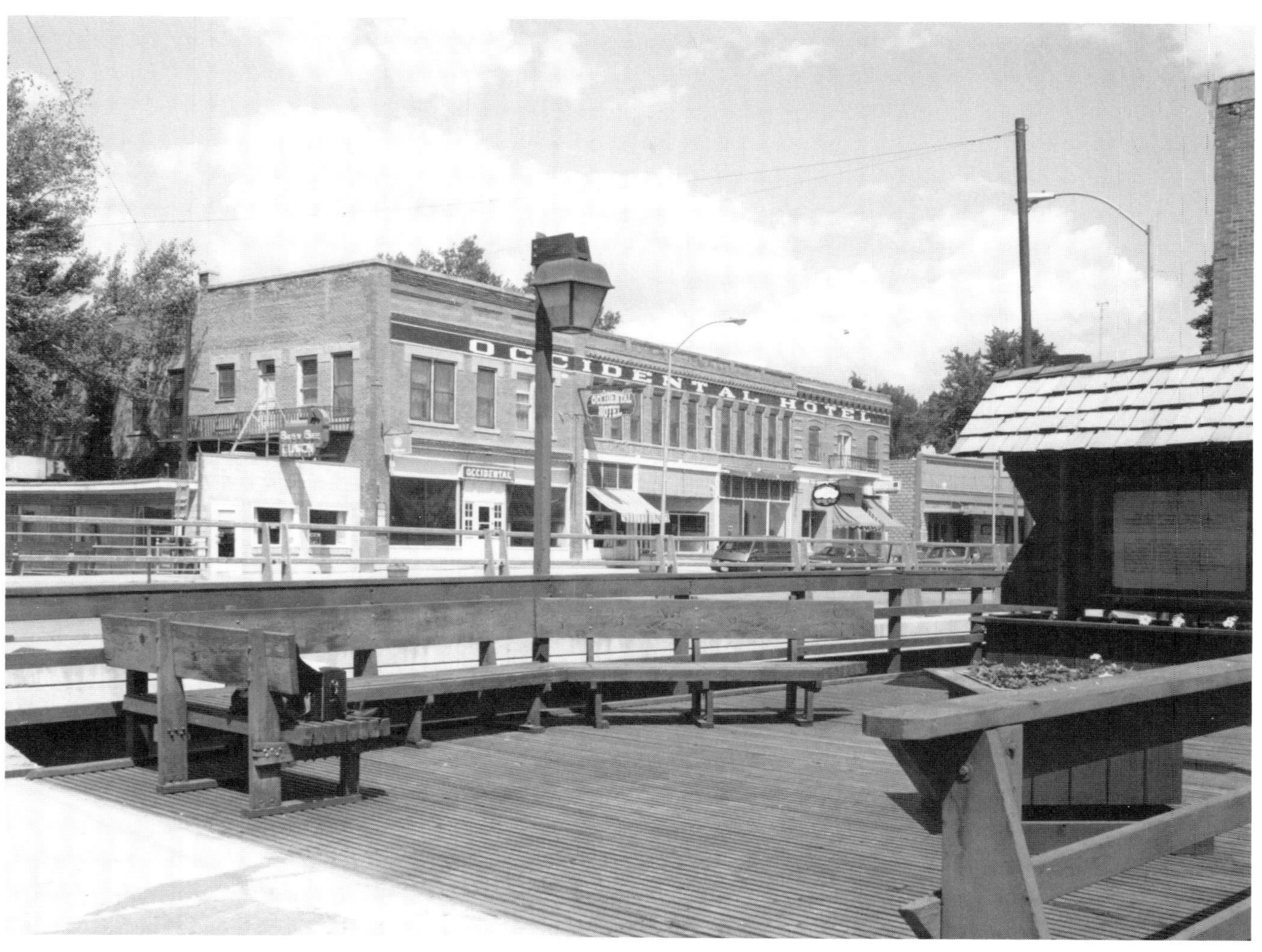
OCCIDENTAL HOTEL
OCCIDENTAL

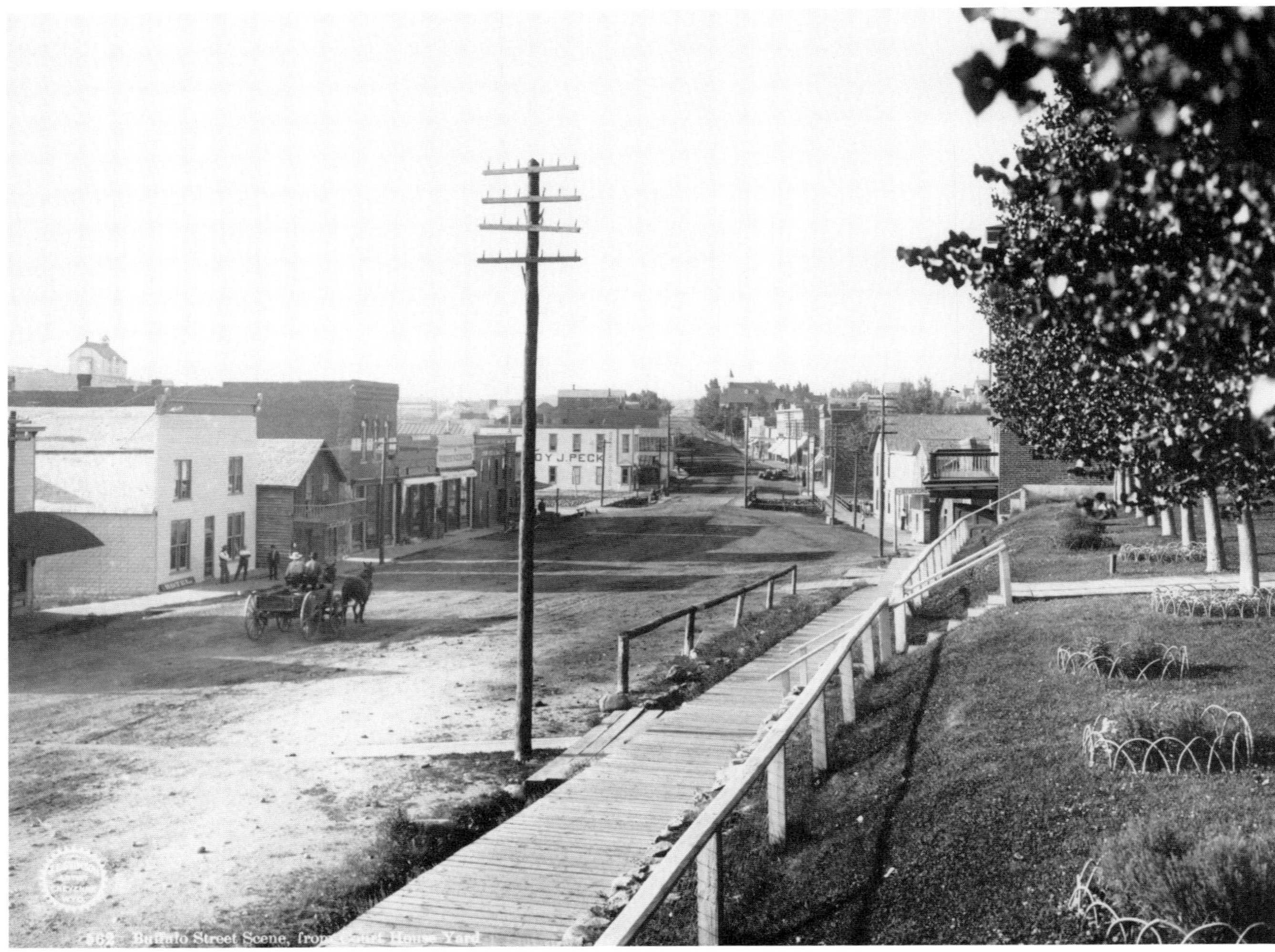

Fig. 83. Street scene from courthouse yard, Buffalo, 1903.

This view, from the courthouse lawn, shows the winding main street in downtown Buffalo. The courthouse was constructed in 1888. In Stimson's photo, a balcony from the old Occidental Hotel can be seen at right center. The modern view shows the newer hotel. The three-windowed building immediately across the street from the hotel with the Curry's Clothier sign, left center, also survives from Stimson's view.

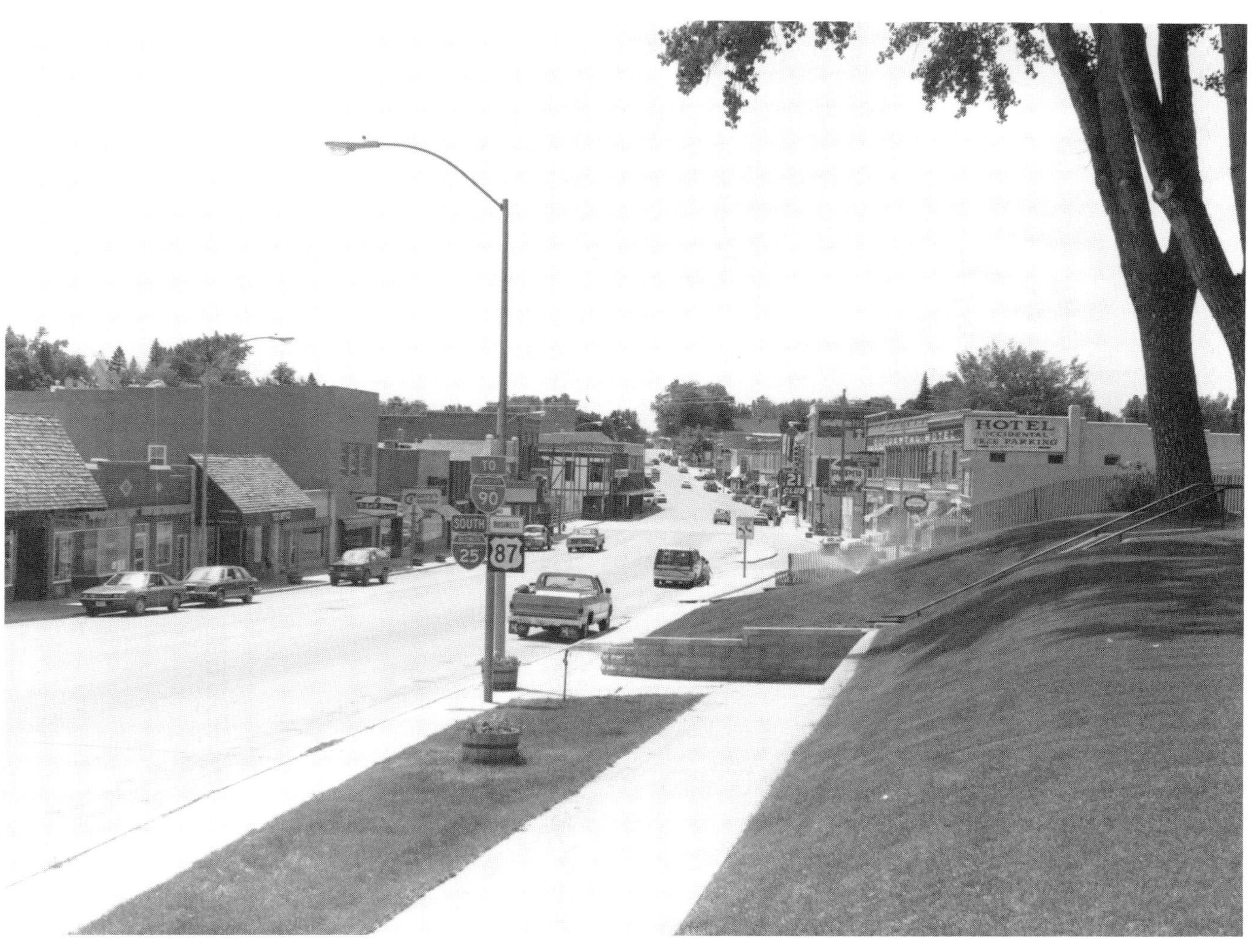
TO
90
SOUTH
25
BUSINESS
87
HOTEL
OCCIDENTAL
FREE PARKING
21
CLUB

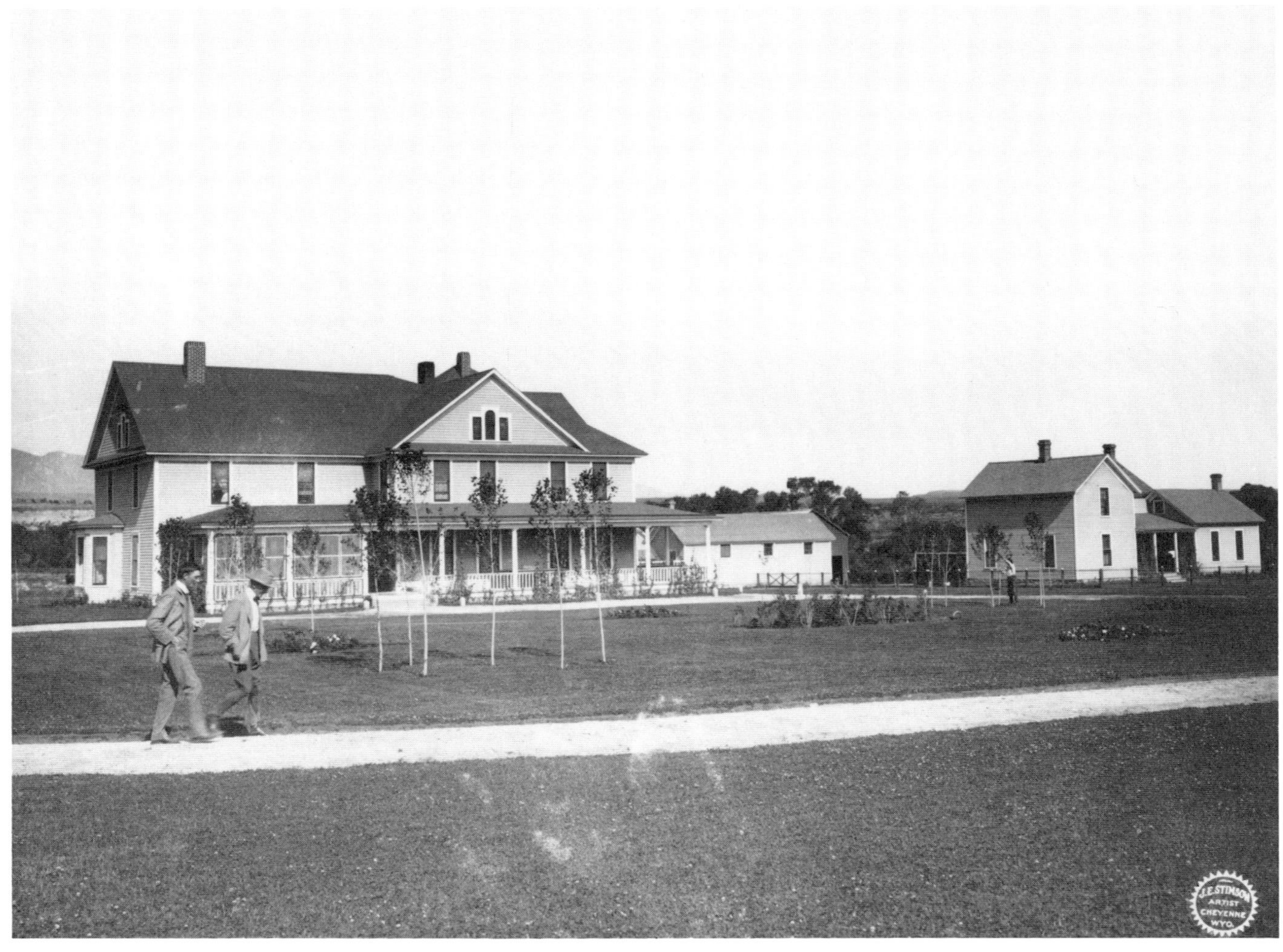

Fig. 84. Moncreiffe Ranch near Big Horn, 1903.

In 1893 William Moncreiffe, the fourth son of the baron of Moncreiffe, established the Quarter Circle A Ranch on the Little Goose Creek near Big Horn City. His younger brother Malcolm soon settled nearby. They built this house together and then lined its driveway with trees. After he returned from the Spanish-American War, William, Malcolm, and another neighbor, Oliver H. Wallop, formed a company that sold saddle-broken horses to the British cavalry for use in the Boer War. From 1899 to 1903, the operation sent more than twenty thousand horses to South Africa from Sheridan. About this same time, the brothers began playing polo on a field at Malcolm's ranch.

In 1923 Bradford Brinton, a director in the Case Threshing Machine Company, bought out William and filled the house with western paintings and sculpture. Like Moncreiffe, Brinton raised thoroughbred horses for polo. After Brinton died in 1936, the ranch was maintained by his sister until 1961, when the Bradford Brinton Memorial was established. The house is now open to the public, and exhibits from Brinton's collections are featured.

Little has changed since Stimson made his photo. An addition has been built onto the back of the house but is not visible from this angle. The foreman's house at right in Stimson's view is still there, behind the trees.

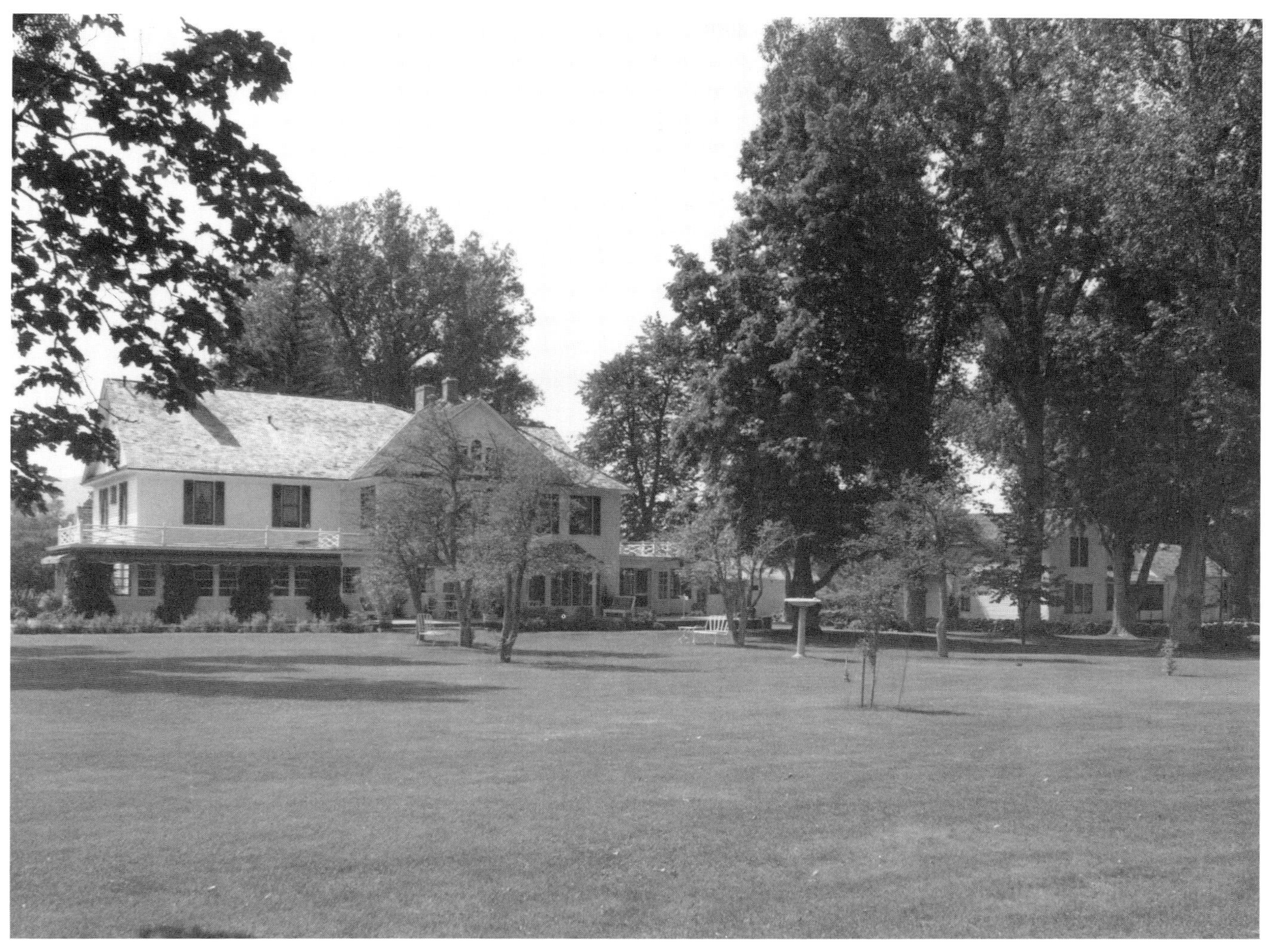

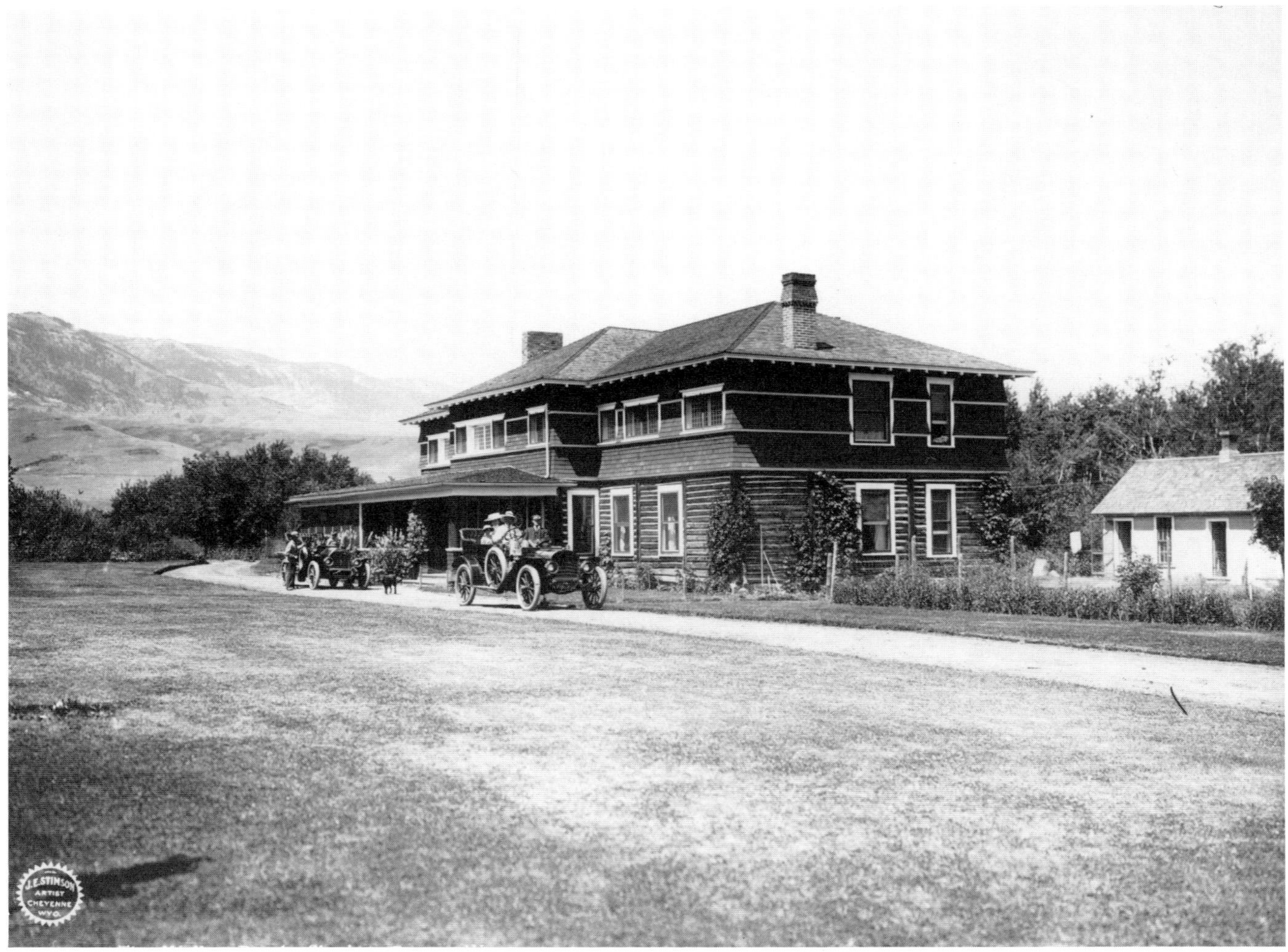

Fig. 85. Wallop Ranch, near Big Horn, 1909.

Oliver Henry Wallop, the third son of the earl of Portsmouth, came to Wyoming in 1891 and settled on the lands of Big Horn pioneer O. P. Hanna. Four years later Wallop bought the Canyon Ranch and moved to the mouth of Little Goose Canyon. At the turn of the century, Wallop went into partnership with his neighbors, the Moncreiffe brothers, to sell mounts to the British cavalry for use in the Boer War. He soon became an American citizen and was elected to the Wyoming House of Representatives in 1908. In 1925 his older brother, then earl of Portsmouth, died in England without any heirs. If the family were to keep their ancestral home and title, Oliver had to go back to England. Following English primogeniture, his eldest son Gerard went with him to England and assumed another family title, Viscount Lymington. Oliver's younger son, Oliver Malcolm Wallop, stayed in America to run the ranch. One of Oliver Malcolm's sons, Malcolm, is currently a U.S. senator from Wyoming.

Although the second story of the Wallop house has been removed, the location of the first story windows show that this is the same house. The top story was removed because it was too difficult to heat. When Queen Elizabeth II visited Sheridan, she stayed at this house.

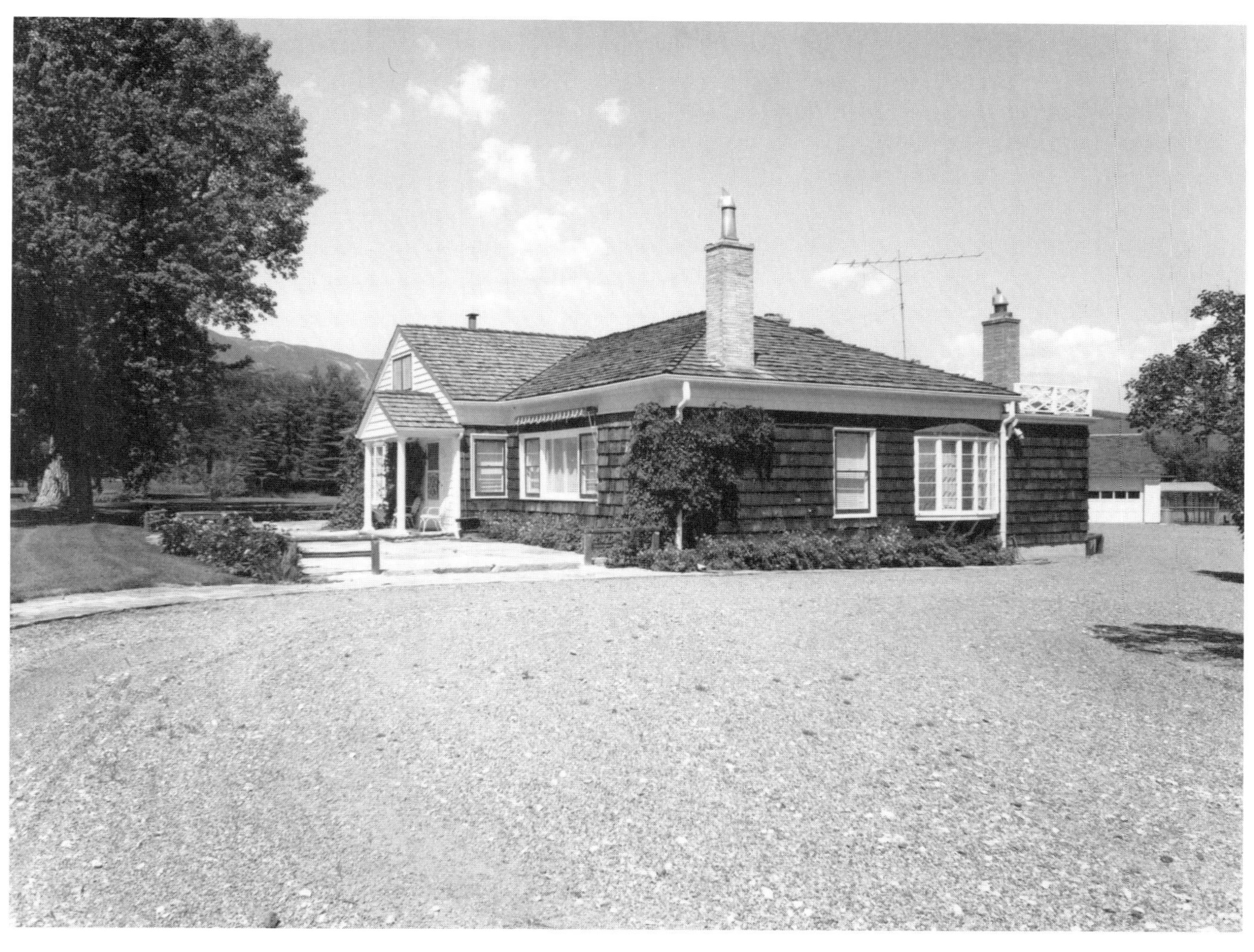

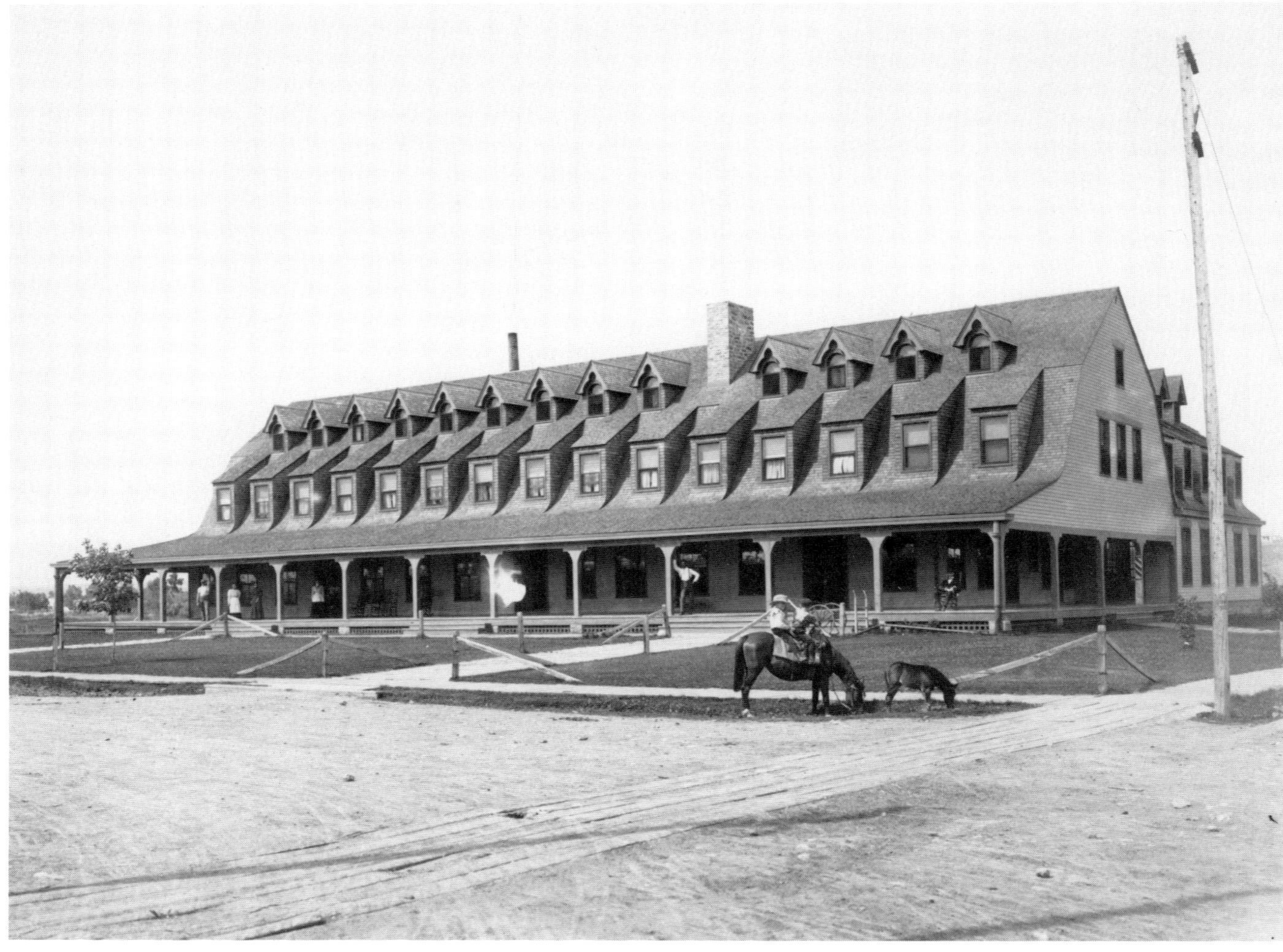

Fig. 86. Sheridan Inn, Sheridan, no date.

The Sheridan Inn was constructed by the Burlington and Missouri Railroad and the Sheridan Land Company in 1892–93 at a cost of $25,000. Thomas R. Kimball, an Omaha architect, modeled the inn after a Scottish inn he had once visited. When the inn opened in June 1893, it housed the first bathtub and electric lights in Sheridan. There were sixty-two guest rooms, a dining room, a saloon, and a lobby. Buffalo Bill Cody operated the inn from 1894 to 1896. Through the years, several presidents stayed at the inn while traveling across the country. Many sportsmen have also stayed on their way to big game hunts in the Bighorns. The inn was designated a national historic landmark in 1964 but ceased to operate as a hotel the following year. In 1967 the property was condemned. The inn was then saved from destruction and partially restored that same year.

Though much of the inn looks the same as in Stimson's view, the saplings at left tower above the inn today.

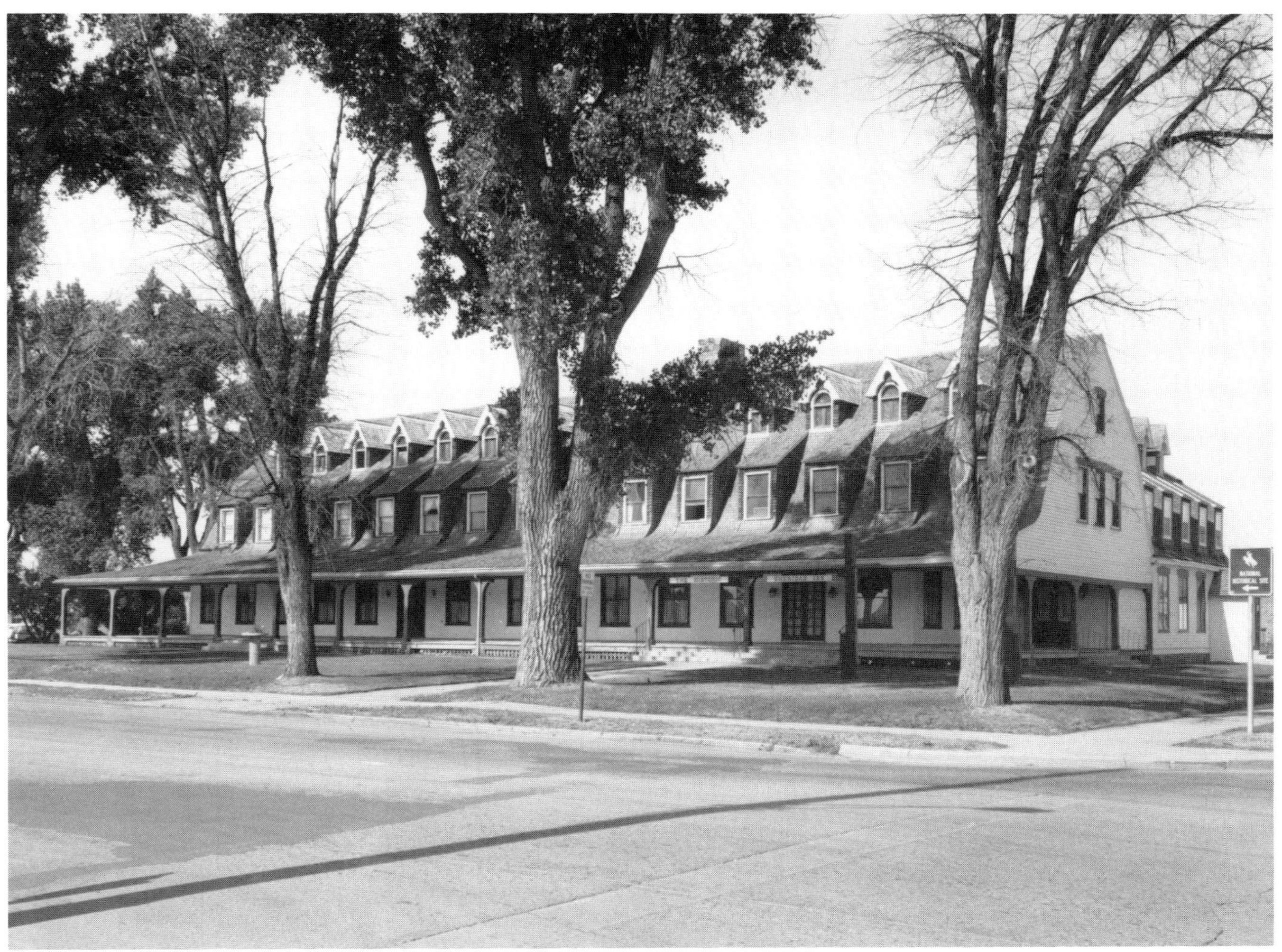

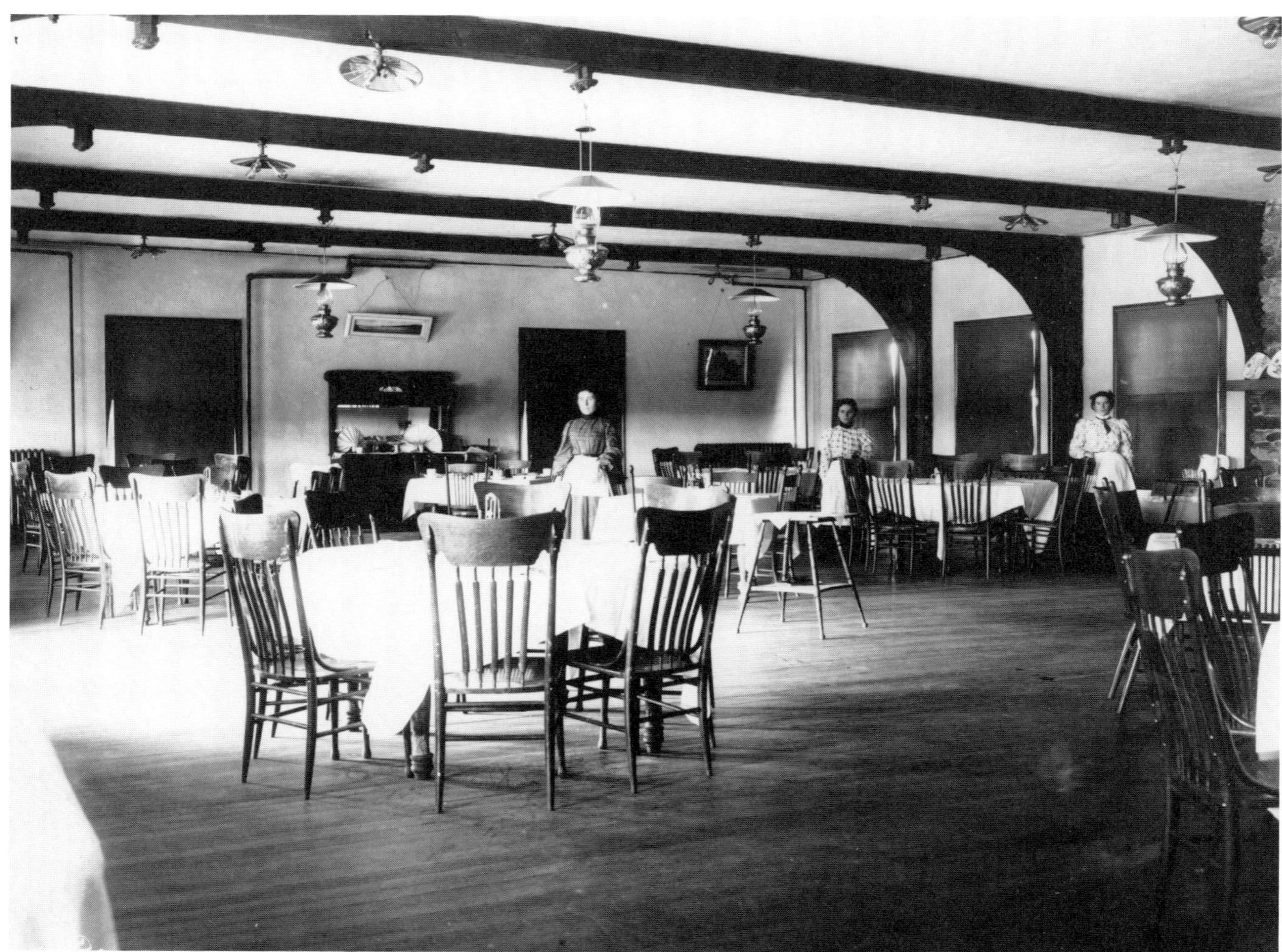

Fig. 87. Dining room at Sheridan Inn, Sheridan, 1899.

The dining room of the Sheridan Inn had a seating capacity of 150 people. Breakfast was priced at twenty-five cents, with lunch and supper at fifty cents each. Meal tickets for locals were also sold at the rate of seven dollars for twenty-one meals.

The room provided one of the largest ballrooms in Sheridan and was the site of many grand balls and parties. The ceiling beams were made of locally cut, hand-hewn logs. The fireplace, right, was constructed of native cobblestone at a price of one thousand dollars.

Today only the beams, windows, and fireplace remain.

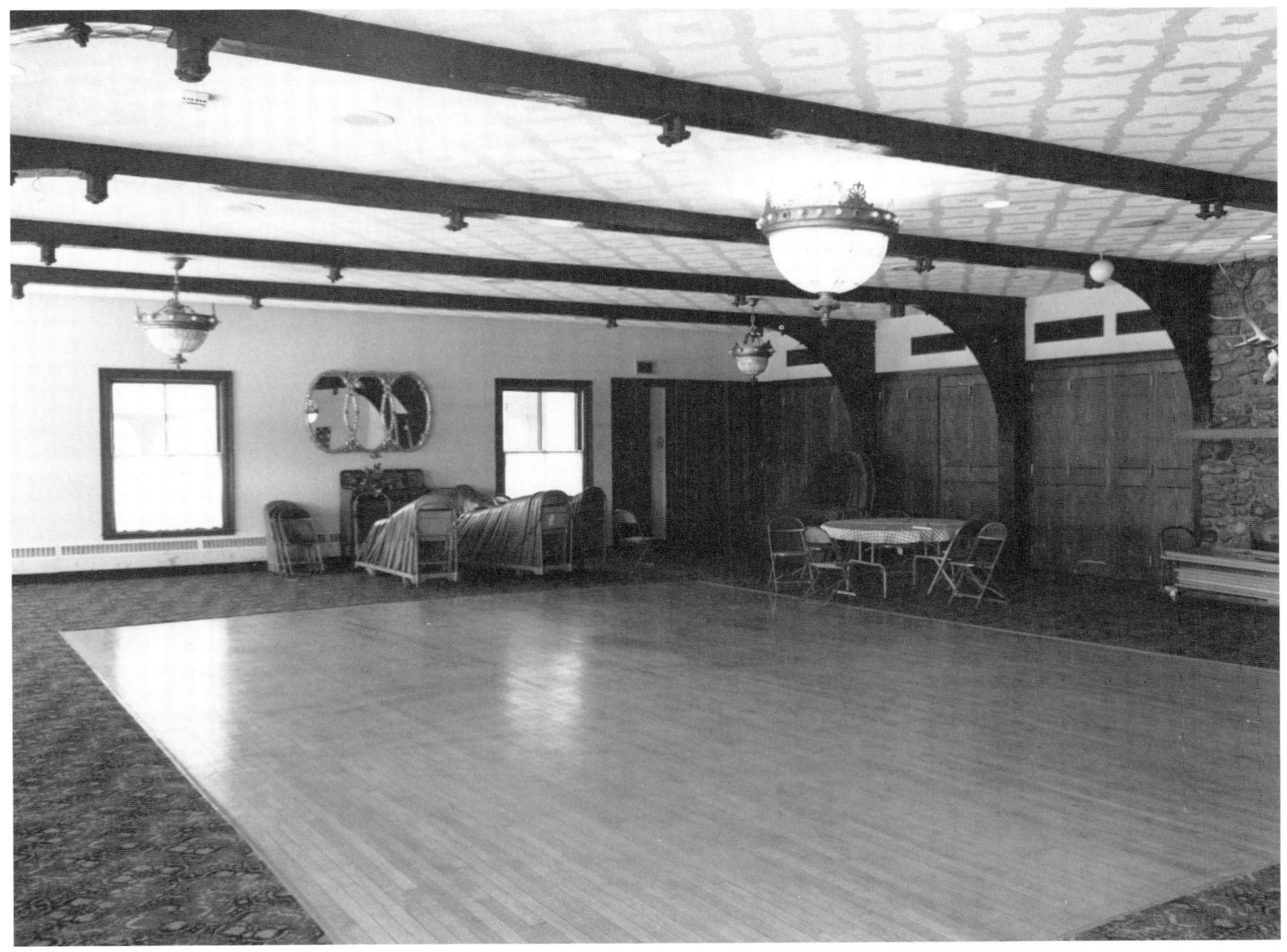

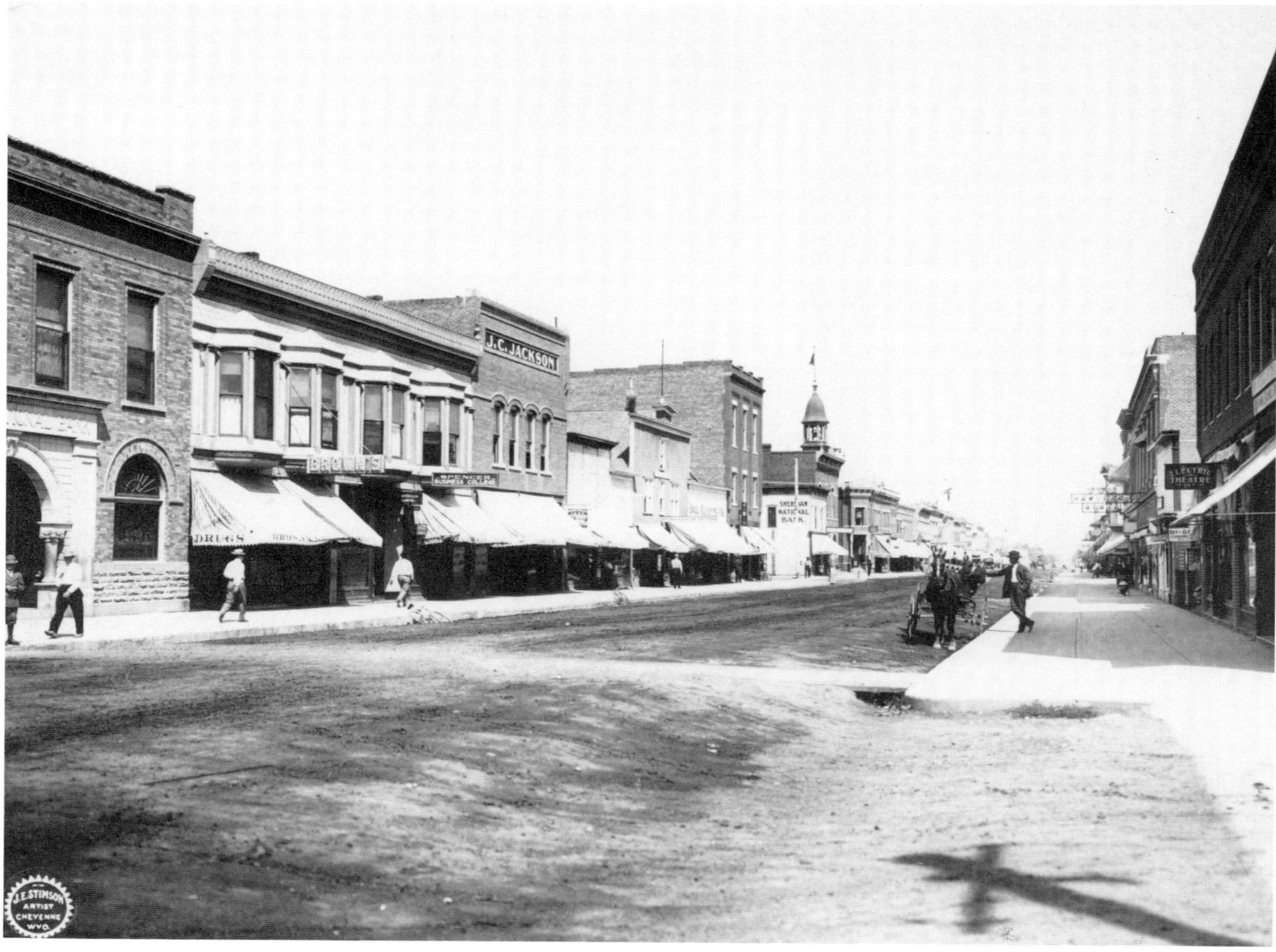

Fig. 88. Main Street, Sheridan, 1910.

The town of Sheridan was named for Civil War general Philip Sheridan, and the first cabin there was constructed at the confluence of the Big Goose and Little Goose creeks in 1879. It was incorporated in 1883, and the Burlington and Missouri Railroad reached the town ten years later. At an elevation of 3,745 feet, Sheridan is the lowest town in Wyoming.

The tower in the old photo sat atop City Hall.

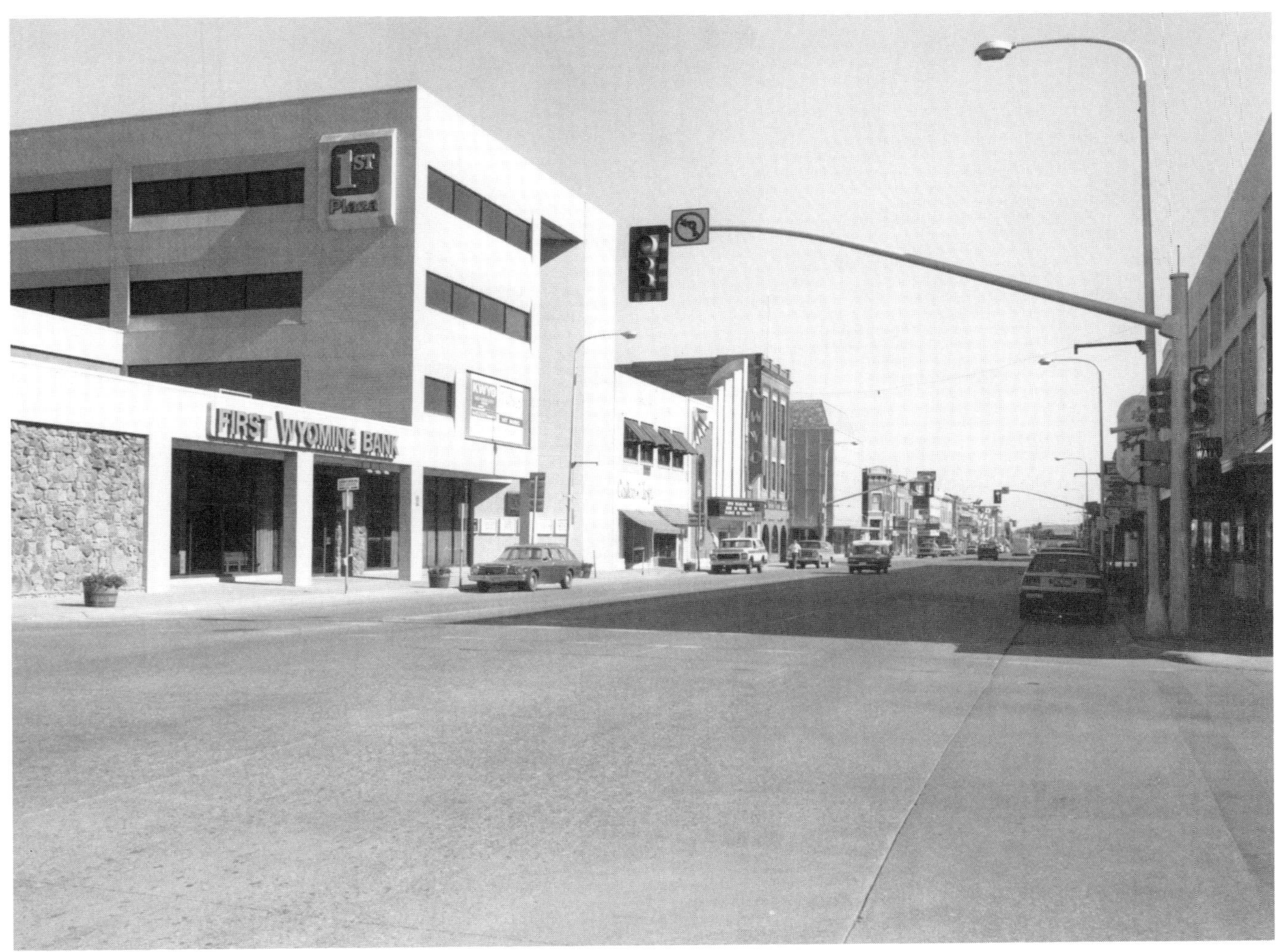
1ST
Plaza
FIRST WYOMING BANK

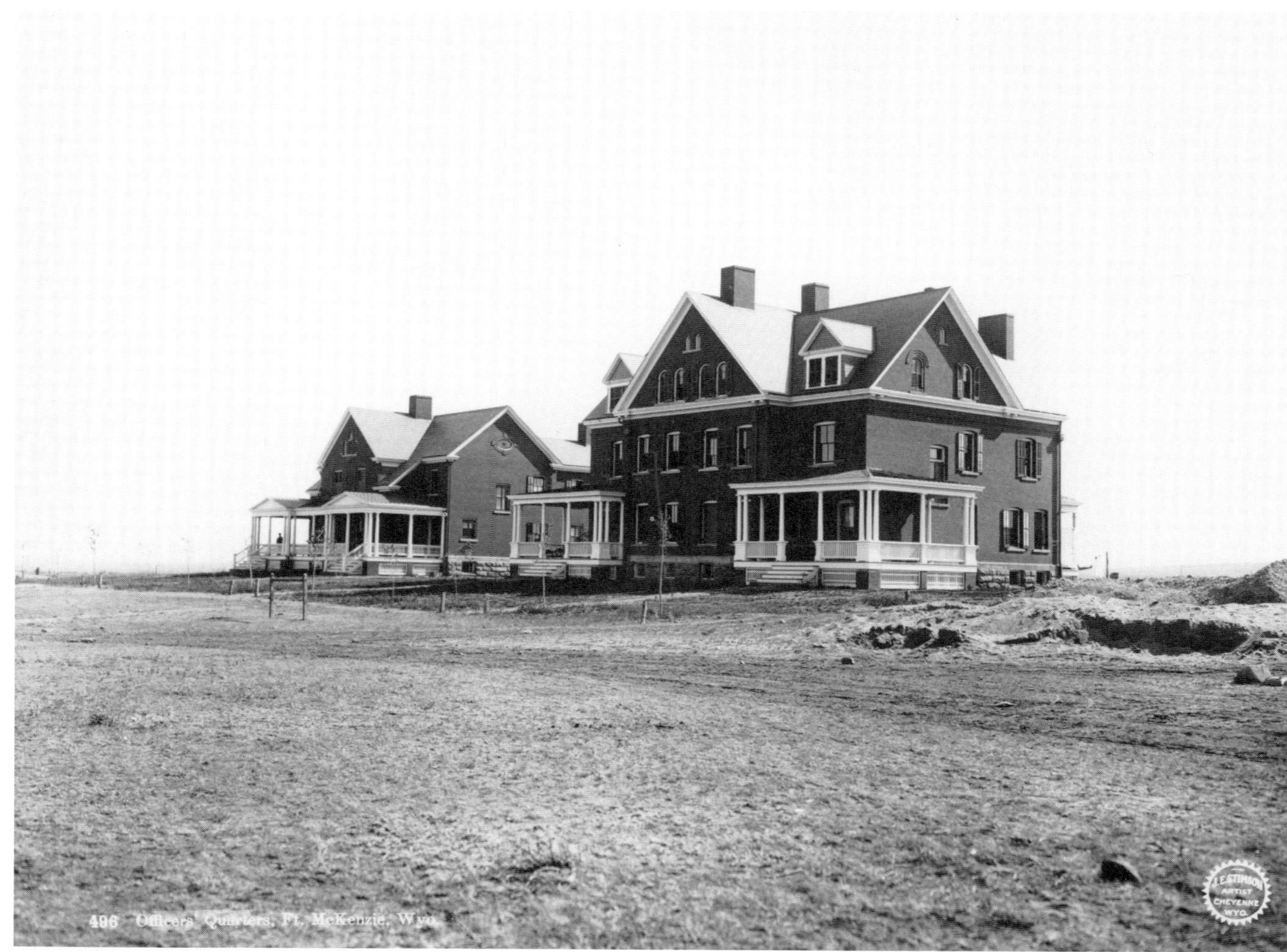

Fig. 89. Officers' quarters at Fort MacKenzie, near Sheridan, 1903.

Because of the large population of Indians on nearby reservations, Fort MacKenzie was established near Sheridan, on Soldier Creek, in 1897. The fort was constructed of red brick in a typical military neoclassical style. The post remained in operation until 1918 when the army abandoned the grounds. The site was unused until 1922 when it was converted to a veterans' hospital.

The two officers' quarters were built in 1902 and remain much the same today as when Stimson photographed the site eighty-six years earlier. The sapling at right in the early view now rises out of the modern photo. The eye-shaped window on the right side of the left building, left center, can still be seen amid the branches of the third tree from right.

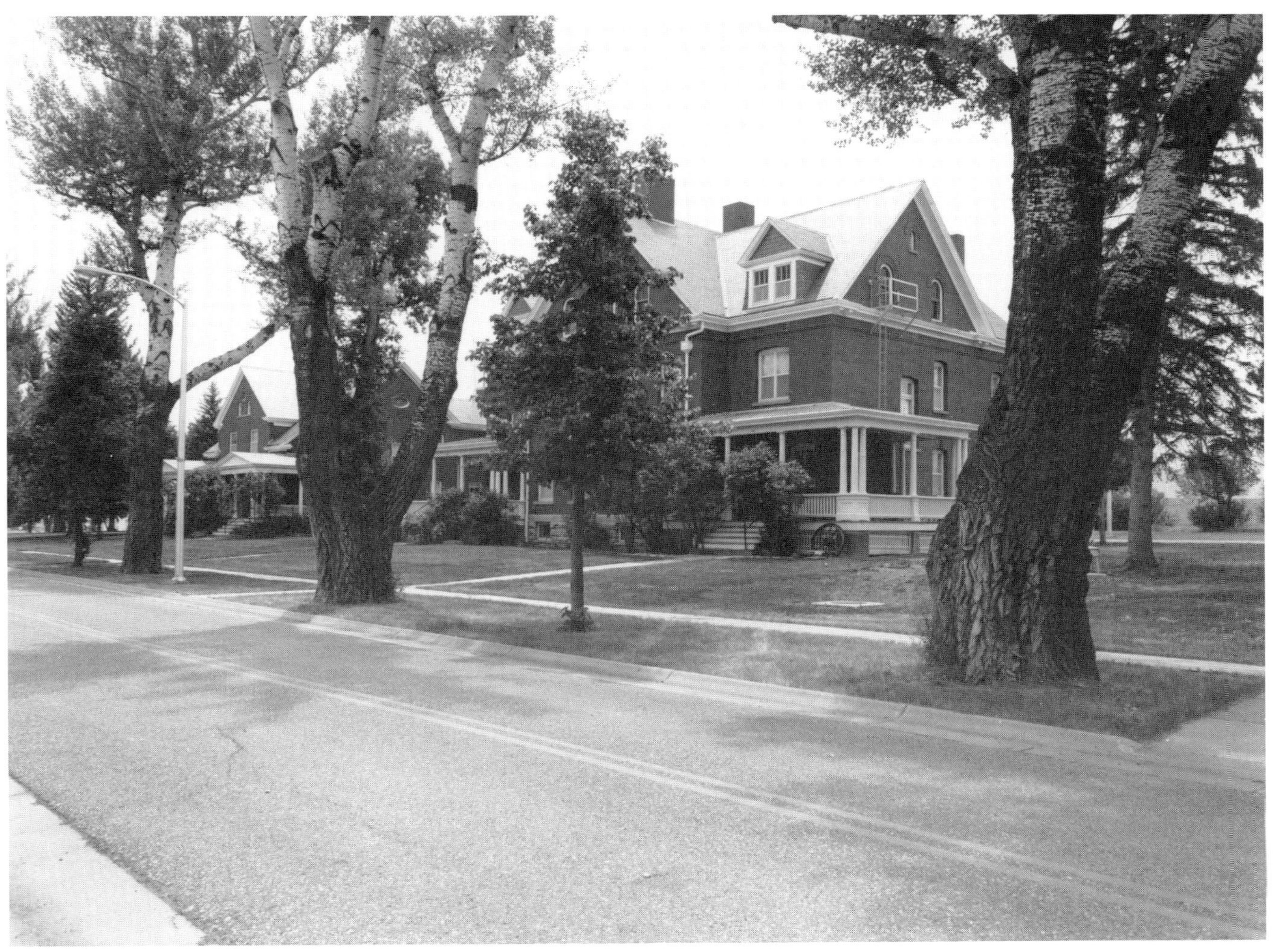

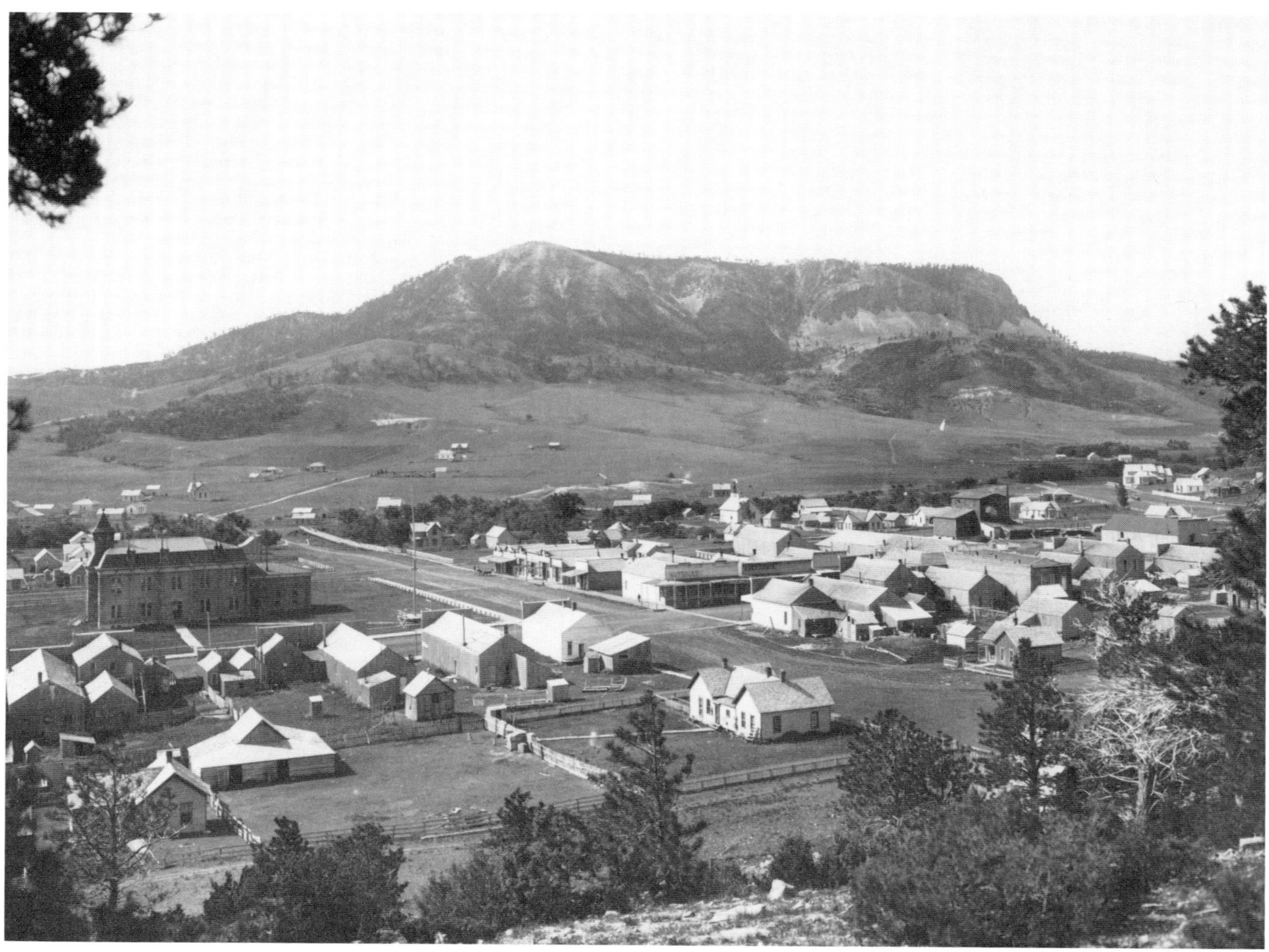

Fig. 90. City of Sundance and Sundance Mountain, 1903.

Nestled under the shadow of Sundance Mountain, the town of Sundance was established in 1879 as a supply center for cattle ranches. A newspaper, the *Sundance Gazette,* began operation in the 1880s. The Crook County Courthouse, left center in Stimson's photograph, was dedicated in 1887 and survived three roofs before being replaced by the new courthouse in 1968. Harry Longabaugh, the Sundance Kid, was tried and convicted here of robbery in 1892 but escaped.

The duplex at lower center in Stimson's view remains today.

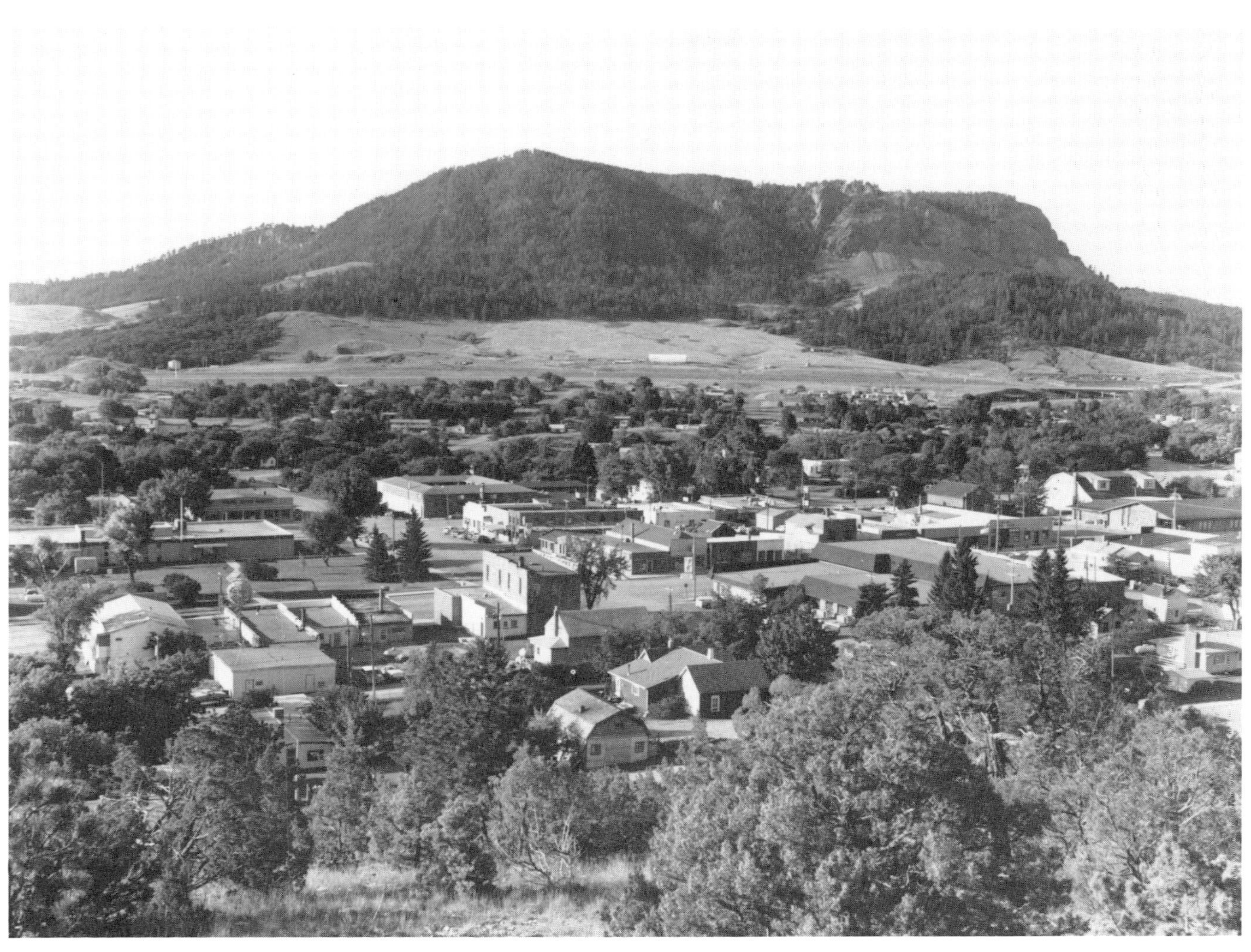

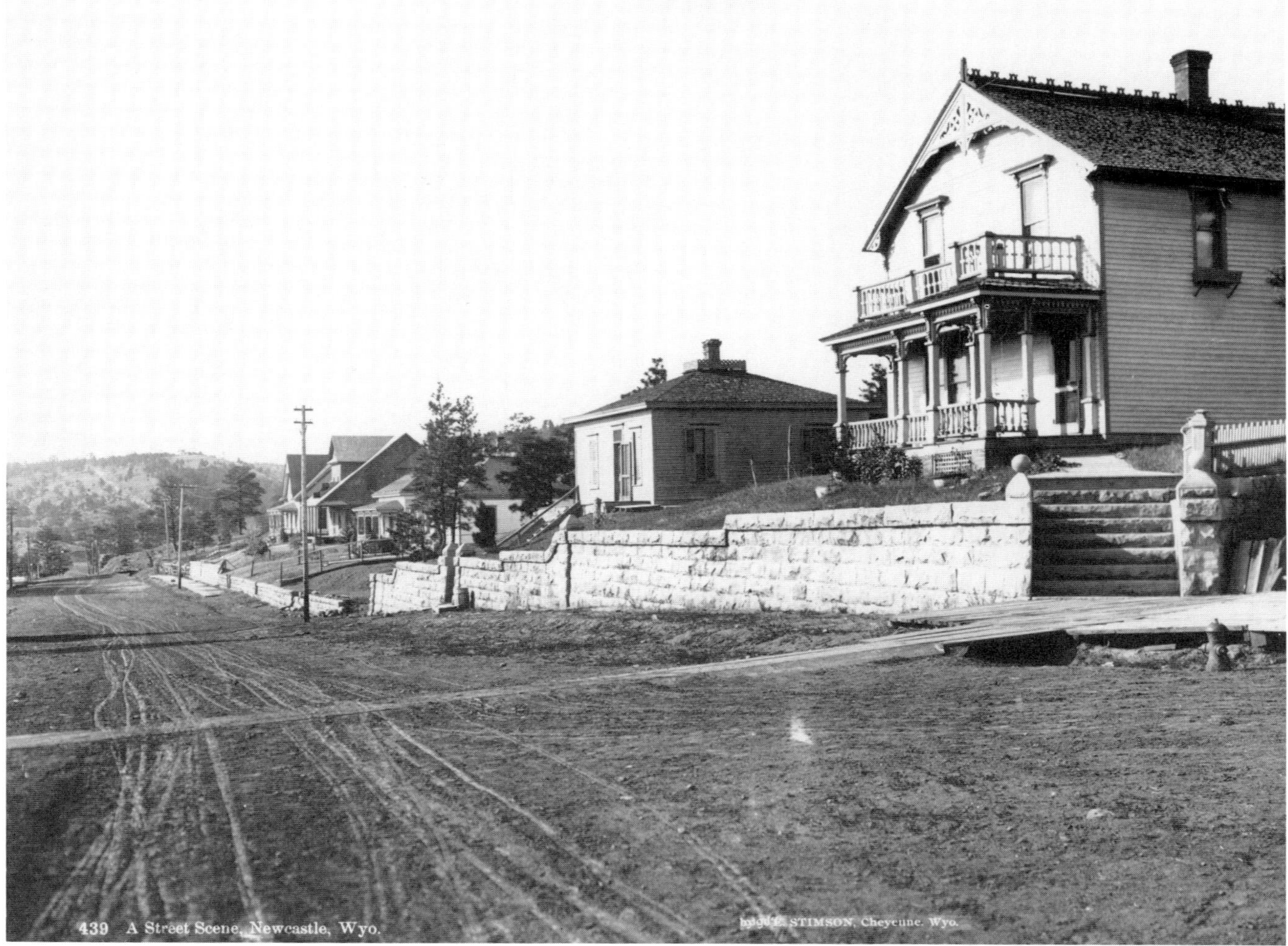

Fig. 91. Street scene, Newcastle, 1903.

Named for the English coal town of Newcastle-upon-Tyne, Newcastle was established as the western terminus of the Burlington and Missouri Railroad in 1889. A railroad spur was then built to the coal mines of Cambria. Today the town is known as the Western Gateway to the Black Hills.

The stone steps and wall that flank Summit Street, as well as the house at right center, minus the gingerbread, remain from Stimson's photo.

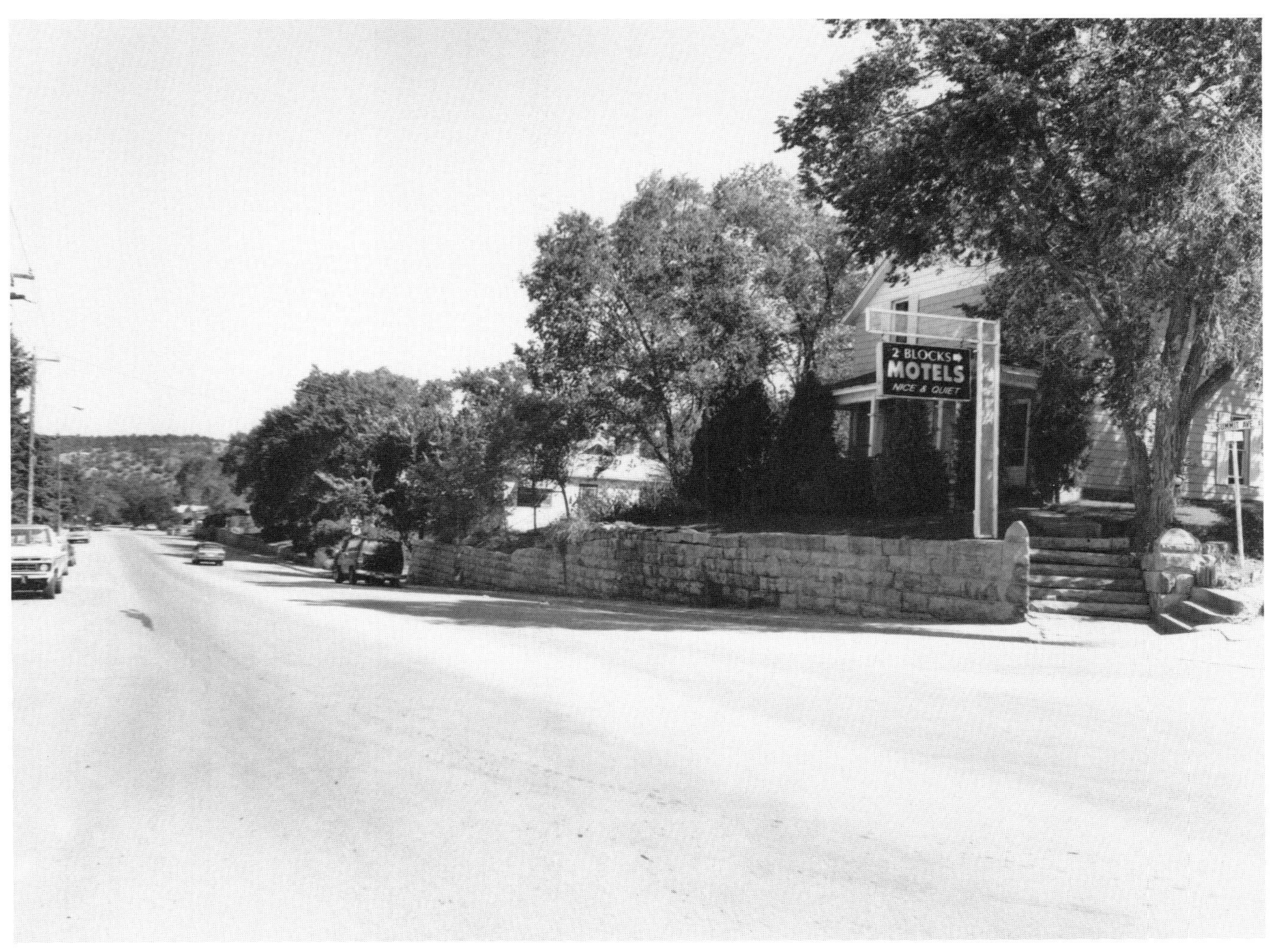
2 BLOCKS
MOTELS
NICE & QUIET
SUMMIT AVE

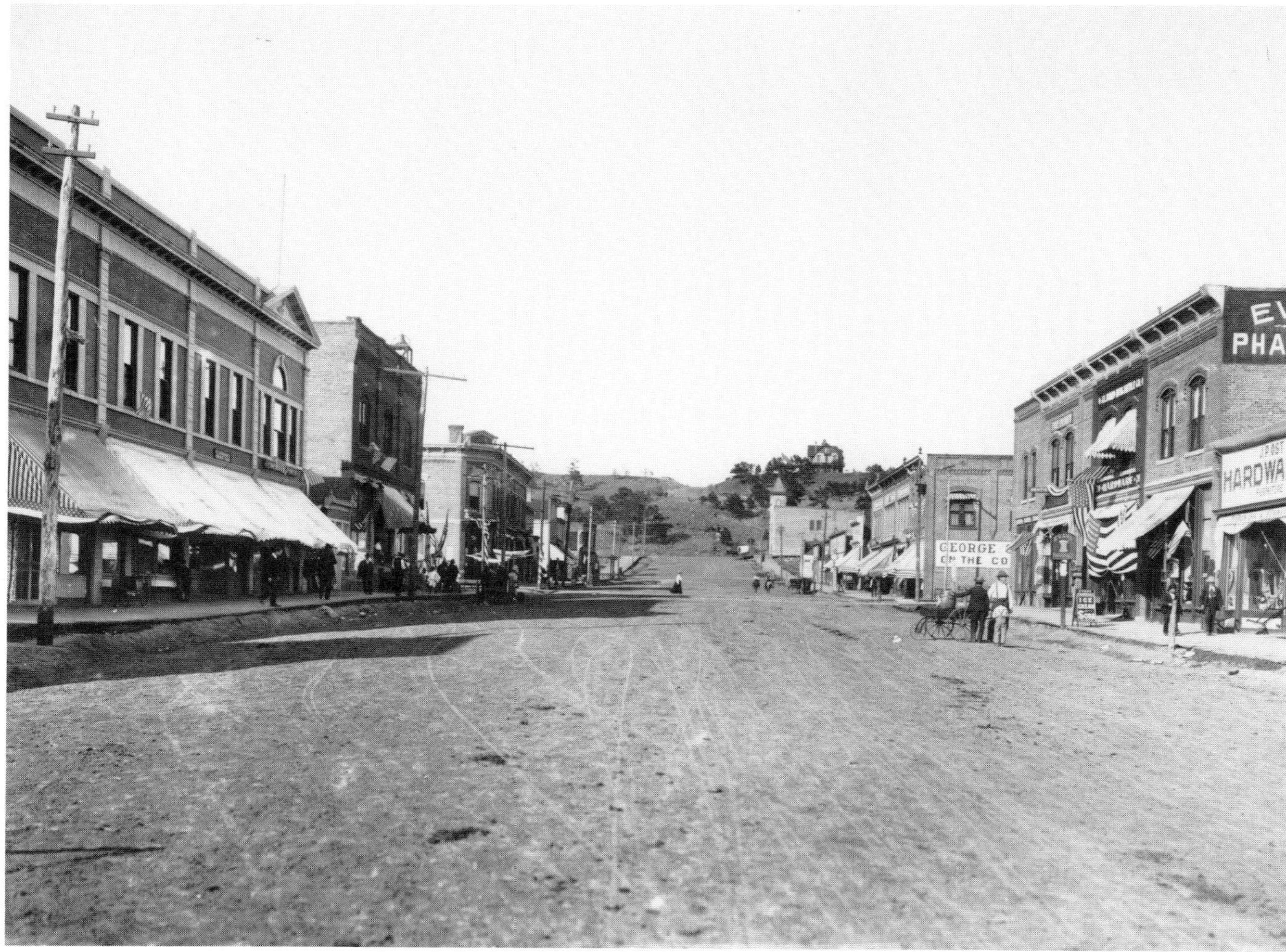

Fig. 92. Main Street, Newcastle, 1903.

The house of Senator Frank Mondell is no longer on the hill at center in this view of Newcastle. Several buildings can still be seen on Main Street.

The white lines in the foreground of this shot identify this location as the very center of Main Street. Because it was taken on a Saturday morning, I asked a police officer to direct traffic around me so that I could take this shot.

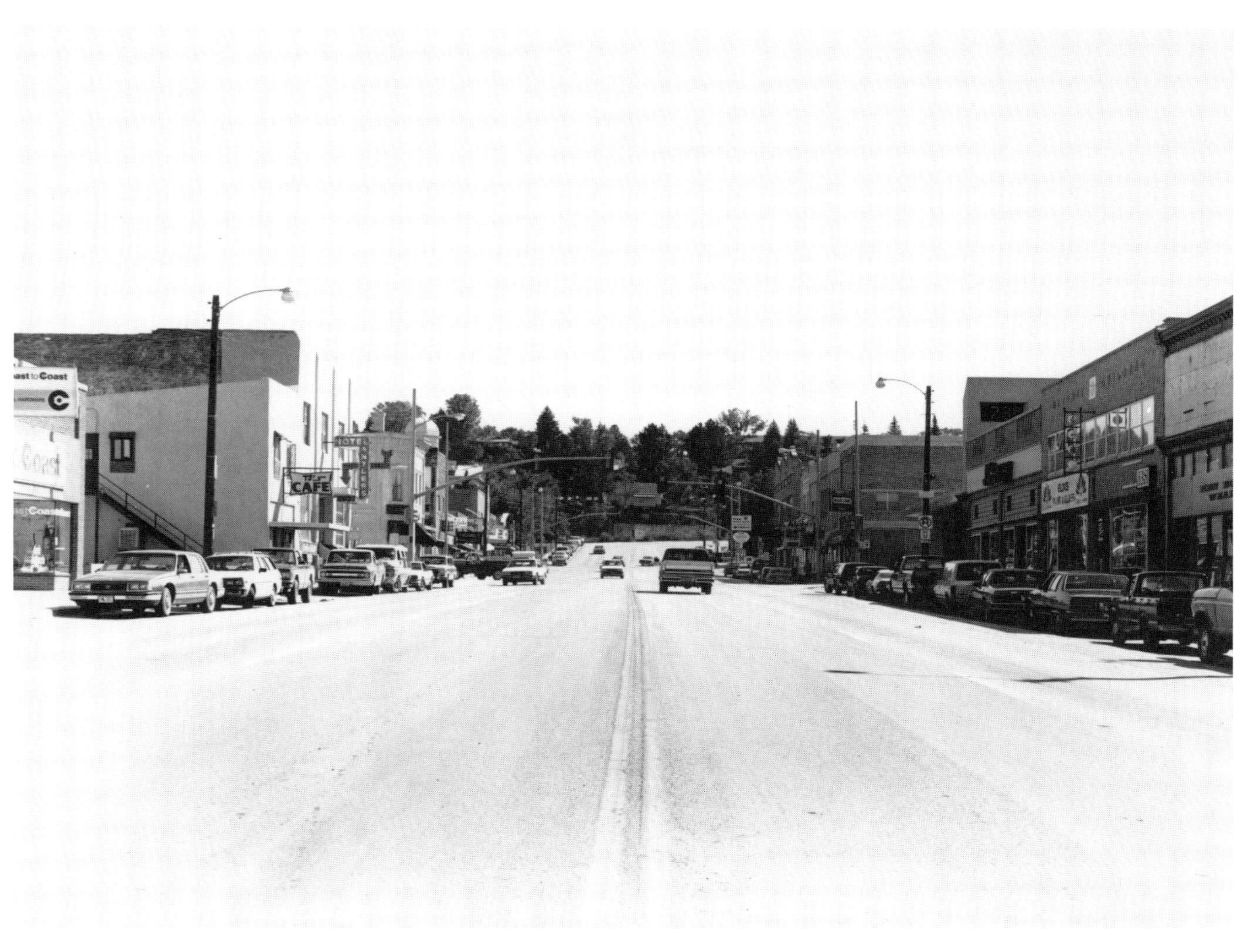
CAFE

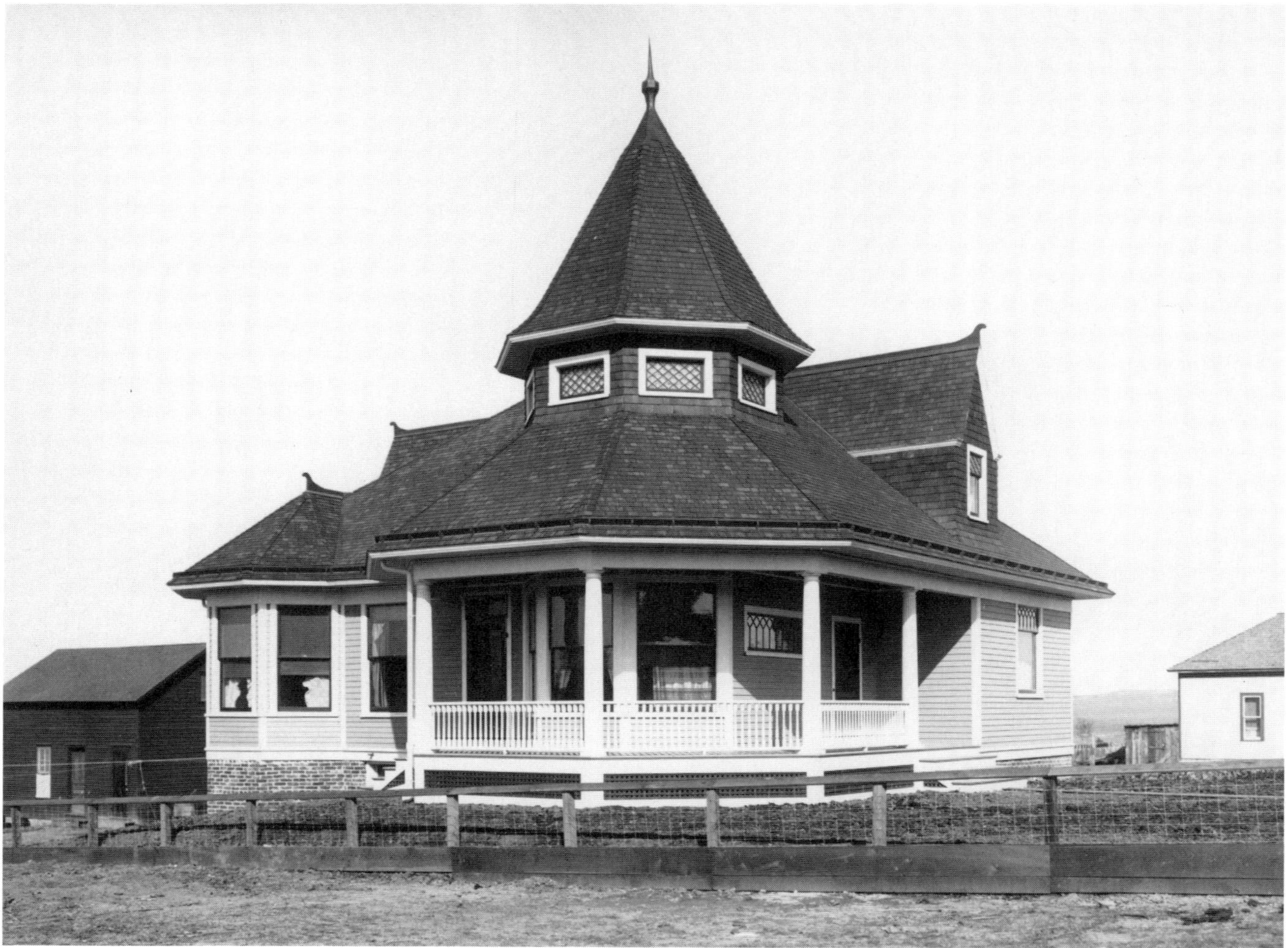

Fig. 93. The Douglas Hospital, 1903.

The town of Douglas was named for Senator Stephen Douglas of Illinois. It was established in 1886 and was home to Bill Barlow, "the Sagebrush Philosopher." The first state fair was held in Douglas in 1905. Today the town is widely known as a favorite haunt of the mythical jackalope.

The hospital, now a vacant house, was built around the turn of the century and remained in operation until after World War II. The tree at left in the modern view is not even visible in Stimson's photograph.

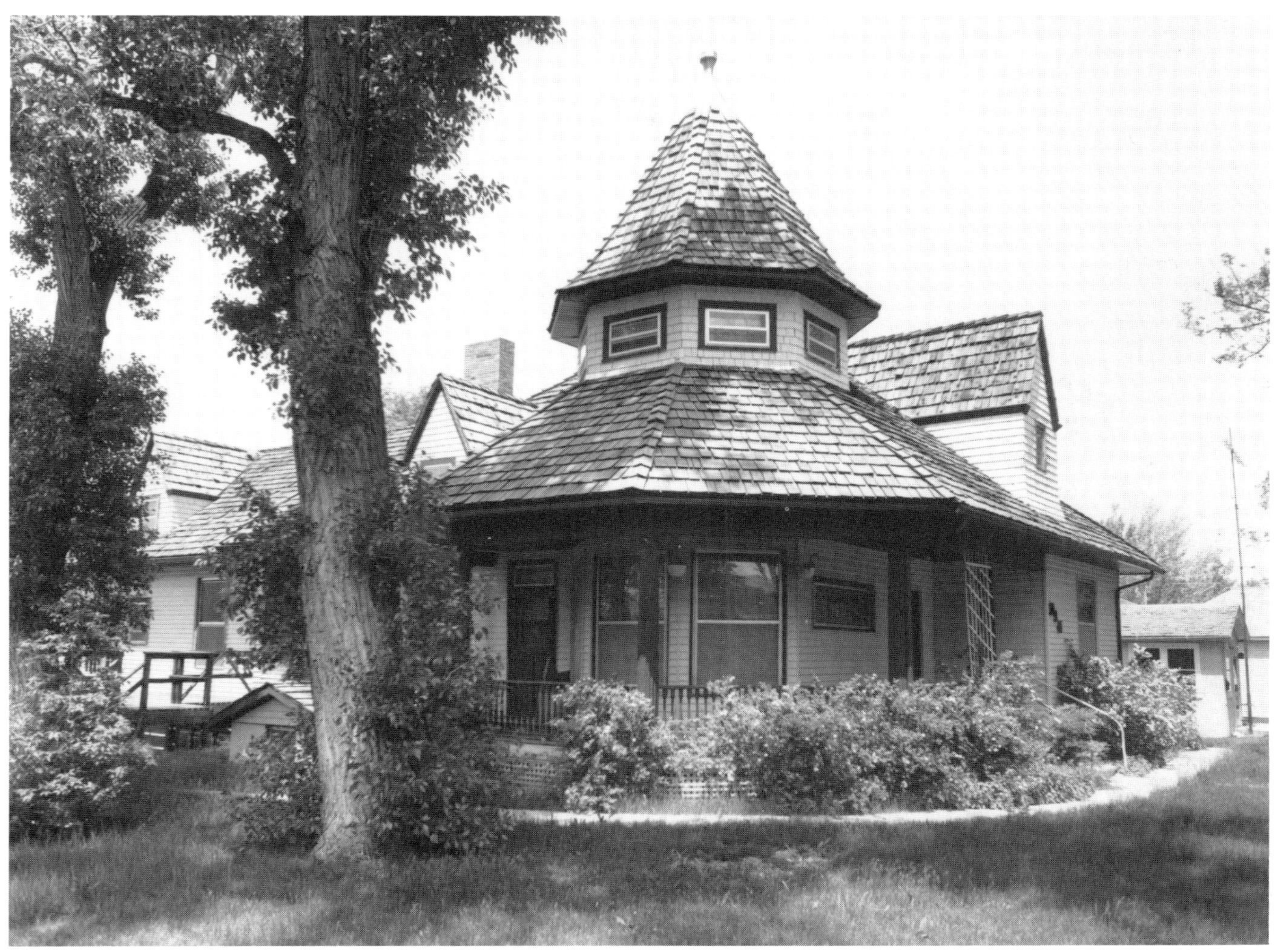

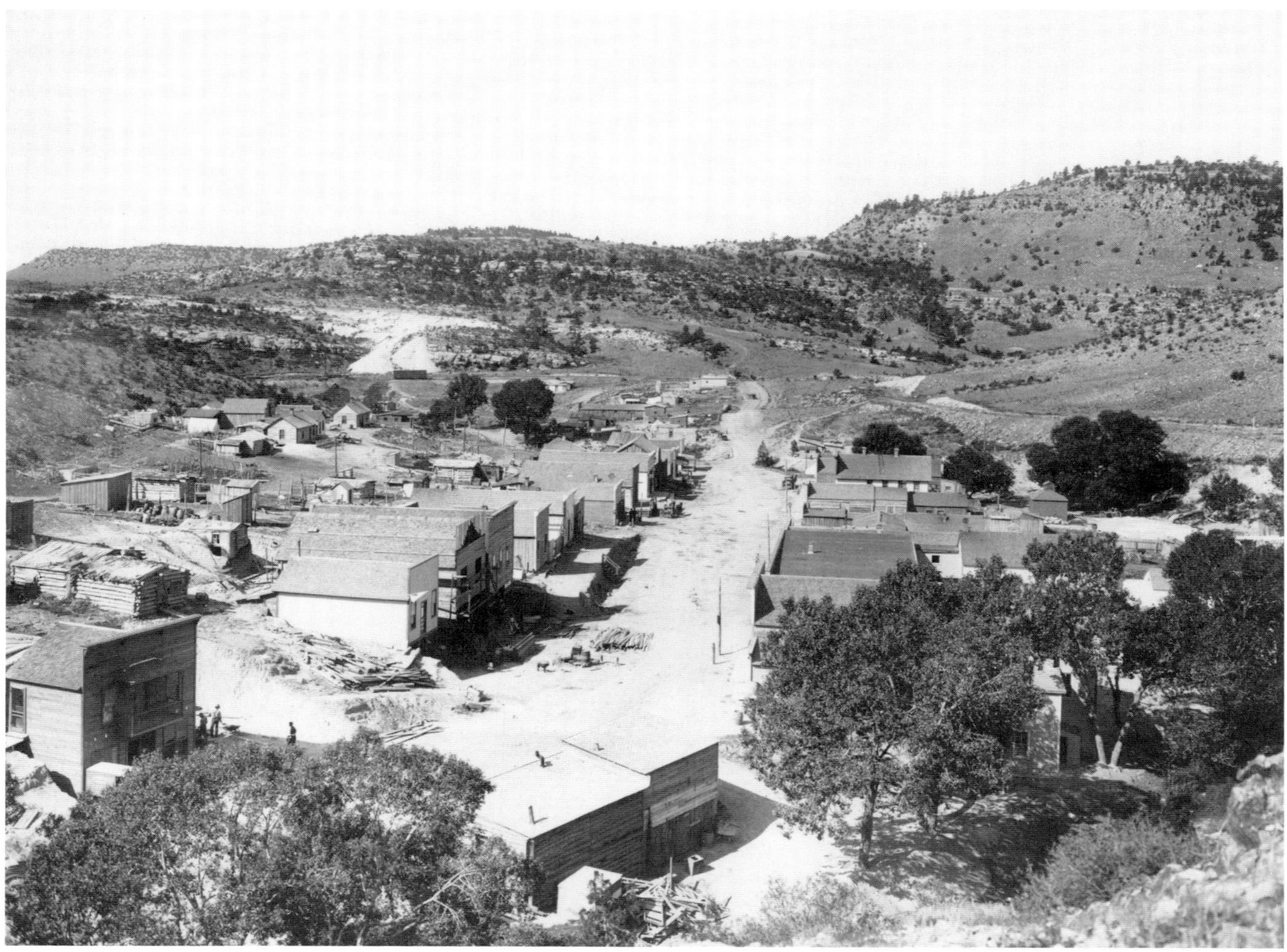

Fig. 94. Hartville, 1907.

The town of Hartville is located five miles north of Guernsey and has been the home of iron, copper, and limestone mining. The town was started in 1881 when copper ore was found nearby. Populated with miners from the Black Hills, the town had a wide-open reputation during its earliest days. Hartville boomed again after the Burlington Railroad built a branch to the Sunrise mines three miles away.

In the modern photo, the three-windowed building, left center, remains from the old view. A railroad cut can also be found at left center.

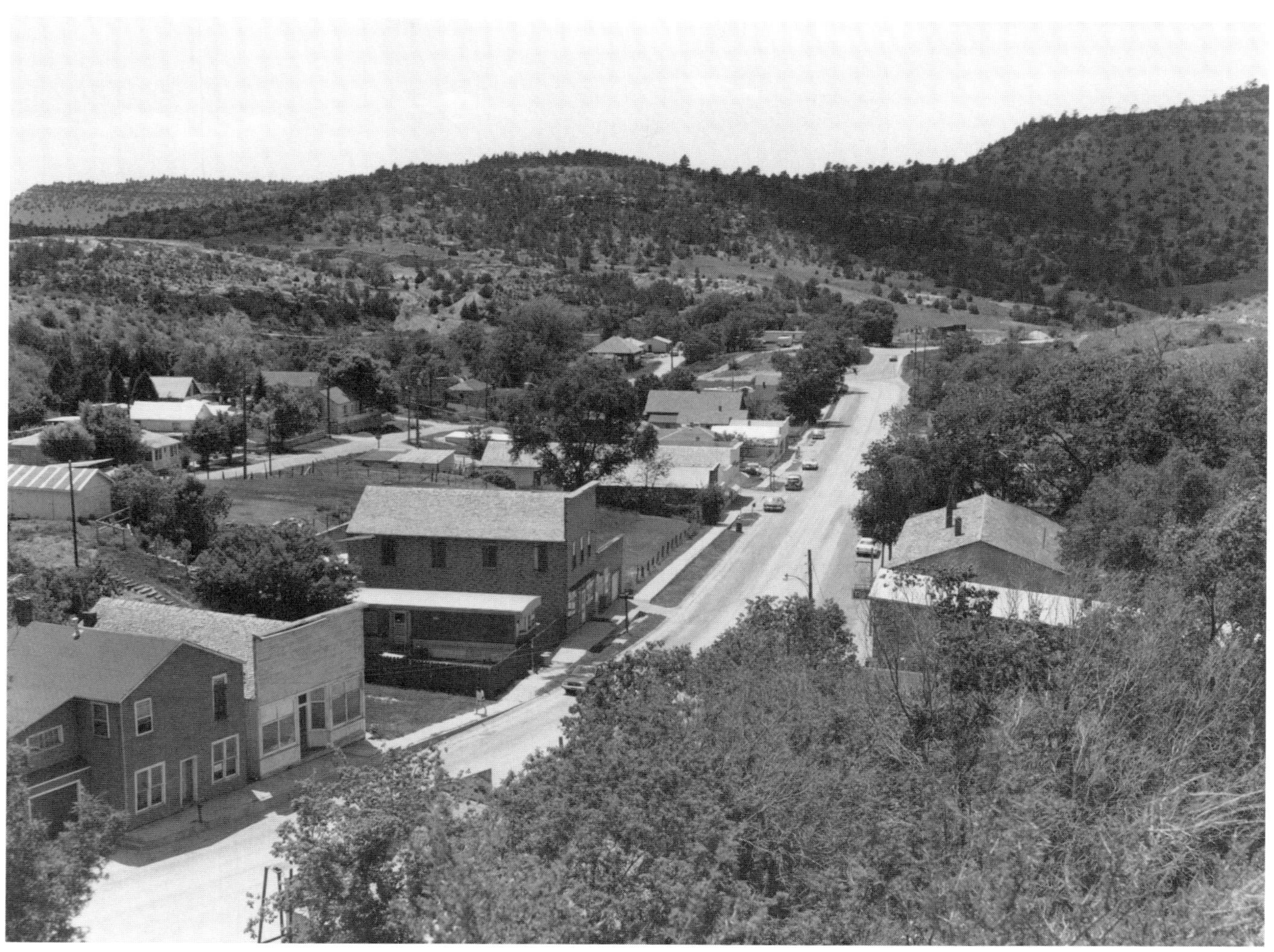

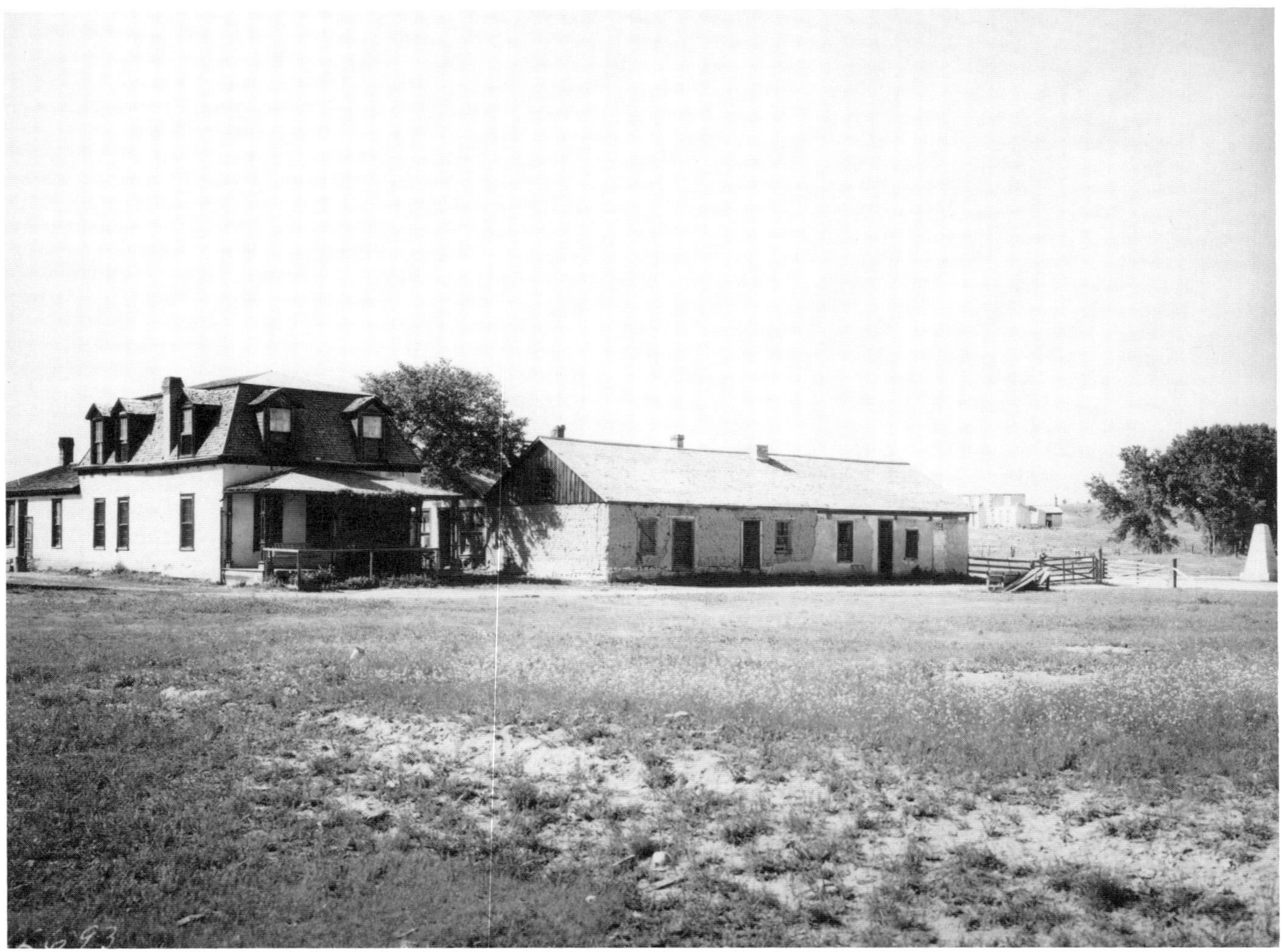

Fig. 95. Sutler's store, Fort Laramie, 1930.

One of the oldest buildings in Wyoming, part of the sutler's store at Fort Laramie was built in the 1830s. The walls are made of adobe twenty-seven inches thick, with a covering of stucco. The northern half of the store was built in 1852, and the rear portion, the enlisted men's bar and officer's bar, were completed in 1883. The sutler, a civilian post trader, sold a variety of goods. The building was restored between 1951 and 1955 and refurnished six years later in 1961. A new roof was added in 1974.

The Burt House, left, was built in 1885 by the Army Corps of Engineers. It served as living quarters for two of the post's families. The white obelisk, at right center, was erected in 1915 by a group of concerned Wyoming historians, including Grace Raymond Hebard, to mark the site of the decaying fort.

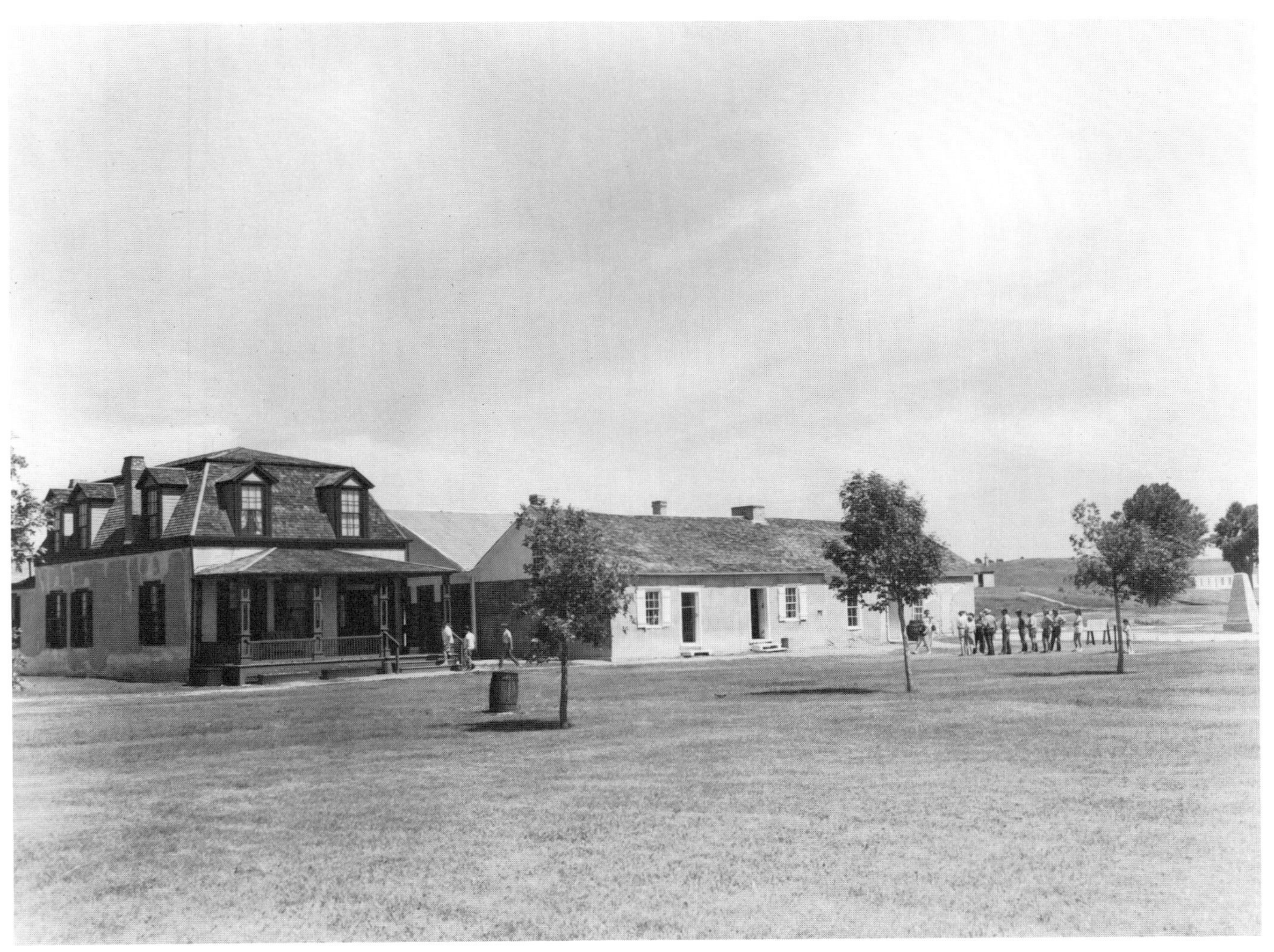

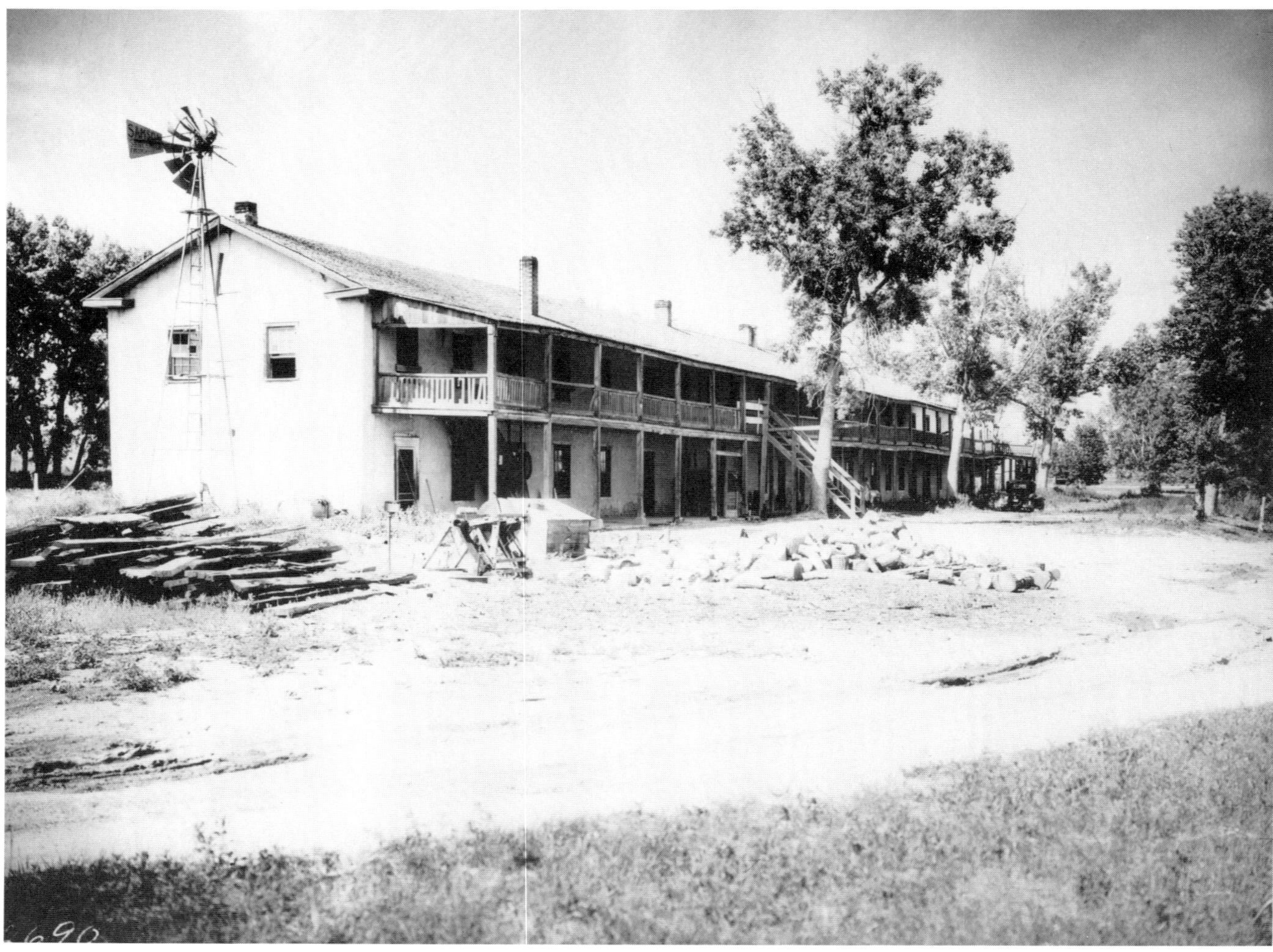

Fig. 96. Cavalry barracks, Fort Laramie, 1930.

The cavalry barracks were built in 1874 by the Army Corps of Engineers. The building material used was a form of lime grout. It is 270 feet long by 26 feet wide. The building housed cavalry troopers from its construction until 1883. During the previous winter, the veranda was added, and infantrymen then occupied the barracks until the fort was closed in 1890. During the early twentieth century, the barracks was converted into an automobile motel. It has recently been restored to its 1876 condition.

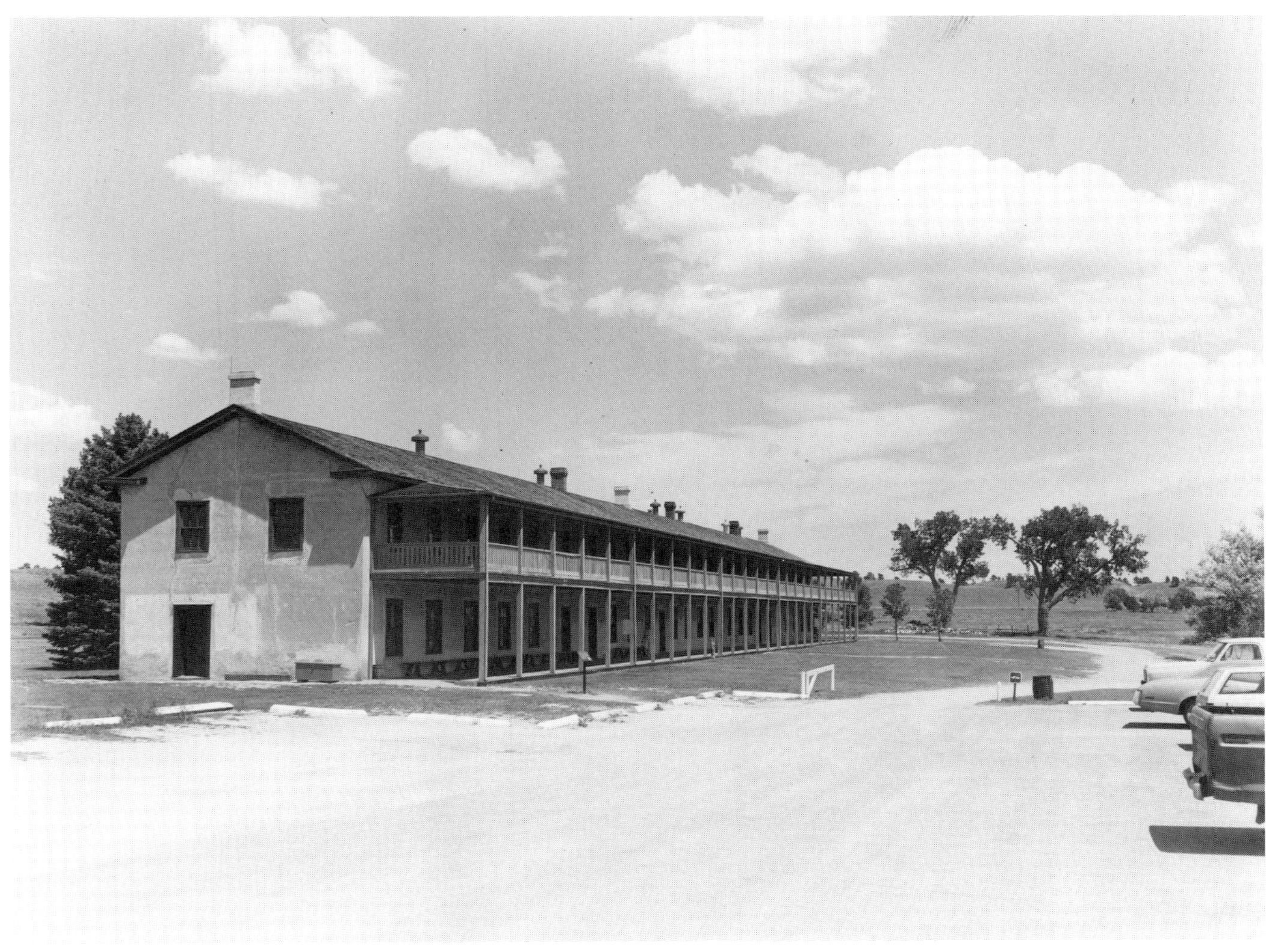

A Closer Look: Interpretive Rephotography

This set of photographs could have fit into any of the three main themes of this book. Instead, because of some fairly obvious characteristics, the photos have been included in their own chapter to show how rephotography can yield answers to the question of how Wyoming has changed since Stimson's day. All of the pairs of photographs in this book suggest something about time's effect on Wyoming.

In the first chapter, man's impact on the environment is slight. Some scenes, like the Yellowstone Falls, seem ageless. Other views, like Dome Lake, show how quickly a forest can take hold of the land. The land is altered for convenience but not destroyed. The next chapter takes the opposite view and looks at how the environment makes an impact on the people of Wyoming. The views of the Forgotten Past hint at the omnipresent boom-bust economy that raises hopes only to frustrate them. The Encampment smelter and the towns of Dietz and Carneyville attest to this pattern in Wyoming's economy. The third chapter takes yet another view by examining man's impact on man. As the years go by, each generation finds a new use for the leftover man-built environment of its predecessors. The changing shops along Cheyenne's streets reflect this dynamic.

This chapter, then, will try to go beyond the themes of previous chapters to show more subtle yet deeper roots that characterize Wyoming in the twentieth century. If J. E. Stimson photographed Wyoming's best in his time, these photographs, more than any others, will show what has become of that Wyoming.

Although my views are not meant to place a value on the changes that have taken place but merely to point out some of the differences, I am reminded of Mark Klett's words describing the Rephotographic Survey Project's work on the photographs of William Henry Jackson and other photographers.

Klett said that each pair of photographs not only presents a detailed image of each scene as viewed by the photographer but also contains a deeper, cultural meaning that goes beyond the image itself. By making the photographs as close as possible to the originals, the rephotographer has brought each scene to life. Klett said:

> Side by side, the pairs suggest movement—the growth, development and dissolution that occurred after the nineteenth century photographers made their pictures.

In a sense, I have tried to bring to life the Wyoming of J. E. Stimson, and this final chapter goes the furthest toward helping us to understand how the state is both different and similar to the Wyoming of almost a century ago.

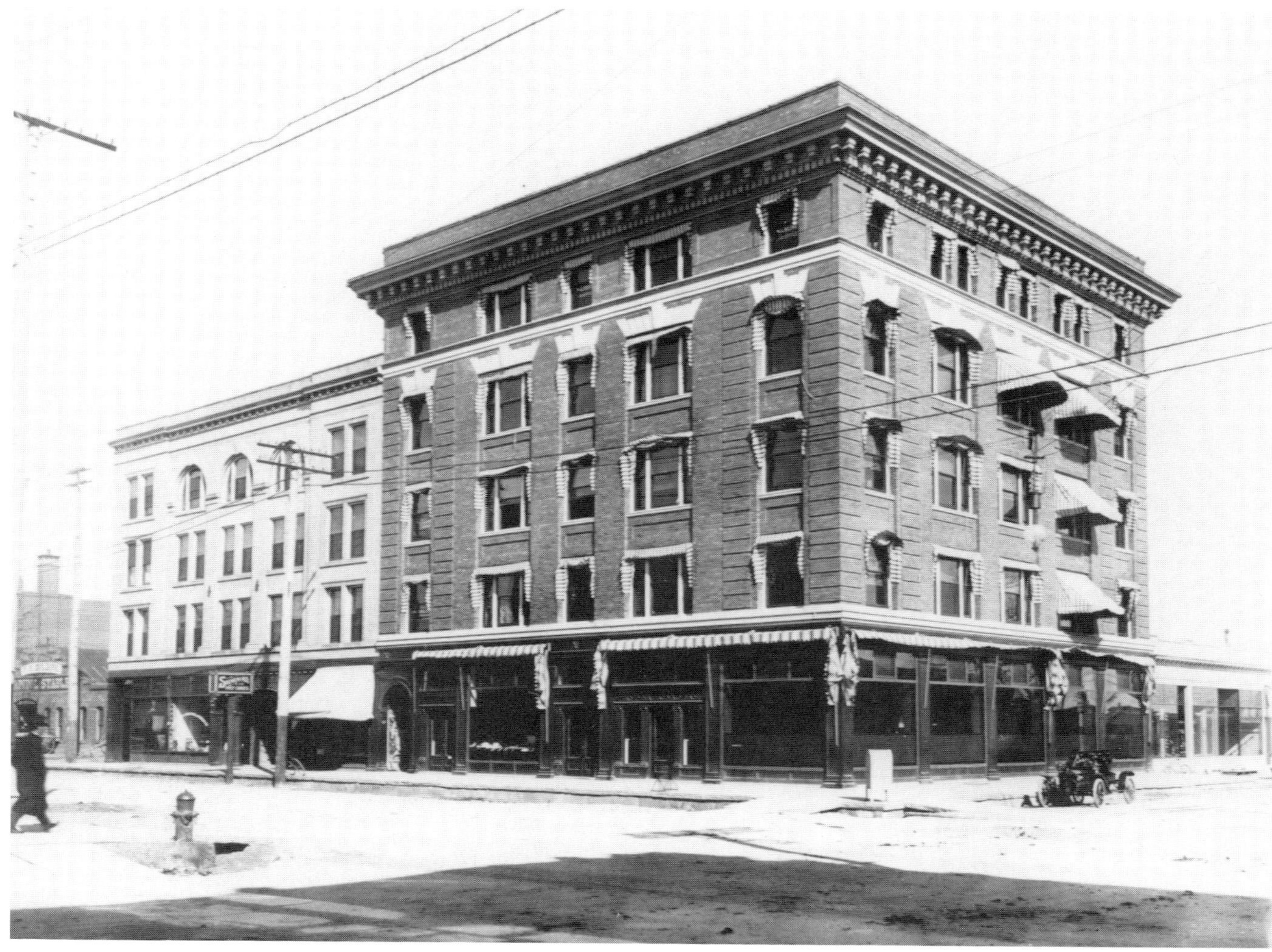

Fig. 97. First National Bank building, Cheyenne, 1908.

This view of the First National Bank building, on the northeast corner of Capitol Avenue and Sixteenth Street, is a classic Stimson view. When compared to the modern photo, many interesting details reflect the changes that have occurred over the years.

On many of the south-facing windows of the bank building in Stimson's shot can be found awnings to provide shade. In the modern photo, the awnings are gone, but many of the windows now have air-conditioners! At right center of the modern photo can be found the west wing of the Plains Hotel. The telephone wires and cable car cables from Stimson's view also no longer exist. Finally, I parked my Ford pickup in the same place that Stimson had parked his Model T.

But by far the most interesting comparison can be found on the Majestic Theater building to the left of the bank building. In Stimson's view, a small sign can be found under the middle pair of windows. It reads:

Souvenirs
Post Cards

In the modern photo, at the same location, can be found another sign. Certainly the message attests to the societal changes that have occurred since Stimson's day. The new sign reads:

Naughty Greeting Cards

This simple change of signs clearly shows that times have changed in Wyoming since Stimson's day. With its modern buildings and cable car, downtown Cheyenne reflected the pulse of the capitol city. Indeed, Stimson's view of the First National Bank was taken soon after the bank opened—a testimony to the city's progressive leaders. A photo like this one would help bring investors to Cheyenne and, in turn, the Union Pacific. I doubt if the city fathers would have allowed such a risqué sign to hang in the heart of their city.

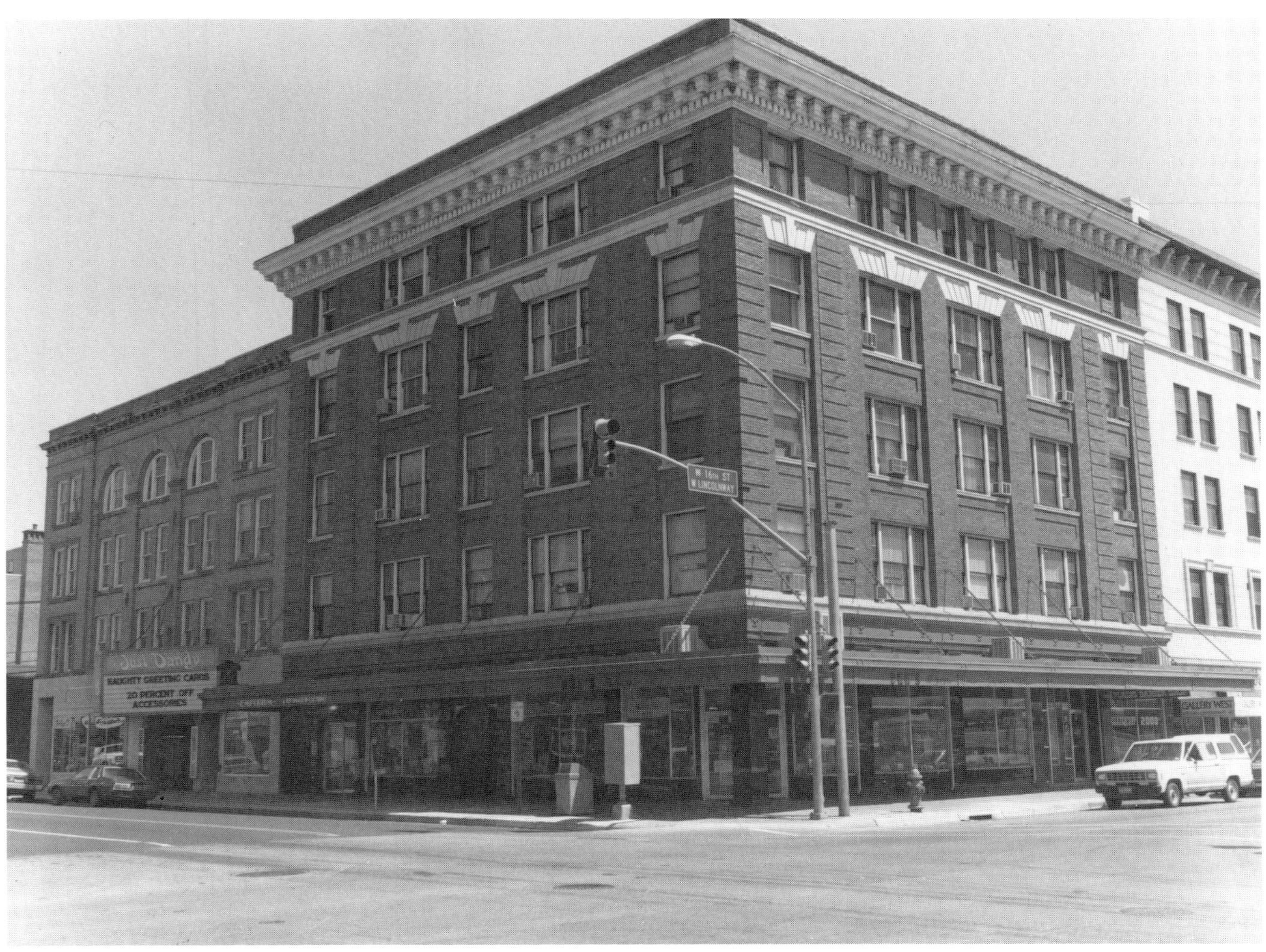

In the modern view, the old downtown is no longer the center of Cheyenne. Instead, the commercial interests are focused on the Frontier Mall on the north side of town. Because fewer people might view this sign and possibly object to its content, the sign is allowed to stay. This pair of photographs, then, not only shows society's changing values but also the shift in commercial focus away from the downtown.

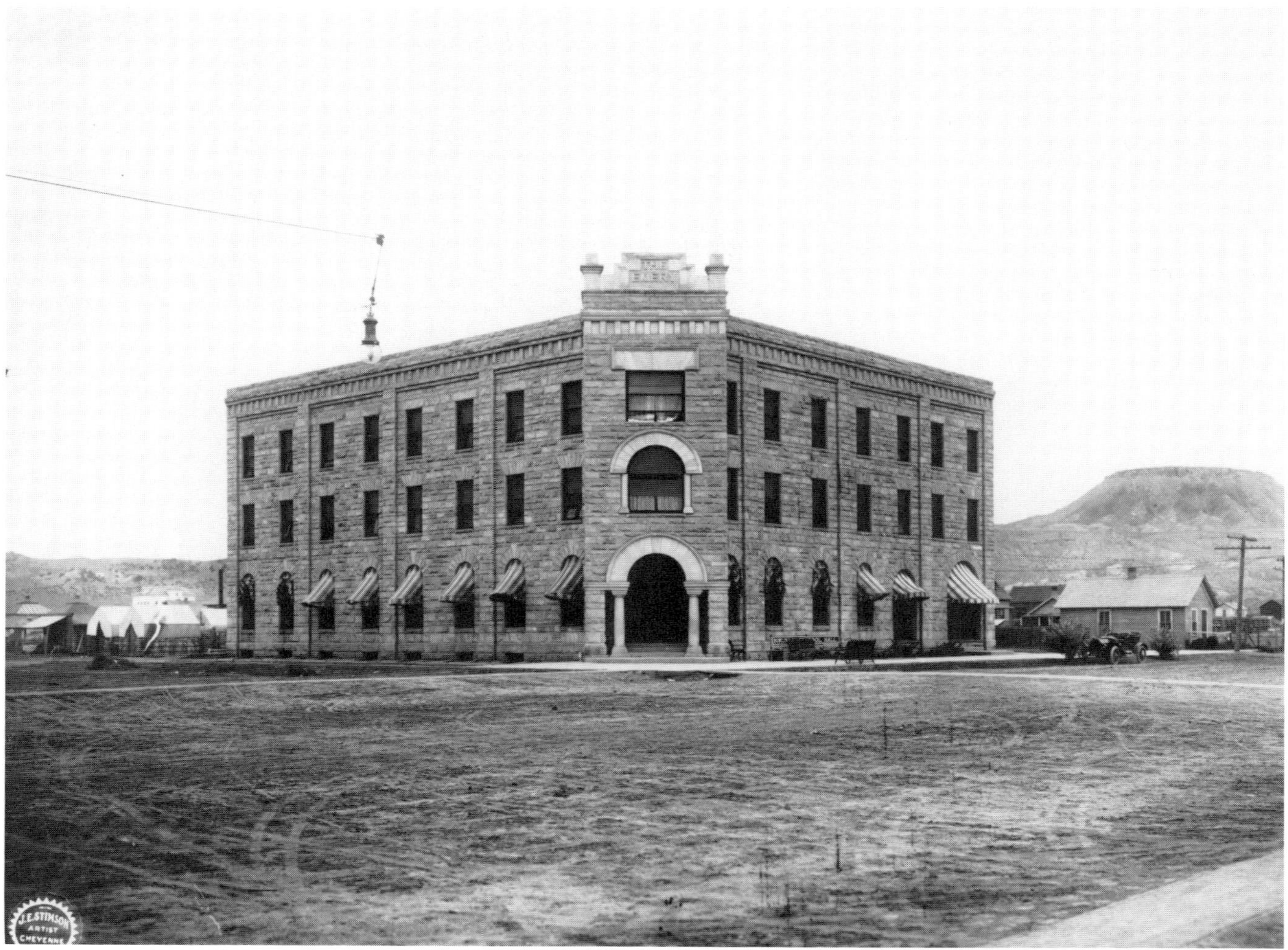

Fig. 98. The Emery Hotel, Thermopolis, 1910.

The Emery Hotel was opened in 1906 by H. O. Emery. Constructed of native stone and locally cut timber, the Emery had forty rooms, a bar, and a restaurant. During the 1930s, famed cowboy Nick Knight and his wife operated the hotel. In 1963, to keep up with the growing trend of limited service automobile motels, the Emery was torn down and replaced by the Moonlighter Motel. Special demolition equipment had to be brought from Denver to accomplish the destruction of the hotel.

Like the previous photograph, this pair of photos hint at more than just the replacement of an old hotel with a modern motel. During its heyday, the Emery was the focal point of Thermopolis for locals and tourists alike. For the latter group, which came to Thermopolis to enjoy the soothing waters of the town's hot springs, the Emery was a home away from home. A place to sleep, a restaurant to eat in, a bar, and even a pool hall and bowling alley (note sign in old photo) were all within easy reach.

The demolition of the Emery in 1963 reflects not only the growing popularity of automobiles and auto motels but also the changing American attitude toward commercial lodgings. It is ironic that in a town known for its hot springs, the Moonlighter boasts a heated swimming pool. The Moonlighter, like most motels, maintains no restaurant, bar, pool hall, or bowling alley. Food and entertainment must be acquired someplace else. The home away from home atmosphere that the Emery offered is no longer available.

A close look at the modern photograph suggests an alternative, or compromise, between the Emery and Moonlighter. At the corner, right center, can be found a mobile home. Complete with bed, kitchen, and possibly a portable bar, television, and VCR, the motor home synthesizes the Emery and Moonlighter into a modern, if not future, form of accommodation.

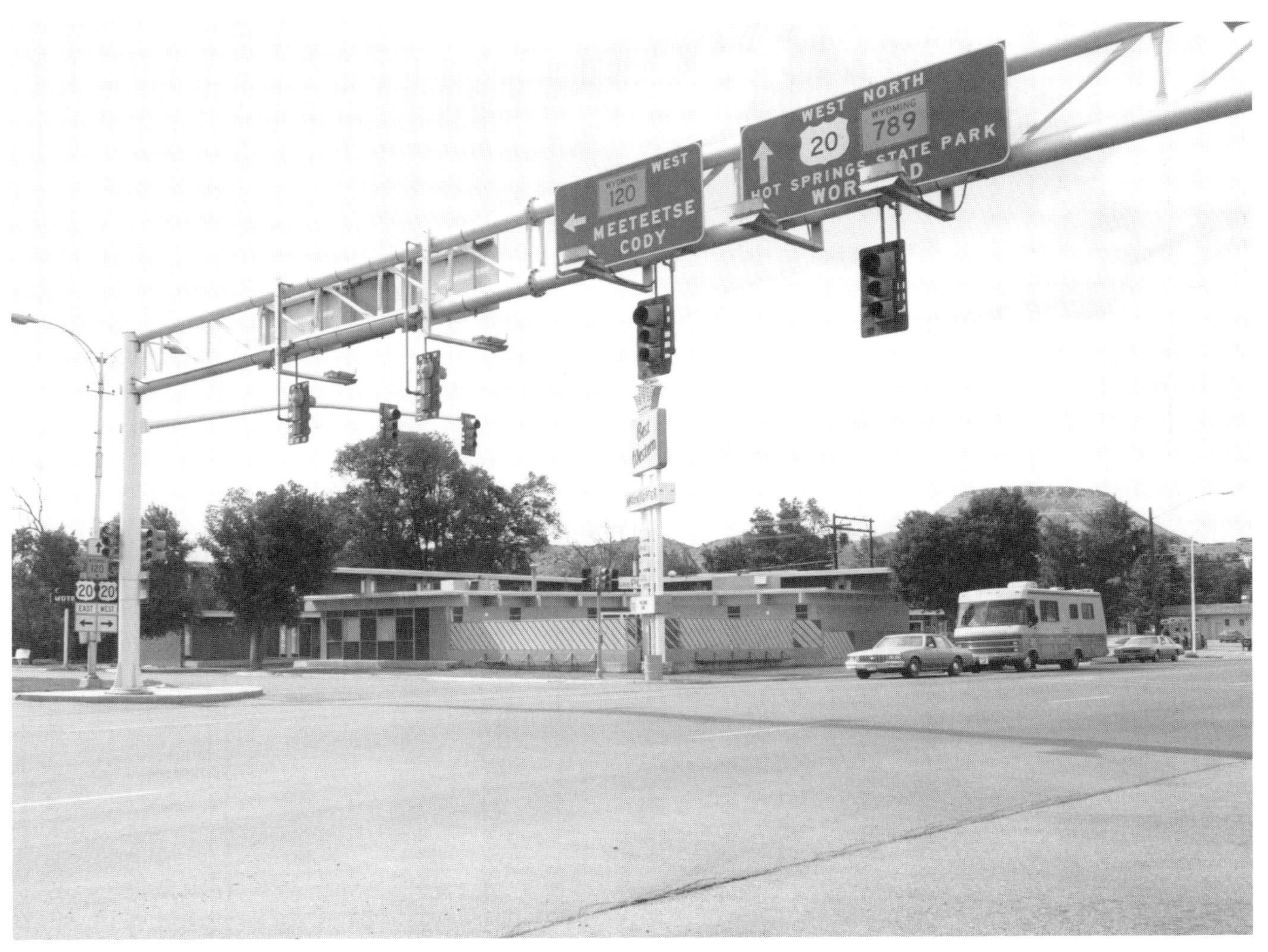
WEST
WYOMING
120
MEETEETSE
CODY
WEST NORTH
20
WYOMING
789
HOT SPRINGS STATE PARK

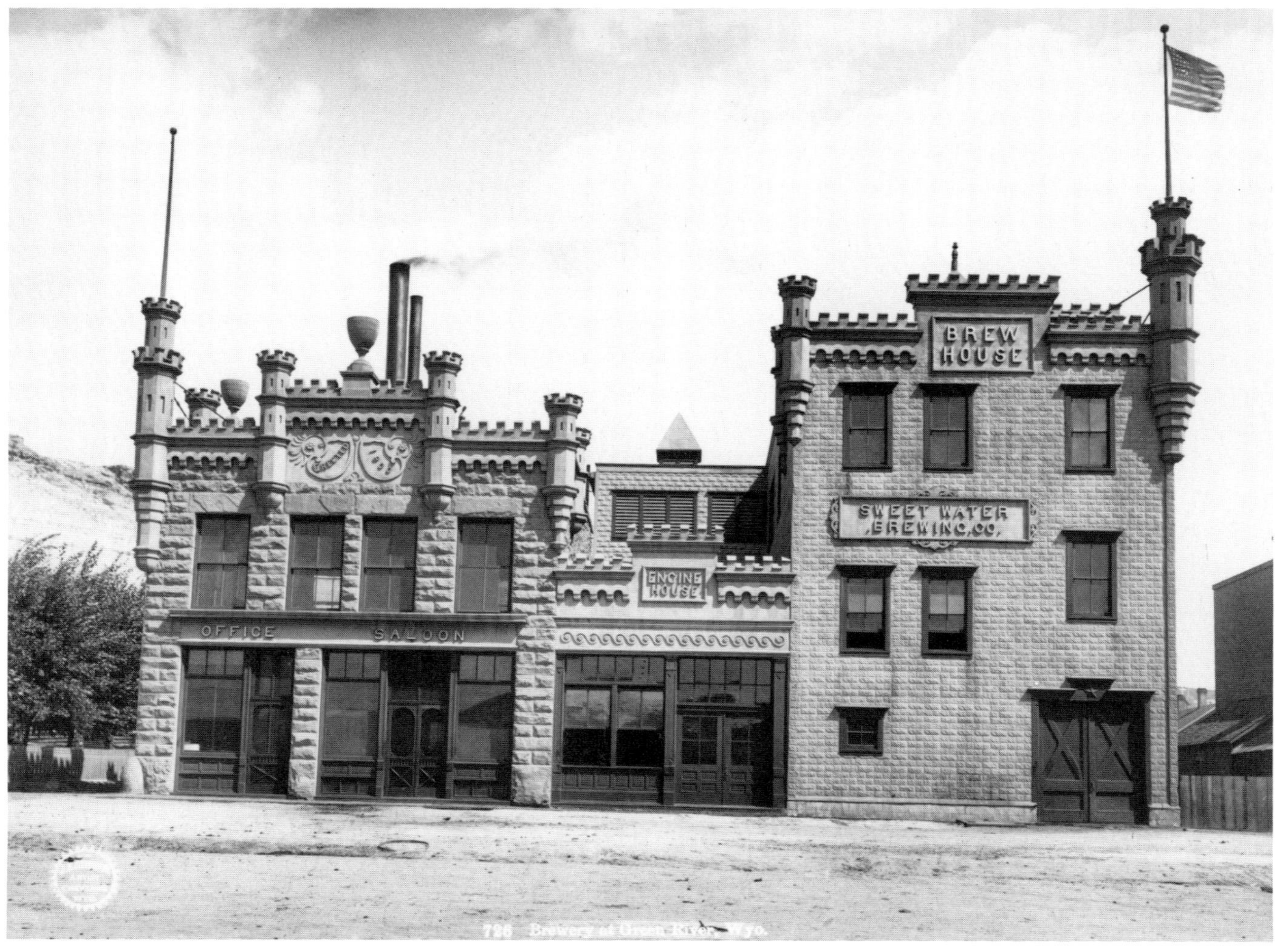

Fig. 99. Brewery at Green River, 1903.

The first brewery in Green River was opened in 1872, before either a school or a courthouse had been constructed. By 1879 the brewery was purchased by a man named Karl Spinner. Business increased to the point where five thousand barrels of beer were produced each year. During Spinner's tenure, the name Green River Brewery was adopted, and the brewery began to ship its product across the country. After placing second at the 1890 Columbia Exposition, the beer became known as Columbia Beer.

The modern era began in 1891 when the brewery was purchased by brewmaster Hugo Gaensslen. A graduate of the United States Brewery Academy in New York City, Gaensslen oversaw the construction of a three-story frame building with tin siding. The operation was expanded and incorporated, and the name was changed to Sweetwater Brewing Company. A new name for the beer, "The Pioneer Wyoming Brew," was also adopted during this time. In 1900 the stone structure seen in Stimson's photo was built. Patterned after the famous Chicago Water Tower, the new building incorporated four towers with merlons, crenels, and coping. Large stone urns that resemble beer glasses were placed atop each high point, and a beer barrel was carved into the stone on the side.

In 1904 and 1905, The Pioneer Wyoming Brew won medals at the St. Louis Exposition and Lewis and Clark Exposition in Portland, Oregon. The saloon, left center in the old photo, was leased to private individuals so that Gaensslen could concentrate on his brewing. An icehouse, essential in prepasteurization days, was also maintained nearby.

During Prohibition, various citrus crushes, a nonalcoholic near beer known as Wyoming Beverage, and a lemon-lime drink named Green River, were produced. But because of local moonshining, the near beer never became very popular. In 1931 Gaensslen died, and the operation closed

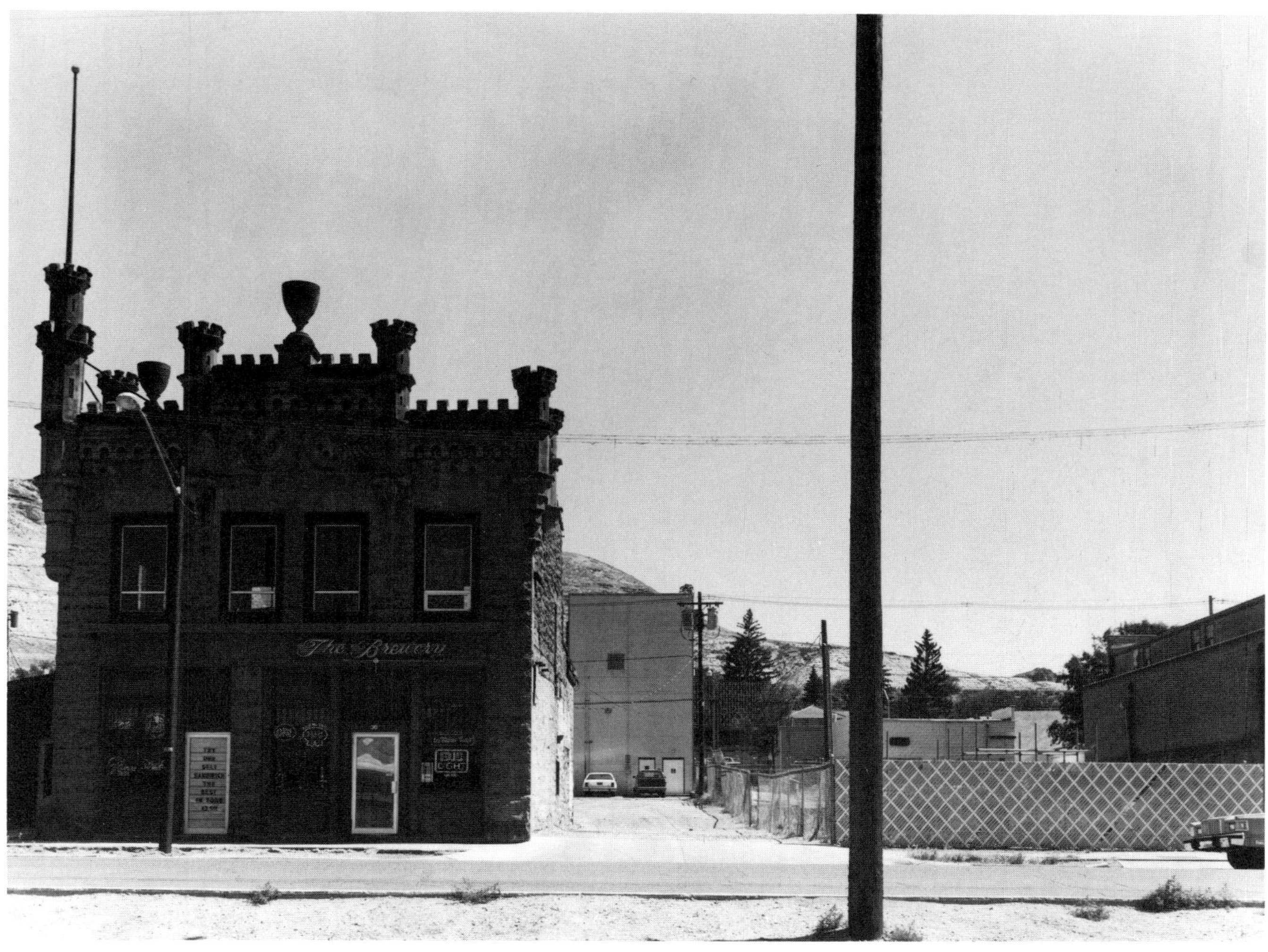

two years before Prohibition ended. In 1936 the brewery operated for a short time before being permanently closed.

Local history aside, this pair of photographs hints at the homogenization and consumer culture that have changed America since the early photo was taken. When J. E. Stimson visited Green River in 1903, he could go to the Sweetwater Brewery and get a mug of the locally produced Pioneer Wyoming Brew. He could visit with Gaensslen and see local workers making a local product.

Today the scene is very different. Only one-third of the original structure has survived. The section of the old brewery marked "saloon" now houses a saloon called The Brewery. If someone were to buy a beer at The Brewery, he would not be able to find a local product. Instead, he would get the same kind of beer in Green River as he could get nearly anywhere else in the country. Large corporations with beers such as "Oly" and Bud Light (note signs in the window of the modern photo) have driven the local products off the market. Our country is much more homogenized today; things are the same everywhere you go. Most foods are available anywhere in the country. This trend assures the consumer of a similar product throughout the country, but it contributes to the loss of the small-town atmosphere that many people have experienced.

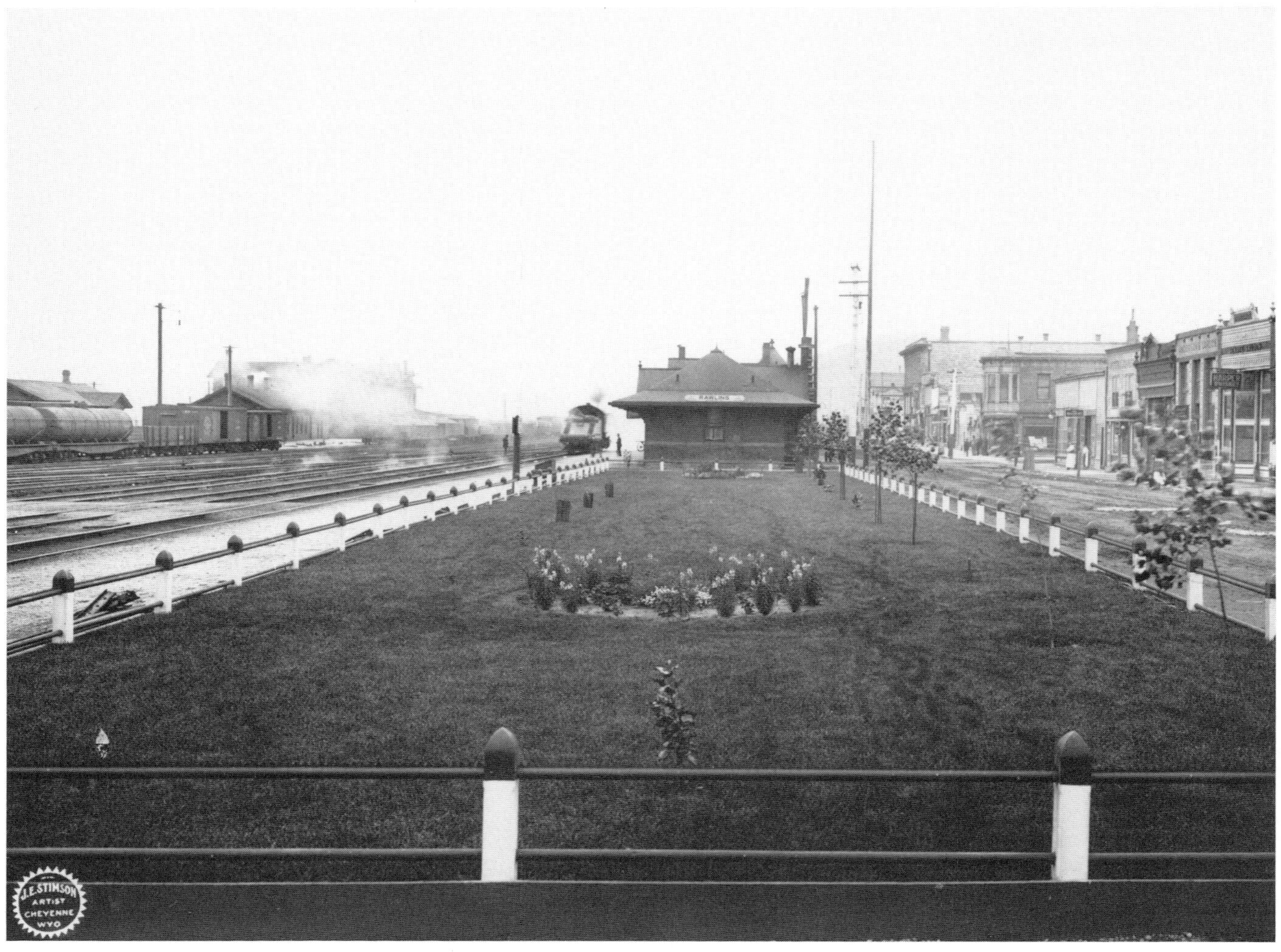

Fig. 100. Union Pacific Depot and Park, Rawlins, 1909.

Probably more than any other set of photographs, this pair of the Rawlins Depot and park exemplifies what has become of J. E. Stimson's best of Wyoming.

For visitors traveling eastward on the Union Pacific, the Rawlins Depot must have seemed a virtual oasis in the Red Desert. As in all UP towns, the depot was the first place that visitors saw when they got off their train. It was their first impression, and it was important for the Union Pacific to make this impression a positive one. The task was accomplished in part by providing a permanent, stylish depot. Built of brick, the Rawlins Depot met this basic criterion. Another crucial element was for the railroad to beautify the grounds around the depot so that passengers would have a comfortable place to stretch their legs. The UP did this by landscaping beautiful parks near each station. Cheyenne, Laramie, Rawlins, Rock Springs, Green River, and Evanston all had parks. With elaborate (at least for arid Wyoming) rock gardens, deciduous trees, flowers, lawns, and fences, the parks also became a place for locals to picnic and train watch. Together, the depot and the depot park served as a transition between the mechanized railroad and the town.

Joseph Stimson's job was to capture this important public-relations device on film. It was hoped that his shots of a town's depot and park would attract investors. These investors would then help to build up the downtown commercial district seen at the right side of Stimson's view. In turn, these investors would bring more business to the Union Pacific. Like so many of his photographs, this luscious Stimson view of Rawlins certainly was not typical of the town. Instead this photo is a prime example of Stimson's view of Wyoming's finest.

Today the view in Rawlins is very different. The Rawlins Depot is no longer the first thing that visitors see when they arrive. In fact, passenger trains no longer travel the Union Pacific lines. Because of this, the Union Pacific,

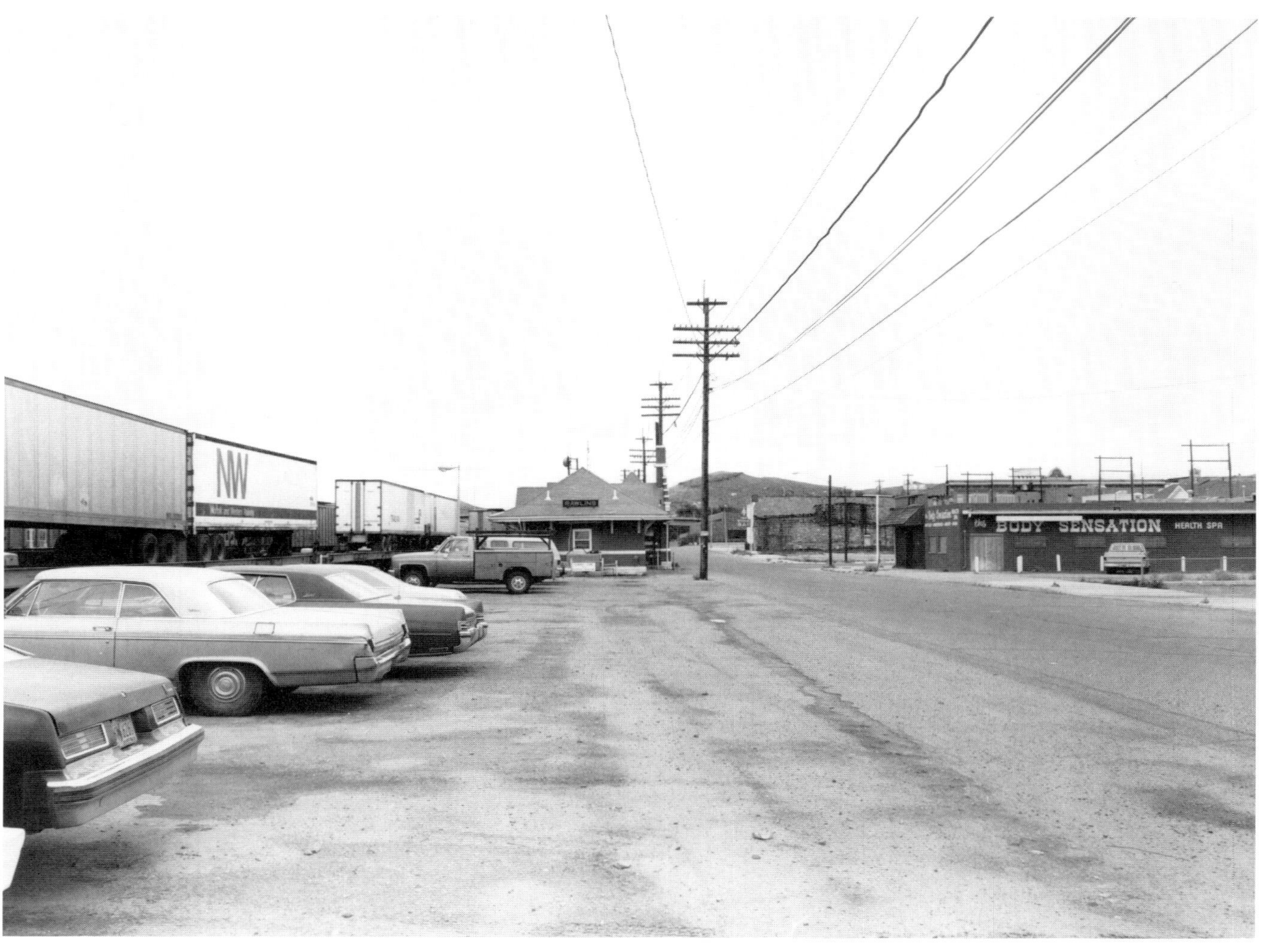

as well as the railroad towns along its path, do not have a direct interest in maintaining either their depots or the adjacent parks. Many of the old depots are gone; the Rawlins Depot is closed. Likewise, nearly all of the beautiful depot parks that Stimson photographed are gone today. Dusty parking lots like this one now occupy the grounds.

A direct result of this lost highway is the slow destruction of the downtown commercial center. The modern view shows that very few of the Front Street buildings remain from Stimson's photo. With less depot traffic, many businesses have either closed down or moved out to the highway to try to lure business from more modern transportation lines.

A scene similar to Stimson's view can be found in Rawlins, but at the site that provides the modern parallel to the depot of eighty years ago. As with the relocated commercial areas, a good place to look is Interstate 80. Following much of the same trail that the UP blazed one hundred years earlier, Interstate 80 is also a large people-mover. Businesses near the highway provide the same first impression and transition function that the depot and park once did. A stop at McDonald's offers the appropriate parallel scene, with its trees and grass and playground for the kids. Like the depot and park, the restaurant is often the first impression of Rawlins for many travelers.

Many of the photographs in this book could be interpreted in the same detail as these last four. If Stimson photographed the best of Wyoming to promote investment and tourism, it is interesting to speculate about what he would photograph today. With its important function and scenic grounds, perhaps McDonald's would have been included.

Appendix A

Photo References

This table includes the figure number of each pair of rephotographs, a description of the site, date of the original Stimson photograph, date of the modern photograph, and finally the Stimson collection archives number of each print. Using this identification number, specific Stimson photographs may be purchased from the Department of Commerce, Division of Parks and Cultural Resources, Museums Division/Photographs.

Fig. No.	Description	Date of Original	Date of Rephoto	Archives No.
1.	Granite Springs outing	1908	1987	2233
2.	Vedauwoo rock formation	c. 1910	1988	6021
3.	Red Buttes country	1906	1988	1423
4.	Sphinx Rock	1906	1988	1426
5.	Castle Dome	1906	1988	1409
6.	Maine Rock	1906	1988	1417
7.	Beehive Rocks	1906	1988	1420
8.	La Prele Dam	1910	1988	2931
9.	Natural Bridge	1903	1988	820
10.	Wind River Canyon	c. 1925	1988	5921
11.	Thermopolis Fountain	1910	1988	3129
12.	Devil's Tower	1903	1988	470
13.	Spillway	1909	1988	2633
14.	Dome Lake Club House	1899	1988	E49
15.	Holdridge's Cottage	1899	1988	E6
16.	West view, Dome Lake Club House	1909	1988	2631
17.	Guests at Dome Lake	1909	1988	2635
18.	Eaton Bros. Ranch	1909	1988	2603
19.	Shoshone Canyon and Tunnel	1910	1988	3156
20.	Shoshone Dam	1911	1988	3157
21.	Diablo Castle	1903	1988	610
22.	Silver Gate	1902	1988	363
23.	Yellowstone Canyon	1907	1988	2063
24.	Yellowstone Falls	1902	1988	309
25.	Brink of Falls	1902	1988	341
26.	Giant Geyser	1907	1988	2079
27.	Castle Geyser	1907	1988	2091
28.	Grotto Geyser	1907	1988	2099
29.	Old Faithful Inn	1907	1988	2092
30.	Chimney and fireplace, Old Faithful Inn	1907	1988	2070
31.	Lake Hotel	1907	1988	3011
32.	Lobby, Lake Hotel	1907	1988	3004
33.	Yellowstone Lake boat	1907	1988	2073
34.	Colonel Meldrum's house	1902	1988	345
35.	Colonel Meldrum's office	1902	1988	304
36.	Grand Tetons from Bar BC	1924	1988	4471
37.	Menor's Ferry	1899	1988	E85
38.	Chapel of Transfiguration	1930	1988	4741
39.	Cambria coal camp	1903	1988	446
40.	Sunrise	1907	1987	1953
41.	Dietz	1903	1988	493
42.	Street scene, Dietz	1903	1988	492
43.	Kearney coal camp	1909	1988	2593
44.	Walcott Station	1901	1987	150
45.	Smelter, Grand Encampment	1903	1987	765a
46.	Mill at Hecla Mine	1902	1990	290
47.	Interior, Hecla Mill	1902	1990	298
48.	Dale Creek Bridge	1901	1987	247
49.	Dismantling Dale Creek Bridge	1901	1987	171
50.	Rocky Mountain Bell Telephone Co.	1906	1990	1753
51.	Nagle residence, Cheyenne	n.d.	1987	6485
52.	Masonic Temple, Cheyenne	1903	1987	374
53.	Sixteenth Street, looking east	1908	1987	4040
54.	Cheyenne, looking up Randall Avenue	1910	1987	2849
55.	Capitol Avenue, looking south	1898	1987	5704
56.	Cheyenne west from UP Depot	1910	1987	2845

Photo References

Fig. No.	Description	Date of Original	Date of Rephoto	Archives No.
57.	Panorama of Cheyenne	1910	1987	2873
58.	Panorama of Cheyenne	1910	1987	2845
59.	Lakeview Cemetery	1911	1990	3424
60.	Residence of James Mathison	1905	1987	1150
61.	Old Main, University of Wyoming	1922	1987	7045
62.	Science Hall, University of Wyoming	1903	1987	772
63.	Merica Hall, University of Wyoming	1922	1987	7049
64.	Street scene, Saratoga	1907	1987	1972
65.	Osborne Building, Rawlins	1905	1987	989
66.	The Ferris Hotel, Rawlins	1905	1987	988
67.	Green River from UP gate tower	1903	1987	728
68.	Green River	1903	1987	724
69.	Pilot Rock, Green River	1899	1987	E84
70.	South Pass City	1903	1987	647
71.	Atlantic City	1903	1987	650
72.	Street scene, Evanston	1905	1987	996
73.	Diamondville	1903	1987	719
74.	Street scene, Kemmerer	1903	1987	715
75.	Bird's-eye view of Cody	1903	1988	613
76.	Irma Hotel, Cody	1903	1988	615
77.	Panorama, Meeteetse City	1903	1988	645
78.	Bird's-eye view of Thermopolis	1910	1988	3126
79.	Street scene, Worland	1910	1988	3143
80.	Panoramic view of Buffalo	1903	1988	557
81.	Panoramic view of Buffalo	1903	1988	557
82.	The Occidental Hotel, Buffalo	1910	1988	2954
83.	Street scene, Buffalo	1903	1988	562
84.	Moncreiffe Ranch	1903	1988	480
85.	Wallop Ranch	1909	1988	2594
86.	Sheridan Inn	ca. 1899	1988	5747
87.	Dining room at Sheridan Inn	1899	1988	E22
88.	Main Street, Sheridan	1910	1988	2949
89.	Officer's quarters at Fort MacKenzie	1903	1988	496
90.	Sundance	1903	1988	471
91.	Street scene, Newcastle	1903	1988	439
92.	Main Street, Newcastle	1903	1988	438
93.	The Douglas Hospital	1903	1988	821
94.	Hartville	1907	1987	1946
95.	Sutler's store, Fort Laramie	1930	1987	4693
96.	Cavalry barracks, Fort Laramie	1930	1987	4690
97.	First National Bank building, Cheyenne	1908	1987	4038
98.	The Emery Hotel, Thermopolis	1910	1988	3131
99.	Brewery at Green River	1903	1987	726
100.	UP Depot and Park, Rawlins	1909	1987	2659

Appendix B

Site Location Maps

The Natural Landscape

YELLOWSTONE NATIONAL PARK
Shoshone River
Bighorn River
Cody
Sheridan
Buffalo
Powder River
Belle Fourche River
Gillette
Worland
Newcastle
Thermopolis
Jackson
Snake River
Wind River
Riverton
Casper
South Pass City
Sweetwater River
North Platte River
Wheatland
Laramie River
Kemmerer
Green River
Rock Springs
Green River
Rawlins
Saratoga
Encampment
Laramie
Cheyenne
Evanston
0 10 20 30 40 50 Miles

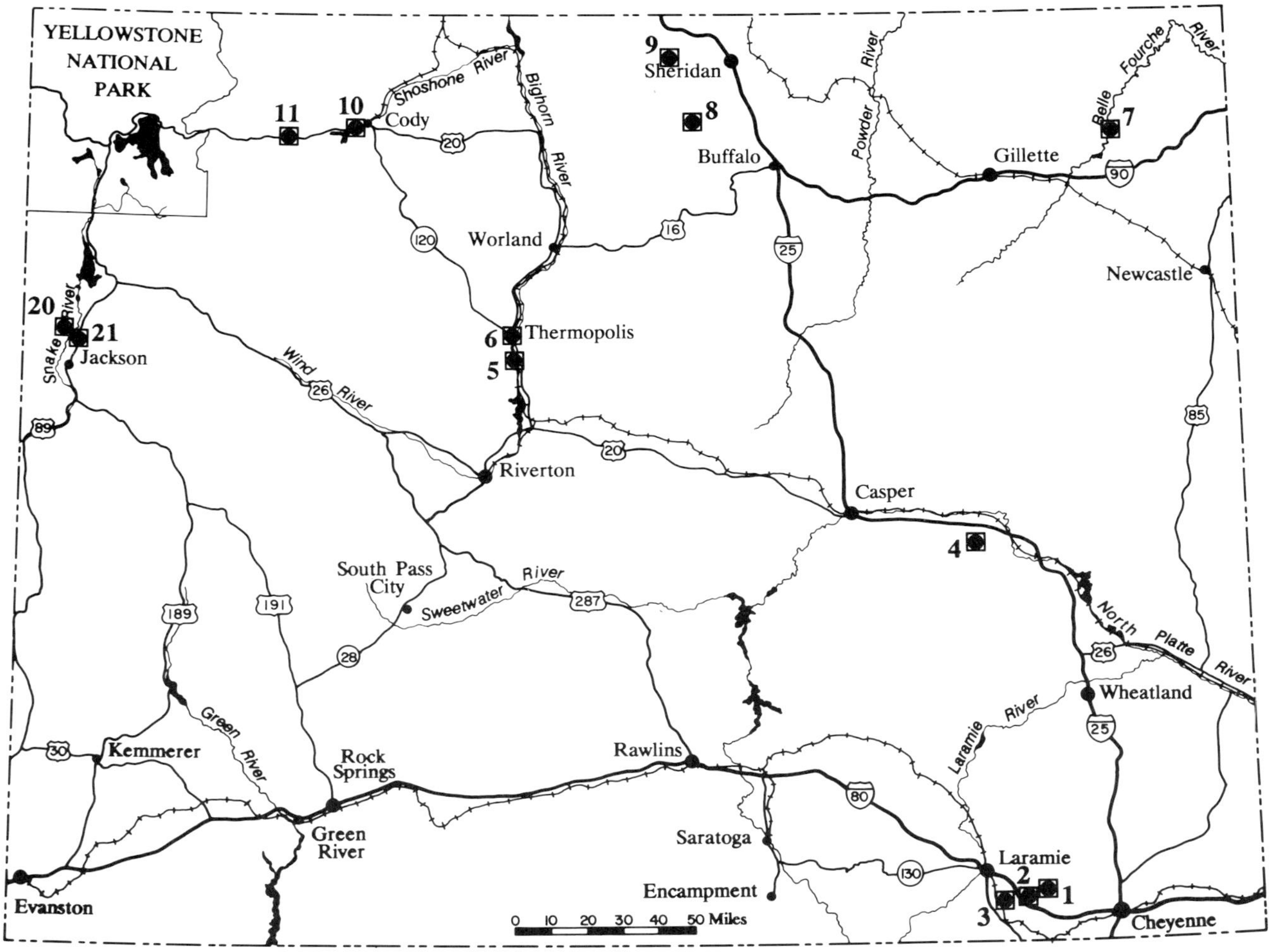

The Natural Landscape

Site No. Location	Figure Nos.
1. Granite Reservoir	1
2. Vedauwoo	2
3. Red Buttes	3–7
4. La Prele Creek	8,9
5. Wind River Canyon	10
6. Thermopolis	11
7. Devil's Tower	12
8. Dome Lake	13–17
9. Eaton Ranch	18
10. Shoshone Canyon	19,20
11. Diablo Castle	21
12. Silver Gate, Yellowstone National Park	22
13. Artist Point, Yellowstone National Park	23
14. Lower Falls, Yellowstone National Park	24, 25
15. Upper Geyser Basin, Yellowstone National Park	26–28
16. Old Faithful Inn, Yellowstone National Park	29,30
17. Lake Hotel, Yellowstone National Park	31,32
18. West Thumb, Yellowstone National Park	33
19. Mammoth Hot Springs, Yellowstone National Park	34, 35
20. Bar BC	36
21. Moose	37,38

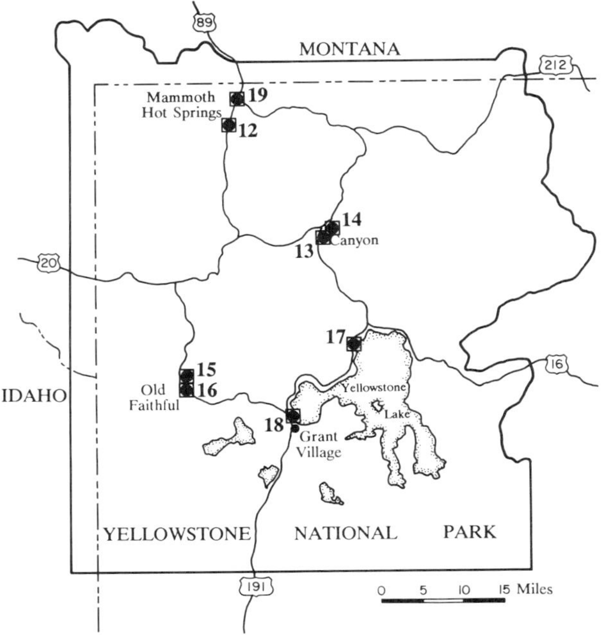

The Forgotten Past

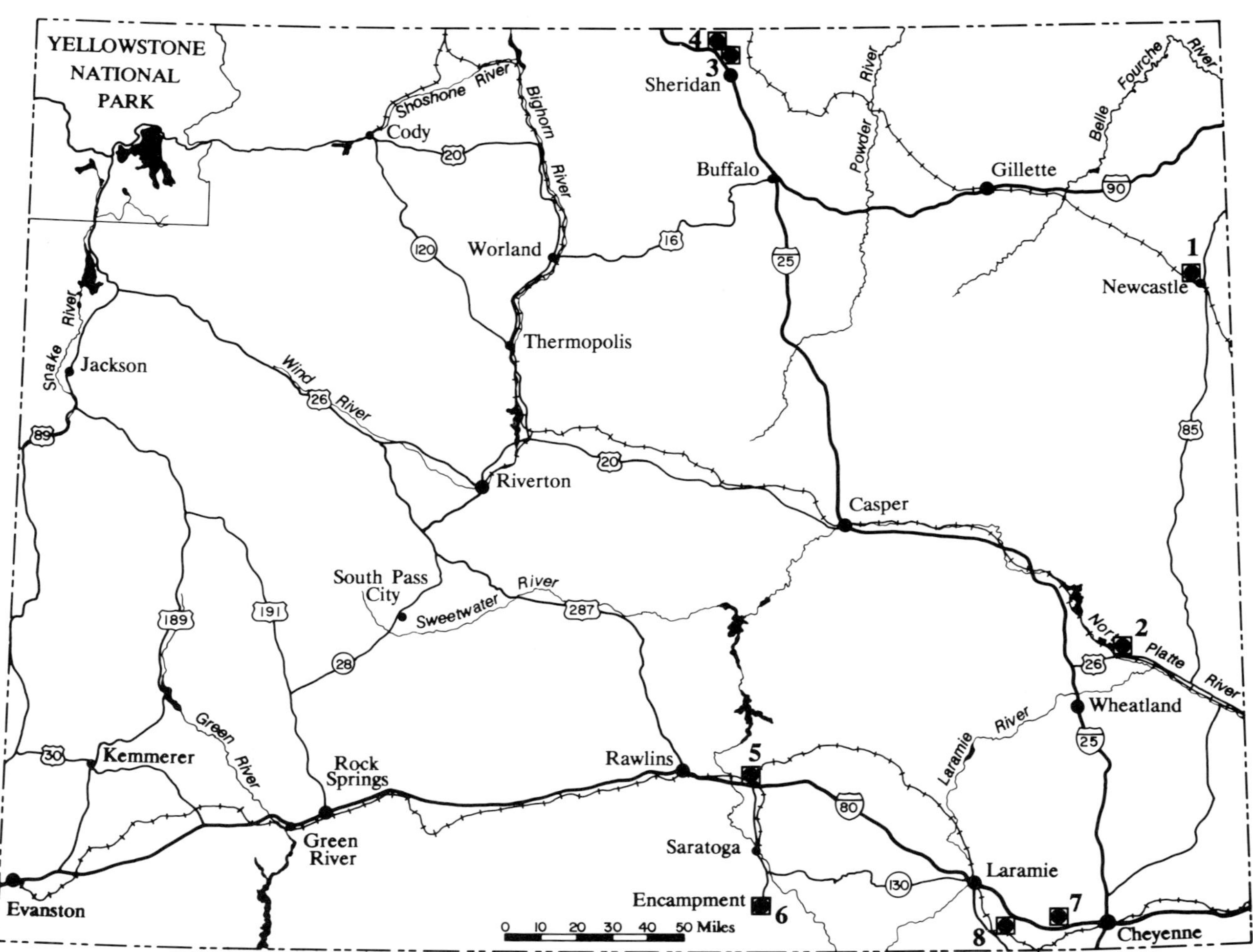

The Forgotten Past

Site No.	Location	Figure Nos.
1.	Cambria	39
2.	Sunrise	40
3.	Dietz	41,42
4.	Kearney	43
5.	Walcott	44
6.	Encampment	45
7.	Hecla	46,47
8.	Dale Creek	48,49

The Dynamic Townscape

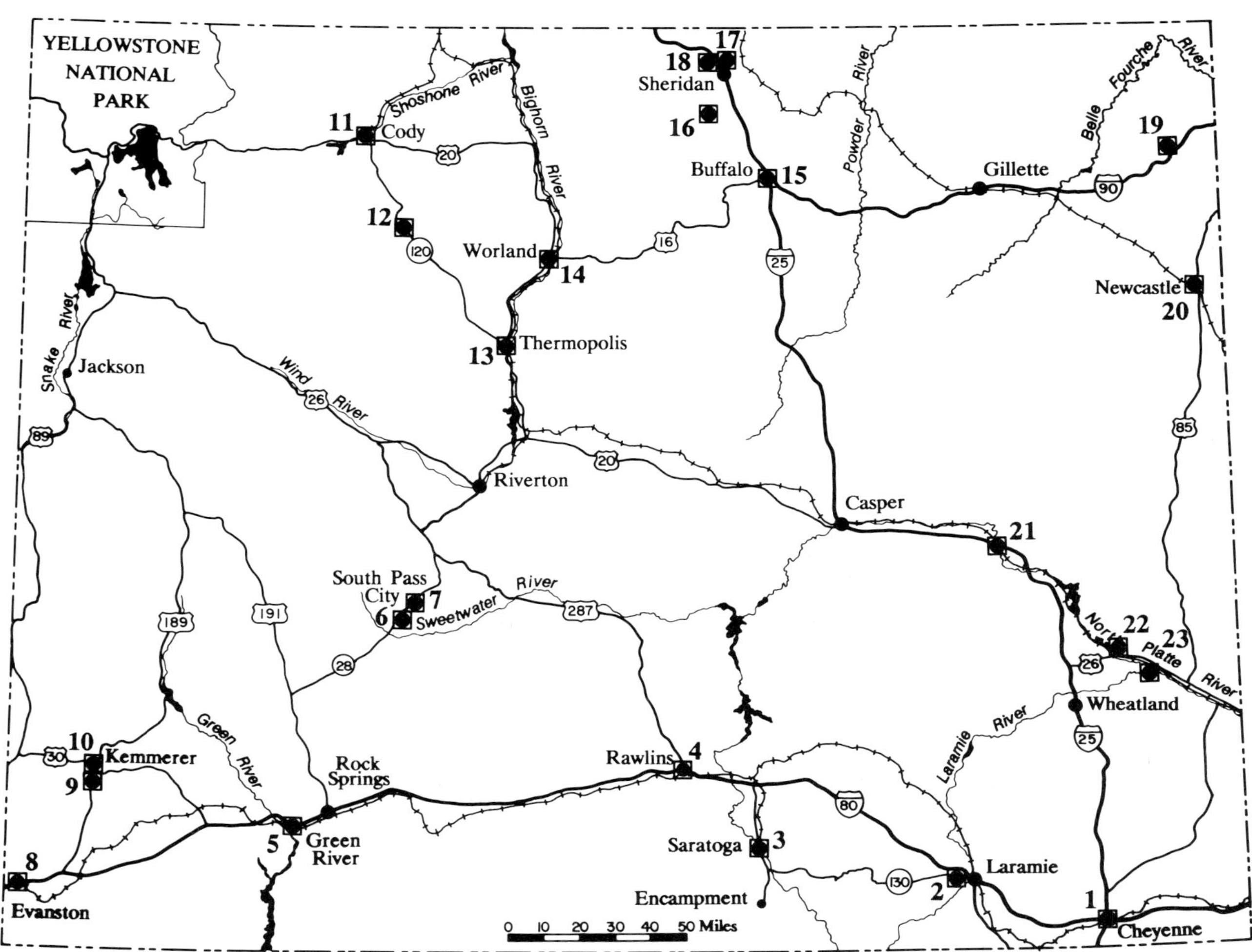

The Dynamic Townscape

Site No. Location	Figure Nos.
1. Cheyenne	50–59
2. Laramie	60–63
4. Saratoga	64
4. Rawlins	65,66
5. Green River	67–69
6. South Pass City	70
7. Atlantic City	71
8. Evanston	72
9. Diamondville	73
10. Kemmerer	74
11. Cody	75,76
12. Meeteetse	77
13. Thermopolis	78
14. Worland	79
15. Buffalo	80–83
16. Little Goose Valley	84,85
17. Sheridan	86–88
18. Fort MacKenzie	89
19. Sundance	90
20. Newcastle	91,92
21. Douglas	93
22. Hartville	94
23. Fort Laramie	95,96

A Closer Look: *Interpretive Rephotography*

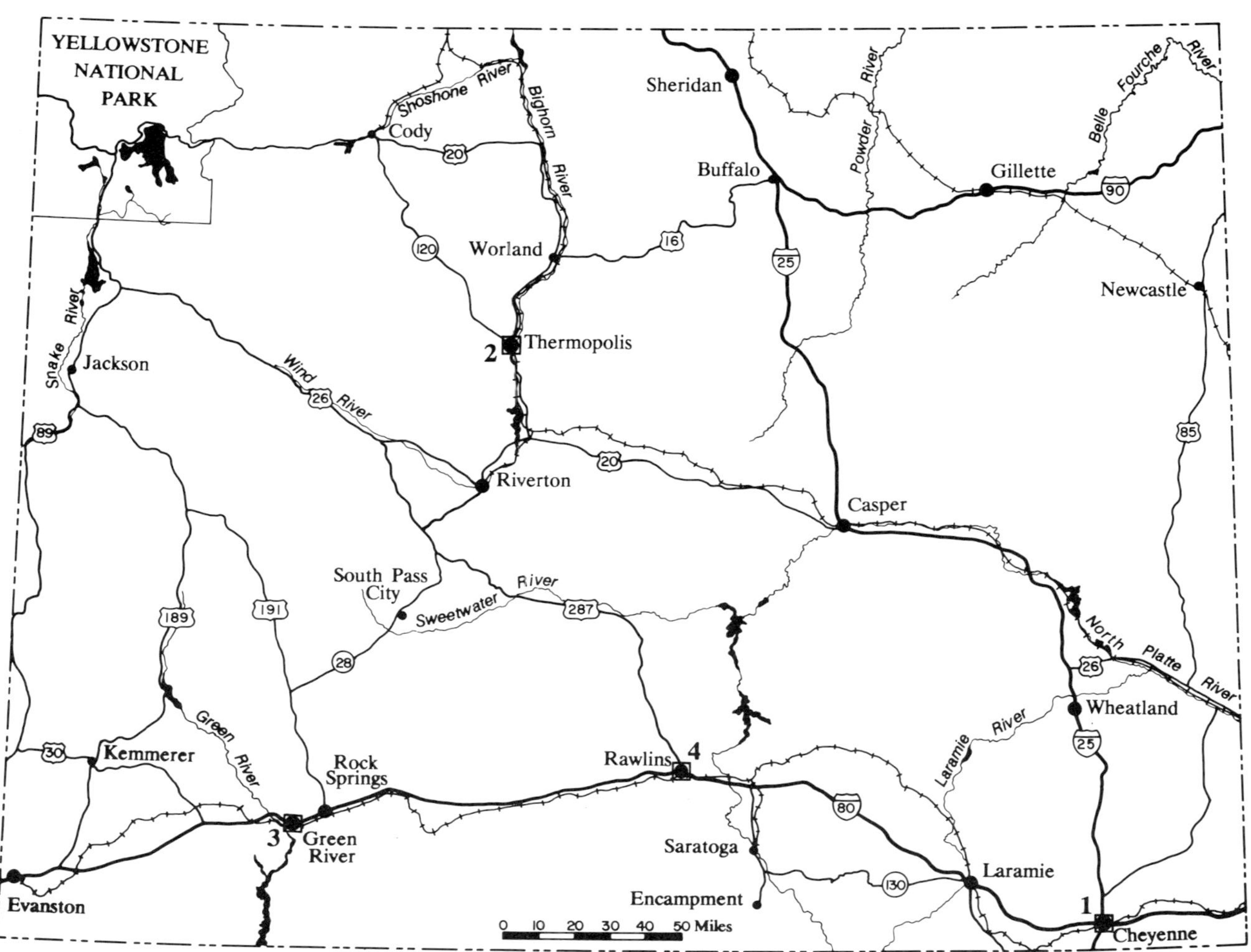

A Closer Look: *Interpretive Rephotography*

Site No.	Location	Figure Nos.
1.	Cheyenne	97
2.	Thermopolis	98
3.	Green River	99
4.	Rawlins	100

Bibliography

The information for the biography is taken from Mark Junge's book on J. E. Stimson as well as from my own interviews with Stimson's daughter, Josephine Love, and his grandson, Richard A. Patterson. For the introduction to rephotography, several rephotography books, particularly Mark Klett's *Rephotographic Survey Project* and Kendall Johnson's *Rangeland Through Time,* were used and are cited at the end of this note. The quote on history and travel is from Carla Davidson's introduction to the April 1988 edition of *American Heritage.*

For the most part, the information that is contained in the four chapters of this book was gleaned from the same variety of sources used to locate the original Stimson vantage points. These include several books: Urbanek's *Wyoming Place Names,* Bartlett's *History of Wyoming,* and the WPA's *Wyoming: A Guide to Its History, Highways, and People.* Also, many of the sources listed in the acknowledgments deserve mention here for not only showing me where to find each desired site but also telling me what they knew of each location. For many of the sites, these introductions provided a good place to begin further research. I also picked up bits and pieces of the puzzle from many brochures that I found in the museums, libraries, and sites along the way. Finally, the Wyoming State Archives in Cheyenne provided me copies of the Wyoming entries to the National Register of Historic Places list. In many cases, the information for the photo captions was either written or double-checked from these brief but thorough studies.

Bartlett, I. S. *History of Wyoming.* Vol. 1. Chicago: S. J. Clarke Publishing Company, 1918.

Chittenden, Hiram Martin. *The Yellowstone National Park.* Cincinnati: Stewart and Kidd Company, 1915.

Dittl, Barbara, and Joanne Mallmann. *The Story of the Lake Hotel.* Boulder, Colo.: Roberts Rinehart, Inc., 1987.

Hatfield, William F. *Geyserland and Wonderland: A View and Guide Book of the Yellowstone National Park.* San Francisco: Press of the Hicks-Judd Company, 1902.

Johnson, Kendall. *Rangeland Through Time.* Laramie: University of Wyoming Agricultural Experiment Station, 1987.

Junge, Mark, *J. E. Stimson: Photographer of the West.* Lincoln: University of Nebraska Press, 1985.

Klett, Mark et al. *Second View: The Rephotographic Survey Project.* Albuquerque: University of New Mexico Press, 1984.

Kuzara, Stanley A. *Black Diamonds of Sheridan: A Facet of Wyoming History.* Cheyenne: Pioneer Printing, 1977.

Laramie County Historical Society. *Early Cheyenne Homes.* Cheyenne: Pioneer Printing and Stationery Company, 1964.

Larson, T. A. *History of Wyoming.* Lincoln: University of Nebraska Press, 1978.

Le Roy, Bruce. *H. M. Chittenden: A Western Epic.* Tacoma: Washington State Historical Society, 1961.

McWilliams, Esther. *Eatons' Ranch.* Privately published, 1981.

Redford, Robert. *The Outlaw Trail.* New York: Grosset and Dunlap, 1976.

Robertson, C. F. *Development of the Worland Valley. Historical Review, 1941.*

Scofield, Susan C. The Inn at Old Faithful. Crownset Associates, 1979.

Stephens, Hal G. *In the Footsteps of John Wesley Powell: An Album of Comparative Photographs of the Green and Colorado Rivers, 1871–72 and 1968.* Boulder, Colo.: Johnson Books; Denver: The Powell Society, 1987.

Stilgoe, John R. *Metropolitan Corridor: Railroads and the American Scene.* New Haven: Yale University Press, 1983.

Urbanek, Mae. *Wyoming Place Names.* Missoula, Mont.: Mountain Press Publishing Company, 1988.

Whitman, Walt. "Passage to India." In *Leaves of Grass, The Collected Poems of Walt Whitman.* New York: The Book League of America, 1942.

Work Projects Administration. *Wyoming: A Guide to Its History, Highways, and People.* New York: Oxford University Press, 1941.

Wyoming Recreation Commission. *Wyoming: A Guide to Historic Sites.* Basin, Wyo.: Big Horn Publishers, 1976.

Wyoming State Historical Society. *Re-Discovering the Big Horns.* Wyoming Bicentennial Project, 1976.

Index

This index contains information found only in the text of this book. For photo locations, consult the site location maps and Appendix A.